The Postwar Yankees

THE POSTWAR
YANKEES

BASEBALL'S GOLDEN AGE REVISITED • DAVID G. SURDAM

University of Nebraska Press • Lincoln & London

Parts of chapters 2 and 7, as well as tables
2.1, 2.2, 7.1, and 7.2, originally appeared in
"The Coase Theorem and Player Movement
in Major League Baseball," *Journal of Sports
Economics* 7, no. 2 (May 2006): 201–21.

Chapter 5 and tables 5.3–5.5 originally
appeared in "Television and Minor League
Baseball: Changing Patterns of Leisure
in Postwar America," *Journal of Sports
Economics* 6, no. 1 (February 2005): 61–77.

Chapter 6 and tables 6.1–6.4 originally appeared in "The American 'Not-So-Socialist'
League in the Postwar Era: The Limitations of
Gate-Sharing in Reducing Revenue Disparity
in Baseball," *Journal of Sports Economics* 3,
no. 3 (February 2002): 264–90.

Library of Congress Cataloging-in-
Publication Data
Surdam, David G. (David George)
The postwar Yankees: baseball's golden age
revisited / David G. Surdam.
p. cm.
Includes bibliographical references and index.
ISBN 978-0-8032-1789-8 (cloth: alk. paper)
1. New York Yankees (Baseball team)—
History—20th century. I. Title.
GV875.N4S87 2008
796.357'64097471—dc22
2008012923

Set in Sabon.

Contents

Acknowledgments vii

Introduction: *What Golden Age?* 1

1. Those Damn Yankees:
   Dominance and Submission in the American League 11

2. Player Movement and Building the Yankees:
   Leaving Soon from a (Small) City near You 32

3. The Game on the Ledger: *Doldrums amid Prosperity* 59

4. Changing Demographics, Suburbia, and Leisure Patterns:
   Why Did Baseball Attendance Fall? 85

5. Television and Baseball:
   The New Technology, Friend or Foe? 126

6. Where Is Robin Hood When You Need Him?
   Revenue Sharing in the American League 163

7. Isn't Anybody Going to Help That Game?
   Baseball Attempts to Rejuvenate Its Popularity 181

8. The Major League Cartel: *Keeping Out the Interlopers* 209

9. The Sixteen-Headed Hydra:
   The Cartel Faces the Enmity Within 244

10. The Yankees' Dynasty:
    Did Success Spoil the Team and Its Fans? 278

    Epilogue: *What If the Golden Age Ended and
    Nobody Cared?* 303

    Appendix of Tables 307

    Notes 353

    Bibliography 403

    Index 411

Acknowledgments

Writing this book was truly a team effort. I've been helped by the kindness of friends as well as that of strangers.

I thank Phil Greiner for his help in compiling Yankees/Athletics trade data. John Kuenster, editor of *Baseball Digest*, generously allowed me to browse through the magazine's back issues and make copious photocopies of useful articles. The staff at the Chicago Historical Society and Notre Dame library supplied me with the *Sporting News*. George Rugg, curator of the Joyce Sports Collection at Notre Dame, was particularly helpful. He suggested using scorecards as primary materials, and the suggestion paid off. In addition, we would often go to lunch and commiserate as only fellow Red Sox fans can. The University of Oregon library staff, including Mark Watson, Ted Smith, and Thomas Stave, helped me locate important government documents. The Multnomah County Public Library in Portland, Oregon, contained several useful reference works on the Minor Leagues, and the staff was helpful in photocopying material.

Professor Louis Cain advised and encouraged me to switch research agendas from the American Civil War to the economics of professional sports. His advice was certainly fruitful. Mike Haupert's thorough reading and comments have greatly improved the manuscript.

Participants at a number of conferences, including the Illinois Economic Association, Southern Economics Association, and Western International Economics Association, and workshops at the University of Northern Iowa, Northwestern University, Bowling Green State University, University of Oregon, and University of Chicago economics departments made sagacious comments. Columnist George Will provided encouragement along the way. Professors Paul Gabriel, David Galenson, John Hoag, Jerome Klinkowitz, Anthony Krautman, Richard

Lindholm, Sandy Mazzola, and Kevin Quinn provided useful comments. Attendees at the Learning-in-Retirement program at the University of Oregon were attentive and supportive. Several anonymous referees made excellent suggestions for revisions. The University of Chicago Graduate School of Business provided funding throughout the research and writing stages of the book. Loyola University of Chicago Graduate School of Business also provided support during the early stages of research. The economics faculty at the University of Northern Iowa offered encouragement during the final stages of this project.

While the members of my dissertation committee at the University of Chicago—Robert Fogel, David Galenson, and the late D. Gale Johnson—did not supervise this effort, I thank them for instilling the unquenchable thirst for more data to analyze and willingness to reconsider entrenched historical ideas.

The late sportswriter Leonard Koppett's articles and books inspired a lasting interest in sports statistics, an interest whetted by my experiences playing Strat-O-Matic Baseball. The game's creator, Harold Richman, provided me with many hours of amusement and started my investigations and analysis of baseball statistics. In addition, the Springfield, Oregon, public library had a copy of the first edition *Macmillan Baseball Encyclopedia*, a true treasure trove.

I thank Robert Taylor, acquisitions editor at the University of Nebraska Press, for his encouragement and support of this book.

Sara Springsteen, project editor, and Elizabeth Gratch, copy editor, were enjoyable to work with and helped improve this work.

I would also like to thank Roger Buchholz, designer; Kim Essman, compositor; and Alison Rold, production manager, for their efforts.

Sarah Statz Cords compiled yet another excellent index and, as always, was a pleasure to work with.

I remain grateful to two mentors: my "surrogate" grandfather, Bryan O. Wilson, who long encouraged me to study mathematics, and my high school accounting teacher and longtime friend, Bert Kronmiller, who helped foster my interest in sports statistics. Mary Bogard urged me to get on National Public Radio to publicize my ideas, an idea whose time has yet to come. I also thank my Robert D. Clark Honors College senior thesis committee: Professors Paul Speckman, Richard Koch, and the late Edward Diller. Their advice and encouragement of my thesis, "Baseball Run Production," fueled my interest in sports statistics a quarter of a century ago.

My parents, George and Thelma, have long tolerated and even spurred my interest in baseball statistics and history.

I dedicate this book to Gary Lewis, the best friend a fellow could ever have. Gary and Paul Dowdy were gracious Yankees fans who did not gloat after the unfortunate incident in October 1978.

The Postwar Yankees

Introduction

What Golden Age?

The New York Yankees have dominated Major League Baseball in recent years, leaving many fans waxing nostalgic about a time when the sport was not ruled by teams with large payrolls. Many fans born just before and during the postwar baby boom remember the era fondly. Major League Baseball of that time conjures images of a golden age filled with great new stars—Mickey Mantle, Willie Mays, and Duke Snider—as well as holdovers such as Bob Feller, Joe DiMaggio, Ted Williams, and Stan Musial. Roger Kahn's poignant *The Boys of Summer* (1972) captures the mood of the Brooklyn borough during the early 1950s. More recently, Doris Kearns Goodwin's memoir, *Wait till Next Year* (1997), describes the pains and joys of growing up rooting for the Dodgers. Gary David Goldberg's television show *Brooklyn Bridge*, which aired from 1991 to 1993, also recalled growing up rooting for the Bums. In 1968 songwriter Paul Simon celebrated Joe DiMaggio in "Mrs. Robinson," while a decade later his contemporary Dion DiMucci recorded the nostalgic tune "(I Used to Be a) Brooklyn Dodger." New York Giants fans savored Bobby Thomson's playoff-winning home run in 1951 and Willie Mays's wondrous catch in the 1954 World Series. Rooting for the New York Yankees, with their cool efficiency and large payrolls, was likened to rooting for U.S. Steel, although in

2001 actor Billy Crystal paid tribute to two beloved members of the team, Roger Maris and Mickey Mantle, in his movie *61**.

These heroics played out against a backdrop of changing social and economic patterns. Higher incomes, greater racial equality, changing gender roles, technological changes, and major demographic shifts transformed the nation, even affecting baseball.

Cold war metaphors colored attitudes about the game, with baseball owners lashing out at "socialism," whether Soviet-style or within the national pastime. Baseball assumed mythic proportions. United States senators imbued baseball with the ability to combat the godless Reds; Senator Karl Mundt of South Dakota claimed, "I believe baseball has become very definitely a factor in the cold war we are fighting because we have sent baseball teams abroad with universally useful results."[1] Nor was baseball's power relegated to fighting communism; it was also fighting the good fight against that other scourge of the 1950s—the juvenile delinquent. The inanity reached a peak in an exchange during a Senate hearing, when Wisconsin Senator Alexander Wiley asserted, "Public interest is a matter of keeping the youth in action, keeping them mentally alert, particularly now when we are talking about this Khrushchev problem. We can't be diverted from the big issue, which is maintaining the peace." To which baseball entrepreneur William Shea responded, "You, sir, know that baseball probably constitutes one of the greatest deterrents to juvenile delinquency, because baseball is played, primarily, during the summer when the youths are out from school; when they don't have the day-to-day activity of going to school."[2]

If the American legislators seemed to be employing hyperbole, their Soviet counterparts were acting just as silly. During the middle of September 1952 the *New York Times*, along with other major American newspapers, reported that a Russian magazine, *Smena*, claimed that "Beizbol" was a "Yankee perversion of an ancient Russian village sport called lapta." Presumably, the perversion consisted of the Americans transforming the quaint village sport into a "beastly battle, a bloody fight with mayhem and murder." Although Americans cherished the sport's ability to inculcate (good) character among its youth, the Russian reporter claimed, "American businessmen 'intensively implanted' this bloody sport among 14-year-old and 15-year-old adolescents who 'supplemented their lack of technique by a surplus of rough play.'" While lamenting the sad fate of "Tai Kopb" (Ty Cobb), whose body was "covered from head to foot with scars," the article excoriated the Yankee businessmen for exploiting athletes.[3]

Today's readers might respond to this depiction with amusement and perhaps derision, as did the *Chicago Tribune*, inserting editorial comments about the Soviet penchant for claiming priority of many inventions. American government officials, however, reacted with alacrity. While the secretary of defense took a humorous view of the Russian article, the State Department claimed it was part of the Soviet's "Hate America" campaign. Adding to the farcical nature of the situation, the new Soviet ambassador stated he would attend a baseball game.[4] If he had attended a New York Yankees game, he would have found much propaganda fodder. Unless the Yankees played the Browns, White Sox, or Indians, for example, the ambassador would not have seen any black players. Indeed, during the following December Jackie Robinson created a stir by his blunt answer to the question of whether New York Yankees management was prejudiced toward black players, given that the team did not have any at the time: "Yes, I think they are."[5] Hollywood audiences were already familiar with the dichotomy of blacks being shut out of good jobs but being drafted to fight and, possibly, die for the nation. In films portraying the Korean War, such as *The Steel Helmet* and *Pork Chop Hill*, the black GI often confronted a disturbing question, whether posed by a wily Commie captive or upon a character's own introspection: Why was he fighting for America when he was denied civil rights at home? The black GI character often responded by killing "Reds" because being an American, with all of its imperfections, was better than being Red. It was a good thing that the ambassador did not attend a Yankees game in 1927, with the famed "Murderer's Row" of Babe Ruth and Lou Gehrig. By the time of escalating United States involvement in Vietnam, the golden age of baseball was in eclipse. No senator would assert that baseball could convert the Viet Cong or deter hippies and yippies from their sometimes violent political demonstrations.

Entire constituencies of Major League Baseball fans might find reasons to think of the legacy of the golden age as having been tarnished. Seven Major League franchises—Baltimore/St. Louis, Kansas City/Philadelphia, Washington, Chicago Cubs, Cincinnati, Philadelphia, and Pittsburgh—combined for five .500 and nine winning seasons during the 1951–60 period. In other words, each of these franchises averaged two seasons of .500 or better ball during the decade. There are no literary paeans to growing up in, say, Pittsburgh and rooting for the Pirates.

If you were a player, you were undoubtedly exploited, in the sense of having your pay determined in a rigged market. If you were an African-American player, you had to struggle harder to gain acceptance while enduring separate lodging and dining facilities during spring training. And while the owners might elicit little sympathy from many readers, the era was punctuated by almost annual congressional hearings challenging, if not threatening, their hallowed antitrust exemption.

The signs of decline, in retrospect, were obvious. The postwar era was a golden age primarily if you were a New York baseball fan. The New York Yankees and their National League neighbors, the Dodgers and Giants, dominated the game much as the Yankees (and in terms of payrolls, also the New York Mets) do today. Aside from the eras of Columbia Broadcasting System CBS ownership and George Steinbrenner's exile from active management of the Yankees during the late 1980s, the Yankees have been paramount. The postwar era epitomized Yankee superiority. If you lived outside the area, in what New Yorkers considered the hinterlands, the era probably did not appear so golden. From 1949 to 1964 the only World Series not to feature a New York team was the 1959 match-up between the Chicago White Sox and the Los Angeles Dodgers—and of course, the Dodgers were formerly a New York baseball team. In the ten series held between 1949 and 1958 not only was there a New York team in every World

Series, but six of them were played by two New York teams. Of the remaining thirteen teams only the Philadelphia Phillies, Cleveland Indians, and Milwaukee Braves appeared in the World Series during these ten years.

Even after the Dodgers and Giants vacated New York, the original New York franchises dominated the game. From 1959 through 1966 at least one of the three teams was in the World Series, and twice the series had two of the three teams.

The American League was essentially a variation of the Yankees and the Seven Dwarfs. Bottom-feeding teams, such as the St. Louis Browns, Philadelphia Athletics, and Washington Senators, began each season hoping to finish within thirty games of the Yankees. Fan apathy to such mediocrity across these cities induced all three of them to relocate by 1961. After trying to bankroll a winning team in Boston, owner Thomas Yawkey gave up during the 1950s, and the Red Sox settled into a shabby genteel mediocrity. The 1954 season represented the culmination of American League imbalance. The Yankees won 103 games, their best record between 1943 and 1960, but the Cleveland Indians won 111 games. Five teams finished more than forty games behind the Indians, including the Senators, Orioles, and Athletics. These three teams finished a combined 162 games behind the Indians. New York, Cleveland, and Chicago never finished below fourth place and often finished first, second, or third between 1951 and 1960, aside from 1957.

Not only did the Yankees routinely win pennants; they allegedly did so by pilfering star players from some of their hapless rivals. When Arnold Johnson purchased the Athletics and transferred the team to Kansas City, a series of trades with the Yankees induced fears that the Athletics were now lackeys of the Bronx Bombers. Such exploitative relationships between teams, however, were not new.

In the National League the Pittsburgh Pirates went eight consecutive seasons without rising above seventh place in an eight-team league. About the time that Roberto Clemente and others resurrected the Pirates, their cross-state rivals, the Philadelphia Phillies, fell into a four-year skein as the worst team in the National League. The Cincinnati Reds sported losing records for every season between 1945 and 1955. Between 1947 and 1966 the Chicago Cubs had one winning season, going 82-80 in 1963, and one .500 season, in 1952. Without the magic of Branch Rickey's farm system, the St. Louis Cardinals became mediocre, despite the presence of Stan Musial. Yet unlike the American League, every National League team had at least a brief taste of championship success, as every one of the original eight franchises won a pennant between 1945 and 1964, including six different pennant winners between 1945 and 1951.

Even in New York City, however, epicenter of the golden age, fan apathy and frustration began to develop. Indeed, for Dodgers and Giants fans the so-called golden age had ended prematurely, when their beloved teams moved west after 1957. Even the haughty New York Yankees saw attendance fall by more than a third between the immediate postwar years to the mid-1950s. The monopolization of the city might have boosted attendance at Yankee Stadium during the last years of the 1950s, but any boost proved disappointingly small. In the hinterlands disappointment lurked. For Milwaukee Braves fans the era ended with the city retaining only a tenuous hold upon the team, while Kansas City fans waited for Charlie Finley to abscond with the Athletics.

Thus, by 1964 the Major Leagues were in turmoil. Television had proven to be an ally of dubious worth, bringing in revenue but also promoting competition from soap operas, situation comedies, westerns, professional wrestling, and professional football, which was capturing the imaginations of growing numbers of fans. An increasing proportion of Americans earned college degrees and worked in white-collar jobs with rising incomes and security. Americans left the inner cities in droves for the burgeoning suburbs. Greater proportions of Americans owned cars and enjoyed wider choices of leisure activities. The baby boom promised to deliver more fans but only at some indefinite future time. Initially, the baby boom may have altered leisure patterns of millions of young married adult fans. While black players now appeared in the Major Leagues, the transformation was uneven. The Yankees and other American League teams delayed signing black players. In addition, the original sixteen teams played in old stadiums located in stagnating or declining neighborhoods; many of the stadiums lacked amenities that modern fans take for granted.

The Columbia Broadcasting System's purchase of the New York Yankees in 1964 seemed to exemplify the growing reach of corporate America. With its deep, deep pockets CBS seemed well positioned to extend the Yankees' dominance. After all, CBS was the nation's leading television network. Ironically, however, the purchase marked the end of the era.

What follows is a reexamination of Major League Baseball between 1946 and 1964 through the eyes of an economist. While an economist might not be most readers' first choice of whom they'd like to spend an afternoon with at the ballpark, economists can provide uncommon, and at times highly contentious, insights into the game. In particular, economists tend to view the reserve clause and drafts of amateur players with skepticism, being dubious of the need for "territorial exclusivity" for franchises, and they often view rising player salaries as a manifestation of rising revenues and ticket prices rather than as the factor triggering higher ticket prices.

Although it is easy enough to demonstrate that New York City baseball fans have been the chief beneficiaries of any hallowed age, important questions remain. Would players, for instance, have regarded the era as golden? During the postwar period and remaining a fixture of player's contracts until it was struck down in 1975, Major League Baseball owners enforced a reserve clause giving them the right to retain a player after his contract had expired during the postwar period. Owners and players testified before Congress that the reserve clause was crucial in maintaining competitive balance. Unlike many people, economists tend to believe that the distribution of playing talent to a large degree should be similar under either the reserve clause or free agency. Most economists believe that a crucial attraction of the reserve clause to owners was its diminution of a player's bargaining power.

Because teams could not merely sign established stars who were free agents, how did the Yankees maintain their competitive edge? Did they buy or trade for established stars, or did they sign the best amateur talent? If your team was not very competitive, could you at least hope to see your favorite hometown hero throughout his entire career? Was the comforting belief that teams had roster stability during the pre–free agency period true?

For baseball owners the golden age certainly lost much of its luster after the immediate postwar attendance boom between 1946 and 1950. Indeed, it was reasonable to ask, "What if the baseball gods put on a golden age and nobody came?" The "Boys of Summer" Dodgers played to just over a million fans per season during the 1950s. During their two pennant-winning seasons in 1951 and 1954, the New York Giants averaged just 1.1 million fans per season. For their final three seasons at the Polo Grounds the Giants averaged only seven hundred thousand fans, despite the marvels of Willie Mays. Indeed, it is fair to ask whether contemporary fans, even those residing in New York City, behaved as though they were living in a wondrous age. During the 1950s attendance fell off in both leagues, although the National League rebounded nicely as the decade unfolded.

What factors may have accounted for the attendance doldrums? Did owners, seeing the initial attendance boom, decide to exploit the increased demand and raise ticket prices? Did changing technology and demographic shifts affect attendance? Did television kill Minor League Baseball, or was the new medium falsely accused of "murder"? Did the growing ownership of automobiles and the concurrent shift to suburban living expand people's choices of leisure activities and affect the ease of attending Major League Baseball games at downtown stadiums? In addition to being able to drive to games and finding readily available parking, what other amenities did fans want? Did the baby boom affect the leisure activities of American adults? How did owners respond to these changes?

If the attendance stagnation in the American League was due in part to the monotonous success of the New York Yankees during the

1950s, what steps did rival American League teams take in attempting to redress the imbalance? Did revenue sharing shrink the income gap between the wealthy Yankees and the ne'er-do-well Browns, Athletics, and Senators? Given the access to a new pool of talented black players, did American League rivals attempt to improve themselves via this relatively cheap source?

What if you lived in a burgeoning city in the West or South and wanted big league baseball? What chances did your city have of attracting a team, given baseball's long-standing sixteen-team, ten-city organization?

Unlike most businesses, Major League Baseball owners operated within a cartel, which barred the entry of new teams and should have bolstered the members' collective profits. Yet within the cartel teams had a good deal of discretion over quality and prices. The group also tried to prevent individual teams from acting in ways that could damage the other members. During the 1950s, however, issues arose that threatened the cartel's stability. Wealthy sportsmen throughout the country wanted their own teams. The scramble for the players that enjoyed the last vestige of a free market—talented amateurs—triggered escalating bonus payments. Teams in smaller or declining cities coveted new locales, especially the growing cities of the West Coast and Southeast, all the while cognizant of the fact that moving teams prematurely might injure the cartel by raising travel costs, generating public ill will, or, worst of all, encouraging congressional scrutiny.

All of these issues echo even today. Studying the past may help us understand how we got here, and fortunately, there is a wealth of data available for the period. Two congressional hearings required team owners to present financial data for several seasons between 1946 and 1956. Various sporting publications at the time also reported attendance, ticket prices, media coverage, and other relevant data. And teams produced more informative scorecards during the postwar era than they had previously.

This book differs from other discussions of the era in its greater reliance upon data, buttressed by statistical and economic analysis.

The most technical material can be found in the notes, so as to not disrupt the text. Because baseball fans in general appear to be comfortable with numbers, they will perhaps find that looking at financial and other data opens new vistas for thinking about the game. In addition, throughout the story the opinions of contemporary observers provide color and, more important, truer glimpses into the attitudes pervading the game.

Those Damn Yankees

Dominance and Submission in the American League

Almost every American has heard of the mighty New York Yankees. Even those who are not baseball fans know that the Yankees epitomize championship baseball. The team's resurgence beginning in 1996 has created the usual hand-wringing and cries to "break up the Yankees." Yet the current team has a long way to go before rivaling the records of past Yankee teams, particularly those that won fifteen pennants in eighteen seasons between 1947 and 1964. The Boston Celtics' eleven National Basketball Association titles in thirteen years is the only skein in professional sports that comes close to rivaling the Yankees. Between 1996 and 2003 the Yankees appeared in six World Series, winning four of them. Since then, the team has disappointed its owner, George Steinbrenner, and its fans, despite its gaudy collection of stars (with matching salaries). Judging from statistical data drawn from the Yankees championship runs, the current streak of success is not as illustrious as previous streaks have been, especially in terms of win-loss records (see table 1.1 in the appendix). The "games ahead" figures for both the 1976–78 and 1998–2001 eras in table 1.1 are inflated by the divisional structure, in which only four to six teams compete directly for a divisional title instead of eight to ten teams competing for a league title. At least the current Yankees dominance over baseball has paid off in terms of attendance.

This chapter provides a brief history of the New York Yankees, from their modest beginnings through the Jacob Ruppert ownership and Babe Ruth. I examine the team's record on the field during the postwar era and consider the effect of the team's repeated pennant success on fans' interest and appreciation. Despite being the only team at the time in New York City, having four more home games than in previous seasons, and featuring Mickey Mantle's and Roger Maris's pursuit of Babe Ruth's single-season homerun mark, attendance at Yankee Stadium in 1961 failed to recover to the levels of 1946–51.

The New York Yankees' Early Record

The New York Yankees' early history was one of disappointment. The team failed to win any pennants during the American League's first two decades. From 1903 to 1918 the Yankees won fewer than 48 percent of their games. Thanks to the alleged impecuniousness of Boston Red Sox owner, Harry Frazee, the new Yankee owners, Capt. Tillinghast Huston and Col. Jacob Ruppert, were able to buy virtually an entire starting lineup and pitching staff. The Red Sox had been the American League's most victorious franchise between 1903 and 1918. According to legend, in 1920 Frazee supposedly needed money to fund his Broadway efforts, so he sold Babe Ruth for a reputed $125,000 (plus a $300,000 loan). In fact, according to the New York Yankees' financial records, the team paid four installments of $25,000 for Ruth, and there is no evidence of a loan.[1] Before this sale, the Yankees had purchased Duffy Lewis, Carl Mays and Ernie Shore from the Red Sox for a combined $55,000; the Yankees also threw in some players who would help the Red Sox to second-division finishes. After purchasing Ruth, the Yankees bought Joe Dugan, Herb Pennock, George Pipgras, and Elmer Smith and traded for Waite Hoyt and Wally Schang. Many of these players joined holdovers Frank Baker, Wally Pipp, and Bob Shawkey, who had been purchased from the Philadelphia Athletics and Detroit Tigers, to form the bulk of the Yankees' first pennant-winning squad in 1921. Later the Yankees would buy Red Ruffing from the Red Sox.[2]

The Yankees began successfully to introduce new talent such as Bob

Meusel and, later, Lou Gehrig and Tony Lazzeri. By the 1930s the growing Yankees farm system and judicious purchases of some Minor League players produced Bill Dickey, Lefty Gomez, and Joe DiMaggio as well as a host of lesser-known players. The talent probably peaked with the 1936–39 editions, led by DiMaggio and Dickey (see table 1.1 in the appendix). In each of the four years the Yankees led the league not only in scoring but also in fewest runs allowed. The Yankees also outscored their opponents by 2.14 runs per game during this period, topped by the 1939 edition that outscored its foes by 2.72 runs per game; even the storied 1927 Yankees had only outscored their foes by 2.44 runs per game. These Yankees also led the league in homeruns and earned run average (ERA) in each of the four seasons. The 1927 Yankees had dominated in such a fashion, but the 1926 and 1928 teams had struggled to finish first, although the latter team won 101 games. The 1936–39 Yankees were the class of the baseball world, yet falling attendance was a troubling aspect of the streak. Not only did the league's attendance fall by 10 percent between 1937 and 1939, but the Yankees' attendance fell by almost 14 percent during the same period. The 1941–43 teams did quite well too, winning by an average of over thirteen games per season. Again, while both the league's and Yankees' attendance fell between 1941 and 1943, the Yankees' attendance fell by a greater proportion. Clearly, repeated championships did not necessarily deliver greater attendance. During the latter half of the American involvement in World War II, the Yankees fell to third and fourth places in 1944 and 1945, but their attendance perked up considerably. The war reduced the disparity between incomes for Americans in general and, in the American League, created the most radical "income redistribution" of all—the moribund St. Louis Browns won their only pennant in 1944.

The Postwar Yankees and Attendance Trends

Major League Baseball enjoyed a stunning resurgence of popularity immediately after the war. The two leagues attracted more than twice as many fans per season during 1946–50 as during the previous boom of the late 1920s. The Yankees had their first attendance of over two million in 1946, despite the fact that the team finished a distant third (perhaps fittingly) to the Boston Red Sox (see table 1.2 in the appendix). In each of the five seasons from 1946 to 1950 the Yankees attracted over two million customers. Unfortunately for subsequent Yankee owners, the franchise would not attain this level again for another twenty-five years, and in one year attendance would actually drop below one million, albeit in the slightly strike-shortened 1972 season. The Yankees attendance peaked in 1948 at 2.37 million fans. Ironically, the team finished third that season, only two and a half games behind the Cleveland Indians, as the tight pennant race spurred attendance.

The Yankees hit their stride in 1949, en route to five consecutive pennants. The team was initially centered around aging veteran Joe DiMaggio, who had had a superb year in 1948 but was simply not the same player that he had been before the war. By 1949 injuries and aging limited him to half the season. Still, the Yankees rallied around Yogi Berra, Tommy Henrich, and Phil Rizzuto as well as pitchers Eddie Lopat, Vic Raschi, and Allie Reynolds. Relief pitcher Joe Page led the league in saves. This team won the pennant after a torrid race with the Boston Red Sox, an arguably more talented team. Author David Halberstam wonderfully recounts the pennant race in *Summer of '49*. He chronicled how the Yankee players were especially motivated by World Series money to supplement their paychecks.[3]

None of the subsequent eight pennant-winning teams crushed the opposition in the fashion of the 1936–39 squads, nor were these Yankees loaded with "superstars." What the Casey Stengel and George Weiss Yankees had was a balance of hitting, fielding, and pitching. In some cases the Yankees would have five or six hitters with more than ten homeruns as well as five or more pitchers with ten or more wins. Just once during the five pennants between 1949 and 1953 did the famed "Bronx Bombers" lead the league in homeruns. In fact, the Yankees of the postwar era were almost as likely to boast the league's best earned run average (ERA) as they were to lead the league in homeruns. The team's hitters led the league in homeruns seven times, while its pitchers recorded the lowest ERA six times during the 1946–64 era. The five pennant-winning teams of 1949–53 won by an average of just under four games per season and never cracked the one-hundred-win barrier. Casey Stengel's best record with the Yankees occurred in 1954, when the team won 103 games. The Cleveland Indians won 111 games that year, however, burying the Yankees. The Indians had set an American League attendance record in 1948 with 2.6 million fans, but the team drew just half this number in its pennant-winning season of 1954.

By the mid-1950s the disparity between the Yankees and the rest of the American League clubs was entrenched. Only a super year by the Cleveland Indians in 1954 prevented ten consecutive Yankee pennants from 1949 to 1958. *Sports Illustrated* commented,

> Bluntly, the Athletics of 1954 somehow managed to be terribly terrible in the horribly weak American League, which only half deserved to be called a major league. Only the Indians, the New York Yankees and Chicago White Sox consistently played big-league baseball last summer. No wonder disenchantment struck fans in Baltimore, boredom entered the Washington scene, and absenteeism was rife in Philadelphia. . . . The fans did not weary of major-league baseball. They wearied of the dreary games played by the A's against rivals almost as dreary. . . . The feeble American League can be just as feeble with the A's in Kansas City or Wounded Knee.[4]

The New York Yankees had enough good pitchers that Whitey Ford, arguably their best pitcher ever, made more than thirty starts in only one season between 1953 and 1960. He made thirty-three starts in 1955, pitching 253 innings; in the other seasons between 1953 and 1960 he never threw for more than 225 innings. When Ralph Houk became the manager in 1961, Ford's starts jumped to thirty-nine. He averaged thirty-seven starts and almost 260 innings per season between 1961 and 1965. The longer season probably accounted for two extra starts per season, but Ford clearly worked more during the waning days of the Yankees' postwar dynasty.

During the 1946–54 period the American League had three relatively weak franchises in the Philadelphia Athletics, St. Louis Browns, and Washington Senators (see table 1.3 in the appendix). Note that these prolonged disparities occurred in the absence of free agency. The first two teams shared their cities with National League teams. The Boston Red Sox, Cleveland Indians, and New York Yankees consistently finished with winning records. The Chicago White Sox and Detroit Tigers fielded mediocre teams throughout the nine years, although the two teams were heading in opposite directions, as the White Sox improved between 1950 and 1954. The 1955–64 era saw a tightening of the win-loss distributions, after netting out games with the expansion Los Angeles Angels and Washington Senators. The standard deviation in win-loss percentage shrank between 1946–54 and 1955–64, from .088 to .068.

Although the league became a little more competitive in the later period (1955–64), even as the Yankees continued to dominate, there were some significant shifts. While the Browns/Orioles improvement was not surprising, the declines of Boston and Cleveland were marked. Chicago improved dramatically. All three cities shrank in population between 1950 and 1960, although the metropolitan areas grew. Boston shrank by about one-eighth in population, but the Red Sox were now the sole Major League occupants of the city because the National League Boston Braves relocated.

The Yankees' domination of the American League occurred as attendance was falling throughout the league. The cry "Break up the Yankees" assumes a plaintive aspect in light of the dwindling attendance. Both leagues enjoyed large attendance gains after the war; after drawing over ten million fans in both 1948 and 1949, however, American League attendance fell below seven million in 1953, the last of five straight Yankee pennant years. The American League, which usually had higher attendance, fell behind the National League that year. Although the novelty of a new pennant winner in 1954 bolstered American League attendance by almost one million and the tight race of 1955 increased it by another million, the National League recaptured the attendance lead in 1956 and would maintain it, with one exception, for another twenty seasons.[5] The exception to larger National League attendance occurred in 1961, when the expanded American League drew more total fans than the still eight-team National League. Yet the National League still attracted more on a per-team basis. While American League attendance peaked again in 1955, being higher than any season since 1950, the next three years concluding a Yankee four-year pennant run saw attendance plunge by over 18 percent between 1955 and 1958.

The Chicago White Sox's surprise pennant of 1959 bolstered attendance by 25 percent, with the Chicago franchise alone drawing 625,000 more fans in 1959 than in 1958. The attendance hike held during the 1960 season, even with the return of the Yankees to the top. New York's attendance reached 1.63 million in 1960. This Yankee team—with Mantle, Maris, and Ford—was beginning the last Yankee championship streak until the late 1970s. The first four pennants (1960–63) were won by an average of eight games per season. The 1961 Yankees feasted on the diluted talent of the expanded American League and won 109 games out of the lengthened 162-game schedule. The Detroit Tigers finished eight games back, but now there were six teams finishing over thirty games behind the Yankees. While overall league attendance rose by nine hundred thousand, attendance fell slightly on a per-team basis. By 1964, even with a tight pennant race, which the Yankees won by a single game over the Chicago White Sox, the attendance was at the same level as in 1960, despite the two additional teams. In spite of the collapse of the Yankees and a new champion in Minnesota in 1965, overall league attendance continued to drop, reaching 8.86 million. This attendance level was the lowest of the original expansion era of 1961–68.

The National League did not have such a dominant team; the Dodgers were the closest approximation during the 1950s and 1960s. After 1956 the National League consistently drew more fans than did the American League, reaching a peak in 1965–66, when the National League drew almost five million more fans per season.

What was the game like on the field? Did changing the balance between pitchers and batters affect attendance? Table 1.4 shows summary statistics for the National and American leagues during the years 1946–64 (see appendix). For comparison three recent National League seasons are included; modern American League statistics are not used for comparison because of the designated hitter rule. Baseball in recent years has featured high levels of homeruns and respectably high numbers of stolen bases, a mix not found during the postwar period, when other features of the game were emphasized.

National League batters hit more homeruns than did the American League hitters in every season between 1947 and 1959; eventually, the American League became the homerun league, especially in 1964. Although the National League often featured more stolen bases than did the American League, the differences were usually small. The influx of black players did not immediately transform the National League into a base-stealing league, despite Jackie Robinson's base-running exploits. Maury Wills and, later, Lou Brock helped widen the National League's advantage in stolen bases, but stolen bases were much rarer during the postwar era than they are in today's game.

The postwar American League game relied on high on-base percentages from many walks and a reasonable amount of homeruns, especially in 1950. Today's baseball officials who rely on on-base and slugging averages, such as general managers Theo Epstein and Billy Beane, would have embraced 1950s-style baseball. Slow-footed sluggers found their niche during the postwar era.

As the Yankees' excellence waned toward the end of the postwar era, the game itself changed. During the 1960s baseball in general was entering an offensive "ice age." After the homerun binge of 1961 in the American League, both leagues watched offensive numbers plummet in 1963. Through July 1963 hitters in both leagues were putting up the lowest batting averages since 1908–9. *Sports Illustrated* hired Joseph S. Ward and Associates, engineering consultants, to test baseballs. The firm found that the balls were heavier, bouncier, and firmer in 1961 than in previous seasons.[6] A similar set of tests done in 1963, however, revealed that the newer balls were lighter than in

1961. According to the engineer testing the balls, "A lighter ball is a deader ball." The engineer concluded that "5% of the old bounce is definitely not there. This means that a ball Roger Maris hit into the seats 400 feet away in 1961 would fall 20 feet short of the seats today."[7] In addition, baseball tinkered with the strike zone before the 1963 season: "Officially, the top of the strike zone was raised from the letters on the uniform to the top of the shoulder." Philadelphia Phillies manager Gene Mauch claimed, "The new strike zone is helping the pitchers, all right. The batters are panicking on that high pitch. They don't know whether to swing or not."[8] By 1968 American League hitters would set records for futility; the season would be known as the "Season of the Pitcher." Despite the low offensive numbers, attendance was higher on a per-team basis in 1968 than in 1961. The anemic offensive numbers did not appear to be the main culprit of the American League's attendance woes of the early 1960s, as the league's attendance rebounded when different teams won pennants during the worst of the offensive slump of 1965–68.

The Effect of Pennant Races on Attendance

By the late 1950s attendance at Yankee Stadium had settled around 1.5 million. While many baseball fans viewed themselves as "Yankee haters," the team's drawing power on the road was on the rise. As New York sportswriter Til Ferdenzi observed, "It would appear that every knocker is becoming a booster for the hated Yankees." The Yankees road attendance accounted for 24 percent of the league's total attendance.[9] Even so, too much dominance within a season and across seasons eventually discouraged fans. An examination of some pennant races illuminates the phenomenon.

The Yankees sprinted to the pennant in 1958. With the Dodgers and Giants gone from the city, the Yankees expected a big increase in attendance. Unfortunately for the team, it ran away and was ten games ahead of the Chicago White Sox on September 12. A late-season slump and fan disinterest combined to curb attendance. When the season finished, Yankee officials were bemoaning a drop in season attendance of seventy thousand. As to compensate for the disappointing gate, Yankee management hoped to use the late-season swoon to ratchet down salaries. Even Mickey Mantle, the 1958 homerun leader with forty-two, would have to fight hard to get a pay raise.[10]

The Yankees faded to third place in 1959. The team was eliminated on September 9 and ended up fifteen games behind Chicago. Surprisingly, the Yankees drew 120,000 more fans in 1959 than in 1958. Although attendance slackened after the Yankees were eliminated from contention, the attendance figures compared favorably with the 1954 season when the Yankees did not win the pennant, and the team drew fewer than thirty-six thousand fans for the final six home games (although those games were against lackluster Washington and Philadelphia).

Paul Richards was not the only observer wondering if the Yankees' dynasty was over after the 1959 season: "It was no fluke season for the Yankees. They simply don't have it and it's my prediction they'll be several years back as bona fide pennant contenders. Their pitching staff is shot and most of their power gone. For the Yanks to pull back they're going to need five more pitchers and a slugger to help out Mickey Mantle. . . . I mean that clubs today are better stocked generally than ever before and cut deeply into the Yanks' one-time superiority."[11] In response to an observation that the Yankees had "not sent up a first-class rookie in three years," George Weiss admitted that the team suffered "a decline in the caliber of [its] rookies": "The farm system has been hit hard by the cutback in minor leagues all along the line." In addition, the Yankees were particularly unable to develop durable pitchers: "I'll admit our farms have not been turning out pitchers, but they have yielded infielders and outfielders and catchers other clubs want [and trade pitchers for]."[12]

New York sportswriter Dan Daniel made the interesting observation that Casey Stengel had less trouble with the 1959 squad than in previous years: "This is a well-behaved Yankee roster."[13] Daniel claimed to have see harbingers of the 1959 fiasco as early as the 1958 slump: "They had shown signs of damaging pre-occupation with things having nothing whatever to do with winning games. I made it emphatic that if the Bombers did not pay closer attention to baseball, the White Sox, hungry, desperate, in a city without a pennant since 1919, would win."[14] Weiss made eerily similar comments: "Maybe [the Yankee players] weren't hungry enough . . . maybe the Yankees had too many outside interests on their minds. All the key men are independently wealthy from the high salaries and the World Series shares. . . . The attention they gave to personal activities might have detracted from their concentration on baseball."[15] Daniel wrote that at least "Yankee-Haters" had a banner season in 1959.[16]

The Yankees won both the 1960 and 1961 pennants by eight games, but the 1960 campaign was suspenseful for longer. The Yankees dropped three straight games in Baltimore during the first weekend of September to fall behind the Orioles. Despite the novelty of the Orioles being in a pennant race, the three games drew a total of only 114,604 fans, or just a little more than 38,000 per game in a stadium seating up to 48,000. New York struggled to catch the Baltimore Orioles. By September 15 the Yankees were just one game ahead of Baltimore and two games ahead of Cleveland. The Orioles came to Yankee Stadium for four games over the weekend of September 16–18. With the pennant hotly contested, the four-game series, including a Sunday doubleheader, drew 142,749 fans, or fewer than 48,000 per day. The Yankees won all four games to all but eliminate Baltimore. In fact, the Yankees would not lose again during the regular season, ending the season with fifteen consecutive wins. After clinching the pennant with six games remaining, the Yankees watched attendance plunge, as fewer than ten thousand fans per game bothered to show up. Despite the disappointing crowds at the end of the season, the Yankees home attendance was the highest since 1952.

During the late 1950s the Yankees' chief rival was the Chicago White Sox. The Sox drew over 1.6 million fans in 1960, the team's highest turnout ever. Bill Veeck, always responding to the fans' desires, increased the number of night games for the 1961 season. An average of 26,640 fans showed up for night games versus 15,264 for day games. In addition, the Sox played better at night. The White Sox had similar attendance numbers as the Yankees in 1960, despite sharing a much smaller city with the Chicago Cubs. Shortly thereafter, Veeck sold his interest in the team because of failing health. He earned $370,000 profit on the $1.1 million sales price, after taxes.[17]

The American League expanded from eight teams to ten teams in 1961, while the National League waited until the 1962 season to expand. The additional fifty players added to the game in 1961 meant that the Major Leagues were digging deeper into the talent pool.[18] Because of the diluted pitching talent available in the American League during 1961, established homerun hitters had banner years. In 1960 Mickey Mantle led the league in homeruns with 40. Roger Maris had 39. Other sluggers with more than thirty homeruns included Jim Lemon (38), Rocky Colavito (35), and Harmon Killebrew (31). In 1961 Maris and Mantle combined for 115 homeruns. Colavito hit 45 homeruns. Jim Gentile finished third in the homerun race with 46, twenty-five more than he hit in 1960. Harmon Killebrew increased his homerun total to 46 in 1961. Norm Cash hit 41 homeruns, twenty-three more than in 1960. Jim Lemon slumped to 14 homeruns, as his career collapsed. After these six players, Bob Allison's 29 homeruns ranked seventh. Of these six sluggers with forty or more homeruns in 1961, only Harmon Killebrew ever attained that plateau again.

Given today's concerns regarding steroid use, perhaps one should ponder whether facing 25 percent new, less-talented pitchers was a bigger advantage than using steroids. Of course, expansion pitchers were legal. Even though Mantle and Maris were relatively fast base runners, both hit only sixteen doubles during 1961. In 1960 the two combined for just thirty-five doubles. Of the top six homerun hitters in 1961, the average number of doubles was less than twenty-two. The American League, as a whole, averaged around 220 doubles per team during 1960–61. This average was quite low, as every National League team had more doubles in 2000 than any team in the American League had in either 1960 or 1961. Thus, the American League game continued to revolve around slow-footed sluggers.

In 1961 the Yankees entered September holding a slim game-and-a-half lead over Detroit. The Tigers came to Yankee Stadium for three games and ended up losing all three of them before a total of 171,500 fans. Notice that the three-game attendance was almost thirty thousand greater than the pivotal home series against Baltimore in mid-September 1960. The Tigers series was just the start of a thirteen-game Yankee winning streak that broke the pennant race open. By the time the winning streak ended, New York had a comfortable ten-and-a-half game lead over the Tigers. The two teams split four games in Detroit over the September 15–17 weekend. Over 126,000 fans showed up for the series, even though the Tigers were essentially eliminated from contention. The Yankees clinched the pennant during the next series at Baltimore.

Of course, 1961 is revered as the year Roger Maris broke Babe Ruth's single-season homerun record. Indeed, forty years later the Home Box Office television channel featured a movie titled 61*. The film was actor Billy Crystal's homage to Maris's feat. As with other aspects of baseball's golden age, however, here nostalgia diverges from reality.

Mickey Mantle and, after a slow start, Roger Maris began hitting homeruns at a record pace. Mantle, of course, had hit fifty-two homeruns in 1956, so his challenge to Babe Ruth's single-season record was no surprise. Maris's high was his thirty-nine homeruns in 1960, so his bid was a surprise. By mid-July people began to speculate whether the two Yankees would break the record.

Because the season now consisted of 162 instead of 154 games, the question arose whether it would be fair for either Yankee to break the record after the 154th game. Baseball commissioner Ford Frick, a crony of Babe Ruth, ruled on July 17 that "no batter would be credited with breaking the record unless he did it in 154 games." Frick stated that breaking the record after 154 games would earn a "distinctive mark" in the record book to account for the extra games.[19] Although he did not use the term *asterisk*, he will forever be associated with the typographical character. Indeed, rarely has a typographical character ever achieved such infamy. While there was a strong argument that a distinction should be made, Frick weakened his case by initially focusing on the homerun record, to the exclusion of other possible records.

Frick's ruling caused much controversy, and even after Maris failed to break the record in the 154th game, the commissioner was still on the defensive. He reiterated his position that if Maris hit homeruns sixty and sixty-one in the remaining eight games, he would go into the record book as the homerun king for a 162-game season. The *New York Times* reported that according to Frick, "As for that star or asterisk business, I don't know how that cropped up or was attributed to me, because I never said it. I certainly never meant to belittle Maris's feat should he wind up with more than sixty. Both names will appear in the book as having set records, but under different conditions."[20] Frick continued by maintaining that all records would be subject to the same condition. He also mentioned that he believed the 162-game season was an anomaly and that the Major Leagues would soon return to the old 154-game season. Another *New York Times* article suggested that a majority of fans, even among a small sample of New York fans, backed Frick.[21]

Writers in the *Sporting News* backed Frick's decision, thirty-seven to eighteen.[22] Mickey Mantle said, "If I should break it in the one hundred and fifty-fifth game, I wouldn't want the record."[23] Columnist James Reston disputed Frick's decision denying Maris the record. Maris's achievements not only "take your mind off Nikita Khrushchev," he argued, "but because, unlike international politics, they are tangible and definite . . . Maris is more than a ball player. He is a momentary antidote to the confusion of our times, a brief escape from frustration and a particularly attractive figure as the symbol of bad luck."[24] He concluded that, while Frick's argument was correct in the "mathematics," it was incorrect in the philosophy and psychology, as Maris had to pursue Ruth, while Ruth merely swung with a "free mind."

Maris hit his fifty-fifth homerun against Cleveland in game 141. According to Bill Veeck, Maris's pursuit of Babe Ruth's record should have been a box office bonanza instead of another fumble by baseball's hierarchy:

This dream situation, this promotional fairy tale, is exactly what fell into the laps of the Yankees in 1961. And in flat defiance of all laws of promotion and probability, it did not even cause a minor traffic problem around Yankee Stadium. Commissioner Frick had come to the aid of the Traffic Department earlier by issuing an edict [here Veeck referred to an asterisk]. . . . What he did, in that one brilliant stroke, was to build the interest up to that 154th game and throw the final 8 games out in the wash with the baby. What he did was to turn what should have been a thrilling cliff-hanger lasting over the full final week of the season into a crashing anticlimax. He did even more. By focusing all attention onto the 154th game, he turned Maris's run for the record into a defeat—another anticlimax—instead of the victory that would have left everybody, except old Babe Ruth ghost-writers like Frick, glowing in satisfaction and feeling most kindly toward baseball.[25]

A contemporary observer disagreed with Veeck's gloomy prognosis. This observer claimed that Maris's chase was a "commercial success of huge proportions. There has hardly been an empty seat at a Yankee game in weeks. . . . Four-dollar tickets that a scalper couldn't have sold for $3 a month ago are now going for $30 and $40 apiece."[26]

As mentioned, the Yankees split four games with Detroit in the middle of September. Maris belted homeruns fifty-seven and fifty-eight against the Tigers in games 150 and 151 (note that in addition to these games, Maris played in a game ending in a tie, so the Yankees had actually played 152 games at this point). On Tuesday, September 19, the Yankees played a doubleheader in Baltimore. The team split the games, with the Yankees clinching a tie for the pennant. Some 31,317 fans attended the doubleheader. Maris failed to hit a homerun. On Wednesday, September 20, Maris had his last chance to break Ruth's record in 154 games. He hit homerun number fifty-nine early in the game. The crowd was sparse, only twenty-one thousand. He failed to get another homerun in the game, so, officially, the homerun race was over.

The anticlimax was not apparent, however, in the Baltimore attendance figures. On Thursday, September 21, the Yankees concluded their series in Baltimore, losing before twenty thousand fans. After a rare Friday off-day, the Yankees spent the weekend playing the Red Sox in Fenway Park. The Yankees won both games, playing before a combined fifty-nine thousand fans. The Sunday game was the second largest crowd at Fenway for the season. Maris did not hit any homeruns in the series.

The Yankees returned to Yankee Stadium for the final five games of the season. They had clinched the pennant during the Baltimore series, so the only remaining excitement was Maris's pursuit of homeruns sixty and sixty-one. Third-place Baltimore came to New York for a midweek two-game set. The teams split the games, and Maris hit homerun number sixty in game 157. Veeck's observation now rings true. The two games with Baltimore attracted a total of fewer than twenty-seven thousand fans. A good opponent and Maris's homerun exploits failed to generate a large crowd. The final three-game set with the ninth-place Red Sox over the weekend of September 29 through October 1 drew a total of 63,700 paying fans. Indeed, the Saturday game included free tickets for nine thousand children.[27] Somewhere, nine thousand baby boomers and their slightly older siblings can wax nostalgic about seeing Maris fail to hit homerun sixty-one in the 161st game of the season.

Maris, of course, hit homerun number sixty-one against Tracy Stallard early in the last game. The game had 23,154 in attendance.[28] Compared to the season-ending series against the Boston Red Sox at Yankee Stadium in 1960 (which Ted Williams had sat out), the Yankees drew 26,510 more paying customers. Yes, Maris's homerun chase arguably accounted for most of these additional customers during the three-game set, but Veeck's point remains valid. Despite four additional home games, the Yankees drew just 120,000 more fans in 1961 than in 1960. The attendance figures were not affected by changes in ticket prices. The Yankees had raised ticket prices in 1959 but had kept the prices constant through 1963. For the American League as a whole, only the Boston Red Sox raised ticket prices for the 1961 season.

The Yankees road attendance was another indication of the tepid response to Maris's homerun pursuit. The Yankees drew 1,946,674 fans on the road during the 1961 season compared with 1,859,008 in 1960. Given that there were four more road games during 1961, the per-game attendance was about the same during both seasons.

The National League expanded to ten teams for the 1962 season. Major League owners worried about attendance during that season. Expansion and the longer season were not hiking attendance as they had hoped. The longer schedule and additional teams diluted the best draws, such as the Dodgers versus the Giants. Instead of playing each other twenty-two times, the two National League powerhouses only met eighteen times. In addition, bad weather in the first part of April hurt attendance early in the season; a proposal to shift the season two weeks later meant competing with professional football in October. Owners also feared the problem of ten-team leagues: too many teams out of contention early.[29]

New York entered the 1962 Labor Day Weekend two games ahead of Minnesota and three games up on the surprising Los Angeles Angels. The Los Angeles Angels, still in the pennant race, came into Yankee Stadium for a Labor Day doubleheader. Over fifty five thousand fans attended the games. The remaining two games of the series drew fewer than twenty-nine thousand. The following weekend the Boston Red Sox played three games with the Yankees, but fewer than eighty-one thousand showed up for the pennant race weekend. Thereafter, the Yankees went on the road for their next eleven games. As befits the best draw on the road, the Yankees played to an average of over twenty thousand customers per game. The team clinched a tie for the pennant in the last game of the road trip. Upon their return to Yankee Stadium, the team clinched the pennant by beating the Washington Senators eight to three. The fans had already decided that the game was meaningless; certainly, the opponent did not elicit much excitement, so fewer than eleven thousand came to the stadium. The Wednesday game with the Senators was even worse, drawing only 3,623 patrons. A final weekend series with the Chicago White Sox attracted less than thirty-seven thousand fans combined.

American League attendance was stagnating; the two expansion teams had difficulty attracting fans. Only Calvin Griffith of the Minnesota Twins had reason to smile. During the off-season the Twins sold six hundred thousand tickets. Club officials predicted a total gate of 1.5 million for the 1963 season. The Twins did particularly well with out-of-state patrons.[30]

The Dodgers and Yankees threatened to run away from their competitors during the 1963 season. Such a possibility again worried owners. Sportswriter Joe King attributed the American League's lackluster attendance in 1963 to the Yankees' continued dominance, the league's failure to place a team in California first, and public relations fiascoes perpetrated by Oakland Athletics owner Charlie Finley.[31]

The Yankees drew almost 185,000 fewer fans to home games in 1963 than in 1962. The team's road attendance fell to just under two million. Still, the team attracted 690,000 more fans on the road than at home. Nor was the team's attendance advantage enhanced by higher ticket prices as much as in the past, as its ticket prices were no longer higher than all of its rivals' ticket prices. New York's boxes still ranked as the most expensive in the league, but some teams charged the same amount for reserved grandstand, and most charged a higher price for general admission tickets. Four rivals charged $2.50 for reserved grandstand, just as the Yankees did. In fact, only Baltimore and New York failed to charge the league-wide $1.50 for general admission.[32]

Toward the end of August 1963 the Yankees held an eleven-game lead over the Chicago White Sox. Although the pennant race was not officially over, most Yankees fans were not enticed to attend games at Yankee Stadium. Less than eleven thousand watched a game with the Red Sox on August 29. The Yankees went to Baltimore and Detroit for five playing dates (six games). Over 127,000 customers attended these games, despite both the Tigers and Orioles being well out of the race. The Yankees won the next five home games, drawing only fifty-five thousand fans.

The Yankees then went to the Twin Cities for four games with the second-place Twins. The Twins, however, were already thirteen games out of first place, with fourteen games left to play. The crowds were respectable, averaging thirty-five thousand per game. Although the Yankees won the first game and clinched the pennant, the remaining three games each drew more than the opening game. The remaining nine games at Yankee Stadium played to puny crowds totaling less than sixty thousand for seven playing dates (including a doubleheader and a game that was rained out). One might argue that clinching the pennant early cost New York at least ten thousand fans per game, but the events of 1964 make this prediction tenuous. Had the race been less lopsided, the Yankees might have matched their tepid home gate of 1962.

In 1964 the Yankees discovered the answer to the question "What if the Yankees were in a real, honest-to-goodness, down-to-the-wire, pennant race?" The Yankees found themselves in third place entering September. In fact, they remained in third place until September 16, when Baltimore and Chicago were tied for first, with New York a half-game back. The Yankees then went on one of their patented late-season winning streaks, winning eleven games in a row. By September 27, when the streak ended, New York was three games ahead of both Baltimore and Chicago. Yet the Yankees did not clinch the pennant until the final Saturday, with only one game remaining. Despite the tightness of the race, the team attracted just sixty-six thousand fans during the final seven games, including two doubleheaders. The Yankees played before fewer than eight thousand fans both for a doubleheader against Detroit on the final Thursday of the season and a single game against Cleveland on the next day. Only 26,600 showed up to watch the Saturday and Sunday games. The gate may have been suppressed because the Yankees did not play Baltimore or Chicago during September. Nevertheless, the Yankees' dynasty ended in the face of fan indifference.

Rival Forms of Entertainment in New York City

There is another factor to consider in examining attendance at Yankees games in the postwar period. The Yankees, of course, faced greater competition from other forms of entertainment than did their rivals, so a better comparison of their ticket prices might be with Broadway shows or even more highbrow entertainment. Because few teams in other cities faced such an intimidating roster of rival entertainment venues, the Yankees risked losing patrons if fans did not find the pennant race exciting. New Yorkers thinking about paying $2.50 for a reserved grandstand seat in 1963 could see in the October 1 issue of the *New York Times* that attending a motion picture, including such fare as *How the West Was Won*, with an all-star cast including John Wayne, Jimmy Stewart, Debbie Reynolds, and Gregory Peck, would cost between $2.50 and $3.50 on the weekends. New Yorkers could choose between two staples of the American musical stage: *A Funny Thing Happened on the Way to the Forum* with Zero Mostel or *How to Succeed in Business without Really Trying* with Rudy Vallee. Good mezzanine seats cost up to $7.50 for either show. Finally, if New Yorkers sniffed at the rather common entertainment found at the musical theater, they could treat themselves to the visiting Bolshoi Ballet at Madison Square Garden, for which tickets ranged from $2.00 to $6.50.

Because a reserved grandstand seat cost $2.00 in 1950 and $2.50 in 1963, was the 25 percent increase in price between 1950 and 1963 extraordinary? In other words, had the Yankees reserved seat prices risen faster than prices of rival forms of entertainment between 1950 and 1963? Again, looking at the October 1, 1950, edition of the *New York Times*, one can gauge the change in prices of theater and music tickets. A New Yorker could purchase tickets to see Laurence Olivier in *Henry V* for $1.80 to $2.40 or to listen to Jascha Heifetz perform for $1.80 to $3.00. The Ballet Russe charged $1.50 to $4.00. Unfortunately, the motion picture theaters did not list prices in 1950, so these figures are not available. These limited examples, however, show little evidence that the Yankees raised prices faster than other forms of entertainment.

Despite a tight pennant race in the American League in 1964, attendance figures were disappointing. Perhaps American League fans had a certain fatalism about the race's outcome, despite its closeness. Part of the problem began during the preseason, when American League teams failed to improve their season ticket sales. By 1964, then, the American League clearly lagged in attendance, while the National League remained healthy and competitive. The National League had a tight pennant race and strong attendance in 1964. The St. Louis Cardinals finally overtook the Philadelphia Phillies during the last week of the season. In addition, other teams finished close to these two clubs. The defending champion Dodgers also attracted large crowds.[33]

For the Yankees the dwindling attendance after 1961 was vexing. In some years the team squelched attendance by running away with the pennant. In others fans appear to have simply tired of the seeming inevitability of another Yankee pennant.

Player Movement and Building the Yankees

Leaving Soon from a (Small) City near You

During the postwar era Major League ballclubs depended upon their farm systems, trades, and purchases to stock their teams. Despite the rise of free agency in the 1970s, not much has changed in terms of player distribution. As with today's game, good players tended to end up with wealthier teams, as poorer teams traded or sold their stars. Once the free agency system began, many people feared that wealthy teams, such as the Yankees, would simply "buy" pennants by signing the best free agents. But the Yankees had been able to maintain their superiority during the postwar era in the absence of free agency.

Examining player movement during the postwar period offers valuable insights for economists and for baseball fans. Economists would not be surprised by the movement of star players from teams in smaller cities to larger cities during the postwar era. They adapted a theory developed by Ronald Coase, Nobel Prize–winner in economics, in suggesting that the distribution of players should be similar under either the old reserve clause or the free agency regimes.[1] Suppose the St. Louis Browns had signed Mickey Mantle. Mantle might have improved the Browns' record and, as he developed into a threat to Babe Ruth's homerun record, become a marquee player attracting additional fans. Perhaps Mantle might have boosted the Browns' gate and television revenues by, say, $150,000 per season. A previously Mantle-less Yankees team, however, might have received a revenue boost of $350,000 per season by acquiring him in his prime. There would be an arbitrage opportunity: by transferring Mantle to the Yankees, the two teams could split the benefits of having $200,000 more in gate revenues per season. So far our story is no different whether it took place in 1951 or 2001—a star player often generates more revenue in a larger city than a smaller one. The key difference would be the mechanics of transferring Mantle. Under the reserve clause owners in St. Louis might sell Mantle to the Yankees or, to assuage fan outrage, might camouflage the deal by getting Yankee farmhands, as well as cash, for Mantle. Today New York might offer the most attractive compensation package to Mantle and sign him away from St. Louis. Notice that under the reserve clause the owners share the benefits of Mantle's productivity, whereas under free agency Mantle captures more of the benefits from his productivity via a higher salary.

There are, of course, countervailing forces. In either 1951 or 2001 the Yankees would not find it desirable to sign every star player available. First, the additional star players, with their attendant higher salaries and purchase prices, while improving the team's record, would likely do so at a diminishing rate. Second, as the team's record improves, at some point a super team turns the pennant race into shambles. An early clinching of the pennant has typically proven to diminish the gate for the remaining games. During the 1930s, for instance, the Yankees typically saw home receipts fall off after they clinched the pennant or were eliminated from the race. Aside from avoiding "games that don't matter," fans demonstrate complex preferences. While fans prefer uncertainty in the outcome of a particular game, as shown in economists Glenn Knowles, Keith Sherony, and Michael Haupert's examination of demand for games in 1988, they also like to see the "best" team (i.e., a strong visiting team) in games in which the pennant race is still uncertain.[2] Thus, a team will likely find it disadvantageous to become too powerful. Third, across seasons fans may tire of one team continually winning the pennant races. As we have seen, repeated Yankees pennants often occurred concurrently with falling attendance. Thus, there are limits to any team's willingness to sign productive players. One can conclude that regardless of almost any plausible set of rules governing player acquisition and transfer, the Yankees would be likely to do well, given reasonably adroit deployment of their abundant resources.

Building the Yankees

How did the Yankees build their teams in the absence of free agency? The 1953 roster provides clues. The Yankees farm system produced seven of the eight regulars and two of the key starting pitchers. The eighth regular, Gene Woodling, debuted with Cleveland in 1943; the Yankees apparently picked him up on waivers or as a free agent (there were occasional free agents well before the 1970s), given that there is no record of them trading for him. Half of the reserves debuted with the Yankees. The Yankees purchased Johnny Mize in 1949 from St. Louis. Mize was primarily a pinch hitter and is often cited as the sort of veteran help the Yankees regularly obtained during the pennant race. Mize's debut with the Yankees in 1949 was not productive, however, although his later career with the team was more useful.

The team acquired seven pitchers via trades or purchases. Eddie Lopat came from the Chicago White Sox and cost the Yankees Aaron Robinson, which was a fairly good swap, given that he won 113 games with the team. Because the Yankees promoted Yogi Berra at catcher, Robinson was expendable. Cleveland traded Allie Reynolds to the Yankees for veteran infielder Joe Gordon. Reynolds won 141 games for New York, but Gordon was a key player in Cleveland's 1948 pennant. The Cincinnati Reds traded Ewell Blackwell to the Yankees for infielder Jim Greengrass. Greengrass ended up having a couple of decent seasons for the Reds, but Ewell was a bust for the Yankees, winning just three games. Jim McDonald cost the Yankees perennial journeyman Clint Courtney. The Senators received three mediocre pitchers for Bob Kuzava. Between them McDonald and Kuzava won thirty-nine games for the Bronx Bombers. The Yankees purchased

Ray Scarborough from the Red Sox, but he only won seven games for New York. Last, but perhaps most costly, veteran Johnny Sain cost the Yankees Lew Burdette. Sain won 33 games for the Yankees, but Burdette won 203 games lifetime. Among the homegrown pitchers Whitey Ford was the gem.

After retiring, George Weiss, general manager of the Yankees for most of the postwar era, explained the team's philosophy about acquiring players: "Because the Yankees were substantially built on developed players, we seldom did any trading for front-line men. Pitchers were the exception . . . we had trouble developing good pitchers. . . . We were fortunate that we had good men we could spare to get these men we wanted, which is another tribute to our system." He added, "It's no accident that defense has probably been the most consistent factor in our success, notwithstanding our great slugging reputation." Weiss summed up the team's trading philosophy, except in the case of pitchers, as "one of trying to get a man to fill a needed gap, often short-term, without helping the opposition too much, and without trading away a star."[3]

When Cleveland won the pennant in 1954, the Yankees responded by making several roster moves during 1954 and 1955. Farm products Bob Cerv, Jerry Coleman, Bob Grim, Elston Howard, Johnny Kucks, Tom Morgan, Bill Skowron, and Tom Sturdivant replaced players from the 1953 roster. New York bought veteran relief pitcher Jim Konstanty from the Philadelphia Phillies during the 1954 season; he won eight games and saved fifteen others for the Yankees. The team acquired Billy Hunter, Don Larsen, and Bob Turley from the Baltimore Orioles in return for Harry Byrd, Jim McDonald, Willie Miranda, Hal Smith, Gus Triandos, and Gene Woodling. Enos Slaughter appeared to be another valuable late-season veteran pickup for the Yankees, but he did little in his New York debut in 1954. He was more productive during his second stint with the team in the late 1950s. In order to get Slaughter, New York relinquished Bill Virdon, who would enjoy a lengthy career as a slick-fielding outfielder with a modest bat. In another trade New York received Eddie Robinson, Harry Byrd, and three other players from the Athletics in return for Don Bollweg, Jim Finigan, Vic Power, and three others after the 1953 season.

Thus, the Yankees were able to reload their team primarily by introducing young players, including several pitchers. The young pitchers each had seasons of glory for the Yankees. Grim won twenty games in his 1954 rookie year, Sturdivant won sixteen games in both the 1956 and 1957 seasons, and Kucks won eighteen games in 1956. Yet each of them quickly faded. Coleman, Howard, and Skowron were solid Major Leaguers, but none of them became a dominant player. The farm system also produced Bobby Richardson and Tony Kubek, who became the double-play combination for the 1960–64 squads. Jim Bouton, Al Downing, Joe Pepitone, Mel Stottlemyre, and Tom Tresh came up through the system during the early 1960s.

Running a farm system was costly. From 1952 through 1956 the Yankees typically reported the largest net loss of farm club subsidiaries. During the five-year period the team reported a loss of $925,237, including a gain of $8,071 in 1953. The Chicago White Sox reported a cumulative loss of $742,182, while Cleveland reported only $82,000 in losses.[4] Yet Chicago and New York represented stark contrasts in producing big league players, with the White Sox farm system being one of the least productive. Although the Yankees farm system was beginning to develop fewer good players, it still produced many Major Leaguers during the mid-1950s, so the $40,000 extra subsidy per season to its farm system compared with Chicago's appears to have been well spent. The Detroit Tigers' experiences demonstrate the costliness of running a farm system. Between January 1, 1950, until September 30, 1957, the Tigers spent $2.27 million for scouts, salaries, and expenses, plus signing bonuses for 632 players. In September 1957 there remained 54 players of "value" left in the system, with a collective worth of $2.16 million. The Tiger management estimated that each Major League regular, not star, cost $100,000 in development costs.[5]

The Yankees typically operated the largest farm system in the American League, although other teams were developing their own systems.[6] In 1953 the Yankees owned three Minor League teams and had affiliations with ten more. The St. Louis Browns had the second largest system, as they owned one team and had affiliations with eleven others. Five of the American League teams had eight or fewer Minor League teams, owned or affiliated: Boston, Chicago, Detroit, Philadelphia, and Washington. By 1955 the Yankees owned only one Minor League team and had affiliations with ten other teams. Cleveland, Detroit, and Baltimore had at least nine Minor League teams each. Boston, Chicago, Kansas City, and Washington each had seven or fewer Minor League teams.[7]

To examine the productivity of the Yankees farm system, I will use the "total baseball rankings" (TBR) system. Baseball statisticians John Thorn and Pete Palmer, along with other researchers, attempted to adjust player performances for differences in ballparks, in playing rules, and other factors. The (TBR) is in a sense a marginal productivity measure. It gives a rough idea of how many wins the player would add to an average team. In many cases a player's (TBR) may be negative. One drawback of the (TBR) is that players who see very little action may receive a rating near zero; a below-average regular may receive a negative number and thus appear worse than the seldom-used player.

The Yankees scouts and George Weiss made several astute signings of young players up to the early 1950s. When young Joe DiMaggio injured his leg, the San Francisco Seals saw bidding by Major League teams diminish. The Yankees purchased DiMaggio for $25,000. Mickey Mantle got an initial bonus of $1,000, which was double what Yogi Berra signed for. Collegiate star Charley Keller got a $5,000 bonus, while Tommy Henrich cost $20,000. Gil McDougald received a $1,500 bonus, but Phil Rizzuto signed for practically nothing.[8]

Although the Yankees introduced four to five times as many top players as some of their American League rivals between 1919 and 1945, their edge was shrinking. During the postwar era the Yankees fell behind the Cleveland Indians in introducing productive players, although the Indians developed a large number of solid but not spectacular players (see table 2.1 in the appendix). New York's productivity was nearly triple that of the least fecund farm system, the Philadelphia/

Kansas City Athletics. Of New York's six star debuts three—Mickey Mantle, Whitey Ford, and Yogi Berra—accounted for 154 of the 194.4 in total baseball rankings. Jackie Jensen and Gil McDougald were two other star players introduced by the Yankees (in 1950 and 1951); after making only a brief appearance with the team, Jensen was traded. After 1951 the Yankees farm system did not introduce any players with high (TBR)'s until Mel Stottlemyre's rookie season in 1964.

During the 1919–45 period two National League teams, the New York Giants and St. Louis Cardinals, approached New York's record for introducing star players. In the postwar years, however, the Giants and Boston/Milwaukee Braves far outpaced the Yankees. The Braves, late-comers to developing a farm system, poured hundreds of thousands of dollars into their postwar system.[9] The Dodgers were also more productive. All three teams introduced great black players such as Henry "Hank" Aaron, Roy Campanella, Willie Mays, Willie McCovey and Jackie Robinson.

The Brooklyn Dodgers and New York Giants mirrored the Yankees' acumen in signing good young players. The players on the 1954 New York Giants apparently cost $150,000 in bonuses, purchases, and draft prices, while the 1955 Dodgers cost $90,000.[10] Jackie Robinson signed for nothing, while Roy Campanella cost the Dodgers $1,700.

When the Giants relocated to San Francisco and began earning larger profits, the team plowed much of the returns into its scouting and player development. The Giants paid $184,300 for their entire 1959 roster. Many of the key players hailed from the Caribbean: the Alou brothers, Felipe, Jesus, and Matty; Orlando Cepeda; and Juan Marichal. Willie McCovey signed for a bus ticket. The Giants paid the Birmingham Negro League team $10,000 for Willie Mays. Only Mike McCormick signed a big bonus of $65,000.[11]

In a 1958 *Baseball Digest* article author Bill Bryson showed that the New York Yankees, Brooklyn Dodgers, and Boston Red Sox had signed 112 of the 318 regular Major League players. The Yankees signed the most eventual Major Leaguers with forty-three. Although some of these players made their Major League debuts with other teams, the author felt that tracing the player to the team with which he initially signed gave a better representation of the various teams' farm systems. The Yankees produced more Major Leaguers than the combined farm systems of the Athletics, Orioles, Phillies, and White Sox, but, again, after 1951 none of these Yankees boasted high productivity ratings. The White Sox produced only eleven of the Major League regulars playing at that time.[12]

Another Approach to Building a Strong Team

The Chicago White Sox represented another approach to building a good team. As noted, the White Sox's farm system was not impressive. Yet the White Sox went from 60-94 in 1950 to 81-73 in both 1951 and 1952 to 89-65 in 1953. The team would peak at 94-60 in both 1954 and 1959 and would not have a losing season until a collapse in 1968.

How did the White Sox improve so quickly, building a team that finished in the top three for most of the 1950s? The team introduced only one productive player between Luke Appling in 1930 and Earl Battey in 1955—Eddie Lopat in 1944—and he went to New York after the war. The White Sox introduced Luis Aparicio in 1956; Johnny Callison, Norm Cash, and Johnny Romano in 1958; and Gary Peters in 1959. Clearly, the farm system did not catapult the Sox into respectability.

The White Sox used a series of trades and purchases. Although fans believe that the Yankees built their success on the backs of their weaker brethren, the Chicago White Sox actually epitomized such "rapacity." The team did not make many deals with the New York Yankees after the Eddie Lopat deal, but it stripped its downtrodden American League rivals. Six of the eight regulars and four of the top five pitchers hailed from the Athletics, Browns, and Senators. The White Sox obtained Nellie Fox, Sherm Lollar, Minnie Minoso, and Jim Rivera as relatively untried players.

To compete with Cleveland and New York after 1954, the White Sox picked up Dick Donovan and Jack Harshman for nothing except possibly the waiver price or Minor League draft price. The two combined for twenty-six wins in 1955. The team acquired George Kell, veteran star third baseman; Kell cost the Sox Grady Hatton and $100,000. Jim Busby cost three benchwarmers. Although Chicago acquired some players from Boston and Detroit, the Athletics, Orioles, and Senators accounted for six of the players acquired after 1953.[13] Thus, the 1955 White Sox had seven regulars obtained from other teams, as only shortstop Chico Carrasquel was originally a White Sox. Luis Aparicio would replace Carrasquel the following season. Only one of the nine top pitchers began with the White Sox.

Chicago, then, represented the antithesis of the New York Yankees. As baseball writer Bryson pointed out, "If the [small number of future Major Leaguers signed by the White Sox] is an indictment of [them] as farmers, though, at the same time it is proof positive of their genius as traders."[14] A team could be successful in the absence of both free agency and a good farm system. The White Sox were unique, however, in their success in improving their team. Many baseball fans will recall that Tom Yawkey of the Boston Red Sox attempted to buy a pennant. When his efforts to win the pennant with purchased former St. Louis Browns players failed, Yawkey decided to invest in a farm system.[15] The new Baltimore Orioles owners, citing a convenient tax-free $500,000 worth of income, announced to the fans their intention of buying players. Given that Baltimore did not win its first pennant until 1966, twelve years later, one can assume that the planned spending spree failed.[16]

Player Movement during the Postwar Era

Although modern fans bemoan small-city teams losing star players via trades, cash sales, or free agency, the phenomenon is not new. In discussing the movement of players, I turn again to the Thorn/Palmer total baseball rankings.

During the postwar period the teams in the larger cities tended to have surplus players to sell to teams in the smaller cities. The New York Yankees and Brooklyn Dodgers sold or traded many players to their poorer brethren. Of course, these players were usually less productive than those retained by the Yankees and Dodgers. Conversely, the St. Louis Browns were notorious for selling their best players to wealthier teams; sometimes the wealthier teams sent players to the Browns, but they were typically marginal prospects at best. In terms of net productivity the teams in the larger and medium-sized cities gained from teams in the smaller cities (see table 2.2 in the appendix). The Indians and Giants gained the most productivity in terms of the TBR ratings from cash transactions between 1946 and 1960. The Browns/Orioles, Tigers, and Braves lost the most productivity. When the Browns moved to Baltimore, however, the loss of productivity slowed, if not reversed.

There was a marked similarity between the 1946–60 and 1974–92 eras in terms of the quality of players involved in cash transactions. The players sold in the later era were a year and a half younger on average than in the earlier cohort. The average player involved in cash transactions in both eras was below average in terms of productivity.[17] There was also a strong similarity between the 1946–60 and 1974–92 eras in terms of the amount of talent moving from smaller cities to larger cities via cash and, in the later period, free agency. Again, teams in the larger cities tended to gain productivity from teams in the smaller cities. On a per-team basis the amounts of productivity shifted were similar across eras.

The change in property rights to a player's labor between the 1946–60 reserve clause and the post-1975 free agency eras did not significantly alter the overall pattern of the flow of talent. The evidence also suggests that the movement of players was not so dramatic as to explain the Yankees' domination of the American League for over forty seasons between 1921 and 1964 or the Dodgers' success for thirty seasons (1947–78). Nor can the pattern of player movements explain how a small-city franchise such as the St. Louis Cardinals could do so well for twenty years (1926–46). The Cardinals farm system was so fecund that at one time ninety current Major Leaguers hailed from the system.[18] Successful farm systems may have reduced the need for big-city teams, such as the Yankees and Dodgers, to acquire productive players from teams in the smaller cities, as during the 1946–60 era, with the reserve clause. The Dodgers sold many of their excess players; in a series of deals they received $700,000 from the player-starved Pittsburgh Pirates.[19] Conversely, the free agency era has allowed some franchises, particularly the Yankees, to improve its talent rapidly in a way that had usually eluded teams in the past.

As the Coase theorem predicts, during the 1950s the Athletics, Browns/Orioles, and Senators rarely kept their best young players. The Athletics kept Ferris Fain and Bobby Shantz for many of their best years but traded Clete Boyer and Nellie Fox early in their careers. The Browns kept Ned Garver and Roy Sievers for a number of years, but they traded Ellis Kinder almost immediately. After moving to Baltimore, the franchise kept its next four stars—Brooks Robinson, Milt Pappas, Ron Hansen, and Boog Powell—for most or all of their strongest seasons. The Washington Senators/Minnesota Twins were not overly successful in introducing new stars. Between 1946 and 1964 the franchise developed Camilo Pascual, Harmon Killebrew, Bob Allison, Jim Kaat, and Tony Oliva. The team kept Allison and Oliva for their entire Major League careers; Killebrew stayed with the team until his final season in 1975, when he signed with Kansas City. The franchise traded Kaat and Pascual during the middle of their careers. Robinson, Allison, Oliva and Robinson were the only three of the eighteen stars produced by the three franchises to remain with their original team. Even a strong team such as the White Sox did not always retain its star players. The postwar White Sox did not produce any star players until 1955. The team held on to Luis Aparicio and Earl Battey for many of their best years. Conversely, the team traded its trio of 1958 rookies (Johnny Callison, Norm Cash, and Johnny Romano) to Cleveland and Philadelphia in 1959.

The New York/Kansas City Shuttle: Exploitation of a Lackey?

In the public's perception perhaps nothing exemplified the almost vassal-like relationship between the rich Yankees ball club and the destitute members of the American League as the player conduit between the

Yankees and the Kansas City Athletics. The sale of the Philadelphia Athletics to Arnold Johnson in 1954 triggered fears that the close relationship between Johnson and the Yankee ownership would be detrimental to baseball.

The National League in its early days had battled public distrust emanating from its interlocking ownerships, whereby some owners had interests in more than one team. Such conflicts of interests led to unsavory manipulations of player rosters. These shenanigans reverberated in the widespread belief about the relationship between the transplanted Athletics and the Yankees. Historian Charles Alexander wrote, "Season by season, the Athletics' best players went to New York in exchange for 'promising youngsters' who usually settled into mediocrity. Kansas City was officially a big-league city, but plenty of people there and elsewhere wondered whether the ball club wasn't still effectively a Yankees farm." Another historian echoed Alexander's statement: "[Kansas City was] a steady supplier of talent to the Yankees, accepting in return batches of players the Yankees had no further use for."[20] Given the issue of interlocking directorates, the congressional hearings of 1957 paid a great deal of attention to the relationship between the Yankees and the Athletics.[21]

Certainly, there were elements of the relationship that provided combustibles for conspiratorial fires. The *Chicago Tribune* and *New York Times* covered the controversy. At the time of the sale Johnson owned Yankee Stadium and the baseball park in Kansas City where the Yankees farm team played. In addition, Washington Senators owner Clark Griffith claimed, "I also have heard Johnson and Dan Topping are business associates in a large corporation."[22] Griffith complained that the Yankees "tried to railroad this Kansas City thing through" the league meeting.[23] In addition, he pointed out that Johnson's ownership of Yankee Stadium would make his ownership of Kansas City a violation of the league rules against having direct or indirect interests in multiple teams. Griffith, however, may have been influenced by his fears that a Philadelphia shift would mean that the new Baltimore team would be considered an "eastern" team and thereby share more playing dates with the Senators.[24] Even former Athletics owner Connie Mack's wife complained about the Yankees' involvement in the deal: "New York wants this club to go to Kansas City and when New York's in the back and pushing it, well, there's your answer."[25]

The Yankees' co-owner Dan Topping energetically backed Johnson's attempt to move the Athletics, and he even claimed that he would not ask for any compensation for the Yankees' Kansas City Minor League territory. Johnson had to compensate the remainder of the American Association for the loss of the territory. Topping stood by his support for the transfer: "There's been no secret about our position. We think it would be best for the American League and best for us to move the A's to Kansas City."[26] He further maintained that "Philadelphia has been a real white elephant in our league for fifteen years and I can't see how things will get better there."[27] Arch Ward, a *Chicago Tribune* sportswriter, was also less suspicious about the move: "[The] addition of Kansas City . . . will strengthen [the league]. Philadelphia was a terrific liability. . . . Its new owner, Arnold Johnson of Chicago, is solid financially and a sportsman at heart."[28] To allay fears of interlocking ownership, Johnson divested his holdings in Yankee Stadium.[29]

Although the previous owners of the Athletics had recently completed two trades with the Yankees, the pace picked up after 1954 and continued until Charles O. Finley purchased the Athletics upon Johnson's death in 1960. The two teams made seventeen player transactions between 1955 and 1960, although one of the trades basically unraveled. Given the Athletics' relative poverty, the fact that the Yankees sold more players to Kansas City than they bought from them is surprising. How much cash changed hands is ambiguous. The *Macmillan Baseball Encyclopedia* listed only the $50,000 sale of Ewell Blackwell, Dick Kryhoski, and Tom Gorman. All of the other transactions involving cash did not specify the amount, so we do not know which team gained cash overall.

The Yankees received many players who would never wear the pinstripes. Of the twenty-seven players the Yankees received from Kansas City during Johnson's ownership, over one-third failed to make the team. Others, such as Joe DeMaestri, Murray Dickson, Sonny Dixon, Kent Hadley, and Virgil Trucks, appeared only briefly as Yankees. Dickson and Trucks had been star pitchers but were well past their primes.

Who were the useful acquisitions for the Yankees? Clete Boyer became a fixture at third base for the Yankees during their last run of pennants. He was an excellent defensive player with a below-average bat. Bob Cerv, Hector Lopez, and Enos Slaughter became useful reserves. Roger Maris was of course the most notorious Yankee acquisition during this era. Maris had shown flashes of power during his first three seasons with Cleveland and Kansas City, hitting twenty-eight homeruns in 1958. Yet he had performed very erratically in 1959. Although he underwent an appendectomy in May, he was hitting .344 as late as July 29. Thereafter, he slumped badly, finishing the season at .273. One observer thought that Maris was disappointed that a proposed deal sending him to the Yankees had fallen through. Scouting reports on Maris quoted by the *Baseball Digest* read, "Most baseball men have been viewing Roger Maris with covetous eyes for the past few seasons. From a theoretical point of view, he represents the ideal young player. . . . He can run, throw, and hit with power. . . . Maris has talent but has failed to produce consistently." He had three great seasons, winning two Most Valuable Player awards, and was a coup for the Yankees. Injuries robbed him of a greater career, and the Yankees traded him to the Cardinals after the 1966 season.

At the time of Maris's trade from Kansas City to New York, some reporters believed that the Athletics had gotten the better of the deal. New York sportswriter Dan Daniel claimed that "there is considerable feeling here that the Bombers gave up too much in this transaction. . . . The four men whom Kansas City got in the trade will improve that club tremendously." Kansas City sportswriter, Ernest Mehl, while addressing the fans' suspicions of the Yankee/Athletic conduit, seconded Daniel's impression: "A great many others believe the A's made a deal which could help them. They recognize the fact that Siebern, without all of Maris' interesting possibilities, may be a more consistent hitter."[30] George Weiss claimed in 1961 that Pittsburgh offered Bill Virdon, Dick Groat, and Ron Kline for Maris but backed out at the last minute.[31]

Of the pitchers acquired by the Yankees, Ryne Duren harnessed his wildness and became a good relief pitcher.[32] Ralph Terry was another solid acquisition. After bouncing between the Athletics and Yankees, he returned to New York for good in 1959. Casey Stengel hoped that a "change of scenery" would benefit Terry: "He looked like a fine prospect with us a few years ago, but I understand that after we traded [him] to the A's, [manager] Harry Craft never was quite satisfied with him. Maybe, with a fresh start in New York, he'll do better. At least, I hope so."[33] During the last four pennant seasons of the Mickey Mantle/Whitey Ford era, Terry won sixty-six games. If he was not the ace of the staff, he was a strong number-two starter.

The other pitchers acquired by the Yankees, such as Art Ditmar, Duke Maas, and Bobby Shantz, typically turned in a season or two of good backup work. The Ditmar trade provoked much negative comment. Some rival owners cited the trade as proof of the Yankees' control over the Kansas City franchise. Arnold Johnson retorted, however, that other teams had offered less for Ditmar and did not think of him as a potential star until he became a Yankee. These pitchers performed better with the Yankees than with the Athletics.[34]

In evaluating the pitchers whom the Yankees acquired, one might also consider that pitching for the Yankees was beneficial not only for a pitcher's win-loss record but also for his earned run average ERA. Sportswriters commented on the way that pitchers improved after being traded to the Yankees. George Weiss claimed that he selected pitchers who possessed "courage." He could presumably note their courage in facing Mickey Mantle and Yogi Berra before trading for them.[35] The pitchers' improvement after joining for the Yankees may be explained partially by the superior fielding possessed by the New York team and the fact that these pitchers no longer had to face the Yankees' hitters.

The Yankees, then, had acquired a potential Hall of Fame player, had his career not been disrupted by injuries, in Maris; a front-line starter in Terry; a regular in Boyer; several effective reserve outfielders; and a two-year wonder reliever in Ryne Duren. The team also got a few good years from second-line starters Ditmar, Maas, and Shantz. According to baseball historians, the Athletics received in return a motley collection of players, although not all of them were chaff. Jerry Lumpe hit well for a second baseman. Deron Johnson later became a solid power-hitting first baseman, and his 245 career homeruns were, surprisingly, only 30 fewer than Roger Maris hit. Unfortunately, Kansas City released him after the 1962 season, as he showed little promise in 1961–62. Hank Bauer was clearly ending a solid career as a middling outfielder. He was, however, comparable as a reserve to the reserve outfielders the Yankees obtained.

The Athletics received some promising younger outfielders from the Yankees. Norm Siebern was one of the more useful former Yankees. The Yankees were the only team interested in signing Siebern as a amateur, but by 1958 he was a top-ranked rookie prospect.[36] He had hit .300 in 1958 for the Yankees, and the *New York Times* columnist John Drebinger described him as a "potentially great" outfielder. Apparently, a knee injury and, later, fielding miscues in the 1958 World Series hampered Siebern, who "never seemed to recover from the criticism he suffered."[37] During his four seasons with Kansas City he hit over .272 in each season and clubbed a total of seventy-eight homeruns. Siebern was one of the six players in the Roger Maris trade. Obviously, Most Valuable Player Maris was the superior player in 1960 and 1961, but Siebern's 1962 season was comparable, if not better. Siebern and Maris each earned a Gold Glove award while with the Yankees.

Bob Cerv had played sparingly for the Yankees in the early 1950s but hit over .300 in 1955–56 with some power. In his three full seasons with the Athletics he belted sixty-nine homeruns, including thirty-eight in 1958, and hit about .290. He gave the Athletics a good bat for three seasons and outproduced all of the hitters that the Yankees received, aside from Roger Maris. The Athletics got one good half-season out of Lou Skizas. The outfielder was a bust for the Yankees, but he hit .316

for the Athletics during the second half of the 1956 season. He blasted eighteen homeruns in 1957 for the Athletics, who then traded him, while his value was highest, to Detroit in the Billy Martin deal. Skizas had one homerun left in him and retired after the 1959 season.

Woodie Held was another good young player relinquished by the Yankees. He played a total of five games for them in 1954 and 1957 before being traded to the Athletics. Although he hit twenty homeruns in 1957, the Athletics traded him to Cleveland in return for, among others, Roger Maris. Cleveland converted him into a shortstop, and he averaged over twenty homeruns per season during his first seven full seasons with the Indians. Most of the other hitters were of limited value, even for the Athletics. Among them was the famous "Marvelous" Marv Throneberry. Before becoming an original member of the twentieth-century New York Mets and a stalwart for Miller Beer ads, Throneberry had languished on the Yankees bench, although he had batted 1.000 in his 1955 debut of two at bats. Throneberry had his first mediocre season while playing for Kansas City, hitting .250 with eleven homeruns. He had his best season playing for the pathetic Mets in 1962, but he was out of the Majors early in the 1963 season.

The Kansas City A's did not fare as well with the pitchers they received from the Yankees. Ewell Blackwell, Murray Dickson, and Johnny Sain were all experienced hurlers with almost four hundred big-league wins among them. Unfortunately, they were all at the end of their careers, and even the Athletics, with their mediocre pitchers, used them for only one or two seasons each. The trio earned only thirteen of their lifetime wins with the Athletics. Blackwell had a sore arm and had been on the "voluntarily retired" list before the trade.[38] Art Ditmar pitched more effectively for the Yankees than he did for the Athletics during his two stints there. According to Lou Boudreau, Athletics manager, Ditmar was "rated one of the brightest prospects in baseball. The White Sox tried to land him last winter [1957]." George Weiss seconded Boudreau's opinion: "[Ditmar] is the ace in the deal."[39] The Athletics reacquired him in 1961, but he immediately lost his effectiveness, losing his final seven big-league decisions.

The Athletics picked up several relatively young pitchers—Bob Grim, Johnny Kucks, Tom Morgan, and Tom Sturdivant—from the Yankees, but although these pitchers had had brief success in New York, they could not replicate their effectiveness with the Athletics. The A's obtained Sturdivant, Kucks, and Jerry Lumpe during the 1958 season. Casey Stengel commented that "all are in excellent physical shape, but the two pitchers, Kucks and Sturdivant, just couldn't get going for me, and I felt we had to do something. Maybe a change of scenery will do them good."[40] Sturdivant did nothing for the Athletics and was traded to Boston. He later turned in two decent seasons as a relief pitcher. Even so, the acquisition of Kucks, Sturdivant, and Lumpe for Hector Lopez and Ralph Terry turned out to be a dubious one. Lumpe was a good-hitting second baseman, but Terry turned in some very fine seasons for the Yankees.

Most of the pitchers acquired by the Athletics did poorly with their new team. Jack Urban gave the Athletics a decent rookie year in 1957, going 7-4 with a 3.34 ERA. Unfortunately, he quickly lost his effectiveness. A possible explanation was his age, as he was a twenty-eight-year-old rookie.

The Athletics thus erred badly in their pitching acquisitions from the Yankees. Grim, Kucks, Larsen, Morgan and Sturdivant all had their moments of brilliance with the Yankees, and the Athletics picked them up a year or two too late in every case. Conversely, the Athletics could not harness Duren's fastball, and they traded Terry too soon. They got two decent half-seasons from Tom Gorman and Jack Urban, but these successes were small offsets to Duren, Terry, and other Yankee pitching acquisitions from the Athletics.

The two teams' frequent transactions during Arnold Johnson's ownership of the Athletics elicited much commentary. The *New York Times* columnist John Drebinger wryly remarked on the conduit: "Balked at every other port of call, the Yankees yesterday turned to their old standbys in the trading mart to swing that long-awaited deal," and, "The Yankees finally broke the trading barrier yesterday and no one need more than a single guess to name the party of the second part."[41]

He further remarked on complaints about all of the trades by rival officials from the White Sox and Indians, Bill Veeck and Frank Lane. The *Times* repeatedly printed all of the trades from previous years. The Associated Press led off a trade story with "The slumping New York Yankees again turned to Kansas City . . . for help. . . . The Kansas City–New York shuffles, starting shortly after the Athletics moved west in 1955 into former Yankee farm territory, have involved 52 players."[42] Chicago sports columnist Edward Prell was less gracious: "The [Boyer/Ditmar] deal added fuel to previous complaints by rival American League club officials that the Athletics, in effect, are a farm club of the Yankees."[43] Prell also remarked that Athletics official Parke Carroll had held a similar position with the Yankees' former Kansas City Minor League team.

The Athletics denied any impropriety, with their manager, Lou Boudreau, claiming, "We went to every [team]. The Yankees had the players we wanted. The others did not."[44] Given the Yankees' fecundity in producing Major League players during this era, Boudreau's remarks were plausible. A Kansas City sportswriter, Ernest Mehl, even acknowledged as much in his column. Arnold Johnson also angrily denied any improper relations between the two teams, and he voluntarily appeared before the congressional committee investigating professional team sports to refute any such rumors. Weiss and Johnson also cited the fact that Kansas City had made trades with other American League teams (such as acquiring Maris from Cleveland and selling Harry Chiti to Detroit). Yet Chicago White Sox vice president Charles Comiskey claimed that his team had offered the Athletics a similar but better deal for Boyer and Ditmar. Ironically, this initial wave of criticism during 1957 occurred before the Yankees had reaped much, if any, advantage from their trades with the Athletics.

Yet not all of the contemporary observers thought that the Yankees were exploiting the Athletics. Indeed before the Ryne Duren, Roger Maris, and Ralph Terry deals, the Yankees had little to show for their trades with the Athletics. As one sportswriter put it, "If previous deals between the Athletics and Yankees are any criterion, the

A's will eventually get the better of the latest multi-player swap. . . . With the exception of Enos Slaughter, all Kaycee players acquired by the Yankees in their previous deals with the A's have been assigned to minor league affiliates of the New York club or dealt eventually." The columnist was reviewing the evidence up to the Art Ditmar trade. Two weeks later another columnist remarked that many of the Yankees' trades with Kansas City and other teams were for short-term help. The Yankees farm system was deep enough that the Yankees could afford to relinquish young players who became solid performers—Lew Burdette, Jim Greengrass, Vic Power, and Bill Virdon, for instance—in order to get veterans to help win a particular pennant.[45]

Of course, if the Athletics and other teams received inferior players from the Yankees, these players might still continue to be performers for those teams, while they might have languished in the Yankees farm system. Therefore, the continued presence in the Major Leagues of the Yankees' castoffs was not necessarily definitive evidence that the Yankees got less than they gave. Nevertheless, even as late as 1961, Kansas City sportswriter Ernest Mehl defended the trades: "Despite the popular feeling that the Yankees gained the upper hand in their dealings with the A's, the facts do not bear this out. On the present roster of the Yankees there are five players obtained from the A's. They are Hector Lopez, Roger Maris, Joe DeMaestri, Cletis Boyer and Art Ditmar. Either directly or indirectly as the result of these trades, the squad of the present Athletics include 14 players."[46] Curiously, Mehl neglected to add Ralph Terry to the list of players acquired from the Athletics.

Mehl lauded Arnold Johnson and his general manager, Parke Carroll: "In all fairness . . . what has been done to improve a team labeled in 1953 as the worst ever to compete in the American League, would have been tried by anyone else. To their credit, they have continued to make their moves in the face of all the opposition."[47] Sportswriter Dan Daniel reported that many New York writers thought the Yankees' reacquisition of Ralph Terry and Hector Lopez was not very valuable, while the reaction in Kansas City was positive: "The fact is, the fans [in Kansas City] almost unanimously rated this as one of the better deals the club has made."[48] The Roger Maris trade was of course the most memorable one. Dan Daniel cited another reason why New York fans disavowed the Maris trade: "Many of them deplore the invitation to the [Yankee] Haters which stems from the trade. They would much rather not deal with the Athletics. . . . It would appear that the connection with the Yankees hardly has been a handicap and deterrent to Kansas City progress. But the Yankee haters are hollering, and they won't be stilled."[49]

Aside from fans and sportswriters, baseball officials had mixed feelings about the trades. In 1957 two rival baseball officials defended the conduit. John McHale, general manager of the Detroit Tigers, stated, "There is nothing illegal or unethical about the trading between the Yankees and the Athletics. . . . [Arnold Johnson] took a ball club that had nothing and made it into a ball club that is tough to beat. Arnold and I were on the phone at least 25 times since the opening of the season. We just couldn't trade because we didn't have the extra ballplayers to offer. We don't have depth and that's no secret." McHale's counterpart in Baltimore, Paul Richards, claimed, "[Johnson had] to get ballplayers. The most logical source is the team that has the most, and that is the Yankees. Kansas City would be trading with, say, Chicago if the White Sox were the team overloaded with talent."[50] It is important to note that both of them were commenting in 1957, before the most infamous trades took place.

The Yankees reaped a greater advantage from the later deals, starting with the Boyer trade. The Maris trade, in particular, irked rival American League owners and officials, especially Frank Lane and Bill Veeck, with Veeck lashing out against the "unholy alliance" between the Yankees and the Athletics. He claimed that the Yankees got Maris for "some players the Yankees didn't need." He characterized Maris as someone who would "be around Yankee Stadium for a long time, and DeMaestri . . . is the league's third best shortstop." He thought the Athletics were offered more by other teams: "Only this morning, Detroit asked for Maris, and was told that he was too valuable to put in any transaction that didn't include Harvey Kuenn. . . . Whenever [Arnold] Johnson talks to us, his players are suddenly more valuable. Either that or our opinion of some of the Yankees he gets is far from correct." He continued his tirade by claiming that "this kind of thing comes under the heading of conduct detrimental to baseball. What will this do to the Kansas City fan? Just look at that club. Who on the Kansas City roster didn't come from New York?" Then, in a burst of prescience, he added, "Now I'm just afraid Bud Daley will be next. The Yankees say they need a left handed pitcher." Veeck concluded by hoping that the other owners would do something to stop these "brutal transactions."[51] A cynic might notice that Veeck and Lane represented the two teams with the most hope of beating the Yankees.

Is there a more objective way to analyze these trades? The Yankees acquired players from Kansas City during the Johnson era with a combined total baseball rating of 24.5 during their services with the team. The Athletics got players with a combined TBR of –18 during their stints in Kansas City. At first glance, then, the Yankees appear to have gained 42.5 in TBR. From 1955 to 1962 this would represent a gain of 5 points per season, or roughly five more wins per season than an average group of players would win. The key trade for the Yankees, however, was the one involving Clete Boyer, Art Ditmar, Bobby Shantz, and three other players for a group of mediocre players including Billy Hunter, Tom Morgan, Irv Noren, and Jack Urban. The Yankees picked up the most TBR points from this trade, with the Maris trade a distant second. Only the Ryne Duren swap was another definite gain for the Yankees. Thus, until the Boyer trade the Yankees had very little to show for their trades with the Athletics, and Boyer would not become a regular until 1960.

Moreover, many of the Yankees' acquisitions never played for them, while many of the Athletics' acquisitions played for several, admittedly mediocre, seasons. Another way to look at the trades is to look at the top six producers for each team—that is, every player with a positive TBR during his time with his new team. The six productive Yankees players included Clete Boyer (12.6), Roger Maris (10.5),

Bobby Shantz (6.6), Ryne Duren (3.2), Art Ditmar (2.8), and Ralph Terry (1.6); these players had a combined 37.3 TBR with the Yankees. The Athletics' six most productive pickups included Bob Cerv (5.3), Norm Siebern (5.1), Jerry Lumpe (3.3), Tom Gorman (1.2), Woody Held (0.5), and Enos Slaughter (0); these players had a combined TBR of 15.4. The difference thus comes down to Maris and Boyer versus the advantage in second-line players held by the Athletics.

Certainly, the Yankees/Athletics trading conduit was unusual. Although the Yankees had purchased Bob Shawkey and Frank "Home Run" Baker from Connie Mack during the dismantling of the 1910–14 Athletics, they did not purchase any Athletics players during the second dismantling in the mid-1930s. Nor did the Yankees and Athletics engage in many trades before Johnson took over as owner. The two teams did engineer a massive trade at the end of 1953, with the Yankees receiving pitcher Harry Byrd and veteran first baseman Eddie Robinson, whom they later traded back to Kansas City. In return the Athletics picked up Vic Power, Jim Finigan, and four others.

At the time Yankee officials almost gloated about the trade: "The deal looks mighty good for us because we did not give up a regular and got two in return." They acknowledged that they "gave up some young players who could become great stars." The Athletics were enthusiastic too: "It is a good start toward a faster, younger, stronger defensive team that will return the Athletics to first division." While the Athletics did not return to "first division," they arguably gained more from the trade than the Yankees did. The New York Times commented on the trade the next year: "Although the Yankee package deal with the Athletics a year ago was ridiculed as being lopsidedly in favor of the Bombers, it didn't work out that way at all. . . . The A's got the better of the exchange."[52] Robinson hit sixteen homeruns during his second campaign with the Yankees, but he was no longer a consistent performer. Byrd had a decent season with the Yankees as a second-line starting pitcher before being traded. Power became an All-Star, and Jim Finigan shone briefly by hitting .302 in 1954. Yankee manager Casey Stengel even selected him for the 1954 All-Star game.

His performance prompted the *New York Times* to claim that the Yankees would "pay heavily to get him back."[53] Perhaps the Athletics should have traded him back, given that his performance promptly deteriorated. Thus, the Yankees got one decent reserve performance each from Eddie Robinson and Harry Byrd in return for an All-Star and a one-year wonder.

The Browns sold an inordinately large number of players between 1947 and 1953. Surprisingly, the Yankees did not frequently purchase or trade for any major players from the Browns during this period. In the only major deal between the two teams the Browns sent the Yankees Fred Sanford and Roy Partee in exchange for Red Embree, Sherm Lollar, Dick Starr, and $100,000. George Weiss later reflected on the trade: "I went for a big money deal only once and I got singed so badly I was afraid to go near the fire again. . . . Even now, 13 years later, the memory of that deal [buying Fred Sanford from the Browns for $100,000 plus Sherm Lollar] gives me the creeps."[54] In the other deals all of the players, except Tommy Byrne, were busts. The Yankees did not buy any players from the American League's other shaky franchise, the Washington Senators, during the postwar era and sold that club just one player, journeyman hurler Al Cicotte.

Another franchise that was notorious for player sales, the Philadelphia Phillies, sold only three significant players to the Yankees between 1930 and 1960: Blondy Ryan in 1935, Nick Etten (as well as other lesser, fringe players) in 1943, and Jim Konstanty in 1954. The Phillies sold many players during the 1930s and 1940s in order to remain solvent. The team's player sales elicited a 1941 article in the *Saturday Evening Post*. The National League, however, bought out impecunious Phillies owner Gerald Nugent in 1943.[55] When Bob Carpenter purchased the team in the late 1940s, the sales slowed.

Many baseball fans, remembering late-season Yankee acquisitions during the postwar era, will be surprised to learn that the Yankees often used interleague transactions to fill their needs. They acquired Enos Slaughter from the Cardinals, Johnny Mize from the cross-town Giants, Johnny Sain from Boston, Jim Konstanty from Philadelphia,

Johnny Hopp from Pittsburgh, Lon Frey from Chicago, and Dale Long from San Francisco. Slaughter, Mize, and Sain were the most famous acquisitions.

While the Yankees-Athletics activities were unusual, the activities were not unique. The St. Louis Cardinals sold seven players to the Boston Braves right after World War II. The Cardinals received $205,000 in the series of transactions while relinquishing Johnny Beazley, Morton Cooper, Johnny Hopp, and others. The Cardinals certainly were not poverty-stricken, as they had won the 1946 World Series.[56] Their farm system was so prolific, however, that they had surplus players to sell. Their cross-town rivals, the Browns, sold a large number of players to the Boston Red Sox between 1947 and 1952. The Browns received cash from the Red Sox in six transactions for Denny Galehouse, Ellis Kinder, Jack Kramer, Vern Stephens, Al Zarilla, and others. Shortstop Stephens drove in 440 runs in three seasons for the Red Sox. Stephens and Kinder had greater combined total baseball ratings for the Red Sox than did Boyer, Maris, and Duren for the Yankees. The Red Sox had earlier purchased Lefty Grove and Jimmie Foxx from the Athletics during the 1930s, and either player was superior to any player the Yankees received from the Athletics during the Johnson era.

The Browns' trades with the Red Sox worried fellow American League owners. To prevent the Red Sox from getting even more Browns players, Bill Veeck and the Indians swung a deal "in self-defense."[57] Yankees owner, Dan Topping, wanted commissioner "Happy" Chandler to investigate: "We are not concerned with the acquisition of these players by the Boston Red Sox and Cleveland Indians, but are concerned with the effect it has on the St. Louis situation—which is not good at best—and believe something radical must be done to bring about discontinuation of these trades. We, on our part, do not want to see the American League become a seven-club league."[58]

Nevertheless, it was the Yankees-Athletics conduit that especially irritated fans and fellow owners. After yet another New York–Kansas City trade in 1959, rival owners agitated for a five-year ban on such trades. As one sportswriter commented, "There is a feeling around the American League that the third-place Yankees must be kept down, because a third-place club in New York proved profitable in 1959 and a share-the-wealth era appeared to be in prospect for New York's opposition."[59] There was precedence for such a ban. When the 1939 Yankees completed their fourth runaway pennant, fellow American League owners voted a ban on pennant winners making any trades for the following year. The rule lasted just one season before being rescinded. Even the Yankees recognized the ill will inherent in the trades. After retiring as general manager, Weiss claimed that Topping had nixed a proposed deal with Kansas City: Duke Maas for Ned Garver. Topping reportedly told Weiss, "No, we don't want to make any more deals with Kansas City."[60]

As a postscript to the Yankees-Athletics relationship during the Johnson ownership era, Charles Finley, the new owner of the A's, was cognizant of the suspicions surrounding the frequent trades. He immediately claimed, "Kansas City will no longer be regarded as a Yankee farm team. We'll trade with every club in the league if we think we're getting a fair deal."[61] He went even further the following spring, after firing general manager, Parke Carroll, who had once worked for the Yankees, and replacing him with Frank Lane. "I don't care what the Yankees offer, I wouldn't even trade our two bat boys for Mickey Mantle. I made a promise to our fans in Kansas City."[62] Lane had already indicated his willingness to trade with the Yankees, if necessary. Finley reiterated his promise in June 1961: "There have been too many trades made between these two clubs already. As a result, Kansas City became known as a farm club of the Yankees—and rightly so. Frank Lane would like to trade with the Yankees, but I have overruled him. I have promised our fans we would have nothing to do with the Yankees this year and I won't go back on my promise."[63] As fans would learn, Finley's words and his actions did not always coincide. A week later he traded Bud Daley to the Yankees for Deron Johnson and Art Ditmar. Finley explained his volte-face this way: "I also must keep in mind at all times that I can't stand on a principle if it's going to hurt the ball club in the end."[64]

Today's fans are accustomed to the New York Yankees signing top free agents to maintain their excellence on the playing field, but in the past the team employed different methods in building pennant winners. From Ruppert's initial spending sprees that transferred the power in the American League from Boston to New York; through Ed Barrow's astute signing of Minor League and amateur stars such as Lou Gehrig, Bill Dickey, and Joe DiMaggio; to George Weiss's productive farm system (at least through 1951), the Yankees remained at the top.

Aside from Whitey Ford and Lefty Gomez, the franchise had difficulty developing durable pitching stars, so the team had to trade or buy pitchers. But its pitching acquisitions usually worked, as the team frequently led the league in earned run average.

While fans and pundits may attribute the Yankees' resurgence in the late 1970s to free agency, the team had amply proved that it could acquire sufficient reinforcements during the reserve clause era to supplement its farm system. The Coase theorem was operating in Major League Baseball before and after free agency. So, what is the difference between past incarnations of the Yankees and those of today? In recent years the Yankees must pay top dollar for the team's superiority, as its burgeoning payrolls of the past few years demonstrate. In the past the team could maintain its edge with a much smaller payroll relative to those of its rivals. For Yankee haters perhaps the team's current spending offers solace of a sort.

The Game on the Ledger

Doldrums amid Prosperity

The dominance of the New York Yankees from 1921 through 1964 eventually weakened the American League on the field and in the stands. The Yankees' almost monotonous success in the late 1940s through the mid-1960s exemplified the dangers of having a single team dominate the sport. The team's supremacy was most deleterious to league attendance during its pennant runs between 1941 and 1964.

Of course, the Yankees' on-the-field superiority might not be the only factor explaining the league's problems at the gate. Moreover, just because attendance fell during the early 1950s does not necessarily mean revenues and profits fell. Owners might have raised ticket prices or gained sufficiently increased television revenue to offset the shrinking attendance numbers. Owners might have used their bargaining leverage to drive down salaries. With these possibilities they might have maintained their profit levels. Was falling attendance, then, associated with falling profits and franchise values? If so, were owners caught in a squeeze between stagnant revenues and rising player salaries?

To address the financial issues, I will rely primarily upon data presented to congressional hearings held in 1951 and 1957. As with all financial data pertaining to professional sports, one must maintain an air of skepticism, given the possibility of camouflaging revenue and profits while exaggerating costs. Given the forum in which the information was delivered, however, the data appear to be reasonably accurate. In the case of the Chicago White Sox financial data for 1956 presented during a probate court proceeding corroborated the data presented to Congress.[1]

Ticket Prices and New Ways of Marketing Tickets

Could some of the diminution in attendance between 1946 and 1956 be attributed to rising ticket prices? Most of the increase in average ticket prices were offset by increases in the consumer price index (CPI). In the American League average real (adjusted for changes in the CPI) ticket prices generally increased by less than 10 percent. The average ticket price was obtained by dividing the team's home revenue by home attendance. To this figure is added twenty-nine cents to account for the American League's revenue-sharing plan. For most of the teams in 1955 the average ticket prices fell between the general admission and reserved ticket prices. Between 1946 and 1956 only the Athletics had greater than a 15 percent increase in real average ticket prices (see table 3.1 in the appendix). Some of the other teams had almost no increase over the period. Aside from the Athletics, then, rising real ticket prices probably explained only a modest proportion of the decrease in attendance figures.

Several of the American League teams raised ticket prices during the late 1940s in the face of the attendance boom. Yet whether such increases were the chief culprits behind the later attendance decline is debatable. The Yankees and Red Sox did not hike ticket prices between 1949 and 1953, yet both teams witnessed similar proportional drops in attendance as other teams. By the mid-1950s ticket prices were relatively stable. According to published ticket prices listed in the *Sporting News Baseball Dope, American League Red Book,* and various team scorecards, no Major League team changed its ticket prices between 1955 and 1956. Nine teams continued to maintain their ticket prices between 1956 and 1957, including the New York Yankees. Table 3.2 shows ticket price changes during the postwar era (see appendix).

One possible reason for rising average ticket prices in the face of stagnant posted prices might have been reclassifying the seats or building new box and reserved seats. I did not find seating arrangements for 1946 through 1949. Between 1955 and 1964, however, such reclassifications were relatively small in the National League but more significant in the American League. In the National League Philadelphia, Pittsburgh, St. Louis, and Cincinnati increased their numbers of box seats. The Reds reduced their general admission and bleacher sections; the other teams simply increased the number of box seats while maintaining the same numbers of other seats. In the American League Baltimore, Boston, Cleveland, Detroit, and Kansas City increased their number of box seats. Cleveland had a large change, creating almost 3,600 more box seats and 7,000 general admission seats out of its reserved seating capacities (with a small reduction in bleacher seats). Kansas City essentially eliminated almost all of its general admission seats to increase its numbers of box and reserved seats.[2]

Although winning a pennant usually boosted attendance, Major League owners appeared reticent about exploiting a pennant winner by raising ticket prices in the following season, as most champions did not raise their prices (see table 3.3 in the appendix). The Yankees, with fourteen pennants between 1949 and 1964, only raised prices in 1954, 1955, 1959, and 1964. Despite these occasional price hikes, Yankees ticket prices barely kept up with the change in the CPI between 1949 and 1964. Increases in real ticket prices tended to be small, so the increases probably did not account for much of the mid-1950s slump at the gate.

To boost ticket sales, the Yankees aggressively marketed their games. The team located ticket offices in Newark and provided buses to bring New Jersey fans to Yankee Stadium.[3] It created the Yankee Stadium Club in 1946 as a way to attract season ticket holders who would pay before the season began. For a set fee, depending on the number of seats in the box, a fan had the box for the entire season as well as access to a lounge, bar, and restaurant facilities. Sportswriter Red Smith characterized the program as "the biggest thing in baseball merchandising since invention of the rain check." A box with six seats cost $900, or $150 per seat. Because box seats went for $3.00 per game, the season ticket holder received a discount lowering the per-game price to roughly $2.25. Smith cited rumors that gamblers and other unsavory characters bought many of the boxes; Yankees management claimed that bankers were the main purchasers, as the team initially marketed the plan to banks.[4] An article in *Forbes* stated that the Yankee organization reaped $850,000 in advance sales of its box seats for the 1950 season. It is not surprising that the team converted some of its grandstand seats into boxes, as four American League teams had home gate revenues, after paying the gate sharing proceeds, of less than $850,000.[5]

In 1960 the Yankees devised a new way to tap wealthy fans. The team constructed new loges containing 135 seats. The ultra-luxurious boxes had swivel chairs and attendants. The team planned to pass the $65,000 construction costs directly to the ticket holder. Each customer buying a box containing at least eight seats was to pay $4,480 the first season and $1,080 the second and third seasons, yielding construction costs and advance payments on the usual cost of season tickets for the second and third seasons. After the third season the seats would cost, on average, $275 instead of $225 per seat.[6] With their proximity to the large business community and the "subsidy" afforded to entertainment by the high corporate tax rate, the Yankees were well positioned to exploit season ticket demand.

Other teams quickly imitated the Yankees and promoted season tickets. While Baltimore did not draw as many fans as hoped during its inaugural season, the team showed a profit. Assistant general manager Art Ehlers believed that the team's success depended upon season tickets: "The season ticket sale is the only salvation for a club. If a club goes bad, it still has that money in the bank along about August, when interest would normally die in a loser. . . . There's another windfall in season tickets. The visiting club averages 30 cents an admission. But if the people with tickets don't show up, we don't have to pay the visiting club except on the turnstile count. Neither do we pay the five percent cut to the American League."[7] Down the road in Washington DC, Calvin Griffith of the Senators had less success selling season tickets because few big businesses operated in the city.[8]

Sources of Revenue

What happened to total revenues in baseball in the postwar era? Were Major League Baseball's lackluster profits during the early 1950s the result of falling revenues? Teams earned revenues from a variety of sources, including gate sales, concessions, media (radio and television), exhibition games, stadium rentals for non-baseball games, parking, and net sales of players. These sources varied considerably across teams.

Table 3.4 shows real gross operating income and total income for 1946, 1950, and 1952–56 (see appendix). For the two earlier years owners reported "real gross operating income." For the latter five seasons the "total income" includes all income sources reported for 1946 and 1950 as well as "other income." Even counting "other income," real incomes were falling in both leagues between 1946 and 1952. The National League's figures were typically lower than the American League's, but the transfer of the Giants and Dodgers surely boosted the National League's income beyond that of the American League after 1957. While the American League's total income fell by over 7 percent between 1946 and 1952, the Yankees' decline was steeper, about 15 percent. Despite the organization's sagging income between 1946 and 1952, the New York Yankees' income surpassed Brooklyn's by an average of almost $1 million per season. Walter O'Malley had reason to be dissatisfied with his team's ability to generate income in Brooklyn.

The Yankees had one regular revenue source denied its American League rivals, World Series revenue. The team's success on the field during the postwar era also bolstered the team's bottom line. A reporter claimed that the team had earned $3.3 million from its thirteen appearances in the World Series between 1946 and 1962.[9]

In addition to the gate revenue disparities, which will be discussed in greater detail later, the teams had large differences in net concession income. Baseball owner Bill Veeck stated that the typical team got 20 percent of the concessions.[10] Not all of the owners had such arrangements. Harry Stevens paid a per capita fee to the Dodgers, Giants, Pirates, Red Sox, and Yankees for full concession rights to their patrons. These teams, for instance, received seven cents per customer. Stevens also handled the expansion Washington Senators' concessions, albeit for only the team's inaugural season. The Jacobs Brothers operated concessions for the Browns, Indians, and White Sox, paying 20 percent of gross revenues to the teams. Finally, the Cardinals and Cubs ran their own concessions operations.[11] Cubs treasurer Earl Nelson explained the profitability of concessions: "1,342,970 customers consumed 1,368,876 hot dogs at 15 cents each during the 1946 season. Our net profit was $103,760.80 or 7.58 cents per hot dog."[12]

In figures reported to the 1957 congressional investigation, the New York Yankees earned $2.24 million from concessions during 1952–56, an amount almost four times as much as the Indians, Phillies, and Senators each earned (see tables 3.5a and 3.5b in the appendix). On a per admission basis teams earned anywhere from ten cents to almost thirty-six cents. Some of the disparity probably resulted from differences in the concessions contracts and not from greater consumption of concessions in one stadium over another. In addition, teams also had patrons who did not pay full admission and were not included in the admissions figures.[13] Finally, not all teams sold alcoholic beverages, such as teams in Pennsylvania. Despite the lack of beer sales, the Philadelphia Athletics had the highest concessions income per fan during their last three seasons, but when the team moved to Kansas City, the ratio fell sharply. Unless the Philadelphia fans were consuming inordinately huge amounts of concessions, relative to Kansas City fans, the differences can most likely be explained by some of the factors suggested here. The Yankees had the second highest per attendee concession income in the American League.

Did differences in concession prices account for some of the variation in concession incomes reported in tables 3.5a and 3.5b? Table 3.6 shows prices for such basic concessions as soft drinks, hot dogs, and beer (see appendix). The Stevens brothers rarely published concession prices in their scorecards, which accounts for the lack of prices for the three New York clubs and the Boston Red Sox. The only information I could find on concession prices at Yankee Stadium were two photographs in the "Yankee Stadium—Interior" file at the Baseball Hall of Fame. The photos, circa 1947, showed a soft drink vendor whose hat read "10 cents" and a hot dog vendor whose sign read "Frankfurter and Roll—15 cents." These prices were the same as those in 1947 in Chicago's Comiskey Park, where prices tended to be the highest.

As early as 1937, concessions provided a vital secondary source of revenue. A writer for *Fortune* that year offered a calculation, "On a hot day, your average rooter spends eighteen cents, netting your average concessionaire a profit of a dime."[14] Owner Bill Veeck claimed that a team sold more concessions per fan when it won a game instead of when it lost.[15] He explained that fans would be in a good mood and linger after the game. Yet statistical analysis of the admittedly sketchy data does not support Veeck's contention. In order to test his thesis I normalized each team's concession income per attendee by dividing a season's income per attendee by the team's five-year average, thereby reducing the distortion that might arise by different concessions' contracts. I then compared the normalized per fan concession income to the team's win-loss record for each season. If Veeck was correct, the normalized per fan income should have increased when the team's record improved. Yet the win-loss record was inversely related to the concession income per attendee (although the relationship was not statistically significant). Even so, his claim, if accurate, would have provided an additional benefit from a winning team.

A Los Angeles Dodgers concessions manager claimed that games at night hurt soft drink and food sales, as fans arrived having already eaten dinner. In addition, he believed that close games hurt concession sales, as fans tended to remain in their seats. As one sportswriter put it in a 1959 *Sports Illustrated* article, "Your best bet is an 80° doubleheader in the daytime with the Dodgers leading 8–2 in each game. The disappointed fan is likely to become an emotional eater, but on the other hand he's likely to walk out. He never walks out if the home team is ahead. He wants to be in on the kill."[16]

As noted, many teams leased their concessions to firms specializing in providing such services. Walter O'Malley suggested that the concessionaires will "give you more profit than you could make yourself."[17] The Stevens brothers ran the concessions for the New York ball clubs for many years. The brothers created the Yankees Stadium Club, an idea copied by other teams. By 1962 the firm introduced a king-size frankfurter costing thirty-five cents to the Stadium Club. According to Joe Stevens, "[It] is the key to the revised demands of our ball park buying public." In addition, Stevens found that customers were either "hit-and-run" or leisurely, so one floor of the Stadium Club featured counter service, like one finds at a modern fast-food firm. The other floor had sit-down service with buffet and waiter services.[18]

Television was a key factor in the changes taking place between 1949 and 1953 in terms of teams' revenue. Radio and television revenues were only one-thirtieth as much as the gate receipts in 1946, but ten years later such revenues accounted for 30 percent as much as the gate receipts. As with gate receipts, the broadcasting revenues were unevenly distributed across the franchises (see table 3.7 in the appendix). The Yankees typically received the greatest broadcasting revenues, although in the last five years of the data, the Cleveland Indians usually had similar amounts of revenue. The distribution of broadcasting revenue showed no general pattern, although the relative disparity was smallest in the immediate aftermath of relocating the Browns and Athletics.

The clubs in New York and Los Angeles would retain their advantage in television money into the 1960s, when local television revenues reached a plateau. The Yankees received $1.2 million in local television revenue for the 1963 season. The Dodgers and New York Mets each received $1 million, but later figures revealed that the Mets got $1.2 million per season for 1962–66. As early as the 1962 season, the Mets had a lucrative local television contract. The team signed an agreement with Rheingold Brewery. In addition to $1 million for rights to 133 Mets games, the brewery agreed to buy $100,000 worth of the team's tickets.[19]

Rising Costs: Players' Salaries

During the postwar period Major League teams faced escalating costs. When the St. Louis Cardinals decided to raise ticket prices for the 1961 season, the team's business manager, Art Routzong, blamed higher costs: "Everything's gone up over the years—salaries, road expenses and player replacement costs—but the one thing that didn't keep pace was the ticket price. . . . We spent approximately $1.25 million on our player procurement and development program." Routzong estimated that the average team spent $350,000 to $400,000 on scouting.

Cardinals ticket prices were now closer to the prevailing prices throughout the National League. The Cardinals, however, were handicapped by their limited number of box seats, so the team's "per capita income in ticket sales" ranked seventh in the league. The Cardinals had the fewest box seats in the National League in both 1955 and 1964.[20] Sportswriter Robert Coughlan described some of the other costs: "Everything is up—even with discounts, baseballs cost about $1.30 apiece, and the Yankees, for instance, chew them up at the rate of 120 a day. Hotels, food, transportation and other items for the Yankees' customary traveling party of 45 make road expenses average about $1,000 a day." Coughlan also believed that ticket prices did not keep pace, although he noted that owners often reclassified seats.[21]

Owners primarily blamed rising player salaries. Player salaries rose 13.7 percent in the American League between 1952 and 1956, while such salaries rose 12.6 percent in the National League. The figures in the National League are difficult to interpret, as five of the teams reported payroll figures that included salaries of coaches, managers, trainers, and clubhouse personnel. Indeed, although the owners presented team salary information for 1946 and 1950 to Congress in 1951, all of the teams included managers' and coaches' salaries with those of the players, so a direct comparison with 1952–56 is not possible. The New York Giants reported "team salary expense." In any event the

Reds and Braves had increases of greater than one-third; conversely, the Cardinals, Giants, and Pirates had smaller payrolls in 1956 than in 1952. These data are in nominal dollars; the consumer price index was relatively stable between 1952 and 1956 (rising by 2.5 percent over the period). The 13.7 percent and 12.6 percent rates of increase were smaller than the 18.1 percent rise in average hourly earnings in manufacturing over the same period.[22] The player salary increase is intriguing in light of the absence of free agency and stagnant gate revenues. Growing television revenues may have spurred demand for players and helped bolster salaries.

Although the Yankees frequently reported the highest payroll (see table 3.8 in the appendix), the relative disparities were not as large as those reported in the late 1990s. While the Yankees payroll rarely doubled that of the smallest payroll during the mid-1950s, according to information published in July 2000 in *The Report of the Independent Members of the Commissioner's Blue Ribbon Panel on Baseball Economics*, the New York Yankees total payroll for 1995 through 1999 was 4.8 times that of Montreal and four times that of Milwaukee. In some seasons the Yankees payroll was nine times greater than that of the smallest payroll. About one-third of the other Major League teams had payrolls less than half of the Yankees payroll for 1995–99.[23]

Interestingly, two sportswriters of the postwar era claimed that Detroit would have had an advantage under what we now call free agency, as the Tigers were known to be generous with salaries. A writer for *Baseball Digest* said in 1949, "Walter O. Briggs, Jr., . . . probably is the richest club owner in the American League and blinks not a bit at paying the league's biggest salaries."[24] Conversely, the Washington Senators would have been at a disadvantage because, as another *Baseball Digest* writer explained a few years earlier, "Clark Griffith [Washington's owner] doesn't pay good money."[25]

But a more interesting question is: Did the Yankees incur significantly greater player costs, compared to other teams, relative to their win-loss records? Based on statistical analysis, for a given win-loss record, the Yankees incurred a higher payroll cost, amounting to $120,000 or more per season. The result holds whether the current win-loss record or the previous season's win-loss record is used. For most American League teams going from winning half of the games to 60 percent of the games was associated with an increase in payroll costs from between $40,000 to $47,000. Finally, the Washington Senators apparently incurred a payroll cost of $75,000 less than the average American League for any given record. In fact, Washington's inability to match other teams' payroll is understated because the team reported combined players' and coaches' salaries.[26]

Were the higher Yankee payrolls reflective of higher expenses of living in New York City? In its 1964 edition *Statistical Abstract of the United States* carried a calculation for "Annual Budget Costs—City Workers' Families and Retired Couples, 20 Cities." The Bureau of Labor Statistics compiled the numbers for 1959, but it appeared to be a one-time only survey. Clearly, professional baseball players differed from "city workers," so any comparison is tenuous. The survey listed the annual budget cost for New York City workers to be $5,970. The estimated budget was lower in Baltimore, Kansas City, and Philadelphia, but the costs were higher in other cities with Major League teams. The budget costs were highest in Chicago due to that city's high "rent, heat, and utilities" costs. Boston and New York had the highest "food and beverages" costs. Between 1959 and 1963, however, Boston and New York experienced the most rapid increases in their respective consumer price indexes.[27]

Despite the Yankees' relatively large payrolls, the team was not munificent toward its players. General manager George Weiss was an aggressive negotiator. When pitching mainstay Vic Raschi slumped to only thirteen wins in 1953, off from three consecutive twenty-one-win seasons between 1949 and 1951, Weiss offered a contract with the maximum 25 percent cut. He did so, in part, to offer "an object lesson . . . to bring eleven other Yankee holdouts around."[28] Raschi balked, and Weiss sold him to the St. Louis Cardinals for $85,000. Weiss thus maintained his reputation as a tough negotiator who was short on sentiment, and Raschi, it turned out, performed poorly for the Cardinals.[29] Weiss threatened even Yogi Berra and Mickey Mantle with pay cuts, especially when Berra did not repeat his Most Valuable Player performances.

Weiss feared that in order to pay rising salaries, the team would have to raise ticket prices. Economists would claim that Weiss's thinking was backward. Rising television revenue (or increased demand for tickets) would drive up the demand for players and therefore salaries. In any event he frequently lamented the growing salaries in conversations with sportswriters. He tied the rising revenue from television rights to the Yankees' policy of maintaining stable ticket prices: "Well, it is fortunate for us that we have this likelihood of increased revenue, these television sources of higher income, because if it weren't for them we would have had to raise prices long ago."[30] Weiss felt better after the 1958 campaign. The Yankees built a seventeen-game lead early in August and then slumped. Because of the slump, several players had less impressive statistics, leading observers to conclude that Weiss would keep salaries from rising too much.[31] Despite his efforts, Yankees payrolls allegedly increased, year by year. Before the 1958 season headlines screamed, "Yankee Payroll to Hit Record 500 Gs" and "Player Payrolls Rocket to Outer Space," which seem to contradict the player salary information given to the congressional committees.[32] Throughout January and February 1959 Weiss tried to curb salaries. Mickey Mantle was asked to take a cut from $75,000 to $63,000; Ford and Berra were also "invited" to take cuts. Weiss failed to cut Mantle's salary by 20 percent after the 1958 season, and the parties agreed to a modest raise.[33] When the players proved recalcitrant, Weiss spread rumors that some of them had broken training and discipline rules during the previous season, perhaps in the hopes of swaying public opinion toward the team.[34]

When the Yankees failed to win the pennant in 1959, sportswriters speculated on which players would have their pay cut. Before the 1960 season Weiss claimed that salaries had "really" reached their limits: "If we were limited to revenues taken in at the box office, it is conceivable that we would not have a $50,000-a-year player." He again claimed that television income was crucial in maintaining the payroll and farm system, but, he added, "We definitely are near our limit, and salaries will have to level off."[35]

Several factors nevertheless induced players to demand higher salaries. Some observers felt that the signing of untried teenagers for large sums inspired Major League veterans to take a firm stance in negotiating their salaries with the owners, who also assumed some responsibility. Walter O'Malley, owner of the Brooklyn Dodgers, stated (and the reader is entitled to be skeptical), "You see, we who operate major clubs are not businessmen. We are fans. Maybe the designation is something else again. But I don't see these salaries dropping much."[36] Ironically, at the same time O'Malley was bemoaning the high salaries, another baseball official was claiming that the Dodger organization could sell some of its top Minor Leaguers for a combined $2 million.[37] Owners had sold several top players for well over $100,000, and the two leagues' prices for players in the expansion pool also gave the other players an inkling of their value. The players in the expansion pool, typically aging stars or journeymen, cost the new teams $50,000 to $125,000. The burgeoning television money and expansion, in particular, spurred players to demand higher salaries. These calls for better salaries continued through the era.[38] Finally, players were more sophisticated than in the past about negotiating salaries; according to one general manager, "Most of them know the business facts of life well—too damn well. If there's been one big change in the majors in the last twenty years, it's been the ballplayer's ability to take care of himself in the business world."[39]

After claiming that players were paid based upon a club's ability to pay, the player's output, and the player's value as a gate attraction, baseball executive Bill DeWitt predicted a 10 percent increase in salaries for 1962, following the National League's expansion.[40] But the players' salaries were minuscule compared with modern-day players' salaries, even after adjusting for differences in purchasing power. Gil Hodges led the Los Angeles Dodgers in pay with his $39,000 salary in 1961. In today's dollars this would be about $215,000, well below the current Major League minimum salary. Mickey Mantle got only a $13,000 raise after his fabulous 1961 season.[41] As a proportion of club expenses, the salaries of players diminished throughout the first half of the twentieth century: roughly half at the turn of the century; 35.5 percent in 1929; 32.4 percent in 1939; and about 20 percent in 1950.[42] In the American League player salaries as a percentage of total income (revenue from home and away games, exhibition games, radio and television, concessions, and other sources) showed no definite trend between 1952 and 1956. The ratio was highest in 1953, when player salaries equaled 21 percent of total income. This high mark occurred, however, when the 1953 revenues fell. When revenues rebounded in 1954, the ratio fell to 18 percent, and it only reached 17.2 percent in 1956.[43] The Commissioner's Blue Ribbon Panel reported total revenues and player payrolls for the 1995–99 seasons, and in each one player payrolls exceeded 50 percent of revenues, including 66.9 percent in 1995.[44]

After the Yankees sacked Weiss and replaced him with Roy Hamey, the new general manager tried a new tactic to promote harmony for the upcoming 1961 season: no pay cuts. Observers thought that Hamey hoped to foster goodwill after the acrimonious negotiations during the Weiss era. Rival clubs felt aggrieved at this new Yankee trick, fearing that the precedence of allowing no pay cuts even for subpar performance would trigger an escalation of salaries.[45] Hamey's era of good feelings would face a stern test in the wake of the club's smashing 1961 season. Mickey Mantle and Roger Maris expected large raises off their combined 115 homeruns. Mantle eventually settled for $85,000, while Maris received the largest raise in team history, from $38,000 to $70,000. Hamey stated, "The Yankees . . . will open the season well on their way to the $900,000 mark [in player payroll]. If we go right on winning, the move toward $1 million will be speeded up greatly."[46] Although the Yankees won another pennant in 1962, the rate of increase in the top stars' pay slowed considerably. Mantle finally got his $100,000 contract, an increase of $15,000, while Maris's salary remained constant. After yet another pennant in 1963, Maris, becoming plagued by injury, settled for a 10 percent pay cut, to $67,500; although he was listed as making $72,000 for 1963 before the season began, the postseason article claimed he had made $75,000. Apparently, Maris was one of the few Yankees to take a cut for 1964.[47]

Nevertheless, by the mid-1950s not just the Yankees but also other Major League owners were crying that player salaries were too high. With shrill headlines proclaiming, "Spiraling Major Payrolls Near 10 Million," these owners anticipated their descendants' anguish over free agency– and arbitration-inspired salary hikes a quarter-century later. Former player–turned–general manager Joe Cronin claimed, "There have always been more overpaid players than underpaid players. . . . Major league salaries and expenses have reached the saturation point."[48] By 1964 National League teams were beginning to have payrolls rivaling that of the Yankees, helped by their having higher attendance and more top stars than the teams in the American League.[49]

Today's baseball fan might marvel at the relatively low salaries of even top Major League players during the 1950s. The picture was even worse than the raw numbers suggest, however, as these players may have been squeezed by higher taxes and therefore got to keep a smaller proportion of their earnings. Marginal tax rates (the rate applied to the last dollar earned) were much higher during the 1950s than they are today. Like Ronald Reagan twenty years later, in the early 1960s President John F. Kennedy recognized the disincentives inherent in marginal tax rates that approached 90 percent, and he pushed for and got significant cuts in the marginal tax rates. Nevertheless, such relief did not help players during the 1950s, and Major League players at that time sought ways to reduce their tax loads.

To defray his tax bill, Ted Williams received $100,000 for 1959, but $25,000 was placed in a tax-exempt "expense account."[50] Players argued that their years of high earnings were very limited. One possible solution was to expand the "income averaging," whereby income was spread out over three years. Another solution to help players was the (M. Francis) Bravman plan in which citizens would be taxed on "average income," an amount set according to various ages.[51] Other ballplayers sought contracts paying them over an extended period. In 1958 Major League Baseball Players' Association president Bob Feller expressed hope that tax relief was forthcoming, although he suggested that it might take five years. He pointed out that the ballplayers had common cause with other performers in the entertainment industry, such as actors and actresses. He pointed out that a ballplayer's ability was a depletable asset: "A ball player is entitled to spread the depreciation on his muscles just the same as the oil business allows for depletion of oil wells."[52]

Between the relatively low salaries and higher tax rates, players during the 1950s had difficulty stockpiling enough savings to retire not only from baseball but from the working world entirely. Many players held jobs during the winter, a pattern that would hold until the 1970s. Richie Hebner played for the World Champion Pittsburgh Pirates in 1971. In the off-season he worked for his father as a gravedigger, quipping, "It's a quiet job."[53] Players of the 1950s rarely had agents, much less a posse of hangers-on. Still, players got little sympathy for their reserve clause–inspired, artificially low salaries. With hourly earnings in manufacturing of $2.50 in 1962, Gil Hodges's $39,000 salary in 1961 seemed considerable.[54] Yet Hodges's talent was near the apex of a very substantial pyramid of professional baseball players. In addition, hundreds of thousands, if not millions, of Americans were willing to pay money to see Hodges and his teammates play baseball, but few, if any, would have been willing to pay to watch the top manufacturing workers go about their business.

While players were being squeezed by marginal tax rates, owners had tax relief via the player depreciation rule first granted to New York Yankees owners Larry MacPhail, Dan Topping, and Del Webb upon their purchase of the club in 1945 but publicized by Bill Veeck. A new owner, assuming he possessed 80 percent of the club, could write off assumed player contracts as "depreciation," but the players could not depreciate themselves.[55]

Rising Costs: Other Expenses

Teams faced rising expenses throughout the 1950s. These costs were unevenly distributed across teams, just as revenues were. Certainly, payrolls were rising between 1952 and 1956, but they constituted only a relatively small proportion of total expenses. Did expenses rise at the same rate as player salaries?

One significant expense was signing new talent. According to data presented to Congress, between 1952 and 1956 Major League teams paid bonuses to amateur players ranging from a total of $10,000 by Kansas City to $154,000 by Chicago. The New York Yankees paid $54,000 in bonuses to two players.[56] This data, however, does not coincide with data published in a 1958 article by Bill Bryson in the *Baseball Digest*. Major League owners had contended that their fellows had paid bonuses under the table, so any numbers were suspect. Bryson claimed that the Major League teams paid baseball novices $5 million in large bonuses to about one hundred youngsters between 1947 and 1957.[57] Only a handful of the players, roughly one in ten, had made the Majors by 1957. Others, such as Dave Nicholson ($135,000), Frank Baumann ($100,000), Billy Joe Davidson ($100,000), Paul Pettit ($100,000), and Ted Kazanski ($100,000), were expensive baubles. According to Bryson's figures, even the Yankees got burned. The team paid $320,000 in bonuses between 1951 and 1958, but only Andy Carey, Tommy Carroll, and Tom Tresh became big leaguers.[58]

The New York Yankees had three times the total expenses that the Washington Senators had (see table 3.9 in the appendix). Between 1952 and 1956 every team faced higher total expenses, except the New York Giants. Note that the three franchises that relocated during the five-year period had some of the largest hikes in total expenses, with the Braves more than doubling their expenses. Over the ten-year span from 1946 to 1956, Major League total expenses rose by 87.1 percent in nominal terms. The consumer price index climbed by 39.2 percent between 1946 and 1956. Expenses in the Major Leagues thus outstripped the general change in prices.

The components of total expenses accelerated at different rates between 1952 and 1956. The expense data for 1946 and 1950 only listed two categories: operating expenses and player contract purchases and sales. Although Major League officials often blamed escalating player salaries for their doldrums, "other expenses," which included all expenses except players' salaries, players' bonuses, players' contracts purchased and sold, and officers' salaries, accounted for over two-thirds of total expenses. Such expenses accelerated by an average of almost 30 percent during the five seasons, a rate of increase that was much more rapid than that for players' salaries (see table 3.10 in the appendix).

The Yankees did not incur the largest costs for players' salaries, bonuses, and contracts (see table 3.11 in the appendix). The Detroit Tigers and Cleveland Indians usually had greater expenditures on these categories. The American League teams outspent their National League peers in these categories. The Browns/Orioles and Braves were the two teams with the most rapid rise in these expenditures.

Although officials bemoaned rising travel expenses, the data do not support them, at least for the 1952–56 period. Not all teams provided information on their traveling, hotel, and meal expenses. Ten teams showed traveling expenses. On average these expenses rose by one-fifth over the five seasons, although the increase resulted primarily from the Philadelphia/Kansas City Athletics. When the team moved in 1955, its traveling expenses rose from $40,000 per season to over $122,700 in 1956. Some teams included more than rail fares in their transportation category, so direct team comparisons are tenuous. Even so, the evidence shows that three of the teams had decreases in their traveling expenses: the Brooklyn Dodgers, the New York Giants, and the Philadelphia Phillies. In terms of hotel and meal expenses, of the six teams reporting such expenses, the amounts were strikingly similar, generally between $27,000 and $37,000. The Philadelphia/Kansas City Athletics again were the exception. After three years' expenditure of roughly $33,000 per season, when the Athletics moved west, their hotel and meal expenses jumped to $89,280 in 1956. Brooklyn cut its hotel and meal expense by almost one-sixth over the five seasons.

After 1956 rising rail fares and franchise relocation created a shift in transportation. Even before the Dodgers and Giants moved to the West Coast, Major League teams were beginning to use air travel. Most players found air travel more relaxing and less disruptive to their sleep patterns.[59] In addition, the decaying passenger rail system pushed for increased fares during the mid-1950s. The Dodgers road secretary reported, "There definitely is a difference in the cost of traveling by plane right now. The railroads put through a ten percent increase which went into effect for the current season and that means a definite saving by air even on shorter trips. In a trip from Pittsburgh, for example, the basic fare is some $30, plus $8 for Pullman. The plane fare is about $28 and the club saves the meal money for players because the dinner is free on the airplane."[60] Giants secretary Eddie Brannick bemoaned the rising railroad fares. The Pullman fares outstripped the consumer price index between 1947 and 1957. Air travel cost 6.5 cents per mile, so the Giants often found it cheaper to fly. Airlines sometimes had trouble meeting Major League Baseball's travel needs, leading several officials to suggest that Major League Baseball buy a fleet of planes. A few teams hired charters.[61] Hotel charges were also rising, growing by a third between the late 1940s and mid-1950s, slightly faster than the CPI.[62]

The Giants' relocation to San Francisco almost doubled National League travel from 104,426 to 194,890 miles. With the Dodgers moving to Los Angeles, the overall increase was about the same as if the Giants alone had moved, because eastern teams would play the Dodgers and Giants on the same road trip.[63] Chicago Cubs owner Philip Wrigley was concerned that the higher attendance in San Francisco might not cover the added travel expenses. National League teams shared 27.5 cents for each paid admission with the visiting team. The Cubs found their travel costs increased by $26,000,[64] which meant that they had to draw almost ninety-five thousand more fans on the road to cover the higher costs.

Because of the perceived risks from flying, Major League teams also incurred another expense. The teams collectively purchased flight insurance covering players, coaches, and managers worth almost $86 million. Whether the flight insurance simply replaced railroad insurance or some other accident insurance is not apparent. In the expense information provided to Congress several teams listed "insurance" but did not elaborate further. In the event of a fatal crash the American League also had a "rehabilitation plan" calling for each of the remaining seven teams to submit a list of ten players from its twenty-five-player roster. The stricken team could select three players from each of the other seven teams, and these players would cost $75,000 each. The cost of the players would be covered by the league's roughly $1.88 million policy, for which the club was the beneficiary.[65]

In any case combined traveling, hotel, and meal expenses typically amounted to around $100,000 per team per season. Any distress over rising expenditures in these categories was misplaced. Major League teams faced greater challenges from the rapid escalation in so-called other expenses. For some teams, such as the Braves and Browns/Orioles, player development and replacement costs (the costs of signing young players and running the farm system) were the biggest culprits in these spiraling expenses. The Yankees almost doubled their spending on their ballpark in 1954–56 compared with 1952–53; the team also saw "other miscellaneous" costs rise. Conversely, its depreciation expenses fell from $135,000 in 1952 to $24,611 in 1956.

The Philadelphia Phillies took over Connie Mack Stadium in 1955 upon the Athletics' departure. Instead of paying $112,000 in rent, the Phillies paid $525,000 in various grounds expenses; in addition, the team's payroll for its grounds crew rose by over $132,000 between 1954 and 1955. Fortunately for the Phillies, they were able to reduce some of their grounds expenses in 1956. Yet not all teams saw their "other expenses" grow. Between 1952 and 1955 the Pittsburgh Pirates actually cut these expenses, although increases in 1956 restored them to their previous level. The New York Giants also maintained relatively stable "other expenses."

Four National League teams provided information on expenditures on baseball equipment: Brooklyn, Cincinnati, Philadelphia, and

Pittsburgh. These teams reported wildly different changes in expenses for uniforms, bats, and balls. The Dodgers paid roughly $10,000 per season for uniforms, with a low of $6,813 in 1955 and a high of $13,050 in 1954. The team tripled its spending on bats. The Reds reported bizarre figures for baseballs: only $62 in 1952 but $2,327 in 1956. Philadelphia reduced its spending on uniforms and team equipment from $13,215 in 1952 to $9,622 in 1956; the expenditures reached a low point in 1953. The team spent $10,704 on baseballs in 1956, a sixfold rise over 1952. The Pirates cut spending on uniforms between 1952 and 1956, but the team's spending on baseballs and bats grew during the period.

Statistical analysis shows that real total expenses among the ball clubs were positively related to their win-loss records. In addition, the New York Yankees incurred $1.34 million more in real total expenses for any given win-loss record than other teams, although alternative equations suggested that the three New York teams paid, on average, $807,500 more for any win-loss record than other club. Finally, the three franchises that relocated ended up paying $551,500 more than before relocation. Similar results held for "real other expenses" but not for "real player expenses."[66]

Because of rising expenses, owners sought ways to economize. To reduce scouting costs, for example, some officials suggested that a scouting bureau be created. The proposed centralized group would scout amateur players, file reports, and disseminate information to client teams. Teams would then decide which youngsters to scout on their own.[67]

Baseball owners also lobbied Congress to reduce the federal admission tax to 10 percent. Robert Coyne claimed to have lobbied on behalf of baseball both to get the admission tax reduced and to get a bill overtly giving organized baseball immunity from antitrust laws. He presented the owners a bill for $150,000 for his efforts. Commissioner Ford Frick disputed organized baseball's obligation to pay Coyne, despite admitting, "There's no question that he did a good job on the tax thing. It means that you're saving $100,000 on each million attendance." Frick maintained that Coyne was primarily a lobbyist for the motion picture operators, who shared an interest in getting the admission tax lowered. Baseball's attorney, Paul Porter, perhaps more accurately stressed another reason for Frick to repudiate the lobbyist's claim: "If it becomes known that anybody in organized baseball paid a percentage to get the admission tax reduced, it would be very bad."[68]

The Effects of Attendance on Profits

Was the stagnating attendance associated with falling profits? Although baseball profit figures may be misleading, the figures provided to the Subcommittee on the Study of Monopoly Power and other House of Representatives hearings support the idea of American League atrophy. In the discussion that follows, all dollar amounts are in nominal terms. Every American League club reported an after-tax profit in 1946. The free-spending Boston Red Sox reported losses in 1947 and 1948. In 1949 only Washington reported a loss, while Boston and Philadelphia reported losses in 1950. No figures were reported for 1951. In 1952 and 1953 Boston, Philadelphia, and St. Louis lost money in both seasons, while Detroit lost money in 1952. Overall after-tax profits plunged from an average of $381,000 per team in 1946 to a loss of $25,000 per team in 1952. The Indians' surprise pennant in 1954 earned the organization a handsome after-tax profit of $583,000. Every team but the Athletics made money, with the average team earning $191,000. The next season, 1955, was also profitable, but the average team's profits shrank to $107,000. The average team's profits dwindled further to $72,000 the following year.[69] Of course, these figures do not include the implicit capital costs, and the 1950s figures should be adjusted for the higher price levels in the economy as measured by the CPI.

Profit figures were sporadically published after 1956. Some teams were required by their state governments to publish balance sheets each year. Other teams had stockholders and issued yearly reports. According to balance sheets reported by the Boston Red Sox, the club lost $142,000 in 1958 but made a profit of $85,000 the year before. Whether the profit was after taxes was not revealed.[70] The St. Louis Cardinals reported a loss of $37,000 for the 1960 season; the team's Major League operations were profitable, however, due to an 18 percent increase in attendance. The loss was due to the team replacement costs.[71]

According to sportswriter Clifford Kachline, the Los Angeles Dodgers were profitable between 1959 and 1961 while playing in the Los Angeles Coliseum. When the team moved to Chavez Ravine, however, its profits soared. The Dodgers reportedly made over $4 million in profits before taxes in 1962.[72]

Calvin Griffith finally reaped profits during his team's final season in Washington DC. The Senators made $74,000 in 1960, the largest net profit ever under Calvin, who took over the team after the 1955 season upon his uncle Clark Griffith's death. After moving to the Twin Cities, the team made an after-tax profit of $426,000 in 1961. In contrast, the expansion Washington Senators lost $250,000 that year.[73]

The Pittsburgh Pirates drew well in 1962 but still lost money. The team had attendance in excess of one million fans but lost an unspecified amount. A team official cited increased transportation, meal, and hotel costs as the culprits: $166,000 in 1962 versus $81,000 in 1955. Salaries increased by 85 percent over the same period, but, then, the team had better players in the latter year. The team had sold Forbes Field to the city but now had to pay explicit rent.[74]

The Baltimore Orioles lost $53,000 in 1959. The team's second-place finish in 1960 bolstered gate receipts and spurred profits of $318,000 (it is not clear whether they represent before-or after-tax amounts). Due to their strong on-the-field showing, the Orioles sold a greater number of season tickets for the 1961 campaign; indeed, one-third of the 1961 tickets were season tickets. The team made $99,000 on operations in 1963 and $301,000 net profits in 1964. A club official noted that the team spent roughly $1.05 million in player development during 1964.[75]

The San Francisco Giants earned hefty profits, especially after moving into Candlestick Park in 1960. That year the team had after-tax profits of $946,000 and $308,000 in 1961. The profits continued for the next two years, for a combined $1.12 million (initially reported as $1.46 million). The team's initial stock price of $100 in 1958 rose to $800 by 1964. The team's net profit fell to $309,000 in 1964.[76]

Unfortunately, we do not have profit figures for teams such as Cleveland and Detroit, which were stagnating at that time. Presumably management was doing what it could to keep costs down. We know, for instance, that the Detroit Tigers' new owners pursued such economizing measures as cutting its scouting staff in 1959, limiting players to two towels a day, and restricting the free employee lunch program.[77]

While the mid-1950s saw profits fall among most of the American League teams, teams from both leagues that had relocated saw a boost, if only temporarily, in their net incomes.

Franchise Values and Baseball's Profitability

Despite rising expenses and stagnant gate revenues, people still wanted to buy ball clubs. As New York Giants owner Horace Stoneham pointed out, "There is no financial stringency in the majors. How many clubs are for sale? Not one. A certain man with money and eligibility has been canvassing the situation and finds that nobody wants to get out. If there were the reported troubles, would that hold-fast situation exist?"[78] While Stoneham was incorrect that no one was trying to sell, franchise prices should give strong evidence about the game's perceived prospects.

According to economists James Quirk and Rodney Fort, most Major League Baseball franchises appreciated in nominal and real terms during the postwar period. The New York Yankees were sold for $2.88 million in 1945. While many baseball observers felt that the franchise was at a bargain at $2.88 million, the possibility that the 1945 season would be canceled by the federal government cast some doubt on the sale. But Larry MacPhail, one of the partners purchasing the team, was upbeat: "We bought the club because we felt it was a tremendous bargain at the price. We bought it because we knew that Yankee Stadium alone cost more than the sum we paid for a 97 percent control of the entire baseball property."[79] After a disagreement with co-owners Dan Topping and Del Webb, MacPhail sold his share in 1948 for an imputed franchise value of $6.6 million, or a 20 percent real rate of return per year.[80] In 1964 CBS purchased four-fifths of the team for $11.8 million, giving holdover owners Topping and Webb 3 percent earnings per year. Unfortunately for CBS, it could not maintain the team's playing strength and profitability and sold at a loss to George Steinbrenner in 1973. Aside from CBS's sale of the Yankees and the St. Louis Browns' sale in 1949, all postwar franchise sales resulted in at least a nominal appreciation.[81]

Real rates of return varied greatly. In real terms the gains ranged from 2 to almost 23 percent per annum.[82] Veeck's large capital gains from selling Cleveland (1946–49) and Chicago may have resulted from his divesting shortly after pennant-winning seasons, as the teams still sported winning records at the time of the sales. Most other franchises had solid real rates of return of between 5 and 10 percent per year. Still, without the Braves', Browns', and Athletics' impending franchise shifts, the rates of appreciation might have been modest indeed for those teams.

These franchise values were potentially quite volatile. Potential television revenue and changes in the tax code could greatly change franchise values. During the postwar era a clever interpretation of the tax laws enabled owners to depreciate the value of their players. The interpretation required that a new owner acquire at least 80 percent of the ball club. For the following five years the new owner could then depreciate the value of the players at the time of the purchase of the club. Bill Veeck was a pioneer in using this tactic; as he put it, "As a seller [of a franchise], you are selling more than just the franchise and the players. *You are selling the right to depreciate.*"[83]

The new "property right" enhanced the value of owning a franchise, but the right was not secure. Major League owners feared potential new Internal Revenue Service (IRS) interpretations of the depreciation allowance policy. Existing rules allowed owners to depreciate the value of their players over five years; early in 1964 rumors spread that the IRS was going to force baseball owners to depreciate the value over a lengthier period. Owners feared that any dilution of their tax advantage would adversely affect franchise values. The owners persuaded the IRS to retain the status quo. IRS official Mitchell Rogovin stated, "We used to regard a player like a can of corn in a grocery store. Now we're getting around to classifying him like the grocer's cash register." Owners claimed the tax advantage was necessary to induce them to spend money on the risky prospect of developing Major League talent.[84]

Rising television revenues also maintained or raised the value of Major League franchises. As a sportswriter reported in 1965, "The $300,000 per club that ABC is paying this year is only a beginning for the TV deals that are bound to escalate into much higher figures."[85]

Thus, while a share of reported losses were "paper losses," due in part to the "depreciation" of players, most teams reported some profits, and franchises appreciated in value. Profits, however, especially in the American League, did not return to the levels of the immediate postwar period. Major League Baseball teams had notable disparities in profits.

Franchise values may have appreciated during the postwar period, but there is little evidence that the rate of appreciation was particularly robust. Given the American League's dwindling profitability during the mid-1950s, there was little reason for franchise values to rise rapidly unless the new owners could transfer a moribund franchise to a new city or hoped that television revenues would rise. While owners blamed the most publicized expense—players' salaries—for their woes, other costs made up the bulk of expenses and rose more rapidly. Conversely, television income was beginning to constitute a larger share of total revenues. In addition, owners were beginning to exploit the new tax advantage of depreciating their players. The tax advantage enabled owners to convert profits into paper losses. Eventually, when attendance rebounded, especially in the National League, profit figures brightened.

Changing Demographics, Suburbia, and Leisure Patterns

Why Did Baseball Attendance Fall?

The postwar years brought myriad changes to American society, from large-scale movement to the suburbs and a rise in leisure time and spending. Baseball seemingly stood to reap the benefits of a society with more time on its hands and more money for recreational use. But in fact clubs in both leagues experienced a drop in attendance in the years beginning with the Korean War. Aside from competitive imbalance and the modest increases in real ticket prices, what accounts for the rapid drop in attendance at Major League Baseball games? A number of factors can be cited, but the most significant perhaps was the effect of television on the game.

The Changing Society: An Overview

The postwar period was noted for its rising living standards. Given the uncertainty of what would happen during the conversion from a wartime to a peacetime economy, the improved living standards were a welcome development.

Per capita gross national product (GNP) fell between 1945 and 1946 in both nominal and real terms, but, of course, the decrease reflected the vastly diminished government spending. Personal income rose in 1946. Per capita income hovered around $2,200 (in 1958 dollars) between 1946 and 1949 but jumped by one-twelfth in 1950. Real per capita income (adjusted for changes in the price level) rose another one-eighth between 1950 and 1955 but barely changed between 1955 and 1960. Yet the first half of the 1960s saw another surge in real per capita income. Between 1946 and 1965 real per capita income rose by over 40 percent.[1]

After almost four years of war, Americans responded by expanding their real personal consumption by over one-tenth in 1946 compared with the year before. Americans' total recreational spending went up by over one-quarter between 1945 and 1946. Spending on recreation made up 6 percent of personal consumption expenditures and 4 percent of GNP in 1946. In 1945 the respective proportions had been 5 percent and 3 percent. Spending on recreation as a proportion of personal consumption and GNP then diminished for over a decade, reaching lows in 1957.[2] The proportions of the mid-1950s were similar to those during the Great Depression. Could it be that after the initial boom year, Americans retrenched on their leisure spending?

In order to address this question, two caveats should be noted. First, many Americans had more leisure time in the postwar era than they had had before. Manufacturing workers worked three fewer hours per week in 1946 than in the previous year. Wholesale trade and contract construction workers also put in fewer average weekly hours in 1946 than in 1945, and these reductions in work hours continued into the 1950s. Retail trade workers, too, had lower average weekly hours after 1946.[3]

Second, in accounting for leisure spending, the personal consumption expenditures on recreation have some limitations. As their incomes rose and as federal restrictions on gasoline consumption and travel ended, Americans purchased mobility. Passenger car sales tripled between 1946 and 1950 to 6.7 million passenger vehicles. Fuel consumption by passenger vehicles rose by more than half between 1946 and 1953, and the number of passenger miles driven increased correspondingly. Family ownership of automobiles rose from just over half of families in 1948, the first year listed, to almost two-thirds in 1954.[4] Long-distance auto travel gradually became faster and more convenient as highway construction, culminating in the interstate freeway system, girded the nation in asphalt.

Where were Americans going in their cars? As mentioned, the number of passenger miles being driven increased by over half. Urban travel rose by a third, but rural travel increased by three-quarters between 1946 and 1953 (the rise was more dramatic between 1945 and 1953). One possible explanation is that Americans' greater mobility made traveling to scenic and historic sites more feasible. According to the *Historical Statistics of the United States*, between 1942 and 1945 Americans made an average of 9 million visits per year to national parks, monuments, parkways, historical areas, and military areas—11.7 million such visits in 1945 alone. The number of visits doubled in 1946 and tripled by 1950. By 1960 it had reached seventy-nine million. The "spending on recreation" data in the *Historical Statistics* does not include these trips to parks. A similar, if less dramatic, trend occurred for state parks. Americans also took more trips abroad. Aside from military personnel, only 117,000 Americans traveled overseas during the last year of the war in 1945, but the number rose sevenfold by 1953. Total expenditures on travel abroad were $716 million in 1947 (no data was available for 1945 and 1946), but by 1953 the expenditures had increased by more than half in real terms.[5]

But even within the category of "total recreation spending" a major shift occurred between 1946 and 1953 (see table 4.1 in the appendix). Americans shifted their recreation dollars from "public" to "private" forms of recreation. Expenditures on "radio and television receivers, records, and musical instruments" exploded between 1945 and 1953, and this predates the rise of rock 'n' roll. The upswing in the radio/ television category and "radio and television repair" accounted for two-thirds of higher expenditures made on recreation between 1945 and 1953. The two categories encompassing toys accounted for 38 percent of the increased recreational expenditures between 1945 and 1953. Including "books," "magazines," and "gardening" as expenditures for "private" recreation, these categories combined for 114 percent of the overall increase in money spent on recreation and contributed to the rising proportion spent on what was considered private recreation. Participation in "public" forms of recreation such as movies, theater, spectator sports, clubs, amusement parks, and pari-mutuel racetracks either declined sharply or experienced modest increases at best.

Admissions to specified spectator amusements declined in real dollars between 1945 and 1953. This category included motion picture theaters, theater entertainment, and spectator sports.[6] Expenditures on movies were hardest hit. Weekly attendance at motion pictures went up in 1946, but real box office receipts only increased 7.5 percent over 1945. The increase paled against that of total recreational spending, being only one-fourth the rate of change. Real box office receipts fell 17.6 percent in 1947, and by 1949 box office receipts were almost one-third below the 1946 level. In 1953 real box office receipts were just half of the 1946 receipts.[7] Because television was still largely confined to the Northeast and Midwest (where, of course, the bulk of the population lived), it is not compelling as a primary explanation for the decline between 1946 and 1949 in movie theater attendance. Although indoor movie theaters experienced a prolonged postwar slump, the reduced receipts were partially offset by rising receipts at drive-in theaters. Between 1948 and 1954 the number of drive-ins more than quadrupled, while receipts quintupled in nominal terms and more than quadrupled in real terms.[8] The appeal of drive-in theaters, perhaps reflecting Americans' greater mobility, may have also revealed Americans' growing desire for private (at least within their cars) consumption—an antecedent, perhaps, of home videos.

When they were not seeking amusement, more American males were earning bachelor's degrees, spurred in part by the GI Bill. The number of bachelor's degrees awarded to men peaked at 328,841 in 1950, up from 58,664 in 1946. During 1949–51 American males received almost 870,000 bachelor's degrees. Another 123,000 of them completed master's degrees.[9]

Air-conditioning also played a part in Americans' changing leisure-time activities. It had been common in movie theaters and some other public places for many years. The 1950 census did not enumerate air-conditioning in occupied units, whereas the 1960 census showed that only one-eighth of occupied units had air-conditioning. The diffusion of home air conditioners ranged from 18 percent in the South to 9 percent in the West. As more homes got air-conditioning, going to movie theaters and ballgames might have seemed less attractive than staying at home.[10]

Demographics may have played a role in the declining attendance at professional baseball games. Across the country the number of single males, fourteen years old and older, shrank by 18 percent between 1940 and 1950, although the drop was slightly cushioned by a higher number of divorced men. The number of single men between the ages of twenty and forty-four decreased by almost one-quarter and continued to fall between 1950 and 1960 (by 13.3 percent).[11] While there is little direct evidence of what groups made up the bulk of the crowds at the ballpark, the rarity of "Men's Days" is suggestive, at least, of the gender of the key group. Owners apparently did not think they needed to offer special inducements to get men to attend games. If relatively young single men were professional baseball's best customers, their declining number might have contributed to the eventual diminution in attendance at Major League Baseball games.

Between 1940 and 1950 married men had more children, with a more than one-half increase in the number of small children (under five years old) between 1940 and 1950, thus possibly making them less willing or able to attend games. The number of young children increased by an additional one-quarter between 1950 and 1960.[12]

The population of Standard Metropolitan Statistical Areas (SMSA) increased by a third between 1950 and 1960, but the population of central cities only increased by one-sixth.[13] For the ten cities with Major League Baseball teams in 1950, every one lost population between 1950 and 1960; in some cases the SMSA increased in population. Boston, Detroit, New York, and St. Louis all lost at least one hundred thousand people during the decade. The outer areas of all SMSA's increased by over half. By 1970 more people lived outside the central city than within it. The South and West saw the most rapid upward shifts in SMSA population, although in these regions, too, the increase was more rapid outside the central city. What effects the relative growth of the suburbs had on professional baseball attendance is difficult to assess, but it is plausible to speculate that a growing proportion of the suburban population found getting to downtown stadiums less convenient. The rural population in the South barely changed after 1950, however, so Minor League teams in small southern towns likely faced stagnant markets.

The postwar era featured significant demographic shifts that combined with other changes, among which television was an important one, to alter Americans' leisure patterns between 1946 and 1953. Professional baseball faced competition from Americans' greater mobility as well as their growing family responsibilities and activities. Americans appear to have switched away from spectator activities in general after 1946.

Tried-and-True Tactics for Boosting Attendance

When World War II ended, baseball owners worried about whether the game would return to normal and hoped that their longtime constituencies would return. Did postwar fans differ from the prewar fans? Throughout the early years of Major League Baseball most baseball officials believed that blue-collar workers (presumably male) constituted their core fan base. As early as 1957, according to a *Fortune* article, observers noted that, "Most parks are in industrial centers, or in or near lower-class residential sections. This is far from a drawback, for most real rooters are workers and white-collar people."[14] As the inner cities began to stagnate after the war, however, the formerly advantageous ball park locations would become a detriment.

Major League owners were stunned by the resurgence at the gate after World War II. Because they were unsure about the fans' response in 1946, in order to help boost the gate, they had turned to night games and Ladies' Days. The owners were keenly aware that Sundays and holidays were the best-drawing days.[15] Weekday afternoons typically attracted the sparsest crowds. To bulk up the weekday crowds, owners started scheduling more night games during the week. A few teams, especially in particularly hot and humid areas, also scheduled night games in order to make their patrons more comfortable. Larry MacPhail introduced night baseball at the Major League level in 1935, when he ran the Cincinnati Reds. He noticed differences between fans attending day and night games: "The clash over night ball involves something fundamental. Those who favor it, with its 'shopping' type of fan, its brass bands and fireworks, feel they can cash in on baseball as a form of general amusement. But the majority who oppose it see baseball as a tense competition involving violent partisanship, and prefer to put all their eggs in the basket of the staunch partisan. *He* doesn't want brass bands; *he* doesn't think of baseball as just an alternative to the movies; *he* regards it as something permanent in his life."[16]

The American League had begun playing baseball under the lights before World War II. In 1939 Major League teams played a total of twenty-one games at night. Night baseball, like most innovations, triggered much controversy. Purists preferred baseball under natural lighting. Nevertheless, night baseball proved popular with fans. According to sportswriter Ed Rumill, "What the night game has done is to give the magnates the equivalent of Sunday and holiday doubleheaders on week days—or, to be more exact, week nights. No longer need there be slim gatherings on Mondays, Fridays or other lean days between Saturdays, Sundays and holidays. Every day is Sunday when the light switch is thrown."[17]

Ironically, MacPhail consistently urged restraint in the use of night games. During his brief part-ownership of the New York Yankees, the team played only fourteen night games per season, among the lowest number in the American League. "I didn't think greedy club owners would take [night baseball] to such lengths," he remarked. He believed that too much night baseball ruined the remaining day games on weekdays: "The nature of baseball as a game has changed because the kids can't get close enough to it. As a night game, it's not for the kids. They watch it on TV, but that's no substitute for being at the park and smelling baseball and growing up with a love for the game that youths of our generations had."[18] While MacPhail countenanced more night games in St. Louis and Washington DC, because of the extremely humid days, he felt that those teams should have limited their slate to twenty-one games. Finally, he believed that Major League night games hurt the Minor Leagues. New York Giants owner Horace Stoneham disputed MacPhail's opinions: "We only go along with the demand for night baseball in arranging our schedule. . . . We have a clear idea of what is wanted through our advance sale, and we estimate our public is willing to take 20 or 21 night games at this time."[19] Stoneham had figures showing that a day game during the week averaged less than ten thousand fans, while a night game drew twenty-two thousand, which was more than the averages for Sundays and holiday games.

Rumill believed that night baseball attracted a new crowd to the games: people who worked during the day could now attend games. In addition, he claimed, "Night ball is doing more to solidify interest among females than Ladies' Day and radio combined. The busy housewife now finds it possible to regularly spend pleasant evenings watching the heroes she has been reading and hearing about for so long—something that was only occasionally possible in the afternoon."[20] Yet Dodgers owner Walter O'Malley disliked having too many night games, as the games interfered with the team's "Knothole" program, which admitted children for free. "Just figure what social agencies spend for a certain number of child-hours of diversion or instruction," he asserted, "and then consider that we give the kids two and a half hours in the park at no cost whatever in public taxes or contributions."[21]

In 1946 American League teams played 122 games under the lights. By 1948 the number of night games was 188 (see table 4.2 in the appendix). The weakest teams tended to rely on night games more than the others. The Browns, for example, had thirty-nine night games in 1948 that drew a combined 189,258 fans. For the season the team drew 335,564 fans, so the night games attracted about 1,000 more fans per game than did the day games. Of course, a direct comparison is faulty, given that the night games were typically during the week, when attendance would usually be lower than on the weekend. Nevertheless, night baseball appears to have boosted the meager gate for the Browns, but one is entitled to ponder whether the Browns diluted the effectiveness of night games by having so many. For the 1947 to 1964 period the Browns/Orioles drew almost two-thirds of their total attendance from night games, the highest ratio among the eight original franchises (see table 4.3 in the appendix). The Yankees, in contrast, attracted just over a third of its fans to night games at Yankee Stadium, but by 1964 the team had almost half of its gate at night.

Night baseball was not a panacea. The Cleveland Indians, facing a disastrous decline in attendance in the late 1950s and early 1960s, almost doubled the number of night games between 1947 and 1964. Sadly for the Indians, more was not better. The twenty-six night games in 1947 drew 786,179 fans (the 1948 record was even better, with 1.24 million fans showing up for the twenty-six night games), but in 1964 the fifty night games drew only 376,916 fans.

Boston, Detroit, and New York persisted in hosting a minimal number of night games until 1952. In fact, Boston and Detroit only started using lights in 1946 and 1948, respectively, although Detroit used lights temporarily during World War II to accommodate workers.[22] Tigers owner Walter O. Briggs experimented with different lighting to produce a more flattering effect for his female customers. Thereafter, each team gradually increased its night games. Why did these three teams hesitate to increase their slate of night games? Would they have been better off hosting more night games, or did the teams' fan bases prefer day games? One possible clue: the Yankees sold a large number of season box tickets. Initially, at least, businesses in the city purchased many of the season tickets. One can imagine that the huge New York business community could well induce the Yankees to continue hosting its games during daylight.

The Minor Leagues also relied on night games. According to sportswriter Red Smith, night baseball was crucial for many Minor League teams, "where relatively few people have the leisure to attend afternoon games."[23]

Major league teams offered Ladies' Days or Ladies' Nights to attract female fans. The Boston Braves took credit for initiating Ladies' Day, as this blurb from the team's 1946 scorecard attests: "Bob Quinn, formerly president of the Boston club, is responsible for Ladies' Day. The interest shown by women in the National game has extended from coast to coast, and in some cities, on Ladies' Day, it is necessary to limit the number of tickets available."[24] Typically, women would enter a particular gate at a stadium, paying only enough to cover the tax on a regular ticket or some reduced amount, such as fifty cents. The Chicago Cubs charged women only twenty-five cents.[25] Apparently, teams did not have to count such reduced admissions when calculating the gate-sharing amount, nor did these women figure into the "official" attendance. Owners may have hoped, however, that having a wife, mother, or girlfriend attend a game might induce more men to attend or that women would eventually become loyal fans, willing and able to pay full admission. In addition, even women entering for free spent money at the concessions. Because the average fan paid $1.20 in concessions at Chicago's Comiskey Park, for instance, of which 20 percent went to the White Sox, Bill Veeck could hope for twenty to twenty-five cents net per woman. Veeck claimed that the various Ladies' Days, kids' discounts, and other promotions lured almost 4 million people to Cleveland's stadium during the 1948 season, of which some 2.6 million fans paid full admission, so the promotions increased the crowds by half.[26]

The New York Yankees were the last team to begin holding Ladies' Days. According to a 1937 article, every club but the Yankees held such days. Before the war the Chicago Cubs attracted a tremendous number of women. According to a piece in the August 1937 *Fortune* magazine, "Many [of these women] are steady customers; many more are simply Ladies' Day faithfuls who get in free. Ladies' Day at Wrigley Field is so popular that the Cubs now have to limit their passes to 20,000, which sometimes isn't enough to go around."[27] After World

War II most teams held several Ladies' Days each season, although not all teams listed the event in their scorecards. Detroit apparently had not had Ladies' Days for some time, as the team's June 1959 team newsletter stated that the promotion was "being revived." The Tigers also featured "Lutheran Nights" in 1959–61. Sadly, the newsletter did not state how ticket takers would identify Lutherans, there being no national Lutheran ID cards that the author, a lifelong Lutheran, is aware of.

Bill Veeck believed that "once a woman becomes a fan, she is the best fan in the world," so he made sure that "in every possible way we treated women as women." While running the Cleveland Indians, he "wooed women shamelessly." Aside from the usual Ladies' Day promotion, he gave cosmetic kits, orchids, and nylons to female patrons. He made sure that the ladies' rooms were fixed up: "Ladies rooms in most baseball parks are a shame and a disgrace. At Comiskey Park, the facilities were so bad that I forbade Mary Frances [his wife] to use them." Veeck installed vanity tables, "flattering" fluorescent lighting, and full-length mirrors. He also created a nursery with registered nurses and toys. He concluded, "The best thing that can be said about catering to the needs and whimsies of women is that it works. In 1948, we had an unbelievably high ratio of women customers."[28]

Sportswriter William Furlong detailed Veeck's efforts in attracting female fans:

> The impact of his methods was demonstrated in an important area: banishing the historic dislike women had for Comiskey Park. To overcome this attitude, Veeck worked on a variety of details. He stationed ushers just inside the gates to look for women who appeared confused and to escort them personally to their seats. . . . He gave away orchids and roses, let mothers in free on Mother's Day, gave away green stamps (instead of cigars or beer) on certain Sundays. The result was that the number of women attending games at Comiskey Park tripled (to about 420,000) and the proportionate number went up from less than 20% to more than 30%.[29]

Before the 1957 World Series between the Braves and the Yankees, one observer remarked, "The occasional note of shrillness in the crowd's aggregate voice is traceable to the fact that the proportion of women in a County Stadium throng is very high, probably the highest in the major leagues." He continued, "When Pop goes to the ball game, Mom sees to it that it becomes a family outing. This is reflected not only in increased ticket sales, but also in exceptionally high per capita revenue at the concession stands, which feature an extraordinary variety of souvenirs as well as staples like beer and bratwurst."[30] Sportswriter Dan Daniel believed that women had a greater interest in Major League Baseball thanks to increased television exposure, so Major League teams should focus on getting more women to attend games: "If they want to keep pace with the times, if they are to make the most of feminine interest in the game, they must hire women public relations experts to supplement the work of men now employed in such capacities."[31] Given the owners' conservatism, whether any team acted upon his advice is both unknown and unlikely.

Like every other facet of society, baseball was buffeted by the sea changes taking place across the country in the years following World War II. Women were being recognized as valued baseball fans, with the ball clubs focusing marketing efforts on them, such as Ladies' Days. Night games gave more people the opportunity to attend games after work. While these efforts were successful in spurring attendance during the late 1940s, they ultimately failed to prevent a significant drop in attendance the next decade.

Baseball Looks for Answers for the Attendance Decline

The good news was that tens of millions of Americans went to ball-games, even in the mid-1950s. According to an American Institute of Public Opinion survey, the impressive news was that twenty-three million Americans paid to see at least one baseball game during 1957, and nine out of ten of them saw more than one game.[32] The bad news was the rapid loss in attendance at Major League Baseball games, especially in the American League.

By the mid-1950s individual clubs were concerned enough about faltering attendance to take a radical step: they asked their patrons what was on their minds. The Baltimore Orioles, Milwaukee Braves, and the New York clubs conducted polls, of varying reliability. Major League Baseball also commissioned a poll. The Orioles hired a former Gallup pollster to query fans at various Orioles games. The pollster questioned 2,500 randomly selected fans over twenty different playing dates between July 2 and August 20, 1955. Of course, the poll had a built-in bias, as it only polled fans who had attended the game. The poll did not directly address the issue of why potential fans stayed away. Nevertheless, Orioles officials were surprised by the results: "It was a popular conception that the average fan came from below the middle income bracket, that Baltimore had no outlying area from which to draw, that Baltimore might be stealing some fans from Washington, and that the fans didn't know they were inheriting a second-division team from St. Louis. These things are all disproved."[33]

Indeed, less than a quarter of the fans listed skilled and unskilled labor as the "nature of their work." About one-twelfth were retired or unemployed. Less than 4 percent were housewives. About 56 percent were white collar, professional or executive, although white collar included bank teller and secretary. The Orioles drew disproportionately from middle and higher income levels. Almost 95 percent of the fans were high school or college graduates. The survey might be interpreted as indicating that fans with lower income were discouraged by the ticket prices. About 80 percent of the fans lived in Maryland or Pennsylvania. Less than 1 percent of the fans lived in Washington DC. Almost four-fifths of the fans came to the game via automobiles, with another one-eighth arriving via bus or trolley. More than a quarter of the fans traveled more than forty-five minutes by car to the city's boundaries, but the percentage jumped to 41.2 percent for Sunday games. During the week only 18.2 percent drove that far. More than five-sixths of the fans wanted thirty-one or more night games (the team had thirty-two night games scheduled for 1955).[34]

The Milwaukee Braves conducted their own study about their fans by examining their mail-order list for tickets. The club discovered that about a third of their patrons came from more than fifty miles away and that the average out-of-town fan spent almost $11 while in Milwaukee.[35]

The New York Giants hired a professional polling company to question 1,500 fans at the Polo Grounds. The polling company purposely avoided any games between the Dodgers and Giants because "these didn't represent a true cross-section." The pollsters asked fans about television and its effects upon their willingness to come to the ballpark, but the club did not release this part of the poll: "It [the club] was equally quick to announce that this particular portion of the poll would remain under lock and key."[36] The Giants did not reduce the number of televised home games.

Giants vice president Chub Feeney openly discussed other findings. According to sportswriter Harold Rosenthal, the Giants discovered through the polling that "there are more solo admissions in the bleachers than in the reserved sections; that the bleachers and unreserved seats furnish more repeaters than the reserved and unreserved sections, and surprisingly, that the reserved seats attract a younger clientele." In addition, weather was a critical factor, as two-fifths of the attendees decided only on the day of the game whether to trek to the Polo Grounds. "The more distance separating the fan from the ball park, it was found, the greater must be his long-range planning, which means that the large proportion of reserved seat customers will be found in this group."[37]

A later poll revealed other information. "The poll confirmed our thoughts about more and more of our customers coming from the suburbs. And when we saw how many of our customers came by car, we knew we had to do something about parking accommodations." Apparently, 60 percent of the fans arrived by car, while another quarter took the rapid transit system. The remainder either took a bus or a train or they walked. Feeney noted that even many city residents used their cars to get to the games: "One out of four [city residents] comes by car even though the subway entrance is actually on our doorstep.

Only 56 percent use the subway coming from various points in the city; the rest use private cars, taxis and buses. Almost one out of ten walks." In addition to the mode of transportation to get to the game, the poll revealed that the average fan needed almost three-quarters of an hour to get home after a night game, with city customers needing just over a half-hour. There was gratifying news too. The Giants management was pleased that the vast majority of fans found the ballpark employees courteous and helpful.[38]

Indeed, the Giants management reacted to this and other fan surveys. The club moved the new starting time for night games to 8:15, later changing it to 8:00: "The change was made as a result of a poll taken among the Polo Grounds' fans last summer. . . . A huge majority favored the earlier start."[39] The Giants quickly entered into a reciprocal agreement with the New York Yankees to share both clubs' parking facilities.

Ironically, the Giants had been one of the first clubs to discuss how to reach the ballpark and parking in their scorecards. As early as 1947, the club's scorecard discussed how to reach the Polo Grounds via mass transit. The 1949 scorecard informed fans that, "Parking lot for Polo Grounds patrons: Patrons are invited to utilize the parking space for automobiles, located at southeast entrance of the Polo Grounds, 155th Street and Eighth Avenue. This parking space is intended to serve as a convenience for Polo Grounds fans. A one-price 75-cent parking fee has been established."[40] By 1952 the scorecard listed an additional parking area: "Automobile commuters from New Jersey, Westchester and Long Island are invited to avail themselves of the facilities of the Giants parking lot, located directly adjoining and South of the Polo Grounds. A one-price 50-cent fee will be maintained." The team raised the parking fee to a dollar in 1954. The 1956 scorecard informed fans that for night and Sunday games the Yankee Stadium parking lot would be available for Polo Grounds fans.[41]

The Yankees and Dodgers also polled fans during the early 1950s. The teams asked questions regarding television and fan comfort. The Yankees responded to the polls by changing the starting time of day games.[42]

Finally, commissioner Ford Frick hired an agency to survey baseball fans during 1955.[43] Frick wanted to discern why attendance at Major League games was declining. "If they are staying away from games, there must be reason," he said. "We found out that it was not entirely television, or that there was too much baseball on television. People also were watching horse races, horse operas, and 'I Love Lucy.'"[44] The survey queried twenty thousand people across the country. The major findings included establishing that fans stayed away from ballparks because of inadequate parking and other problems in getting to the stadiums. Fans also thought the games were too slow and took too long. Apparently, many fans preferred watching games on television for free. The *Sporting News* editorialized that the owners had previously discounted complaints about the length of the games: "Evidently there is such a relationship. No one wants to sit on the wooden chairs—even with a rented cushion—while nothing is happening on the diamond." While the editors sympathized with the fans, some baseball officials did not. Cincinnati Reds general manager Gabe Paul retorted, "Sure, the seats are hard. . . . A baseball crowd doesn't mind bad seats much, anyway. Every time something happens they all jump up. Besides, they've always got the seventh-inning stretch."[45] The parking problem and fans' preference for television also wrought little optimism from an editorial writer for the *Sporting News*, who cited the difficulty, in general, of getting people to use mass transit in order to conserve scarce parking: "It appears that a percentage of fans who once were willing to wrestle with [parking problems] now are inclined to settle for video instead of personal coverage. . . . Perhaps there isn't much more the clubs can do about television. . . . Television is a full-grown competitor for the attention of the public. If baseball were not available on the silver screens, a great many people undoubtedly would take comedians or drama as TV entertainment."[46]

One question presented people with a list of possible changes to the game; the respondents could check as many as they agreed with. "Better parking facilities" received the largest response (71.25 percent), followed by "More attention to comfort and convenience of spectators" (58 percent) and "Shorter games, faster paced" (55.9 percent). More than a third of the people interviewed chose "Better equalization of competitive strengths between teams." In response to a second, similar question—"If you could make a specific suggestion for the betterment of baseball, what would it be?"—the largest number chose "Improved parking facilities" (67 percent), followed by "More attention to comfort and convenience of spectators" (63 percent). Only a third cited "Less TV coverage." Others cited improved Major-Minor League relations and definite radio-television policy.

Other questions dealt with television. Over a third of the fans approved of pay-as-you-see television at a nominal fee, while half favored blacking out home games on television if such broadcasts hurt the gate. About three-quarters of the respondents thought radio and television increased the general interest in baseball. The interviewees were split on whether broadcasts and telecasts affected attendance at games: two-fifths felt radio and television reduced attendance, while over one-quarter believed it boosted attendance. As reporter Carl Lundquist summarized the results, "People expressed the feeling that it was more comfortable in their living rooms than it was making a long trip to a ball park and sitting in inferior seats."[47] In addition, fans cited increased entertainment opportunities as competition for baseball. These findings conflicted somewhat with the informal poll done by the *Sporting News* in 1954, in which fans expressed their preference for limiting bonus payments to young players, more competitive balance, faster games, and a shorter season.[48]

In addition to the survey data, baseball pundits occasionally resorted to dubious explanations for the drop in attendance. According to J. G. Taylor Spink, editor of the *Sporting News*, "Baseball long has been known as a family sport, and when the kids go back to school, interest wanes. . . . Another factor is the constantly growing interest in football, both professional and college."[49] Spink was trying to explain the attendance doldrums of the American League in 1961. Yet his explanation was suspect, as kids went back to school every year.

In order to bolster sagging attendance, commissioner Ford Frick had earlier designated March 19-26, 1955, as "Let's Play Ball" week. Frick urged Major and Minor League team owners to get governors and local officials to proclaim publicly, "Let's play ball." He also encouraged television and other forms of promotion.[50]

New Competitors in the Market for Leisure

Baseball faced increasing competition from other leisure-time pursuits. In its inaugural issue *Sports Illustrated* ran an article entitled, "The Golden Age Is Now," in which the author chronicled the expanding leisure-time activities being pursued by Americans. In a recent year Americans had obtained some thirty-two million hunting and fishing licenses. Twenty million Americans had bowled. And employers had spent $800 million to sponsor recreational activities.[51] According to economist Richard E. Snyder, however, the recreational sports boom of the postwar era was concentrated among "those affluent metropolitan households, about 10 million families all told . . . [who] instead of concentrating on one sporting activity alone, they go from one to another as the seasons progress."[52]

American males generally devoted more of their time to do-it-yourself home improvement and repair jobs. Magazines featuring articles on such topics, including *Popular Mechanics*, *Popular Science*, and *Better Homes and Gardens*, experienced surges in their subscriptions. The first two magazines almost doubled their circulation between 1946 and 1953, although their numbers fell off by 1957. The third magazine had an 80 percent increase in subscribers between 1946 and 1957.[53]

In addition to television, many youths turned to other forms of recreation: comic books and rock 'n' roll music. Comic book sales skyrocketed during the immediate postwar period. In 1949 the ten comic book groups, each with at least 1 million units sold per month, had a combined 35.6 million in monthly sales.[54] Musical tastes among the young changed markedly during the postwar era, particularly during the mid-and late 1950s.

Little League baseball proved popular. By 1961 there were a million boys playing in the United States and other countries.[55] One former Minor League player blamed Little League for the decline in Minor League attendance: "You know what's killin' the minor leagues? It's not television—it's the damn Little Leagues." As one writer observed, "The average citizen with a choice between watching a minor league game and his son's Little League game would, naturally go out to see his flesh and blood."[56] American Legion and other leagues also grew during the 1950s. Despite the growing number of youths playing Little League and other organized baseball, some health researchers sounded alarms about the country's youth becoming unfit. These researchers claimed that American kids were less flexible and had less muscular strength than their European peers.[57] The burgeoning youth leagues held one promise. According to a 1962 piece in the *Sporting News*, "A special study of youth baseball . . . disclosed that Organized Baseball is in a position to hit the biggest jackpot of talent in its history, with more boys playing on more teams in more games than at any time in diamond annals."[58]

A Cardinals official, Bing Devine, attributed some of the Minor Leagues' doldrums to "backyard barbecue pit and air-conditioning that made staying at home more attractive"; his remarks undoubtedly applied to the Major Leagues, too.[59]

Football loomed as a formidable rival to professional baseball. Bill Veeck believed that college football had an advantage in attracting fans, as it exemplified a sport in which the alumni and current students identify completely with the team. The college student's familiarity with football made him or her a natural patron for professional football.[60] Professional football, as represented by the National Football League, demonstrated steady growth throughout the 1950s. The league's attendance rose from roughly 2 million in 1950 to 3.3 million in 1960. The American Football League began play as the decade ended. The All-American Football Conference folded, however, after 1949. That league had drawn over a million fans during some of its seasons, so the National Football League's attendance gains of the 1950s restored the total professional football attendance to the same levels as had existed during the late 1940s. Football teams may have gained from increased ticket prices. Did the growing popularity of NFL football affect attendance at Major League games? Until 1958 the Los Angeles Rams and San Francisco 49ers were superfluous in addressing the question, seeing as Major League Baseball had yet to claim those cities. Green Bay may have affected the Milwaukee Braves attendance. Major League Baseball teams in Boston, Cincinnati, Kansas City, and St. Louis did not face NFL competition during the 1950s.[61]

In the next decade, however, professional football's success was harder for baseball to ignore. The management of the ailing Cleveland Indians blamed suburbanization for its dwindling attendance, but when eighty-three thousand fans attended a professional football exhibition doubleheader on a rainy day in August 1963, the Indians management's excuse seemed lame. "Obviously, the people of Cleveland still support an *attraction* and, if they are presented with one, they will push the barbecue routines aside and come to town."[62]

Major League Baseball and professional football clashed over playing dates. The National Football League decided to lengthen its season to fourteen games for the 1961 season. The league scheduled its opening games on September 17, a week earlier than in 1960 and two weeks earlier than in most years. This meant that football would overlap the baseball schedule for three weekends instead of the final weekend, in addition to the World Series. Because ten of the NFL teams shared parks with baseball teams, conflicts were inevitable, although typically baseball teams controlled the parks.[63] Some Major League teams, however, accommodated professional football. The Brooklyn Dodgers advertised the upcoming Brooklyn/New York Yankee professional football team's schedule in their 1949 scorecard. The Boston Braves ran an ad for college football in their 1949 and 1950 scorecards. The Athletics ran an article on the National Football League's Philadelphia Eagles in their 1949 team newsletter. Despite these cooperative ventures, football continued to threaten baseball's claim as the national pastime throughout the 1960s.

(Some of) The Owners Respond

Baseball owners could do little to alter changes in society, whether in terms of the movement of people from the central cities to suburban areas, the growing ownership of automobiles, the baby boom, or the changing patterns of recreation. Yet they could try to make their product more convenient or more attractive.

Major League Baseball was a business. As Bill Veeck pointed out, "We are in the entertainment business, competing for the entertainment dollar. Competition is tougher. In 1902, there wasn't much else you could do unless you wanted to stay home and sing along with the player piano. . . . Like everybody else, we are competing with television." Veeck believed that most fans were casual fans: "If you depend solely on people who know and love the game, you will be out of business by Mother's Day." He stated, "I did always try to create the feeling that we were all one big happy family, that we were all out to have a good time together." A team's most important attraction was its ability on the field. The average fan "identifies himself completely with the home team. If the home team wins, he wins. If the home team loses, he loses. It is not pleasant to lose. . . . You cannot expect a man to pay good money to come into your park and be humiliated when it is so easy to stay home."

Although winning was crucial, a baseball promoter sought to enhance any team's ability on the field by providing fans with entertainment and a good time: "[It] softens the blow of losing. It gives the fan something else to think and talk about as he is leaving the park."[64] Veeck characterized baseball's fan base: "Baseball is the workingman's game. A baseball crowd is a beer-drinking crowd [except, officially, in Pennsylvania, where the sale of beer was prohibited], not a mixed-drink crowd. This is why a pennant-winning team can galvanize an entire city the way a football team, with its more limited audience, cannot."[65]

In another interview Veeck did not tout promotion as the critical factor that makes one team more profitable than another; instead, a stadium's location was the key: "That was always important, but now it's crucial. With TV, people can see a ball game at home. If it's a bother to get out to the park—why bother? So the stadium must be tied in completely with good roads and public transportation. The single most important improvement that can be made in baseball today is improved parking."[66]

Veeck owned teams in Chicago, Cleveland, and St. Louis. His observations may not have held as well in New York or Los Angeles. Still, he knew the Chicago fan as well as anyone. The Cubs fan "comes from the suburbs and from out of town. He will come to a Sunday game . . . to relax." The White Sox fan, however, found "nothing casual or relaxing about baseball. . . . The White Sox had long ago tested the loyalty of their rooters; the weak and the faint of heart had fallen by the wayside and only the strong, the dedicated and the masochistic remained." The ballparks seemingly reflected their fan base. Wrigley Field was beautiful and friendly, while Comiskey Park was "in the grimy industrial back-of-the-yards section of the South Side . . . the maintenance had been neglected so completely over the years that it had all the appearance of an outdoor slum." In addition, Comiskey was located in a dubious neighborhood: "You did not walk your dog at night unless you wanted both yourself and the dog mugged." The neighborhood and stadium made attracting women to Comiskey a particular challenge. Veeck made sure that there was plenty of lighting throughout the neighborhood surrounding the ballpark. He cited the efforts of police lieutenant John L. Sullivan and the Andy Frain ushers in helping maintain order: "We kept the rate of rowdyism going down the next year by putting a coat of white paint on everything that didn't move or talk, and over-ushering by 25 percent."[67]

Clearly, the comfort and attractiveness of the stadium mattered. New St. Louis Cardinal owner August Busch purchased the team just as baseball entered its doldrums. He observed, "Major league clubs have got to stop defying the customers to come into their parks. Our magnates must become tidier housekeepers. . . . We must offer fine parks, fine service, sufficient parking, clean and adequate facilities, comfortable seats, clean and attractive approaches and park settings. And baseball initiative and enterprise."[68]

The Major Leagues had experienced a stadium-building frenzy—back in 1909–15. Unfortunately, most of these stadiums were still in use throughout the postwar era. The Pittsburgh Pirates and the four teams in Philadelphia and St. Louis played in stadiums built in 1909. Aside from the Yankees and Indians, all the other teams played in stadiums built between 1910 and 1915. Yankee Stadium dated back to 1923. Cleveland's Municipal Stadium was the newest stadium among the sixteen teams, having been built in 1932. Hence, as the franchise re-location movement started in 1953, every Major League stadium was at least twenty years old, and most were pushing forty. The owners of Wrigley Field in Chicago and Briggs Stadium in Detroit scrupulously maintained their parks throughout the era. Indeed, until very recently, both parks were still in use. Nevertheless, with such an old stock of stadiums, most Major League Baseball owners had to scramble to improve existing facilities or, preferably, obtain new ones.

The older stadiums were lacking in two fundamental ways: they were not situated to handle large volumes of automobile traffic and parking, and they were uncomfortable. Getting to the ballpark had usually been simple enough: mass transit served almost every park in 1950. Yet with suburbanization and growing automobile ownership, fans clamored for improved parking. *Sports Illustrated* included park-ing and mass transit information in its 1957 and 1961 season analyses. The older stadiums typically had "barely adequate" parking at best, but less-complimentary adjectives were more common. Several teams carried information regarding mass transit serving their ballparks.[69]

As shown earlier, Giants owner Horace Stoneham took his fans' wishes seriously. He responded to fan surveys. Despite his efforts, the main problems for the Giants were the location of the team's ballpark and the Polo Grounds Stadium itself. Getting to the stadium was an exercise in frustration: "It is stuck in between a cliff and a river; it has one parking lot, which is designed on the principle of the fun-nel—everything seems to go out through one gate." Once at the game, fans discovered that many seats in the aging stadium had obstructed views. "Watching a game from [the lower stands behind the dugouts] is like watching it through a picket fence, and the people who sit there sway back and forth continuously during a game, first one way to get a glimpse of the pitcher winding up—as the batter disappears behind a post—and then the other way, abruptly dismissing the pitcher, to watch the batter swing. The Polo Grounds is a terrible place to watch a ball game."[70]

Yet the Polo Grounds experience was not unique. What did baseball patrons find at other stadiums? James Murray wrote a satirical article for *Sports Illustrated* in August 1956, before the Dodgers and Giants left New York City. The older stadiums often had obstructing poles, terrible restrooms, and uncomfortable seats. He characterized a hypothetical discussion between husband and wife regarding the evening's entertainment: "The ball park? That filthy hole? Not on your life! We're going down to Loew's [theater]."[71] Murray blamed the owners: "The fans' dissatisfaction with what they get when they've plunked their money down and paid off the parking lot shark and the small boy who wants to watch the car and the bully who beats them into buying a program and the usher who tells them where to go and the usher who dusts off the seat when they finally get to it—well, their dissatisfaction with the whole works is country-wide."[72]

Philadelphia fans feared vandals who flattened their tires or who rioted near Connie Mack Stadium. Cleveland fans faced steep ramps to seats in the upper stands. As with New York Yankee fans, Cleveland fans wondered about favoritism in allocating choice seats: "How come the choice tickets for choice double-headers wind up in the hands of the shady characters on Short Vincent Street?" White Sox fans had to endure stockyard stench, although the closing of the yards during the 1960s ended their misery. Murray concluded that some owners complacently believed that all they had to do to attract fans was to field a good team: "As far as the promoters are concerned, the fans are just a bunch of fair-weather friends and there isn't any reason why a promoter should go out of his way to make the temporary residency of those who pay admission into their arenas any more pleasant. But this is an attitude which is peculiar to the sports industry alone." He also included a jab at potential future fans, my generation—the baby boomers: "You haven't a prayer of capturing the younger generation. They're used to ruffled nurseries, followed in succession by bunk beds, lightweight bikes with gearshifts, fancy automobiles and, at length, air-conditioned offices and restaurants. As far as they're concerned your places of business are just damp, draughty, cramped and cavernous old architectural monstrosities, peopled with hostile or indifferent personnel, insolent vendors and swell-headed performers who won't even sign autograph books."[73]

Murray's fellow *Sports Illustrated* writers echoed his remarks. In the April 15, 1957 season preview, each team's prognosis had a "Spectator's Guide." Fans going to Yankee Stadium, who typically faced "fantastic traffic snarls," were advised, for instance, to "avoid seats toward rear of lower and second decks, since overhang obscures all balls hit skyward." Some ushers required tips; others were prohibited from accepting tips. Comiskey Park featured inadequate parking and restrooms, both in number and cleanliness, and so, "kindled by an abundance of beer, hot tempers often erupt, so brawls are frequent." Briggs Stadium, County Stadium, Fenway Park, Municipal Stadium (Kansas City), and Wrigley Field, at least, got favorable reviews. Because Griffith Stadium was rarely crowded, its small size was not a detriment; indeed, there were hardly any traffic jams on the way to and from the ballpark and few waiting lines for restrooms or concessions. Sportswriters claimed that Ebbets Field had surly ushers, especially when not tipped, and inadequate parking, restrooms, and concessions. But they also felt that "no baseball park is more fun." Even though beer was not sold in Philadelphia's Connie Mack Stadium, patrons brought in copious quantities, occasionally leading to an ugly atmosphere: "Sedate Philadelphia has the rowdiest clientele in major leagues." At the Giants' stadium you would find a fairly clean park and average restrooms. Parking at the Polo Grounds was inadequate, however, and many seats were too far from the action or faced obstructions. The Harry M. Stevens Inc. "handles refreshments without imagination."[74] The Stevens company also provided scorecards for the Dodgers, Giants, and Yankees. These scorecards, while not the worst in the Major Leagues, were not among the better ones, as they were printed on cheaper paper and contained little information.

By 1961 there were old and new things to complain about. Ushers at Yankee Stadium still insisted on being tipped. Griffith Stadium remained in a poor section of town, but Comiskey Park was benefiting from urban renewal. The Giants' new park, Candlestick Park, became a byword for windiness. Willie McCovey bemoaned the conditions, saying, "The wind keeps blowing peanut shells in my eyes."[75]

Several of the teams that relocated during the 1950s responded to the allure of having a new ballpark. Milwaukee enticed the Boston Braves with a relatively new ballpark, County Stadium, which had opened its doors in 1953. The park also had ample cheap parking; fans could park for twenty-five cents, the lowest parking charge in the Major Leagues. Traffic was handled well, too.[76] But compare conditions around County Stadium with a description of getting to Yankee Stadium in 1957: "The stadium . . . is one of the more difficult places in the world to drive a car to. You can come 50 miles over magnificent modern highways to within 300 yards of the stadium in less than an hour, and then spend 40 minutes creeping the last 300 yards to a jammed-up parking space. Parking cost: $2 and up." The writer advocated parking several bocks away and taking the subway the remainder of the distance.[77] The location of the ballpark was a detriment, as Yankee fans increasingly moved to the suburbs. According to sportswriter Harold Rosenthal, "The Yankee trade more and more is a suburban one, coming from New Jersey, Westchester, Connecticut and Long Island, streaming in over bridges, parkways and through tunnels. Yankee Stadium parking is better than that of the other clubs in New York, but it is still woefully inadequate for one of those big Sunday double-headers or an attractive night game."[78]

While fans were usually willing to pay for improved seating and amenities, they occasionally displayed some anomalous preferences. Walter O'Malley pointed out that building general admission and bleacher seats in a new stadium was likely an unprofitable venture:

You're not going to make any money to speak of on those [general admission and bleacher] seats. . . . [After all of the revenue-sharing, league fees, and taxes] leaves you 32.5 cents which might just barely pay out your cost of construction and maintenance someday. And the public doesn't like those seats either. They're very seldom well filled. The public wants reserved seats even if the view sometimes isn't as good—it's some kind of snobbery. I could sell all the general-admission and bleacher seats I don't sell now if I wanted to cheat and raise the price a dollar and make them "reserved." But it's a tradition that you've got to have them. And you figure you're getting some people into the park, kids and others, who otherwise couldn't afford to come to the ball game, and getting their loyalty, and you know they'll climb the ladder to the reserved seats and boxes just as soon as they get the money.[79]

In general fans flocked to newer, more comfortable stadiums. The Dodgers and Giants eventually occupied new stadiums in Los Angeles and San Francisco. The Dodgers' Chavez Ravine, opening in 1962, featured many amenities. There were sixteen thousand parking spaces, with another nine thousand spaces planned. The lots were arranged to be adjacent to seating locations. The Dodgers touted the twenty-seven lanes of traffic leading into and out of the stadium parking area. The stadium featured "modern, form-fitting" seats measuring twenty inches, two inches wider than the seats at Ebbets Field (if you don't think two extra inches matter, get a yardstick and try sitting on it with a friend). There was a stadium club for wealthy patrons; memberships cost $300 per season and quickly sold out.[80] Dodgers management clearly believed that parking, comfortable seats, sufficient and clean restrooms, and unobstructed views were important, as they touted these attributes of the Chavez Ravine stadium, opening soon, in the team's 1961 scorecard. San Francisco built Candlestick Park for the Giants. The parking lot had a capacity of 8,800 cars, and parking cost seventy-five cents or a dollar per car. The stadium seats had wooden backs and armrests and were twenty-one inches wide, as compared to the standard nineteen-inch wide seats.[81]

The expansion teams also had aspirations for fancy new stadiums. The Mets had to use the Polo Grounds for their first two seasons. The stadium still lacked parking, and the neighborhood was not improving: "The area, late at night, is one of the more unattractive portions of the city—did not help the new team attract fans."[82] The Mets' new stadium had much more parking, as well as mass transit, but traffic jams occurred. Officials hoped to avoid a replay of the traffic snarl-up when it hosted the All-Star Game in July 1964.[83]

Washington DC graced the expansion Senators with a new stadium for 1962 with ample parking. The Senators' lease required rental payment of 7 percent of gross, less expenses, or about ten cents per ticket. Unfortunately for the Senators, the Armory, which managed the new stadium, kept all parking revenue, at one dollar per car, and the team did not reap any concessions revenue. It got to keep the television revenue, however, but the team had to agree not to televise more than fifteen home games a season; otherwise, it would have to compensate the Armory for the reduced attendance at the ballpark. Pete Quesada, president of the club, estimated that the team needed seven hundred thousand in attendance to break even in Griffith Stadium but eight hundred thousand in the new stadium.[84]

The Houston Colt .45s (later renamed the Astros) began playing in Colt Stadium. Meanwhile, Houston was building a domed stadium, the famous Astrodome, which would be ready in 1965. The new stadium had a capacity of forty-five thousand and provided thirty thousand parking spaces. It was also air-conditioned and had cushioned, theater-type seats. The team paid a flat $750,000 rent per year.[85]

The other expansion team, the Los Angeles Angels, did not fare as well. The team spent its first seasons playing in a Minor League ball park, Los Angeles's Wrigley Field, and subsequent seasons playing in Chavez Ravine as a tenant of Walter O'Malley's Dodgers. O'Malley charged a rental fee of 10 percent of admission revenues, and the Angels got none of the concessions or parking revenue. Eventually, the team tired of O'Malley's rental terms and the accompanying lack of concessions and parking revenues. As Bill Veeck predicted during the

1950s, Yankees owner Del Webb hoped to get the stadium construction contract for any American League team in Los Angeles. The city of Anaheim agreed to build a new stadium. The stadium had a capacity of forty-five thousand and twelve thousand parking spaces. The Angels would pay Anaheim 7.5 percent of net ticket receipts. The team would keep two-thirds of the net receipts from concessions and half of the net receipts from parking. In addition, the club got two-thirds of the membership fees and net revenues from the stadium club. The city, however, would get part of any pay-TV or free TV revenue.[86] The city manager admitted that even with a gate of 1.5 million a year, the city would have to make up the shortfall in the annual payment on the construction bond.[87]

St. Louis voters approved a bond for constructing a new stadium in 1962, as did Pittsburgh voters in 1964.[88] Between 1966 and 1971 the Cardinals, Phillies, Pirates, and Reds got new ballparks. Thus, the National League would have a complete turnover of stadiums between 1953 and 1970, except for the Chicago Cubs. The American League would continue with existing stadiums in Boston, Chicago, Cleveland, Detroit, and New York.

While owners occupying new stadiums trumpeted the vast parking spaces and easy access, thanks to the expanding freeway system, owners in older stadiums purchased parking lots and publicized parking areas. In a typical "Veeckian" move the White Sox scorecard of 1960 claimed, "The White Sox now have new and improved parking facilities for more than 2,500 cars within a radius of four blocks of Comiskey Park, giving White Sox fans more parking area than any club in the major leagues."[89] Other teams occasionally made similar claims; indeed, the 1958 Baltimore Orioles scorecard boasted that the team had "the most spacious parking lot in the American League." The original Washington Senators began providing a parking map in 1957, which later indicated that 2,600 "licensed, off-street parking" spaces existed in 1959.[90] When the team relocated to Minnesota, it provided similar information. In the American League only the Athletics never provided any parking information. In the National League the Boston

Braves began including parking information in the team's scorecard in 1946: "Ample parking space for automobiles is provided in the rear of the Grandstand."[91] The Giants began describing parking in 1949. Houston and the New York Mets quickly gave information about getting to their stadiums as well as the ample parking to be found at New County Stadium and Flushing Municipal (Shea) Stadium, respectively.[92] The Brooklyn Dodgers, Cardinals, Phillies, and Pirates did not provide parking information in their scorecards.

New White Sox owner Arthur Allyn put $1 million into expanding parking around Comiskey Park. He hoped to expand the number of parking spaces within a four-block radius of the park by 1,400 spaces, to a total of 8,000. Fortunately for Allyn, the new Dan Ryan Expressway was just two blocks away; in addition, the freeway and new apartment housing cleared away many of the decrepit buildings surrounding the park. As one sportswriter put it in December 1962, "Like so many other major league ball parks, [Comiskey Park] was sinking into a blight area, after once being in the center of a middle-class residential location."[93]

In addition to complaints about the lengthy and difficult journey to the ballpark and being uncomfortable while there, baseball fans indicated in surveys during the 1950s and 1960s that they wanted games to be faster paced. The actual length of the game was not the critical issue, but the numerous slow spots, such as time spent changing pitchers, discouraged fans.[94] National League games typically took five minutes longer to complete than American League games, with one key difference being that the American League forced managers to replace a pitcher upon the manager's second visit to the mound.[95] Sportswriter Stanley Frank pointed out that games lasted almost one hour more during 1961 than they had in 1905: "Baseball . . . is infested with pointless loafing that exhausts the patience of its customers."[96] At first some baseball observers dismissed the findings as gripes by "people who had to work" at the ball games, such as reporters, announcers, and park employees, but by 1962 Major League owners recognized that reducing "dead time" in the game would improve the game's attractiveness to fans. The owners implemented such simple remedies as reducing the number of warm-up pitches between innings, requiring the pitcher to be in the on-deck circle for his time at bat, and using carts to bring relief pitchers from the bullpen to the mound to help speed up the games. By the middle of the 1963 season games were an average of ten minutes shorter than they had been in 1962.[97]

Because many baseball owners believed that "people come to a ball park to enjoy the finer technical points of baseball," they downplayed the desirability of creating fun and promoting exciting players.[98] Veteran sportswriter Frederick Lieb cited the need for captivating characters, especially in the television age: "Big-Time baseball more than ever before has become a big, nationwide spectacle—theater if you like—which has plenty of home runs, bases on balls, some fights, pathos, but is lacking in fun, comedy and the colorful figures that once were such an important part of the game. Our top stars . . . possess little of what . . . sportswriters refer to as 'color.'"[99] Another observer blamed the pension fund in wringing out the "color" in baseball: "The pension fund . . . is the greatest incentive to clean living and dull baseball since the invention of house dicks [detectives]. . . . Players are so obsessed now with piling up equity in the pension fund that they studiously suppress any suggestion of individuality that may brand them hard-to-handle oddballs."[100]

Joe Cronin, former player turned general manager, bemoaned players becoming too commercialized. He thought the players' commercial ventures outside of baseball were turning off fans: "Some of them are driving away fans with their attitudes towards the game. . . . They [the players] ought to stop thinking about side money. They ought to stop coasting and start concentrating on baseball."[101] That was easy for Cronin to say, for he had married the boss's daughter (although that did not stop his father-in-law from trading him to the Boston Red Sox). Tony Kubek was one of the players Cronin found vexing. Kubek wanted players to share salary information because secrecy, he felt, only protected the club owner. He wanted a more rational method of setting salaries, rather than forcing players to be sharp negotiators. "I used to think that if you were honest with the front office, they'd be fair with you," he explained. "I found out that isn't so. They simply want to get you as cheaply as they can."[102] Baseball players might have found common ground with that 1950s phenomenon: the organization man. According to William H. Whyte, author of the seminal work by that title, college graduates in 1949 were looking for a calm, good life without risk.[103]

Yet lamentations about the lack of excitement in baseball recurred. The players of a fan's youth always seem to loom as larger-than-life than current players. Although Bill Veeck might wax nostalgic about the "colorful drunks" of his youth, a 1937 article made similar observations: "Old-timers insist that players aren't what they used to be, and that the game is getting too well-behaved . . . most [contemporary] players are in the game for the money. Knowing their playing careers to be limited, they are looking above all for security."[104] One can only wonder what sort of ruffians played in 1910.

Meanwhile, baseball owners were attempting to improve the clientele at their games. The Dodgers, along with several other teams, posted warnings against such vices as gambling and throwing debris onto the field.[105] Nevertheless, there were recurring outbreaks of unruly behavior. Many of the miscreants were youths, prompting concern about whether members of the baby boom generation would become responsible fans. Interspersed with Roger Maris's homerun pursuit in 1961 was a riotous game at Yankee Stadium. On a hot Sunday, September 10, the Yankees swept a doubleheader from Cleveland. Over fifty-seven thousand fans attended the games. Jimmy Piersall created a brouhaha in the opener. In the second game many fans threw debris onto the field. The tumult lasted for seventeen minutes. Dan Daniel attributed most of the trouble to "thousands of the younger customers [who] were looking for mischief." Some fans threw "sandwiches, hot dogs, paper cups in lieu of bottles, beer cans, various parts of clothing and soaking wet balls of newspapers into [sic] the field, mostly aimed at Umpire Frank Umont, working at third base [who apparently blew a call against the Yankees]."[106]

A similar outbreak of rowdyism occurred in Pittsburgh in 1964. The Pirates held a fifty-cent teenager night, attracting over thirteen thousand teenagers. Unruly teens rushed onto the field three times during the game, and the police arrested ten of them. Longtime ushers said they had never seen things get so bad. "This in a ball park that never has sold beer and where no patron is permitted to bring intoxicants."[107]

Finally, some owners had bizarre ideas about how to present baseball as a family pastime. From 1953 through 1956 the Boston Red Sox, in a reminder of the ongoing cold war tension, gave air raid instructions in their scorecards: "In the event of an air raid or an air raid drill, an alert will be sounded over the loudspeaker and a public announcement will be made to the effect than an air raid is in progress." Fans were to go to nearby concrete buildings for safety. The 1962 Houston scorecard featured a Colt .45 on the cover—certainly an anachronistic image.

In addition to wooing families, baseball continued to attract a large crowd of corporate patrons. Because of the high corporate tax rates of the 1950s, corporate purchases of box seats were greatly subsidized by the tax write-offs. Before the 1963 season, however, new Internal Revenue Service interpretations of business entertainment spooked some Major League owners. The IRS, concerned over "extravagant spending for entertainment," tightened its interpretation of legitimate entertainment expenses. A few Major League owners worried that businesses would reduce their purchases of season tickets. William DeWitt, then owner of the Cincinnati Reds, said, "Our advance ticket sale already has suffered. Companies are confused. They don't know whether deductions for season ticket plans are going to be permitted." An IRS official attempted to allay fears: "Where the expenditure is over $25, the companies will have to give names and addresses of those using the tickets. We don't want them handing the tickets out to friends and relatives and then charging the expense off as deductible entertainment."[108]

The tax collectors recognized that the 10 percent tax on tickets to Major League games, as well as the tax on profits, meant that any interpretation that cut deeply into season ticket sales might lead to smaller tax revenues from Major League Baseball. Major League presidents Joe Cronin and Warren Giles also alerted club owners that the new tax regulation actually made season tickets more attractive, explaining that "purchasers of four-seat season boxes need have but one receipt for over 300 tickets. The cost of all these tickets used for entertainment or gifts will be tax deductible. The low cost per ticket permits the use of many tickets for business gifts with the limit of $25 per person per year. No problem of 'lavish' expenditure is raised by the use of baseball tickets."[109] Ultimately, the new tax law had a minimal effect on season ticket sales for the upcoming 1963 season.[110]

Did Owners Practice Variable Pricing?

Modern teams sometimes use variable pricing to reap greater revenues or to expand their fan base. Teams today might charge more for a game with the visiting New York Yankees than with the Tampa Bay Devil Rays or more for a game on Sunday. Today's sportswriters act as though variable pricing is a new and improved method of extracting more money from fans. Owners have long known, however, that games against the Yankees (and Dodgers) bring in the most fans. Did owners during the 1950s and 1960s charge more for games with the Yankees or Dodgers, or did they charge less for games with the Browns and Athletics?

Scorecards and other published material usually provided "list prices" of tickets for the upcoming season, yet owners could still practice a form of variable pricing by offering discounts primarily for games involving (*featuring* might be too strong a word) weaker teams such as the Athletics, Browns/Orioles, and the Senators. Did teams offer Ladies' Days and discounts for children for every visiting team except the Yankees and Dodgers or Giants?

The Brooklyn Dodgers and Cincinnati Reds came closest to an explicit variable pricing scheme. For Sunday, holiday, and night games at Ebbets Field in Brooklyn, the prices were as follows:

Loge and lower box seats	$3.00
Upper stand box seats	$2.50
Reserved seats	$1.25 and $1.75
General admission seats	$1.25
Bleacher seats	$0.60

For all weekday and Saturday afternoon games the prices were the same, but there was a big difference. The Dodgers classified twenty-five thousand seats as general admission for weekday and Saturday games. For Sunday, holiday, and night games the team classified only twelve thousand seats as general admission. Ebbets Field held just over thirty-two thousand fans, so, while many of the seats may have been $1.25 reserved seats, the reclassification was a de facto variable pricing policy. The Dodgers stated this policy in their 1950–55 scorecards. The team also dropped bleacher prices from sixty cents to fifty cents in 1954; the lower price persisted until the team left Brooklyn.[111] In Los Angeles the team did not have bleacher tickets.

The Cincinnati Reds began a variable pricing policy in 1950. The Reds did not just rely upon reclassifying seats but also listed different prices for lower boxes. Lower boxes cost $2.00 for Sunday, holiday, and night games but $1.75 for all other games. The Reds also did not list reserved seating for Saturday and weekday afternoon games.[112] By 1965 the New York Mets and Boston Red Sox also began employing this reclassification policy: "Proportion of reserved and general admission seats . . . dependent upon size of crowd anticipated."[113]

Owners also offered different prices based on the age of their patrons. The Brooklyn Dodgers did not have children's prices, but the team had a special Knothole club, whereby children got free tickets to games. When Walter O'Malley moved the club to Los Angeles, he eventually instituted a half-price general admission ticket for children.[114] The Milwaukee Braves publicized their Knothole Group in the 1958 scorecard: "Since 1954 when the organization was first created in Milwaukee, over 80,000 youngsters—boys between the ages of 10 and 15 years and girls between the ages of 10 and 16 have attended games." The Braves also occasionally had fifty-cent tickets for children under twelve.[115] Most teams had some form of children's prices. The White Sox even reduced its children's price for box seats in 1957, from $1.85 to $1.60.[116] In addition, sponsoring adults had to "see that the children refrain from running through the stands and especially from throwing paper or other debris onto the field."[117] According to the 1957 scorecard, ten thousand youth came to the Kids' Days in 1956. The White Sox did not ignore the baby boom generation. In 1964 the team held two "Teenage Nights" with reduced ticket prices for reserved grandstand seats.

Women and children were not the only beneficiaries of discounted prices. The Los Angeles Angels and Detroit Tigers seized upon another demographic trend: the growing number of "senior citizens." The Angels combined Ladies' and Senior Citizens' nights every Monday during the 1962–64 seasons. The Tigers had six Retirees' Days each season between 1962 and 1964, but none of the discount days coincided with a matchup against the New York Yankees. Even the Yankees took notice of the burgeoning senior citizen population by having a Senior Citizens' Day in 1965.[118]

That younger men were baseball's most reliable customers can be deduced by the paucity of discounts offered to them. The Boston Braves were the only team in 1946 to offer military personnel discounted tickets; in this case the Braves admitted servicemen for free.[119] The Philadelphia Phillies held a Men's Night in 1949, while Cleveland held five such nights during 1952, when the Athletics, Senators, and Tigers were in town for Tuesday or Friday games.[120] Otherwise, men, unless they were senior citizens, rarely got discounted days or nights.

Did Major League teams use Ladies' Days as a form of variable pricing? Did American League teams schedule Ladies' Days primarily on weekday afternoons against the worst teams, such as the Athletics, Browns/Orioles, and Senators? There is evidence among the various team scorecards that some American League teams used Ladies' Days as a modest form of variable pricing. Except for the Detroit Tigers and the expansion Senators, teams almost always scheduled the Yankees for at least one Ladies' Day game per season recorded. Although teams rarely scheduled Ladies' Days on Sundays, the prevalence of Saturday games targeted to women (against such teams as the Athletics, Indians, Orioles, and White Sox) was surprising. After scheduling a few Ladies' Days on Thursdays, the Yankees typically held its Ladies' Days on Saturdays. For most of the years the Yankees would have one Ladies' Day per opponent each season.

In the National League most teams placed their Ladies' Days on weekdays. The Dodgers switched to Saturdays in 1957. The Braves, Cubs, Giants, and Pirates scheduled most of their Ladies' Days on weekdays, although the Giants switched to Saturdays in 1954. The Phillies did not publish much information on Ladies' Days in their scorecards; in 1949 the team had two Saturday games among their six Ladies' Days. The Mets mimicked their cross-town peers by having Saturdays as their Ladies' Day.

National League teams did not discriminate against opponents in scheduling Ladies' Days. Most scheduled the Braves, Dodgers, and Giants as frequently as other opponents. A few teams, such as the Braves and Colt .45s, placed their Ladies' Days early in the season. In the case of the 1959 Braves such a strategy made sense because the Braves were defending champions likely to be involved in a September pennant race.

Overall, then, Ladies' Day did not appear to be a mechanism for variable pricing in the modern sense, except in the sense that such promotions were rarely scheduled on Sundays. Teams did not usually forgo scheduling the promotion when the top rivals came to town. The Dodgers' and Reds' seating policies and the Indians' brief "Men's Night" promotion came closest to being a variable pricing schemes. Unfortunately, there is little available evidence that teams explicitly studied their attendance figures to determine whether their policies were profitable.

Baseball and Blacks

Although Branch Rickey hoped to attract black patrons to baseball in 1945 with his introduction of Jackie Robinson onto the Brooklyn

Dodgers, his fellow owners were less optimistic and enthusiastic about courting black fans. Many owners thought that blacks were unlikely to be strong or desirable patrons of Major League Baseball games; they also did not put much thought into helping their black players. Owners wondered whether blacks would be willing and able to pay full admission to games. Although the Negro Leagues had drawn fairly well on occasion, most black teams charged less than did the white clubs. Because blacks earned less than whites, on average, part of their reticence might have reflected a lack of purchasing power. In addition, until Robinson's debut one might wonder why blacks would patronize a sport that implicitly prohibited their participation on the field.

Some baseball stadiums were located in neighborhoods undergoing a racial transformation. Table 4.4 shows some of the relevant demographic information (see appendix). According to the 1950 census, black median income for 1949 ranged from 58 to 79 percent of that of white median income across the Standard Metropolitan Statistical Areas containing Major League teams. Blacks in Cincinnati and St. Louis had the lowest median incomes relative to whites, while blacks living in Detroit had the highest relative median incomes. Looking at county and city information, Major League stadiums were in counties in which blacks constituted between 4.5 and 35 percent of the residents. The Senators' stadium was in a part of the city that had the greatest number of blacks, while the Braves, Dodgers, Pirates, Red Sox, and Yankees were in counties with less than 8 percent black population. The Giants were in a more heavily black area (19.6 percent). Six teams relocated between 1953 and 1961, and only the St. Louis/Baltimore transfer was to an area with a higher proportion of blacks. The Washington Senators moved from a city with the highest proportion of blacks to one with the lowest proportion.[121]

Would black and white patrons intermingle peacefully? Some owners claimed that their fans might take umbrage at black players. One club owner told Effa Manley, owner of the Newark Eagles of the Negro League, "Many of our fans are white women. It might cause unpleasantness if these women became 'attached' to a Negro home run hitter." Other observers believed that "if Jackie Robinson hits homers and plays a whale of a game for Montreal, the fans will soon lose sight of his color."[122]

When the Braves considered relocating to Atlanta, writer Huston Horn reported that unspecified people were asking south Georgia "rednecks" if "they would drive up the interstate superhighways to attend games in Atlanta, and if they would mind sitting next to Negroes in the city's unsegregated stadium. The answers, by and large, were 'Yes' and 'Not much.'"[123] Such data was tainted, of course, as reasonably savvy respondents knew which answers were the "correct" ones.

Although black players appeared on every Major League roster by 1961, they faced unacceptable conditions. In 1953 a team in Hot Springs, Arkansas, signed two blacks, brothers Jim and Leander Tugerson, but the Cotton States League threatened to revoke the town's franchise in response. Hot Springs complied and sent the two brothers to Knoxville. A judge dismissed Jim Tugerson's eventual civil rights suit against the league.[124] During the 1961 spring training season various groups pressured Major League Baseball teams, including the New York Yankees, to end segregated housing for their black players. Elston Howard, for instance, stayed at a local black physician's home, instead of at the hotel with the other players. In 1961 Dan Topping of the Yankees finally served notice that the Yankees would not continue to train at St. Petersburg, Florida, "unless all our players, colored and white, can be housed under the same roof."[125]

Reporter Robert Boyle examined "the private world of the Negro ballplayer" for *Sports Illustrated* in 1960. He noted friction between American blacks and Latin blacks. Latin blacks were not used to the discrimination that American blacks faced on a daily basis. The racial situation in some of the Minor League towns, being less scrutinized by the national press, was often less pleasant. Black players got smaller bonuses when they originally signed with a Major League team, and they felt a constant pressure to be "better" than white players. There was also controversy about whether black players got as many endorsement opportunities as white players. Black players lamented the lack of advertising endorsements: "Negro players shave, too." Frank Scott, business representative of the Major League players, claimed that black players were not discriminated against. "Not unrelated to the subject, perhaps, is . . . that of the 17,000,000 Negroes in the United States, only one-half of one percent earn over $5,000 annually, indicating a somewhat restricted buying power." Scott strove to make sure blacks got endorsement opportunities. Conversely, black players became "symbols of achievement" and "with their high incomes and conspicuous consumption they are an important part of the bourgeoisie [black] elite." Many contributed generously to the National Association for the Advancement of Colored People. Even so, many felt constrained in their ability to act as individuals in a way that white players did not.[126]

Almost as an afterthought, the Negro League, producer of many great black players, limped to its demise. Before the 1955 season the Indianapolis Clowns and Columbus Clippers folded, leaving four teams.[127] The Kansas City Monarchs sold twelve players, eight to the Majors before the 1956 season. The Monarchs folded shortly thereafter, thus ending an era.[128]

Although most baseball club owners enjoyed booming attendance in the immediate aftermath of World War II, consumers quickly changed their purchasing patterns. Major League Baseball's attendance woes of the early 1950s were not reflective of a significant decline in the population's income, as incomes generally rose during the decades after the war. Owners initially attempted to maintain the attendance boom by offering night baseball and Ladies' Days. They had developed such promotions before the war, although some teams, such as the Red Sox, Tigers, and Yankees were slow to see the light. The Chicago Cubs, of course, continued to play only during the day at Wrigley Field. Owners may have exhausted the gains from both tactics, however, as the Browns' modest attendance increase from night ball demonstrated.

Following the war owners faced significant demographic changes and intensified competition for recreational spending. With their increased incomes and a surfeit of durable consumer goods reaching the markets, American consumers moved to the suburbs and equipped their homes with the latest amenities, such as television and air-conditioning. Of course, moving to the suburbs also spurred consumers to purchase automobiles, giving them a wider range of leisure activities. The postwar marriage and later baby booms likely affected men's ability to attend ballgames, although the data is insufficient to assert this definitively. Professional football probably was not responsible for baseball's doldrums during most of the 1950s, as pro football's overall attendance was about the same between 1949 and 1960. Football's popularity was perhaps more threatening during the 1960s.

Aside from the master innovator Bill Veeck, most owners were somewhat cautious in their responses to dwindling crowds, often relying more upon such proven audience-building techniques as night games and Ladies' Days or variations upon these promotions (such as the intriguing "Lutheran Nights"). Although Veeck proved adept at attracting large crowds in Cleveland and Chicago, his fellow owners disliked him and forced him out during the early 1950s, just when they most needed clever promotional ideas. At least some of the owners recognized the need to increase parking and to maintain the charms of their stadiums. Other owners opted for acquiring new stadiums, especially if it were possible to do at the public's expense. In terms of boosting attendance, if only temporarily, a new stadium has proven consistently successful. Many economists have documented this effect.[129]

Because the National League recovered its attendance more rapidly than did the American League, it was clear that attendance did not have to continue to stagnate. The American League saw evidence that sending fresh faces to the World Series boosted regular season attendance, as in 1954 and 1959. Nevertheless, the owners still had to grapple with the perplexing issues of how to deal with television and competitive imbalance among teams.

Television and Baseball

The New Technology, Friend or Foe?

Television was the newest, and possibly "baddest," entertainment bully on the block during the postwar era. The medium perplexed baseball owners. Detroit Tigers owner John Fetzer had perhaps the most astute observation about television and baseball: "Baseball has been engaged in a constantly changing and developing relationship with the television industry."[1] Did television reduce attendance at Major League Baseball games? In a second plot line did television adversely affect Minor League Baseball?

Television and Major League Baseball

Television Comes to the Majors

During the boom season of 1946 a new specter hung over Major League Baseball. The New York Yankees and Brooklyn Dodgers televised games during the season, and while the telecasts did not turn profits, owners were sensing a new profit-making venture. Indeed, the owners attempted to insert a clause into the standard player contract that would exclude players from television profits.[2] The issue would not die, and as late as 1958, players were demanding 25 percent of each club's radio and television revenue, much to the owners' disgust. Chicago Cubs owner P. K. Wrigley argued, "That's not even profit-sharing. They want a share of the revenue whether there's any profit or not. . . . Radio and TV money keeps them [impecunious owners] alive. And some are even losing money with that additional revenue. Still the players want part of it."[3]

Local broadcasts of Major League games that reached a fifty-mile radius around the stadiums became common in 1947 and 1948, particularly around New York City. Heading into the 1947 season, every Major League team except the Philadelphia teams and the Boston Braves televised home games. Indeed, the teams televising home games jumped in completely, showing their entire home schedule, with the exception of the Cincinnati Reds. The Reds did not show Sunday home games and six of their night games. There was no information about the Boston Red Sox's television plans for 1947.[4] These local broadcasts obviously did not greatly expand the Major Leagues' reach into the southern and western parts of the country. The Columbia Broadcasting System (CBS) and DuMont networks televised the 1949 World Series, but some theaters in Boston, Chicago, Milwaukee, and New York also showed telecasts of the games. The theaters did not always sell out, but the receipts were double or triple the usual amounts. For theater patrons in Scranton, Pennsylvania, the World Series was the town's first taste of television.[5] Today's television viewer would likely be disappointed at the quality of the telecast, as the cameras were slow in picking up shifting activity on the diamond and fought shadows. There was no instant replay, and, of course, the game was in black and white. Most television screens were tiny, so the theater rebroadcasts on 12 x 15 foot or 18 x 20 foot screens held an advantage. CBS, however, featured a split screen, showing batter and pitcher. DuMont employed a bullpen camera with telescopic lens that showed the ball from the pitcher's perspective instead of the usual perspective from behind home plate.

In one of his last acts as commissioner of baseball, Albert "Happy" Chandler negotiated a national television contract. While he boasted about the terms, the reality was that television needed baseball games to fill out its schedule. Some television officials acknowledged as much.

As Bill Veeck pointed out, for the television networks, "baseball happens to be a bargain": "It supplies a daily 3-hour show, and provides its own location, its own actors, and its own pre-packaged audience. Television has to provide nothing except the cameras and cameramen."[6] In addition, baseball came with its own advertising, thanks to daily newspaper coverage. In any case Chandler sold rights to the 1950 World Series for $800,000. He later negotiated a six-year contract for $6 million. The wild card in the deal was the federal government's freeze on television stations. At the time Chandler made the deal, the number of stations was fixed. If the freeze ended sooner than anticipated, his six-year deal looked inept.[7] Cardinals owner Fred Saigh thought Chandler's deal was inadequate: "Television rights worth $1,000,000 today may be worth several million two or three years from now."[8] Other owners thought Chandler had made a good deal.

A decade after the 1946 television experiments, the medium was firmly ensconced at the Major League level. Owners were still trying to assess TV's effects upon gate receipts. By 1956 thirteen of the sixteen Major League teams had local television deals (Kansas City, Milwaukee, and Pittsburgh being the holdouts). The New York teams and Chicago Cubs televised all of their home games, and several teams were increasing telecasts of their road games. Television, clearly, was a growing force for change. Radio and television broadcasting revenues expanded much more rapidly than did gate receipts over this period (see table 3.7 in the appendix).

Baseball was wary of network telecasts. A national *Game of the Week* debuted on Memorial Day 1953 on seventeen stations coast to coast, sponsored by the Falstaff Brewing Corporation and American Safety Razor Corporation. The A's, Indians, and White Sox hosted the games, and each home team received $14,000 per game. Because the games would be broadcast on the West Coast, Pacific Coast League teams protested the incursion, but the overall effects of the telecasts on their attendance was hard to gauge.[9] Later the National Broadcasting Company (NBC) and CBS would take over the *Game of the Week*. Baseball worried about network influence on scheduling and even playing rules. Of course, the networks were interested in having games with top teams. They were also eager to get Major League Baseball to institute interleague games.[10]

Major League commissioner Ford Frick voiced another fear to Roone Arledge, vice president in charge of sports for American Broadcasting Company (ABC) television: "One of the jobs that baseball has to do is keep television from making the show too good. The trouble is that television wants the viewer to see the game better than the fan in the ball park. The view a fan gets at home should not be any better than that of the fan in the worst seat in the ball park."[11] Arledge, himself, viewed baseball as not particularly well suited for television, but the televised game had an advantage over the viewing the game live: "People don't particularly enjoy going to the ball parks, which are often located in out-of-the-way places, or run-down neighborhoods. It's not necessarily a pleasing experience, like driving up to the Yale Bowl."[12]

Who sponsored baseball telecasts? Beer companies were numerically the strongest supporters of baseball telecasts, although oil companies and tobacco companies were also prominent sponsors.[13] By 1961 television and radio broadcasts constituted a greater share of baseball owners' total revenue. Major League Baseball received twice as much revenue from radio and television as they paid for all Major League salaries: $17 million in broadcasting/telecasting revenue versus $8 million in payroll. Air rights totaled $3.8 million in 1952, or 17 percent of income. By 1962 air rights amounted to $20 million, or 40 to 45 percent of income.[14]

Ford Frick announced a renewal of a Gillette and NBC pact in early 1960. The pact was for five years (1962–66), although it retroactively gave the Major Leagues an additional $500,000 for the 1959–61 seasons. Gillette and NBC would pay the Major Leagues $4 million per season. The national television contract financed the players' pension fund, as 60 percent of the money was earmarked for the pension. The players were disappointed, as they thought the deal would bring in $5 million per year.[15]

The Major Leagues also had a contract with ABC to telecast twenty-five Saturday afternoon games, part of a $17 million package with Gillette that included boxing and college football. It is unclear how much money went to baseball. ABC's telecasts did not directly compete with those of NBC and CBS.[16]

Over thirty-two million households watched all or part of at least three World Series games in 1959. The Saturday afternoon national telecasts in New York, Chicago, and Detroit captured 35, 65, and 81 percent, respectively, of the television audience for that time period. *Television Age* claimed, "These soaring home-audience figures would seem to lend weight to the argument of those who contend that video is strictly the villain of the piece when it comes to attendance at the ball parks. But a close appraisal of attendance totals for both Major Leagues over the past four years would seem to signify that in the long haul television has, if anything, helped rather than hurt the gate. The combined turnstile totals for both circuits have shown increases for each year since 1956."[17]

Although these national contracts were lucrative, professional football was doing just as well, if not better, from its contracts. The National Football League (NFL) got $28.2 million over two seasons from CBS The NFL could boast of strong audience ratings: an average of fifteen million per regular season game and thirty-three million for the NFL championship game. The upstart American Football League signed a $36 million, five-year contract with NBC that would begin in 1965. NBC was so determined that the league be a success that the network advanced money to help the AFL sign top collegiate players.[18] Major League Baseball still held the advantage in total television revenue—national and local—with $20 million for 1963.[19]

While baseball and football competed for television revenue, the sports occasionally had common cause. Ford Frick supported New York representative Emanuel Celler's television bill allowing the NFL and AFL to negotiate package deals with networks, as baseball hoped that the antitrust exemption granted to football would also strengthen baseball's.[20]

Baseball envied football's national television contracts. Detroit owner

John Fetzer designed a Monday night *Game of the Week* that would revolutionize baseball programming. The most radical parts of his proposal included the Major Leagues combining to negotiate a single contract with a network, with all teams sharing revenues equally. In many ways Fetzer's plan presaged the NFL's television contract. His plan had the attraction of not upsetting existing television contracts. He intended to set up the schedule so that only two games would be played on Monday nights throughout the season (the regularly scheduled game and a backup "rain game"). Baseball would then offer a package of a three-hour program featuring the game and other promotional items. He believed that such a program could generate an additional $6.5 million in revenue for baseball, or over $300,000 per club.

Fetzer's plan was intended to be a harbinger of including all national games, including the CBS and NBC *Game of the Week*, into one large contract.[21] Even Yankees co-owner Dan Topping and Dodgers owner Walter O'Malley gave some support to the concept of the commissioner's office negotiating national television pacts, with greater, if not equal, revenue sharing.[22] As sportswriter Shirley Povich observed, the Yankees were hesitant to join a package deal: "The Yankees commanded rights fees that ran to $1,500,000 a year because they owned the best show in the majors, and it would not profit them to share the loot in a common pool."[23] Initially, Fetzer's plan hit a snag when ABC announced that it would not bid for the package. NBC was already not considered a bidder because its 1964 schedule was crowded with political conventions and summer Olympics, although its vice president of sports, Carl Lindemann Jr., refused to commit to abstaining. Sports Network Inc. was interested in bidding: "We already send the road games back to the home cities of practically all major league games now."[24] Fetzer and Major League Baseball completed the deal with ABC for $12.2 million over two years, representing eighteen clubs (sans Yankees and Phillies because of their carryover pact for 1965). All clubs would get $300,000 in 1965 and $325,000 in 1966. The pact would eventually lead to a reduced schedule for the CBS and NBC *Game of the Week*. One attractive feature of the pact was that there were almost no blackouts of the games, only in the two participants' cities, which was a factor that encouraged advertisers' willingness to pay.[25]

While Fetzer and Frick were negotiating collective agreements with the networks, Walter O'Malley searched for more lucrative television deals. He wanted to market his Dodgers on television aggressively in ways that were more beneficial to himself. He dreamed of pay television, for which fans would pay fifty cents to watch a game: "I've no idea what a fair price for a subscriber would be, but I'm hoping it wouldn't be more than the lowest-priced seat in the ball park. I like to think of our bleachers as 50-cent seats, the cheapest in town, although the city tax adds to it."[26] Once in Los Angeles, he hoped to televise Dodger games for a fee that was approximately the same as the cheapest seat in the new stadium (roughly $1.50). His dreams awaited approval from the Federal Communications Commission (FCC). Still some observers thought he might get as much as $50,000 a game, even without sponsors. The FCC was not in a hurry to make a decision.[27]

Because watching a number of games on television with a few family members would be much cheaper than attending the games in person, even after factoring in the installation and monthly subscription costs, O'Malley hoped for a large television audience.[28] Using existing technology, including telephone lines and computers, pay television was feasible by the mid-to late 1950s. One possible concern was that subscribers might invite many friends and family to watch the game, all for the same $1.50 charge. O'Malley was not too concerned about this possibility. O'Malley encouraged fellow owner Horace Stoneham of the Giants to develop a similar pay television contract. The two men had previously only telecast road games from each other's stadiums in order to whet California's appetite for televised baseball.[29]

Proponents of pay television faced implacable foes in Congress. Representative Emanuel Celler, chairman of the House Subcommittee on Study of Monopoly Power, testified in 1958: "I defy anyone to tell me that these covetous owners would not, if they could, force all of us to pay a dollar or more to see a game by way of a closed circuit. You should have listened to the testimony of Mr. Walter O'Malley before our committee. He was brash enough to ask why he shouldn't have a closed circuit as far as the Dodgers were concerned. Why shouldn't he blanket out anybody that wants to see the game for nothing."[30] Celler apparently believed in an American's God-given right to free telecasts of Major League Baseball. Throughout the same hearing senators discussed the dire possibility of mixing pay television and baseball.[31] To allay fan fears that they might lose free access to such premier events as the World Series and the All-Star Game, O'Malley repeatedly said that he hoped such games would never appear on pay television.[32]

Major League Baseball was an obvious candidate for pay TV. Subscription Television Inc. (STV), a California company headed by former NBC executive Sylvester "Pat" Weaver, surveyed potential customers in 1964. The company discovered that sports were the most popular programming choice, receiving much greater support than theater and opera. Baseball received the highest support, five out of six of those surveyed indicating an interest in paying for games on television. Professional football had the support of only two out of three of those surveyed, which was roughly double the support given to professional basketball. Of those who favored baseball on the pay television channel, fewer than one in ten said they "frequently" attended ballgames in person, with about a quarter stating that they "occasionally" attended games. Over half of those surveyed said they "never" attended ballgames in person. If the survey was accurate, O'Malley's belief that pay television would not adversely affect his gate receipts looked astute. Of course, interpreting any survey was difficult. Until the customers had to pay $1.50 per game, the results were uncertain.[33]

O'Malley negotiated a better contract with STV than Stoneham did. He arranged to get $200,000 cash up front and one-third of the initial pay TV receipts; the percentage then declined to 31 percent. Stoneham would get 20 percent of the receipts, but his percentage eventually rose to one-third. Both teams agreed to give visiting clubs one-quarter of their pay TV income. Notice that the problem of gauging how many people listened or watched was resolved, making revenue sharing easier. Players, too, sensed an opportunity for enrichment. Tony Kubek, player representative, said the players wanted "a fair share of any extra money which may result from pay-TV. . . . We are unified on this thing, though not formally. I think we are closer now to a ball players' union. . . . We ought to get a piece of the extra money from pay-TV, since we are the performers who make the show go."[34]

STV, in an attempt to create a larger audience, reduced its installation fee from $10 to $5 and waived the dollar-per-month service charge for the first twelve months for the first sixty-five thousand subscribers. Subscribers could watch the first twelve minutes of the game for free before incurring a charge. The company hoped to have 120,000 subscribers within a year and 700,000 after five years.[35]

The bold experiment began during the 1964 season on July 17 in Los Angeles. Before the inaugural game STV had wired only a few thousand homes. A review of the technology indicated that "all fans were enthusiastic with the reception and most observers actually raved about the color, which was noticeably more accurate than the usual color."[36] Unfortunately for STV, a phone workers' strike helped delay installation. The number of subscribers lagged badly and never approached the break-even point, and the company was well on its way to going bankrupt. The company's woes were exacerbated by a California citizens' petition seeking to stop pay TV (Proposition 15), similar to the one that almost stymied O'Malley's acquisition of Chavez Ravine. O'Malley, ardent foe of "baseball socialism," ironically ran afoul of an advertising campaign that (illogically) implied that pay television was a "drift toward socialism." Sportswriter Melvin Durslag lampooned the campaign against pay TV: "Preserve free enterprise—vote Yes on [Proposition] 15."[37] Theater owners, who pioneered pay television by beaming televised championship fights into their theaters and charging $10 to $20 per seat, were the obvious supporters of Proposition 15, but an odd coalition supported the measure, including the California Federation of Women's Clubs—"They wanted to protect the family pocketbooks"—as well as veterans' committees, the state's central labor councils, and hotel and apartment house associations. The proposition passed by a two-to-one margin, and STV suspended operations right after the election.[38]

Television's Effect on Major League Baseball Attendance

Did television affect Major League attendance? Major League owners struggled to ascertain the medium's effects. Night baseball pioneer Larry MacPhail tried to keep the 1947 World Series from being telecast because he feared that televising the games would hurt the gate.[39] Clark Griffith and Bill Veeck thought that televising home games reduced attendance.[40] Veeck argued, "By televising your home games, you're selling your product on one corner and giving it away on another one. I am convinced that television keeps the fans out of the ball park." He continued, "If I had my way, there wouldn't be any home [game] televising. Television in general will make friends for baseball. However, you can stimulate their interest by televising only road games. Ban home telecasts and a lot more people will flock to the ball park."[41] Veeck's fellow owner Fred Saigh, of the Cardinals, pressed for a share of television revenue when playing on the road, especially in New York City, as he, too, believed that television depressed the gate.[42]

While some people pointed out the obvious parallels between radio and television, baseball executive Frank Lane claimed there was a key difference: "Radio aroused the curiosity of people; television satisfies it. Beware!"[43] New Cleveland Indians owner Ellis Ryan opted to televise all home games for a second year in 1951, stating that a one-year test was not definitive: "We feel the pleasure brought into thousands of homes more than balanced any loss of revenue. We're more inclined to attribute the attendance decrease to the team's late August slump and unbelievably poor weather. However, we will keep an eye on the future relation between television and the turnstile."[44] St. Louis Cardinals president Bob Hannegan was more optimistic while conceding the difficulty of gauging television's effect upon gate revenues: "Reduction of the box office count in the face of revenues from television would not bother me. . . . I believe that the ultimate result will be all for the good of the game. Television will increase baseball's publicity beyond comprehension. It will bring into our parks fans who never before went through a turnstile."[45] In 1965 John Fetzer of the Detroit Tigers suggested that "in the more populous markets, television rights commanded prices without adverse effect at the box office, while in smaller major league communities, the rights were not only worth less but their exploitation had a pronounced effect at the turnstiles."[46] Baltimore general manager Paul Richards felt that television was only partly to blame for the American League's steep decline in attendance during the 1950s: "I feel it forms a lesser part of the reason than the recurring absence of a sharp pennant race."[47]

Many of the owners proceeded with caution. They hesitated in signing long-term contracts, fearing that they might sell their rights on the cheap. The television people, of course, hoped to lock in baseball for several years. In addition, the federally imposed freeze on new television stations and the rapidly improving technology made forecasting the future difficult. With eerie parallels to the personal computer revolution of thirty years later, the initial television sets were expensive and unreliable. Would the manufacturers be able to reduce costs and improve quality sufficiently for television to become a mass medium?

What evidence did owners have in assessing the medium's effect on attendance? New York Yankees general manager George Weiss decided to experiment in 1952. He decided to forgo televising a Yankees/Red Sox game at Yankee Stadium. The Monday night game attracted over fifty-one thousand fans, which was both the largest single night game crowd of the year at the stadium and the first night game not televised since 1947. Weiss declined to attribute much significance to the results, however, arguing, "It was not a fair test. Those who had purchased tickets for the rained out game (the previous Friday) used them for this Monday game."[48] By 1955 his attitude had changed, and he asked the Dodgers and Giants to enact a ban on televised night games, although even he did not stop televising night games.[49] Sportswriter Dan Daniel cited the reduction of twenty thousand fans per game in night game attendance at Yankee Stadium between 1947 and 1951, but he exaggerated the extent of the decline. In both 1947 and 1951 the team had fourteen night games at Yankee Stadium. In 1947 the night games had 729,000 in attendance; in 1951 some 563,000 fans showed up. Nevertheless, the rate of decrease in night game attendance was greater than that for all games at Yankee Stadium.[50]

In a poll of Cleveland baseball fans attending games at Municipal Stadium, about a third said telecasts "created a desire to go to the Stadium to see more games." About 60 percent said telecasts had no effect, and less than 6 percent thought telecasts reduced their desire to go to the stadium. Cleveland eventually reduced its slate of televised home games.[51] During the 1949 season attendance at Major League games showed signs of stagnating. Although one reporter believed owners realized that the "turnstile honeymoon" was over and that dollars were not flowing as freely, "some of them are becoming increasingly concerned over the possible adverse effects of television on attendance." The reporter cited the attendance gains made by the Cardinals and Pirates. The Cardinals reduced their number of telecasts of home games during 1949, while the Pirates did not televise any home games. Some of the owners wondered whether they should implement a ban on televising games, similar to the one imposed by the Philadelphia Eagles of the National Football League.[52] Meanwhile, the last-place Detroit Tigers did not televise night, Sunday, and holiday home games, and the team drew well on those dates.[53]

Researcher Jerry N. Jordan discovered that surveys of fans in attendance at Major League Baseball games during the late 1940s showed a higher rate of television ownership among attendees, and that people who owned televisions for two years or more had a higher frequency of attendance than other people. Jordan's research implied that television was a relatively minor factor in determining attendance, trailing team performance, personal income, and team management.[54]

Several owners, particularly the ones in New York, resisted calls to switch telecasts from home games to road games. Apparently, the recalcitrant owners feared the higher costs of telecasting road games, which could amount to $4,000 per game between New York and St. Louis or Milwaukee, although New York to Philadelphia transmissions cost roughly half this amount.[55]

Is there a way to establish statistically television's effects on attendance at Major League Baseball games? The Census Bureau collected statistics on home ownership of television in 1950. The *Historical Statistics of the United States*, published by the Census Bureau under the auspices of the U.S. Department of Commerce, has a time series of "households with television sets" dating back to 1946. The rise of television ownership along with attendance in the Major Leagues is shown in table 5.1 (see appendix). There is no obvious trend, and the decrease in baseball attendance predates the widespread diffusion of televisions, but this is only an impressionistic approach. A congressional investigation of the "status of UHF and multiple ownership of television stations" collected data on television saturation in 1953. By comparing the changes in attendance and win-loss records, we can use statistical analysis to demonstrate television's effects, if any.

In 1950 television ownership rates varied from 13 percent in Pittsburgh to 36 percent in Philadelphia. About a third of homes in New York City had televisions compared to only one-sixth of St. Louis homes. By 1953 the differences in home ownership rates had narrowed considerably. St. Louis had the lowest ownership rate at four-fifths, while nine-tenths of homes in Philadelphia owned sets. Cincinnati and Boston had ownership rates just below nine-tenths. New York City had a modest five-sixths proportion.

Attendance fell by over one-eighth between 1947 and 1950; the attendance in 1953 was over one-fourth below the 1947 level. Changes in a team's win-loss percentage affected the team's attendance. Teams that won pennants could hope for an increase in attendance, but most other teams suffered decreases. Statistical analysis using television ownership rates and changes in win-loss records shows that television did not appear to explain much of the drop in attendance between 1947 and 1950. For the longer period, 1947–53, similar results occurred. The television variable possibly, but not definitively, exerted a negative effect upon Major League attendance.[56] At most, therefore, television exerted an uncertain effect upon Major League attendance.

Indeed, the question of whether televising games made a difference might have missed the real point. Purchasing a television set was an "investment" because the set was a durable good that would provide entertainment for years. The set consumed a large fraction of the recreation budget of many families. According to the Bureau of the Census, the median family income for Brooklyn was about $3,150 in 1950 (see table 4.4 in the appendix). A Brooklyn family perusing the *New York Times* on July 5, 1950, would find Loeser's department store advertising "New! Giant 19" DuMont TV consoles, priced a new low [$495]." You would also get an FM radio in the console, presumably along with the horizontal control knob and the channel dial, but no remote. (Younger readers may need to consult grandparents about the function of the horizontal control knob.) At least the store was honest in conveying the cost of the product, acknowledging that it could take customers "many months to pay for this reliable new DuMont!" By comparison today's consumers can get nineteen-inch color televisions for less than $100, while the median family income is ten times greater than it was in 1950. Thus, whether or not games were televised, people in the 1950s simply had fewer "entertainment dollars" to spend on other forms of amusement, and television may have simply been a manifestation of a desire for "private leisure."

As noted, Major League teams quickly assigned telecast rights to all of their home games (see table 5.2 in the appendix). According to the April 20, 1949, *Sporting News*, five American League and six National League teams planned to telecast all of their home games. Again, in 1953, almost all of the Major League teams broadcast some home games on television. Four teams broadcast all home games, including all of the New York teams and Chicago Cubs. The Pittsburgh Pirates did not telecast any games, while the Milwaukee Braves were uncertain at the beginning of the season. The Braves did not end up telecasting any home games during 1953.[57]

By the late 1950s, however, several teams had mixed feelings about televising home games, and more of them televised road games. In fact, Major League clubs scheduled telecasts of 550 home games and 331 road games for 1957.[58] Indeed, Bill Veeck's argument seemed to have won some adherents, especially in the National League. In both 1958 and 1959 six teams, including five National League teams, chose not to televise any home games. Yet the Chicago Cubs and New York teams were not shy about television, showing all of their home games during the surveyed years; the White Sox showed the majority of their home games during those seasons. No other team came close to showing its entire home slate. Conversely, every team beamed some road games back home in 1965, although the Dodgers and Giants only showed games played between themselves back to Los Angeles or San Francisco.[59]

Did the increased broadcasting rights offset the declining gate revenue? The American League, as a whole, had greater real revenues from gate revenues, both home and away, and broadcasting revenue in 1956 than in 1946. Until their relocation to Baltimore and Kansas City, however, the St. Louis and Philadelphia clubs lagged badly in gate and broadcasting revenues in 1953. The Senators did not relocate until after 1960, and the club's gate and broadcasting revenue fell by a third between 1946 and 1956. In fact, Washington's revenue was lower for every year from 1950 through 1956 than in 1946, except possibly 1951 (for which there was no available data). The three successful teams during the mid-1950s—Chicago, Cleveland, and New York—all had greater combined gate and broadcasting revenues in 1956 than in 1946, but New York's increase was relatively small, less than 5 percent between 1946 and 1956. Although New York's revenues in 1950 and 1954–55 were comparable to that in 1946, there was a sharp diminution in such revenue in 1952–53. Aside from Chicago's dismal 1950 season, both the Indians and White Sox consistently earned more revenue than they did in 1946. The "middle-class" Red Sox and Tigers both earned consistently less in the years after 1946.[60]

Real total gate revenue fell by almost $5 million between 1946 and 1953. Broadcasting revenue, not all of which was from television, rose by $2.4 million between the years, or roughly half of the decrease in gate revenue. The end of the Yankees' five-year reign thus coincided with the increase in television revenues being unable to replace all of the lost gate revenue. The gate revenue rebounded strongly in 1954 and 1955, peaking at $15.46 million in 1955 before falling to $14.90 million in 1956. Conversely, while broadcasting revenues continued to grow between 1953 and 1956, the increase in the league's total revenue was due to the sharp rise in gate revenue for those years. Clearly, the league was still heavily dependent upon good gate revenues in 1956, while broadcasting revenue provided a steadily increasing secondary source of income at best. American League owners had reason to be skeptical of television's ability to offset declining gate revenues.[61]

Television and Minor League Baseball

Baseball historians blame the proliferation of television for the "demise" of Minor League Baseball during the 1950s. Charles Alexander claimed, "Televised major-league baseball directly undercut support for minor-league teams within range of the telecasts."[62] He believed that if the Major Leagues had continued the ban on broadcasts outside a fifty-mile radius, designed to keep broadcast signals from encroaching upon other teams' territories, then the Minors would have fared better. He uses the exits of Newark's and Jersey City's Minor League teams before 1951 to demonstrate the deleterious effects of television (in these cases the teams fell within the fifty-mile radius of New York City). Sportswriter Dan Daniel, writing in 1951, also attributed the demise of Newark's and Jersey City's Minor League teams to television.[63] Sportswriter and baseball historian Leonard Koppett told a similar tale: "In 1952, saturation broadcasting began killing the minors." He, too, used the fate of the Newark Bears team to demonstrate television's killing effect on Minor League teams: "Even the most successful minor league team was dead if it lived in the 'television shadow' of a major league team." He did attribute some of the Minor Leagues' difficulties to radio broadcasts of Major League games.[64]

Table 5.3 shows the rapid expansion and the equally rapid contraction of the Minor Leagues (see appendix). The diminution continued until 1960, when there were only 152 teams left. Thereafter, the addition of four Major League teams with their attendant "farm systems" stabilized the number of Minor League teams. Attendance at Minor League games also increased greatly between 1945 and 1948, quadrupling to forty-one million, albeit partly because of the entry of new teams. By 1951 attendance at Minor League games had fallen by one-third.[65] In data presented to the congressional committee studying monopoly power, teams in the lower classifications earned, on average, $2,000 to $4,400 in 1946 (see table 5.4 in the appendix). Even by 1948, however, many Minor League teams were showing losses.[66] Although professional sports' income figures are sometimes suspect, the Minor League losses are plausible in light of the decline in the number of teams.

How did the new technology affect Minor League Baseball? Certainly, the "television hurt the Minor Leagues" story sounds plausible, but did television in fact trigger the demise of many Minor League teams? Did television affect the Minor Leagues because fans preferred watching Joe DiMaggio and other big league stars on television rather than Minor League players at the local ballpark? Did television hurt Minor League teams by offering indirect competition via general programming, such as the *Texaco Star Theater* with Uncle Miltie (Milton Berle)? Or did television not really contribute to the Minor Leagues' woes?

Professional Baseball's Views of the Minor Leagues' Difficulties

Professional baseball officials sounded warnings about television's deleterious effects upon the Minor Leagues almost immediately. Before the 1949 season Frank Shaughnessy, president of the International League, claimed that television hurt Newark and Jersey City in particular, even though the surveys and polls on telecasts were indecisive. He claimed that television was using baseball to "sell television sets" and that once the market for sets was saturated, the medium would switch to cheaper soap operas.[67]

George Trautman, president of the National Association of

Professional Baseball Clubs, advanced two explanations for the contraction of Minor League Baseball during 1950 and 1951: "There are 1,322 players of last season now in the Armed Forces. . . . We have lost 60 clubs since last year. And it is accounted for . . . by the 1,322 boys that are in the service."[68] He later added, "We are exposed to a saturation of major league broadcasting. We believe there is more broadcasting than our minor league communities can absorb."[69] Ironically, Trautman continued by discussing *radio* broadcasts of Major League games. He bemoaned the Major Leagues' abrogation of the fifty-mile radius protection for Minor League teams: "When you can hear in an afternoon four or five Major League games in one little community, by the time our game starts, everybody is a little tired."[70] Throughout his tenure Trautman continued to cite television and radio as key culprits in the decline of the Minor Leagues, although he included other factors as well.[71] Trautman's successor, Philip Piton, advanced similar arguments about the deleterious effects of television and radio, although he added that "more participation in boating, bowling, touring over the fine new highways that have been built, and other similar factors" hurt Minor League Baseball. He also maintained that the Major League teams' penchant for calling up Minor League players during the season reduced the attendance in the Minor Leagues.[72]

Trautman's initial comments occurred during the congressional hearings on monopoly power and professional baseball in 1951. Other witnesses also raised the subject of radio and television broadcasting of Major League games. The Department of Justice viewed the fifty-mile ban as a violation of antitrust regulations. With the ruling against the restrictions, Major League teams began establishing radio networks to broadcast games throughout the country. During the 1950 season 850 radio stations carried Major League games. In addition, the Mutual and Liberty Broadcasting systems broadcast a *Game of the Day* over 600 stations.[73] In many cases the radio and, later, television broadcasts trespassed upon Minor League teams' territories. In the crowded Northeast Major League teams trespassed upon each other's territory with television broadcasts. The New York Yankees balked, for instance, at the Philadelphia Phillies' plans to broadcast games into New York upon the transfer of the Brooklyn Dodgers and New York Giants to the West Coast.[74]

Former senator Edwin Johnson of Colorado, who was also the president of the Western Association Minor League, testified that television had not injured teams in the association. "When it comes to television we are pretty much in the experimental stage so far. . . . [Minor League teams facing televised Major League games were hurt] because many folks would rather look at a major league game over television than see the minor league play there in the ball park." Johnson continued, now shifting the blame, "Well, I think that radio is very harmful to baseball in a great many communities where they are given too much radio and too much television, we will say, of major league games in minor league territory."[75]

Another Minor League president, A. S. Herlong Jr., also blamed radio broadcasts. "In 1950 they started putting these games of the day on the radio, and people all afternoon would listen to baseball games right in [Leesburg]. They got a tummyful by night and did not go out to the ball game in spite of the fact the announcer did say, 'Patronize your local baseball club.'"[76] Other Minor League officials could not decide whether televised Major League games hurt Minor League attendance. Minor League spokesman Bob Finch indicted television too, but he made contradictory statements. He also said that television did not materially affect Minor League attendance in 1950.[77] Another Minor League official blamed television: "You can't expect fans to look at big league television in the afternoon, hear a game-of-the-day broadcast by radio and then be eager to see a ball game in Class D, or even Class A."[78] Other observers attributed individual Minor League clubs' woes to bad weather.[79]

Howard Green, president of various low Minor Leagues, believed that many Minor League operators failed to promote their clubs. "'Tis sad but true, too, that the vast majority of baseball operators are notoriously lazy . . . lazy both in mind and body. Their business came easy and much of it is going the same way, without a fight on their part to keep it. They were told radio was the reason for all of their troubles and they believed." Green cited successes such as the Temple, Texas, team in the Big State League. Temple, a town with 24,000 people, drew 118,000 in 1951. The owner, O. W. "Bill" Hayes, energetically gave speeches to surrounding towns, produced a film about his team, and held many promotions.[80] Despite Hayes's efforts, Temple's team only played until 1954 and also in 1957 before disappearing.[81]

By 1954 more Minor League officials blamed television. In an informal poll of ten Minor League presidents, all of them cited television. Even Edwin Johnson had altered his stance: "Stop doing it [broadcasting Major League games on television]. This is a plain case of murder." A few of the Minor League officials still did not cite television as the primary culprit in the Minor Leagues' doldrums. Robert Abel, president of the Western International League, stated, "TV hurts, but it's not the main cause of our ills." He blamed a shortage of players, presumably due to the Major League teams' control of the vast majority of players. Howard Green stated, "TV is only one of many factors damaging baseball in the hinterlands. Today's players lack the 'old college try.' Baseball leaders lack courage." Another president stoically said, "TV is certainly hurting the minors. But it's here to stay. We'll have to learn how to live with it. . . . Major leagues should allot a portion of the TV profits to the minors, to keep alive the hand that feeds them."[82] Senator Johnson later proposed an amendment to a sports antitrust exemption bill specifically requiring Major League teams to share their television revenue with Minor League clubs, although Ford Frick was lukewarm about the idea, citing fears of Department of Justice strictures against such arrangements. At this juncture Frick downplayed TV's role, saying, "Television is not the sole rascal in this picture."[83] In a sense, by either owning or affiliating with Minor League teams and paying them subsidies, the Major League teams were already indirectly paying perhaps for damages done. While not explicitly making this connection, Frick emphasized the millions of dollars of subsidies paid by Major League teams to their Minor League cousins.[84] Indeed, such a vertical integration approach to assimilating the external costs between Major and Minor League teams is a common resolution in other industries.

In a later poll conducted by the same journalist, Major League officials addressed the question "What should the Major Leagues do to help save the Minors?" The reader may well guess the attitude of some of the Major League officials. In the manner of the old *Saturday Night Live* "Point/Counterpoint" argument between liberal and conservative pundits, the Major League officials were less than sympathetic to the Minor Leagues' plight. Walter O'Malley declared, "The minors will first have to go back to the old days of hustle and promotion instead of sitting down and complaining about television." Charles Comiskey II, vice president of the Chicago White Sox, was even less sympathetic: "When are the minors going to help themselves? . . . All we hear is that TV is killing them. . . . I don't think TV has hurt as much as they say." Not only officials connected with wealthy Major League teams held this position. Washington Senators treasurer H. Gabriel Murphy said, "We in Washington don't ask for financial help. We just hustle, as the minors should do." George Weiss of the Yankees asked for kudos for his team's public-spiritedness: "The Yankees have sacrificed vast sums by refusing offers for unrestricted TV."

Other officials claimed that no one really knew why the Minors were ailing, so a chorus of "let's appoint a committee" echoed throughout their comments. Other suggestions included limiting the number of Major League night games; implementing a direct subsidy; enacting curbs on televising Major League games; changing the rules pertaining to player control; and broadcasting an annual TV show to raise money for the Minors, sort of a Jerry Lewis Telethon for hurting Minor League kids. Warren C. Giles, president of the National League, offered a self-serving, but revealing, piece of nostalgia for his days as a Minor League owner: "Nothing can replace hustle. . . . I hung on by selling players and asking civic-minded people for money. Also by hustling. Others can do it." Two of the ten officials voiced concerns about concerted action that might trigger a federal antitrust investigation.[85]

William DeWitt, assistant to the New York Yankees general manager and former owner of the St. Louis Browns, viewed the contraction of the Minor Leagues up to 1953 with ambivalence: "This disparity has been cited as an alarming circumstance. That's baseless. The fact that we have lost some 25 minor leagues since the lush peak is not to be deplored. We had far too many leagues. That we may see the present number cut drastically is a possibility that must be viewed with alarm."[86] William McCarthy, general manager of the Minor League Nashville Vols, had a similar opinion: "Of course, that 59 minor leagues that they had in 1947, right after the war, is an inflated figure for the simple reason that a lot of towns had professional baseball that could not possibly support professional baseball, and I would say right now 25 to 30 minor leagues is what would be feasible in professional baseball."[87] He also cited such factors as the Tennessee Valley Authority's creation of water recreation sites as providing competition for Vols games.[88]

Conversely, Washington Senators owner Clark Griffith blamed the farm system as well as the removal of the fifty-mile territorial rights to broadcasting as the culprits for the Minors' troubles. He believed that owners of independent Minor League teams faced an uneven struggle with Minor League teams that were affiliated with Major League teams, so he advocated prohibiting such partnerships.[89] During the 1958 Senate hearings Paul Dixon, counsel for the Senate, observed, "I have been told by minor league managers and owners directly, that the minor league ball clubs started downward and practically disappeared when this unlimited control of ballplayers [i.e., farm system] began to come into major league ball." Dixon found the unlimited control of Minor League players quite interesting and queried other witnesses, including George Trautman, on the topic.[90]

Ford Frick testified before Congress in 1957 that "the minors are being wrecked": "The one thing I want to do is to be able to control, within reason, major league telecasts in minor league territory."[91] Frick hesitated in attributing all of the Minor Leagues' woes upon television, sometimes using the nonsensical figure "60 percent."[92] He did advance one novel idea: "Another problem which is hurting the minor leagues, the matter of parking. Today we are a nation on wheels. People drive to a ball park. Surveys show that you have got 1 car for about every 3 people who come to the ball game. That means if you have got 300 people you probably have got a hundred automobiles. You have got a transportation problem and you have got a parking problem. That has hurt the minor leagues."[93]

Perhaps an earlier opinion from Warren Giles was the most apt: "We had an amusement-hungry public after the war, and some people were very free with their money. As a result, we had abnormally inflated years in 1946, 1947, and 1948. Some people were foolish enough to believe that was the new normal. But I never kidded myself. I knew it couldn't last."[94]

Even in the case of the Newark Bears, sportswriters Frank Graham and John P. Carmichael provided more complicated stories concerning the team's demise. After World War II the Yankees opened a ticket office in the city and offered buses to games. The International League president Frank Shaughnessy bemoaned the Yankees' invasion of its own Minor League team's territory. The Yankees were not the only Major League team striving to attract fans from outside the city; Shaughnessy noted that the Cleveland Indians were drawing about a third of their attendance from outside the city. Graham concluded, "The Newark club, in other words, was caught in the march of progress, which was stepped up when the Yankees started to televise their games. This is no knock on night baseball, a handy ticket office or television. But if you lived in Newark . . . why should you go to see the Bears when you are close to the Yankee Stadium, and can buy your reserved seat tickets just down the street or, if you do not want to make the journey to New York, can see the Yanks on television?"[95] Before the 1949 season the Yankees announced their intention of continuing support for the Newark Bears. Local leaders and club officials worked together to solve some problems facing the team—for example, "to eliminate the smoke, smell and dust nuisances around Ruppert Stadium which Newark club officials contend kept fans away": "The unpleasant odors and smoke resulted from garbage being burned on privately-owned dumps behind the stadium. The mess was solved when the owners of the dump accepted the Commission's 'invitation' to unload their collections on the city lot."[96] In addition, the city attempted to improve the transportation snarl around the stadium. The article made no mention of television as part of the team's problem.

Jersey City had an ironic comeback. Fidel Castro's takeover of Cuba led to the Havana team transferring to Jersey City midway through the 1960 season. A local television station paid for broadcast rights. Although the station eventually stopped broadcasting games during the season, the payment ensured the team's survival.[97]

By early 1955, however, optimistic voices were being raised that the great shake-out had restored stability to the Minors. Even Edwin Johnson was optimistic: "The weaker clubs have disappeared and the stronger clubs are taking a new lease on life. I think that minor league baseball generally is in much more wholesome position than it has been in five years."[98] Johnson's optimism may have been premature. Throughout the remainder of the 1950s and well into the 1960s, headlines in various sports publications warned that the Minors were "doomed unless—." Indeed, an editorial appearing in the same issue that reported Johnson's optimistic appraisal urged "action right now or minors will perish."[99]

Statistical Analysis of the Minor League Contraction, 1946–53

An economist might view the events of 1946 through 1953 as one of entry in response to perceived future profitability between 1946 and 1949 and then exit as the favorable conditions either did not materialize or dissipated during 1949–53 (see table 5.4 in the appendix). The three AAA leagues (twenty-four teams) reported combined net profits of almost $900,000 in 1946, although the Pacific Coast League earned over two-thirds of the profits. By 1950 all three AAA leagues were losing money, a combined $1.4 million. The two AA leagues earned combined net profits for each season during 1946–50, although the Southern Association lost money in 1950. The lower classifications were not so fortunate. Teams in the lower Minor Leagues (A, B, C, and

D classifications) were losing money by 1948. Two years later teams in these lower Minors were hemorrhaging money, and 146 teams in the lower classifications reported a combined loss of almost $2 million, or an average loss of $13,600. Although the report did not list gross operating income for teams in the lower Minor Leagues, teams in AA leagues averaged around $250,000 in gross operating income between 1946 and 1950.[100]

Why did the lower Minor Leagues fare so poorly? The size of the towns possessing Minor League teams is suggestive. In the following discussion data from the 1950 census is used, and only teams in the United States are considered. Table 5.5 shows that the number of Minor League teams increased by roughly half by moving into smaller towns, including some with fewer than ten thousand residents (see appendix). You could revise the vaudeville joke:

"I was in a town so small—"
    "How small was it?"
    "So small that it didn't have its own minor league team in 1949."

Most of these small towns did not sustain their teams. Additional statistical analysis confirms the strong relationship between the population base and a team's survival between 1949 and 1953.[101]

For purposes of discussion "small towns" are those with fewer than fifty thousand inhabitants, while "large towns" are those with more than fifty thousand inhabitants. In 1949, of the 140 American Minor League teams that played in large towns, 102 played in 1953, a survival rate of 73 percent. Conversely, of the 288 American Minor League teams that played in small towns, 135 played in 1953, a survival rate of 47 percent. Population data was unavailable for seven of the teams. The survival rate for teams playing in towns smaller than twenty-five thousand was only two in five.

New teams had a lower rate of survival than the established teams. Of the 448 Minor League teams playing in 1949 (including teams in Canada, Cuba, and Mexico), some 153 began play after the 1946 season. During the 1953 season only 45 percent of these teams survived.

Of the 295 established teams in 1949, 61 percent continued playing through the 1953 season.

The new Minor League teams were frequently independents. Between 1946 and 1949 the Major Leagues increased their affiliation with the Minor Leagues by forty-two teams, while the overall increase in the number of teams was 132 (see table 5.3 in the appendix). Affiliation often included subsidizing players' salaries. In 1946 over three-fifths of the Minor League teams had Major League affiliations. The percentage of teams with Major League affiliations rose to five-sixths in 1960. Teams with affiliations in 1949 were more likely to survive until 1953: 61 to 48 percent. Many of the independent teams, however, played in smaller towns.

Major League teams began broadcasting their games on networks of radio stations in 1950. By 1953 several of the teams had extensive regional networks. Did radio broadcasts in fact affect the viability of Minor League Baseball teams? It should be noted that while Minor League operators protested broadcasts of Major League games into their territories, these operators almost unanimously favored radio broadcasts of their own games, even if they received no compensation.[102]

What were radio's effects upon attendance? Major League radio broadcasts assumed two types: "game of the day" and "affiliated." Several Major League teams combined to broadcast a game each day, often to towns hundreds of miles away from any Major League team. Other Major League teams created affiliations with radio stations, usually in the surrounding area. The St. Louis Cardinals had affiliated stations throughout the Old Southwest and Illinois.

Minor League team owner William McCarthy provided an interesting insight into the difference between the types of broadcasts: "When one particular team broadcasts into your territory and people listening to it build up a loyalty toward one particular major league team [and it hurts attendance]. . . . When there are two different teams playing every day, they listen to it more or less as entertainment and do not become attached or loyal to one ball club and support the local ball club better."[103] Corroborating McCarthy's observation, forty-four of the sixty-three teams facing competition from the game of the day survived between 1949 and 1953, but only thirty-seven out of the eighty-two teams facing similar competition from affiliated broadcasts survived during the same period. Nevertheless, the inclusion of radio broadcasts did not significantly improve the statistical equations' ability to predict which Minor League teams would survive. The population of the town remained the strongest determinant of whether the Minor League team survived in 1953, as the teams that folded while facing game of the day competition played in towns with an average population of only sixteen thousand.[104]

Even without television, then, many of these teams epitomized "shoe-string operations," playing in small towns without subsidization. What were television's effects on Minor League Baseball? The diffusion of television was rapid, astoundingly so. In 1950 one-eighth of American households had a television. Ten years later seven-eighths of households had a television.[105] Contemporary observers, perhaps erroneously, attributed the decline of the movie industry, as well as Minor League Baseball, to the spread of television. The timings of the rise of television and the decline of the Minor Leagues do not coincide.

New York City had seven operating television stations by 1949. According to the 1950 census, about a third of the households in the New York/northeastern New Jersey SMSA possessed televisions. This proportion was one of the highest in the country.[106] Even so, much, if not most, of the diffusion by 1950 occurred in 1949 and 1950. According to the *Historical Statistics of the United States*, households with televisions rose fivefold between 1948 and 1949.[107] Many bars in New York City, as well as Chicago and other large cities, had "big screen" televisions of nineteen to twenty-five inches. These sets cost almost $2,000 in 1947. Bars with television conducted a brisk business, although there were some complaints that the customers spent too much time watching the game and not enough drinking.[108] No one knew whether the bars pulled patrons away from the ballpark or simply deterred them while going home. One can understand why observers attributed the demise of the Newark and Jersey City Minor League teams to television, but New York was not indicative of the nation as a whole.

The federal government froze the assignment of channels to broadcasting companies from September 30, 1948, until April 11, 1952.[109] Before the freeze there were slightly more than one hundred channels with licenses. The freeze meant that television's inroads to the smaller cities and towns slowed. The mountain and southern states, especially, lagged in acquiring television stations. Many of the Minor League teams that folded by 1953 did not face much competition from television. In 1950 almost one-quarter of the households in the northeastern section of the country had television. Fewer than one in twenty households in the South had television. The north-central and western regions had proportions of around one in ten. Outside of Georgia, Louisiana, Texas, and Virginia, all of the states comprising the former Confederacy had rates of less than one in forty. In Louisiana the figure was 2.7 percent, while in Georgia it was 4.2 percent. The Great Plains states were another region where fewer than 3 percent of the households had television. With the freeze on new television stations, the diffusion of television in the South and Plains states undoubtedly continued to lag.[110]

Of the 197 Minor League teams in the United States that folded between 1949 and 1953, 59 were in seven southern states: Alabama, Florida, Georgia, Mississippi, North Carolina, South Carolina, and Tennessee. Most of these teams folded after the 1950 and 1951 seasons. Twelve teams folded in Kansas and Oklahoma. Texas lost 13 teams, and Virginia lost 11 teams. These two states had television ownership rates of 3.2 percent and 6.7 percent, respectively. Thus, almost half of the teams that folded between 1949 and 1953 were in states with low television diffusion in 1950.[111] Aside from the pre-freeze stations in these states, few new stations began operations between 1949 and 1953. Nor did southern Minor League teams face direct competition from Major League teams until the introduction of the Houston Colt .45s in 1962 and the Atlanta Braves in 1966.

In the Northeast television's role as slayer of Minor League Baseball is more plausible. First, there were Major League teams in the area that had sold broadcasting rights to television, so Minor League teams in close proximity to big league cities might have faced direct competition from telecasts of such games. Second, households in the Northeast had some of the highest television saturation rates in the nation. Forty-two teams folded in New Jersey, New York, Ohio, and Pennsylvania. At least one-sixth of the households in these states possessed televisions in 1950. California had a 15.1 percent proportion; ten teams in the state folded.[112] Minor League teams in the four states of New Jersey, New York, Ohio, and Pennsylvania had the lowest survival rate of any region: less than a third of the 61 teams that existed in 1949 played in 1953. In the seven states of the Deep South (Alabama, Florida, Georgia, Mississippi, North Carolina, South Carolina, and Tennessee) slightly more than half of the 129 teams survived. Yet there were several other Minor League teams in the Deep South that began play in 1950 and folded after 1951 or 1952, so the survival rate may be overstated. Over three-fifths of the Minor League teams in Virginia and Texas in 1949 survived until 1953; conversely, only 10 of 22 Minor League teams in television-sparse Kansas and Oklahoma survived until 1953.

Did television affect attendance for the high Minor Leagues (AAA, AA, and A)? For the time period 1947 to 1950 statistical analysis shows that television appeared to have had a negative effect upon attendance, although the impact was not strong. One regression equation suggested, for instance, that a city with 2 percent television ownership rate in 1950 might lose slightly more than 2 percent of its attendance, holding its win-loss record constant. Because many Minor League teams played in areas with very low rates of television ownership, the equation suggests that television exerted a moderate drag at most on Minor League attendance. For the 1947 to 1953 period television appeared to exert an even weaker and statistically insignificant effect upon Minor League attendance.[113]

The experiences of the Southern Association and South Atlantic League demonstrate why the television variable had such low explanatory power. The South Atlantic League (A classification) included Augusta, Columbus, Macon, and Savannah, Georgia; Charleston, Columbia, and Greenville, South Carolina; and Jacksonville, Florida. According to the 1950 census, 4 percent of Jacksonville's reporting households had television. All of the other seven cities had ownership rates of 1 percent or less. Overall, the league attendance declined 35 percent between 1947 and 1950.[114] Clearly, television had a modest effect upon attendance at most, unless one grants a very large "multiplier effect" to the limited number of televisions owned by households or bars. Jacksonville had one television station in 1950 (WMBR, which began operations in 1949). The four Georgia cities did not have any operating stations until 1953.[115] In fact, Atlanta was the only city in Georgia with an operating television station. Of the four Georgia teams Macon was the closest to Atlanta (eighty-one miles), so Atlanta's signal may not have even reached any of these cities. South Carolina did not have an operating station until 1953.

The Southern Association (AA classification) included the cities of Atlanta, Birmingham, Chattanooga, Little Rock, Memphis, Mobile, Nashville, and New Orleans, five of which had operating television stations in 1950. Fourteen percent of Atlanta households reported owning televisions. Of the other cities 9 percent of Memphis, 7.7 percent of New Orleans, and 3.6 percent of Birmingham households had televisions in 1950. Chattanooga, Little Rock, Mobile, and Nashville reported less than 1 percent ownership, with the first three teams not even having an operating station in 1950. While these cities had larger proportions of homes owning television than cities in the South Atlantic League, the league's attendance fell by only one-fifth between 1947 and 1950.[116] Thus, even in the larger southern towns, television was not a compelling explanation for attendance losses.

The Minor Leagues from 1953 to 1964

The Minor Leagues struggled throughout the decade after the 1949–53 contraction. Although Minor and Major League officials often identified television and radio broadcasts as culprits in the Minors' demise, just as many other pundits cited bonus payments made to untried players and other rules pertaining to player procurement. Throughout the era the "death" of the Minors was always imminent. Major League clubs responded by raising their subsidies to Minor Leagues.

The Class AA Southern Association suspended operations before the 1962 season. Officials cited apathetic fans, the rising popularity of outdoor participatory sports, bowling's boom, Major League Baseball telecasts, general television programming, air-conditioning, college and professional football, slower games, poorer teams, and deterioration of Minor League facilities as reasons for the decline. One observer felt that the South's color line had proved fatal. According to Gabe Paul, longtime baseball general manager and future president of the Yankees, "One of the reasons the Southern Association is no longer in existence is the policy of not permitting Negroes to play. It caused a number of Major League organizations to look in other directions for working agreements which otherwise would have been placed with Southern Association clubs."[117] Another observer attributed much of the drop to the wider use of home air-conditioning: "It is much easier all around to sit in an air-conditioned room, especially in the humid weather which afflicted the area in late August, and watch a crucial Major League game than it is to go to the ball park."[118] Other pundits cited Little League baseball as competition. Families who might have watched the local Minor League team now flocked to the neighborhood diamond to watch their children play.

By the late 1950s the surviving Minor Leagues were still facing difficulties. Major League expansion and relocation, television, and the Major Leagues' ever-increasing control of ballplayers made it harder for many Minor League teams to remain viable. Sportswriter Roy Terrell described the situation:

> The problem itself is simple enough: the minor leagues are dying because their two main sources of revenue, admission money and player sales, are drying up fast. Television, the super-highway, Little Leagues and big leagues, outboard motors and hi-fi sets, poor promotion, too

many mosquitoes, rainy weather and the increased cost of living have all combined to keep the fans out of the parks. And the ballplayers which the minors once developed and sold for profit into big time don't even belong to them any more. About 80% of all the players in organized baseball . . . are already owned by major league teams.[119]

The Minor League teams complained of bullying tactics by the Majors, such as their usurpation of Minor League cities; radio and television transmission of Major League games, especially on the weekends and weekday evenings; and Major League's control of players. Independent Minor League teams especially fared poorly without subsidies from a Major League sponsor.

During the 1960 Senate hearings on professional team sports, one remedy put forth was requiring Major League teams to get permission from the affected Minor League team before being able to telecast a game into the Minor League team's territory. George Trautman quickly dismissed the suggestion, claiming, "Some minor league clubs have been almost crucified by local television stations for refusing to consent to the telecasting of major league games when the major league club owning the rights has prohibited such telecasts while the minor league club is actually playing a game at home."[120]

Throughout the discussions of bonus rules and free agent drafts many officials said they believed that the bonus rule injured the Minor Leagues. Rather than Minor League teams scouting and signing talented amateurs, the most promising of whom they would sell to Major League teams, the latter now co-opted the process by signing amateurs directly. The first baseball commissioner, Judge Kenesaw Mountain Landis, bemoaned the "chain-store" approach from its inception, yet he was unable to stop the process. The end result was that Minor League teams lost one of their major revenue sources, as they had few players to sell.[121] Some observers, such as Leslie O'Connor, assistant to Landis, believed that the Minors could develop a young player and sell him to the Major Leagues for about half the cost that a Major League team would incur. He believed that several Major League owners preferred to control the player development process rather than to risk the vagaries of a free market in Minor League players. "It would leave too much to chance," he argued, "and good businessmen like Walter O'Malley of the Dodgers, Lou Perini of the Braves and Del Webb of the Yankees are not going to buy very much of that." The owners also liked the "standardization" process of having their own farm systems, as that way a player would be "indoctrinated thoroughly all his baseball life in the particular style of play and winning psychology of the parent organization."[122]

Throughout the early 1960s the Major Leagues attempted to help the Minor Leagues. They did little, however, to reduce television and radio incursions into Minor League territories. Indeed, the Majors expanded their televising of games on a nationwide basis, with such offerings as the *Game of the Week*, as well as increased the numbers of night games. Eventually, most of the independent Minor League teams folded. The Major League teams streamlined their farm systems and provided various subsidies to the Minor Leagues. Over three years Major League teams paid $2.35 million to the Minor Leagues, in return for which they urged the Minor League teams to do a better job promoting their product. In October 1960 the Majors pumped another $800,000 into the Minors, but more handouts were needed. Ironically, later that year the Minor League teams voted down an amendment aimed at obtaining more monetary aid from the Majors, as the Major League teams apparently pressured their Minor League brethren into voting against the measure.[123]

Major League teams owning Minor League clubs suffered losses too. Financial data presented to a probate court proceeding regarding the Chicago White Sox demonstrated the difficulty of turning a profit on a Minor League team. The Sox owned a team in the Class B, Three-I League: Waterloo in 1956 and Davenport in 1957. Waterloo had drawn 174,000 fans in 1947, but by 1956 the club drew only 46,000. Attendance in Davenport peaked at 133,500 in 1949, before dropping to 72,000 in 1952; the team folded before the 1953 season, only to be resuscitated in 1957. Both teams suffered attendance slides by 1950 and

1951, before many Iowa households possessed televisions. The slide in attendance became precipitous after 1948. During 1956 Waterloo collected only $35,000 in combined gate and concession revenues, an amount barely covering the players' salaries. Sales of players' contracts brought in only $6,000. All told, the White Sox reported a loss of over $100,000 on the team. The Sox lost only $71,500 in Davenport the next year.[124] In order to turn a profit, the Waterloo team needed to quadruple its attendance, while the Davenport team needed to more than double its draw. The ballclubs only saw such levels during the peak of the boom years in 1947 and 1948.

Baseball commissioner Ford Frick blamed the Justice Department for its refusal to allow the Major Leagues to reinstate their ban on Major League broadcasts and telecasts into Minor League territories.[125] George Trautman believed that a curb on broadcasts and telecasts of Major League Baseball games would revitalize Minor League Baseball. He felt, however, that there were other things that Minor League teams needed to do, such as improve fans' comfort, offer more promotions, and speed up the games.[126]

One proposal to help boost attendance at Minor and Major League games was to schedule occasional Major League games in Minor League cities. The Brooklyn Dodgers occasionally played games in Jersey City already. Sportswriter John Holway pointed out that many weekday games drew poorly in Major League cities. These games might have been profitably played in Minor League cities, with proceeds being split between the Minor League team and the two Major League teams.[127] The National Basketball Association occasionally did something similar. Indeed, the famous Wilt Chamberlain one-hundred-point game occurred on a trip to Hershey, Pennsylvania.

The big leagues' incursion into Minor League territories both eliminated larger cities from the Minor Leagues and created a chain reaction as other teams shuffled between leagues. The Minor Leagues wanted to be reimbursed for the violation of their territorial rights. The Pacific Coast League received $900,000 in indemnities from the Dodgers and Giants, when those two teams relocated to California. Calvin Griffith offered $200,000 in indemnities when his Senators moved to the Twin Cities. The American Association wanted $1.6 million but received an amount closer to Griffith's offer.[128]

In the early 1960s the Major Leagues reorganized the Minors into three instead of the existing six classifications. The B, C, and D league classifications disappeared. In addition, the Major Leagues stopped their $800,000 player development funding. The Major League teams instituted instead standard working agreements with fixed cash payments.[129]

The Majors instituted a new plan at their December meetings in 1962. The new arrangement added between $500,000 and $1 million to the cost of developing talent in 1963. The Major Leagues would now contribute $10 million to the Minors. The Majors agreed to guarantee one hundred Minor League teams, or five Minor League teams per big league team.[130] At the December meetings organized baseball also proposed a four-point plan to save the Minor Leagues, including an unrestricted draft and a free agent draft, petitioning Congress for an exemption from antitrust restrictions for all of organized baseball, and realignment.[131]

Is it true that "television killed the Minors"? If not, was there an ulterior motive for promulgating that version of events? Major League owners, concerned with protecting themselves from charges of uncompetitive practices, could use the story to justify their antitrust exemption. Ford Frick stated it explicitly: "But certainly whether we solve radio and television or not, we cannot afford to lose our privilege of a reserve clause, and territorial rights because it is the complete foundation." Benjamin Fiery, counsel for the American League, lauded Rule 1(d) that prohibited Major League teams from trespassing into Minor League territories.[132] Organized baseball's account ran as such: the Minor Leagues and organized baseball were doing just fine; if only the Department of Justice had not opened the floodgates to network television (and radio) broadcasts of Major League games, then more of the Minor Leagues would have survived.

The Minor Leagues were buffeted by a variety of factors. During 1947–49 new owners of Minor League teams flooded the market, but after the 1949 season they, along with incumbent owners, lost their protection from radio broadcasts of Major League Baseball. Competition from these broadcasts, television programming generally, and the appearance of televised Major League games—all of which were felt first in the Northeast and Midwest—put pressure on Minor League ball.

The best overall explanation of the decline of the Minor Leagues between 1949 and 1953 is their overexpansion into smaller towns that proved unable to sustain Minor League teams when the "boom" ended. Indeed, George Trautman commented during a Major League meeting to discuss the Minor Leagues: "We just have to make our product more attractive. . . . We had our boom. At one time there were 59 minor leagues. That's more than there should have been because we got careless. Almost any eight men who came to see us with ties got a league. We didn't consider financial stability. That's one thing we're paying for now."[133] In addition, the Korean War diminished the pool of players. Thus, by 1950 many Minor League teams were weakening. The gradual dissemination of television provided alternative forms of entertainment, and televised Major League Baseball may have delivered the coup de grace for many weak Minor League teams in the post-1953 period. Yet television's role in "killing" the Minor Leagues during the 1949–53 contraction, if any, is plausible mainly for teams in the Northeast.

The Minors eventually adjusted to television. As early as 1948, some Minor League teams began televising home games. In 1949 twelve teams in AAA and AA sold television rights, double the number selling rights in 1948. Teams in Atlanta; Columbus, Ohio; Houston; Hollywood; Los Angeles; Louisville, Kentucky; Milwaukee; and Minneapolis telecast all of their home games, while teams in Baltimore, San Francisco, and Seattle showed at least two games per week. Even Newark considered airing some of its games, but the team failed to complete a deal.[134] Nashville Vols owner McCarthy described his experience in allowing telecasts of six Vols home games per season. He was not sure if the venture was profitable. The broadcasts appeared to hurt attendance on weekday night games but helped to bring fans from a wider radius around Nashville: "We have to draw our attendance on Saturday and Sunday or we just don't draw it, and then 60 to 70 percent of the cars, from checks we have taken, will be outside of Davidson County."[135]

During 1959 at least six Minor League clubs collected $25,000 each from broadcasting and telecasting rights to their games. Another half-dozen earned between $16,000 and $20,000 from such rights.[136] By 1960 most of the teams in the AA and AAA leagues had their own radio broadcasts and, in some cases, television broadcasts. Although the Minor Leagues continued to plead poverty, owners found an element of accommodation with the new medium.[137]

Where Is Robin Hood When You Need Him?

Revenue Sharing in the American League

One potential remedy for the American League doldrums during the 1950s was revenue sharing, in the form of gate sharing between teams. Revenue sharing was not new then—it had been around since the inception of professional baseball. The practice was sometimes controversial, however, given different teams' ability to draw fans at home and away, among other things. Revenue-sharing agreements began informally but have remained a fixture of Major League Baseball. During recent years the issue has come under scrutiny again within Major League Baseball. The *Report of the Independent Members of the Commissioner's Blue Ribbon Panel on Baseball Economics* revisited the topic in 2000 and suggested increasing the amount of revenue sharing, among other changes. Committee members made their recommendations in the hope of increasing the competitive balance within Major League Baseball.[1]

The committee described the current status of Major League Baseball as being a world divided into the "haves," such as the Atlanta Braves, Chicago Cubs, the Los Angeles clubs, and New York Yankees, and the "have-nots," such as the Minnesota Twins, Montreal Expos, Oakland A's, and Pittsburgh Pirates. Shortly after the report's release, the Twins and A's won their divisions. The Expos, however, remained as baseball's charity case and are now, since 2005, the Washington Nationals.

Because the New York Yankees had won three consecutive World Series, the committee members were concerned about the apparently growing competitive imbalance, which they feared could weaken Major League Baseball. In a sense the committee's description echoed those of congressional hearings convened almost fifty years earlier, in 1951 and 1957. During those hearings legislators and some of the witnesses had cited the Yankees' dominance of the American League as being potentially detrimental.

According to data supplied at the congressional hearings and shown in table 6.1, the Yankees sometimes had 3.5 times as much total revenue (gate, concession, and broadcasting revenues) as the Washington Senators (see appendix).[2] The data presented at the investigations was not typically made public, and the baseball researcher is frustrated by the limited number of years for which data was provided. These data are useful in examining how revenue sharing based on gate receipts worked in the past.

The 1950s were a period of anticommunist hysteria in the United States, but that bastion of Americana, Major League Baseball, was in fact practicing a limited form of communal sharing. How well did the policy work? The American League had a revenue-sharing program during the postwar era, but it failed to create even a semblance of revenue parity. Ironically, in 1956 the plan transferred similar amounts of revenue to the Indians, Senators . . . and Yankees, despite those teams' vastly different fortunes on the field and on the ledgers.

Debates about revenue sharing continue today, with new proposals being offered, some of them quite similar to measures undertaken in the past. Thus, besides the historical interest in considering the experiences of the American League during the 1950s, such an examination might provide some clues about the possible effectiveness of current approaches to reducing revenue disparities among Major League teams.

A Brief History of Revenue Sharing in Major League Baseball

Baseball historian Harold Seymour claimed in 1971 that the revenue-sharing rules in early professional baseball leagues arose from informal agreements made between team owners: "Appreciating the results of inequality of markets, the owners tried to compensate by sharing gate receipts, giving 50 percent of the base admission price to visiting teams. Anything above that, taken in through the sale of seats that cost more than the base price, was kept by the home team as an incentive to improve its stands by adding more box and reserved seats."[3] His argument echoed testimony made during the 1951 congressional hearings.[4] Early clubs arranged games and agreed to split the gate. The earliest overtly professional team, the Cincinnati Red Stockings, played almost all of its games on the road. Harry Wright, the manager of the team, negotiated the gate-sharing arrangements with captains of other teams. Because the Red Stockings were a superior team that drew well, Wright was able to get either a relatively large guarantee or a fairly high percentage of the gate.[5]

The professional clubs found the informal method of arranging matches to be inadequate for determining championships. The earliest professional "league," the National Association, was formed in 1871. The requirements for admission into the loose association included a nominal $10 membership fee. The association attempted to have its members charge fifty cents per ticket, but teams in the smaller towns balked and wanted admission to be twenty-five cents. Visiting teams were to get one-third of the total gate receipts. For holidays the gate was to be split evenly between the two teams.[6] Association teams in the smaller cities welcomed the Boston Red Stockings and big-city teams, but these small-town teams were loathe to travel to Boston and other venues. In the 1952 congressional hearings historian Harry Simmons described one situation: "Some [National Association teams] survived only long enough to play a few games at the opening of the season. One such team in 1875 were the Westerns of Keokuk. The Mutuals of New York on their first western trip that season stopped at Keokuk for a pair of games. The Mutuals' share of the gates totaled $35. When it was time for the Westerns to make an eastern swing, the club disbanded. The Mutuals were to use this as an excuse for not making their final trip west in 1876 when the National League played its first season."[7]

Because of the casual nature of the National Association, Chicago White Stockings owner, William Hulbert, wanted to form a new league with teams only from larger cities. In 1876 Hulburt and other owners formed the National League. The new league had a mandatory city population requirement, which was almost immediately ignored, and a requirement that teams play home and away series with each of the other members of the league. The league owners also agreed to a minimum ticket price of fifty cents. According to Seymour, in late 1876 the New York and Philadelphia teams refused to travel west to complete the season, so the league kicked the two teams out. The owner of the Philadelphia team had offered 80 percent of the gate receipts to Chicago and St. Louis if they would have only come east instead of having his team head west.[8] The league formalized its version of gate sharing in 1877 by agreeing that visiting clubs would get fifteen cents, 30 percent of the base admission, for every adult admitted to the park, with attendance monitored by turnstiles.[9]

The American Association was a rival league that operated throughout the 1880s. The league charged twenty-five cents for admission. Its constitution mandated that home teams guarantee $65 to the visiting team, except on holidays, when the gate would be split fifty-fifty.[10]

In both the National League and American Association the percentage gate split generated debate, as some owners favored a fixed guarantee instead of the percentage split. The National League owners resolved the controversy after the 1886 season by instituting a $125 guarantee for the visiting team, except on state and national holidays, when the two teams would split the gate revenue fifty-fifty. The controversy revealed the underlying tensions between the teams. The teams in the smaller cities favored the percentage split, while the owners of teams in the larger cities favored the fixed guarantee. The Detroit manager complained, for instance, "We should be nice suckers . . . to go to Boston or to Washington and put big money in their treasuries for $125." Albert Spalding, owner of the Chicago team, responded that the [wealthier] clubs were "tired of carrying along a club like Detroit."[11] Such comments recurred in the 1950s, as owners of the stronger teams bemoaned having to carry the Philadelphia Athletics and St. Louis Browns. The National League altered the gate-sharing rules again in 1887, granting 12.5 cents per admission to the visiting team as well as a $150 guarantee. By 1891 the National League had a fifty-fifty split of the basic fifty-cent admission, but anything over that was retained by the home team. The Union Association (1884) and Players' League (1890) also had similar gate-sharing policies, although the Players' League mandated a fifty-fifty split of all gate receipts.[12]

At its inception in 1901 the American League instituted gate-sharing rules that were similar to those of the National League. It changed the rules in 1926 by increasing the amount from twenty-five to thirty cents per admission on all but bleacher seats and general admission, and these rules remained essentially the same into the 1950s.[13] A recent collective bargaining agreement between the owners and the players in 1996 included sharing of local revenue (teams earning more than the median revenue would share their revenues with teams earning less than the median) and a tax on player payrolls that exceeded a fixed threshold. Four years later the Blue Ribbon Panel urged an increase in the revenue sharing and a more stringent tax on player payrolls.[14]

The Postwar American League Gate-Sharing Policy

After struggling through the war years, the American League enjoyed a resurgence of popularity in 1946. More than 9.6 million fans enjoyed American League games that season, 4 million more than in any previous season.[15] Yet over the next several years the immediate postwar prosperity began to dwindle (see table 6.1 in the appendix), and by the early 1950s the Philadelphia Athletics and St. Louis Browns were facing financial distress.

The postwar American League had a revenue-sharing plan to help moribund teams. According to the American League bylaws enacted in 1926, "the visiting member shall receive twenty cents each on all bleacher or general admissions and thirty cents each on all other paid admissions."[16] Most of the teams had relatively few bleacher or general admission seats. Using road revenue and road attendance figures, we can deduce the average revenue shared per ticket. The visiting teams received an average of close to twenty-nine cents per admission. This figure was remarkably stable across the decade and between teams. The lack of variance implies that all of the teams were probably paying approximately twenty-nine cents per home admission.[17] A 1962 article in the *Sporting News* supports this assumption: "Figuring twenty-nine cents on every admission—the conventional take for visiting clubs."[18] Bill Veeck cited an average of twenty-eight cents.[19] In the National League the visiting team received 27.5 cents per paid admission.

The National League had elaborate procedures to ensure an accurate count of tickets sold, and that league's bylaws had a section pertaining to turnstiles.[20] Presumably the American League had a similar policy, although the league's bylaws did not contain detailed rules pertaining to the turnstiles. Apparently, this method of gate sharing was easier to implement than a policy based on the actual revenue, although professional football used the percentage of receipts method during this time.

Economists Gerald Scully, James Quirk, and Rodney Fort have created much of the theoretical analysis of revenue sharing in the form of gate sharing. One of their key conclusions is that in the absence of local television revenue such as in the American League in 1946, various forms of gate sharing would not have much effect upon "competitive balance" but that gate sharing might increase the survivability of franchises in smaller cities. Implicit in their arguments and in less well-argued statements by the media and fans is that gate sharing should reduce revenue disparity. Scully, for instance, writes that, "Obviously, the more equal the gate-sharing plan among the teams, the more equal the revenues," while Quirk and Fort conclude that "gate sharing shifts income from strong-drawing teams to weak-drawing teams."[21]

An American League team's gate revenue was simply:

$$\text{Total Gate Revenue} = \text{Gate Revenue at Home} -$$
$$\$0.29 \,(\text{Attendance at Home}) + \$0.29 \,(\text{Attendance on the Road}).$$

Some economic models assume that a strong team will draw less on the road, holding population and other factors fixed, than it does at home. Yet this assumption remains an empirical question. As a redistribution scheme, paying a relatively flat rate per admission seemingly made sense. For a given win-loss record the New York Yankees were likely to draw many more fans to Yankee Stadium than the St. Louis Browns would draw to their park. In economic terms the potential marginal revenue, the change in total revenue, of additional wins was likely to be much greater in New York than in St. Louis, where the Browns shared the relatively small city with the Cardinals of the National League.[22]

Paying a flat rate per admission, however, had a potentially serious drawback. If all of the teams drew equally well on the road, the scheme would redistribute revenue from the Yankees to the Browns. Conversely, if the Yankees drew better on the road than did the Browns, then the potential redistribution would be muted and might even flow in the opposite direction. Such a redistribution would have been contrary to the predictions discussed by Scully, Quirk, and Fort because they assumed that a strong team drew better at home than on the road.[23]

The Postwar American League Experience with Gate Sharing

In an eight-team league equal revenues would mean that each team would have 0.125 of the total revenue. To measure the disparity in total revenue, one can use the standard deviation. Almost two-thirds of the teams would have total revenue shares within one standard deviation (in either direction) from 0.125. The larger the standard deviation, the greater the spread in the distribution of total revenue shares. Gate-sharing rules had different effects upon the standard deviation of the teams' share of the total league gate revenue (mean = .125) and ratios of the top quartile to the bottom quartile (see table 6.2 in the appendix).

The league's gate-sharing plan had its largest effect in 1946 and 1950, when the standard deviation was lowered from 0.068 to 0.058 (1946) and from 0.085 to 0.076 (1950). By 1952 the gate sharing had little effect on the standard deviation. After the Browns and Athletics relocated, the standard deviation shrank. Had there been no gate sharing, the standard deviations would have been almost the same as with gate sharing for those two years. In addition, the gate-sharing plan had a minimal effect on the top and bottom quartile ratios for these years.

Why did the gate-sharing plan have such moderate effects in 1952–54, before the full effects of relocation? There were four factors. First, the rising average price of tickets diluted the relative effectiveness of the flat-rate, gate-sharing method. The average cost of admission was only $1.16 in 1946, but the average ticket price escalated to $1.79 ten years later (a 4 percent annual rate of increase, which slightly exceeded the rise in the consumer price index for the period). Second, the varying average prices of tickets among teams created another dilution of the American League's policy of a flat rate per admission. Throughout the period the New York Yankees received the highest revenue per home admission. The Yankees averaged twenty-two cents more per home admission than did the Philadelphia Athletics in 1946 ($1.29 to $1.07). By 1956 the Yankees had increased their relative advantage ($2.04 to $1.60). Thus, the Yankees shared a smaller proportion of their home revenue than did teams with lower-priced tickets. Third, season box holders who were no-shows did not cost the home team in terms of gate sharing. Given the fact that the majority of season box tickets were purchased by businesses and that New York had the greatest share of business customers, the Yankees had a clear advantage. Fourth, the Yankees were the best road draw in every season surveyed except 1946. Intuitively, when the Yankees played at Philadelphia or St. Louis, fans there could finally see a high-quality Major League team. Detroit, Philadelphia, St. Louis, and Washington typically drew the fewest fans on the road.

Using data for 1950 and 1952–56 (1946 was not included because actual road attendance figures were not available), statistical analysis shows that road attendance was strongly and positively related to a team's playing strength, as measured by win-loss percentage.[24] The National League had a similar relationship between the visiting team's win-loss percentage and its ability to draw crowds while playing on the road.[25]

Although the revenue figures provided to Congress in 1952 did not include revenue paid to visiting teams, the stability of the twenty-nine cents per admission gate sharing allows a quick estimate of the revenue redistribution. As equation 1 shows, one need only examine the difference between home attendance and road attendance. The difference is then multiplied by twenty-nine cents. If the home attendance is greater than the road attendance, the team loses revenue; if the home attendance is less than the road attendance, the team gains revenue. Table 6.3 shows the estimated changes in gate revenue in 1946, 1950, and 1952–56 (see appendix). Even a two-cent deviation in average transfer per admission would change the redistribution by only $20,000 (based on one million in road attendance).

In 1946 the redistribution scheme worked reasonably well. Because the Red Sox, Tigers, and Yankees each retained at least $360,000 more in "games at home" revenue than any of the remaining five clubs, they were prime candidates for redistribution, and indeed, the Yankees lost a large amount due to gate sharing. The Red Sox, however, gained from the plan. The amount of redistribution shrank considerably by 1952, but the Yankees, at least, still lost under the plan. The Chicago White Sox were the most generous donors, while the Browns reaped the largest gain. Yet in 1953 the Browns and Athletics sorely needed infusions of revenue. Between 1952 and 1953 these teams' home attendance had fallen by over 200,000, and their road attendance fell by 175,000 or more for each team. Although the redistribution was limited, the Browns and Athletics gained about 20 percent more in gate revenue than they would have without the agreement.

Nevertheless, the gate sharing program did not prevent a sharp drop in revenues and profits in the American League between 1946 and 1953. The fifth consecutive Yankee pennant did not improve even that franchise's gate revenues or home attendance numbers. Only the White Sox reported higher gate revenues in 1953 than in 1952. But in 1954 two fortuitous events occurred to reverse the decline in the league's incomes temporarily. First, the Cleveland Indians ended the Yankees' string of pennants. Second, the St. Louis Browns moved to

Baltimore. While the Yankees home gate fell slightly in terms of number of fans, the actual home gate revenues increased by almost $400,000 (which could be the result of selling a greater number of reserved and box tickets and a greater number of season ticket no-shows), the team drew almost three hundred thousand more fans on the road in 1954 than in 1953. Thus, finishing second had the ironic result of boosting the Yankees total gate revenue by $470,000 in 1954, even though the pennant race ended with almost two weeks left in the season.

Over time revenue sharing's effects changed dramatically. When the Browns transferred to Baltimore in 1954 and became the Orioles and when the Athletics moved to Kansas City in 1955, both teams' home attendance climbed dramatically; however, the two teams remained poor draws on the road, as their records did not immediately improve. Conversely, by 1954–56 the Yankees were drawing more fans on the road than they did at home. These changes had significant repercussions on the redistribution scheme pursued by the American League.

The transplanted Browns helped the league draw almost a million more customers in 1954 than in 1953, as the Orioles topped the one million attendance figure (some seven hundred thousand more than they had drawn as the Browns in 1953). Although the change appears large, the Browns management was disappointed, having hoped for a total attendance figure of 1.8 million. Despite their attendance boost, the Orioles—as well as the Athletics, Senators, and Tigers—continued to remain behind the Yankees and Indians as road draws. The Browns/Orioles' relocation scrambled the revenue redistribution pattern. With their stronger fan base, the Orioles now became donors instead of recipients. The Athletics continued to be the largest beneficiary. The Tigers continued their generosity. The Yankees became recipients for the first time. The ironic effect of the downtrodden Browns' franchise shift was to increase, albeit modestly, the Yankees' revenue.

Although the Yankees had led the league in road attendance from 1950 on (when data by season became available), usually another contender drew almost as many fans on the road. According to figures listed in *Sports Illustrated*, the Yankees led the American League in total road attendance between 1946 through 1955. Some 15.4 million fans watched the Yankees on the road. Because New York had 19.3 million in home attendance during the period, the team lost over $1.1 million because of revenue sharing. The Indians were a good road draw too, with 14.4 million in road attendance during the ten years.[26] Cleveland's home attendance was only 15.9 million, so the team lost only $430,000 via revenue sharing. Despite the Browns/Orioles' attendance gains for the 1954 and 1955 seasons, the franchise probably gained almost $1.1 million in revenue sharing during the ten years.[27]

The Yankees began a new string of four pennants in 1955. The Philadelphia Athletics finally succumbed to economic reality and switched to Kansas City. The change paid off immediately, as the Athletics drew a million more fans in 1955 than in 1954. Their total gate revenue increased by over $1.8 million. The team improved on the field, too, by winning twelve more games but still finishing in sixth place. In doing well, the Athletics achieved a dubious honor, as the franchise became the league's largest donor for 1955 and 1956. Washington was the largest beneficiary, although the Detroit Tigers also gained (their donation to their peers fell from $97,000 to $26,000). Despite the two franchise relocations, collective net real income across the league fell off from the 1954 level.

The Yankees remained the most popular road team and drew more fans on the road than they did at Yankee Stadium. Their strong appeal to fans in other cities limited the ability of the gate sharing to redistribute money between the weaker teams in the league and them. After the 1954 pennant race, which the Yankees led in road attendance, despite Cleveland's championship, the Yankees increased their road attendance advantage. Between 1953 and 1958 almost 40 percent of all American League attendance was for Yankee games, both at Yankee Stadium and on the road. In 1959, when Chicago won the pennant, the Yankees outdrew both the White Sox and Indians by more than six hundred thousand on the road. When the American League expanded to ten teams in 1961, the Yankees' dominance of road attendance continued. The next year over two million fans in other cities saw the team. In 1962 and 1963 the Yankees drew at least a million more fans on the road than any of its American League opponents.

In fact, of the total American League attendance, over 37 percent of those who came to the ballpark saw a game involving the Yankees.[28] In a ten-team league an average team would attract 10 percent of the total league attendance at home and another 10 percent on the road. Indeed, all of the Yankees' nine opponents drew at least 20 percent of their home attendance via games with New York. The Los Angeles Angels had 36 percent of their attendance for the season from games with the Yankees, while Cleveland had 32 percent. Because New York drew 722,585 more fans on the road than at Yankee Stadium in 1962, the team received a net gain of $209,550 under the gate-sharing plan, more than the combined salaries of Mickey Mantle, Roger Maris, and Whitey Ford. In a sense, then, American League rivals paid for the players who enabled the Yankees to outclass them.

Revenue sharing in the National League had similarly perverse results. In 1955 the pennant-winning Dodgers gained $160,000 from the plan, while the defending champion Giants reaped $103,000. The two teams drew well on the road. Chicago, Cincinnati, Pittsburgh, and St. Louis, the four worst teams, shared $82,000 in net gains. The last-place Pirates only gained $42,000 from the plan, even though their home gate of 469,400 was over 200,000 less than the next-poorest draw. Who paid for the party? Philadelphia lost $46,000. The Milwaukee Braves, however, were the biggest donors by far, as the team lost $300,000 via revenue sharing.[29]

Thus, if road attendance is positively affected by a team's on-field performance, strong teams in large cities may be shielded, to a degree, from the dire effects of some forms of gate sharing. In any case, and for several reasons, the revenue-sharing arrangement in the American League redistributed smaller amounts of revenue during the mid-1950s and early 1960s. Were there better alternatives to the existing policy?

Alternatives to the Existing Plan

Given that existing revenue-sharing policies shifted relatively small amounts of income by 1956, what alternatives did American League teams have? Increasing the flat rate on regular seating from thirty cents to, say, sixty cents, would not have been a panacea. Certainly, a higher flat rate per admission would have amplified the transfers (roughly doubling the figures shown in table 6.3 in the appendix), but such a policy would have increased the gains to the stronger teams from larger cities that happened to draw more fans on the road than at home.

Suppose, instead, that the league assessed a flat percentage rate against the home revenue. St. Louis Browns owner Bill Veeck urged a 60-40 percent split in 1953. The proposal needed the support of six owners, but the Red Sox, Tigers, and Yankees voted it down.[30] Such a policy would have required actual scrutiny of the home team's receipts, including receipts from no-shows, by the visiting team instead of the simple turnstile count, and some teams might have resisted this level of scrutiny.

What might have happened with a fifty-fifty policy (i.e., one based on equal shares)? The fifty-fifty split still has the potential drawback that if a strong team in a large city proves an exceptionally good draw on the road, it could actually gain revenue from such a policy. All that is needed for such a result is for home revenue to be less than road revenue. If the American League's goal was to strengthen the league's weaker franchises by redistributing earnings among teams, would a fifty-fifty split achieve this goal?

In 1956 the hypothetical fifty-fifty policy might have reversed the result of the Yankees being beneficiaries of the actual revenue-sharing plan (see table 6.4 in the appendix). The gate receipts at Yankee Stadium totaled $3.04 million. Under the actual plan the Yankees earned $3.11 million from home and road gate receipts; the gate-sharing plan shifted $65,000 to the Yankees. A fifty-fifty gate split would have redistributed $37,000 from the Yankees to the other franchises. Clearly, the fifty-fifty split would not have necessarily redistributed large amounts of revenue, as long as winning teams from large cities drew well on the road. Indeed, in 1956 such a plan would have had moderate effects on both the standard deviation of the percentage shares of league revenues and the top/bottom quartile ratio.

A "tax" on home revenues, whether a flat rate per admission or a flat percentage of gate revenue, that was *equally* divided among all of the teams would have redistributed larger amounts of revenue to weaker clubs. Such a policy would have mitigated the offsetting effects of strong teams that drew well on the road. In 1956 such a tax would have reduced the standard deviation to roughly half the standard deviation under the existing plan. The 50 percent tax would have almost halved the standard deviation in 1953 too.

Local radio and television revenues were not evenly distributed either. Although earnings from telecasts of games did not make up for the decline in gate revenue, at least an owner did not have to share what he got for television broadcast rights. In theory, even if television adversely affected the gate, an owner seeking his self-interest might still overdo telecasts of home games, reducing the collective revenue while benefiting his individual net revenue. For instance, an owner might have received $200,000 in television revenue (which he did not have to share), at the cost of $225,000 at the gate. Because of the gate-sharing rule, he might have had to pay $40,000 to the visitors, leaving only $185,000. One owner doing this would not be too detrimental, but all owners doing this would leave them worse off individually and collectively. In a sense, then, sharing television revenue might protect the owners from any destructive "beggar-thy-neighbor" temptations.

An extreme form of revenue sharing, such as a 50 percent tax on broadcast revenue, which would then be split evenly between all of the teams, would have narrowed the broadcast revenue disparities. In 1956 such a tax would have reduced Cleveland's revenues from broadcasting by over $250,000, for instance, and increased Kansas City's revenues by $150,000. Sharing broadcasting revenues might have made sense on an abstract level, but implementing such a policy would surely have proven difficult. The gate attendance was reasonably easily monitored. To divide the broadcasting revenues on a similar basis as the gate receipts would have required broadcast ratings information or an examination of a team's audited financial statements. In addition, the owners of teams in larger cities showed little sympathy for their brethren in smaller towns. Walter O'Malley of the Brooklyn Dodgers dismissed fellow owner Fred Saigh's view that his St. Louis Cardinals were entitled to some of the Dodgers' broadcast revenue by characterizing it as "socialism," a most unsavory epithet in the 1950s.[31]

When Bill Veeck, owner of the St. Louis Browns in 1953, challenged New York, Cleveland, and Boston for a share of their television money, the three teams allegedly froze him out by banning night home games with the Browns. The American League president, William Harridge, refused to put the question to a vote of American League owners. The three teams then rearranged their schedules to share more night games among themselves. In addition, Boston and Cleveland did not telecast their home games against St. Louis.[32] Veeck claimed, "On the basis of this disparity in radio-TV receipts alone, the Yankees could sign ten promising young players to each one that the Senators could sign. What chance do the Senators have under that sort of system? This doesn't make the Yankee officials wizards. It just makes them rich and the American League more lopsided each year. . . . One way to help equalize it . . . is to give the visiting club a share of the television loot."[33] Veeck did not mind the Yankees broadcasting games from St. Louis back to New York as, indeed, he claimed they could do for free.

The networks' telecasts of regular season games created additional disparities in revenues among teams. The CBS and NBC *Game of the Week*, for instance, typically shown on weekends, amplified the Yankees' advantage in television earnings. CBS paid $25,000 for each game to the home team, whereas visiting teams received nothing. If all of the teams were equally likely to host telecasts, then the revenue would have been evenly divided. CBS, however, preferred to showcase Yankees home games, and only the fact that the team was on the road for roughly half of the weekends throughout the season kept the Yankees from monopolizing the national telecasts. During the 1963 season CBS showed the Yankees twenty-four times out of forty-seven weekend games. According to Bill MacPhail, vice president of CBS Television Sports, and brother of Lee MacPhail, Yankees official, "We use the

Yankees most of the time because they are the biggest draw. We get a lot of letters saying that the name of the show should be *The Yankee Game of the Week*, but the Yankees are the draw."[34] As it was, CBS signed a five-year contract with the Yankees that devoted $450,000 of the network's $1 million annual budget to the Bronx Bombers. The American League did not have a rule requiring the visiting team to give permission for network television broadcasting of a game, allowing the Yankees to arrange with CBS to televise so many games nationally. Being the best draw guaranteed the team its $25,000 per game, while other teams were being "hammered down to a $10,000 figure."[35]

On NBC the Dodgers and Giants dominated the telecasts. As sportswriter Dick Young sarcastically noted, "This gets to be pretty dull for the Athletics and the Mets and the Senators and Angels—and all the poor slobs who aren't designed to compete with Ben Casey as TV attractions."[36] Occasionally, the Athletics and Senators got to appear as visiting cannon fodder, but of course, they received nothing for their appearances. Naturally, the other teams wanted some of the revenue. Calvin Griffith of the Twins pushed for the visiting team to receive 40 to 50 percent of the television revenue, and he was even willing to let the first division teams get a slightly higher cut. Yankees owner Dan Topping was not sympathetic: "If you carry this percentage thing for the visiting team all the way, you can go too far."[37] Yet by 1965 even the Yankees acceded to paying some of their television money to the visiting team, as the American League decided, in 1964, to grant visiting teams 25 percent of the television revenue from local telecasts.[38]

Finally, as the data demonstrates, the most effective way for moribund franchises to strengthen their financial status was to relocate. The moves to Kansas City and Baltimore improved those franchises' revenues and sharply reduced the standard deviation of team revenues.

Other Forms of Revenue Sharing

American League teams also resorted to their own form of revenue sharing. Between November 17, 1947, and July 1, 1951, the Browns sold twenty of their better players for over $1 million and twenty-eight lesser-known players.[39] The owners of the Browns, the DeWitt brothers, were widely criticized for their player sales, with some rival owners viewing the brothers as "parasites, who feed on the drawing power of the better teams while on the road and keep themselves weak and without support at home."[40] In other cases during the 1930s and 1940s financially stronger teams sometimes made direct cash subsidies or bailouts to the weaker franchises. Even in the postwar period, the American League occasionally made loans to such teams as the Browns.[41] A shift of a few hundred thousand dollars to the weaker franchises might have enabled them to retain rather than to sell a star or two, or the owners of weak franchises might have simply kept the cash and still sold the players.

The Browns' method of remaining solvent was not popular with the other clubs and may have discouraged them from implementing a different revenue-sharing plan. In the same way that politically conservative fears that generous welfare or unemployment benefits will demoralize recipients, baseball owners may have felt that a generous revenue-sharing plan might tempt some of their fellows to save on players' salaries and field a rotten team.

Revenue sharing in the form of gate sharing has the potential to redistribute revenue significantly within a professional sports league. The experience of the postwar American League, however, demonstrates the difficulty in implementing a plan that does not have "perverse" effects. The league's experiences also shows that in some cases a team's playing strength positively affects its ability to draw on the road, contrary to the assumptions economists often make.

Because the perennially strong Yankees drew well on the road, the league's gate-sharing plan had only modest effects on redistributing revenue across the American League. Indeed, such "middle-class" teams as the Chicago White Sox and Detroit Tigers were likely to lose more from the redistribution than the Yankees. A tax that was evenly split among all of the teams in the league, thereby severing the link between a team's playing strength and its ability to draw on the road, offered greater potential for redistributing revenue. Obviously, such a plan also promised to be less viable politically, as the Yankees and other wealthy teams would oppose more effective redistribution. The existing revenue plan had the possibility of helping the Yankees, and perhaps garnering their vote in support, while at most inflicting minor revenue losses on them. Another more effective way to create increased revenue parity was to relocate franchises. Even though the American League missed the opportunity to shift two of its three weakest franchises to Los Angeles and San Francisco, the eventual relocations to Baltimore, Kansas City, and Minneapolis–St. Paul reduced the revenue disparity more than the gate-sharing plan did. Ironically, by playing to larger crowds in the new cities, the Yankees gained from these relocations too.

7

Isn't Anybody Going to Help That Game?

Baseball Attempts to Rejuvenate Its Popularity

Given the Yankees' continued success and its deleterious effect upon attendance, did the rival American League owners attempt any innovations to redress the imbalance? Woeful teams had access to an untapped source of playing talent: black players. The population shifts of the 1940s and 1950s made new cities attractive alternatives to the decaying eastern cities. Finally, poorer teams could push for new rules pertaining to players, especially amateurs. Which innovations did teams use, and how well did these efforts improve their fortunes?

Integration

The National League's Brooklyn Dodgers and their general manager, Branch Rickey, demonstrated the potential gains from hiring black players. Jackie Robinson won the Rookie of the Year award in 1947 while helping the Dodgers to their first pennant since 1941. The team reported growth of over $100,000 in consolidated profits between 1946 and 1947.[1] Yet Robinson did not bolster the Dodgers attendance much, which rose by about eleven thousand compared with the previous season. Unfortunately, the Dodgers did not list their ticket prices for 1946–47, so it is uncertain whether they raised ticket prices for Robinson's debut. While attendance at Ebbets Field did not rise much, the league enjoyed a record-breaking attendance that would not be surpassed until 1960. The Dodgers did set a franchise road attendance record in 1947 by playing before 1.86 million fans.[2] The Dodgers led the Major Leagues in road attendance for the decade 1946–55. The team attracted sixteen million fans on the road, while the St. Louis Cardinals had the second-best road record with only twelve million.

Branch Rickey's acumen paid off for the Dodgers, as they won six pennants in the ten years coinciding with Jackie Robinson's Major League career. The Giants, another early proponent of signing black players, finished first in 1951 and 1954. The 1948 Boston Braves and 1950 Philadelphia Phillies would be the last two National League pennant winners without a black player. The Braves would sign Henry Aaron and Wes Covington and acquire Billy Bruton, and these three played key roles for the Braves' pennant-winning 1957 and 1958 clubs.

Certainly, the pioneer of integration in the American League, Bill Veeck, reaped immediate benefits, winning a title in 1948 and setting attendance records with the help of Larry Doby and an elderly, by baseball standards, Satchel Paige. Veeck had formulated an audacious wartime plan. In 1944 he attempted to buy the Philadelphia Phillies. He hoped to sign a number of black players in an attempt to win the pennant during the talent-starved 1944 season. He made the mistake of informing commissioner Judge Kenesaw Landis of his plan. Shortly thereafter, the Phillies owner sold the team to William Cox, and the integration plan died.[3] The Indians attempted to exploit their connections with black baseball further by signing Luke Easter in 1949, and he had three solid seasons for them. The Indians were pioneers in signing black players, but they were also quick to trade or release them. They signed Sam Jones and Harry Simpson in 1951 but traded both of them by 1955. The Indians also signed Minnie Minoso, but he needed further seasoning before reaping his greatest fame with the Chicago White Sox.

The Browns (1947), White Sox (1951), and Athletics (1953) had little success from their first few black players. The Washington Senators had been pioneers in signing players from the Caribbean, but they were slower in signing black players. Washington owner Clark Griffith was openly dubious of Branch Rickey's integration plan: "Rickey's busting up the Negro leagues. We ain't ready for colored players." Yet Robinson's success changed Griffith's mind, and he pursued such luminaries as Larry Doby.[4] Washington signed Carlos Paula in 1954. Paula had a decent year in 1955, hitting .299, but his batting average and career plunged in 1956. Detroit signed Ozzie Virgil in 1958, while Boston waited until 1959 to play Elijah "Pumpsie" Green. Neither of these players became stars. The Red Sox's problematic relationships with black players is well chronicled in Howard Bryant's book *Shut Out*.[5] Apparently, the Red Sox had opportunities to sign Jackie Robinson and Willie Mays but chose not to.

What about the mighty New York Yankees? They introduced Elston Howard in 1955 and later traded for Harry Simpson and Hector Lopez in 1957 and 1959. The latter two players had respectable careers, and in 1963 Howard became the first black player to win the Most Valuable Player (MVP) Award in the American League. He also won two Gold Gloves for his catching prowess.

In retrospect, however, it is shocking to see how poorly the American League did in signing black players. Doby, Easter, Minoso, and some of the others were solid players (Doby and Minoso were elected to the Hall of Fame), but none of them compiled the numbers or reaped the awards that the early black players did in the National League. Jackie Robinson won the Major Leagues' Rookie of the Year Award in 1947. After Alvin Dark (a southern-born white), black players, including Willie Mays, won the next five Rookie of the Year Awards in the National League. From 1956 through 1959 another three black players won the award, and all reached the Hall of Fame: Frank Robinson, Orlando Cepeda, and Willie McCovey. Given that Hank Aaron, Ernie Banks, and Roberto Clemente did not win the award, one gets the idea of the depth of the talent influx (Aaron and Banks lost out to Wally Moon in 1954, while Clemente lost to Bill Virdon in 1955).

Jackie Robinson was also the first black to win the National League's Most Valuable Player Award in 1949. Again, he was a harbinger, as black players won eight out of the next nine and ten out of the next twelve of the awards between 1951 and 1962. Black players also won five consecutive MVP awards between 1965 and 1969, including Hall of Fame players Mays, Clemente, Cepeda, McCovey, and Bob Gibson. Black players also dominated the National League Gold Glove awards for outfielders, although Ernie Banks, John Roseboro, Bill White, and Maury Wills also won awards as infielders and catchers. While Latin player Luis Aparicio helped make frequent base stealing a weapon again in the Major Leagues, black National League players such as Maury Wills and Lou Brock truly reinvigorated the base-running game. A black Brooklyn Dodger pitcher, Don Newcombe, also won the first Cy Young Award in 1956, but there would be a lengthy wait, twelve years, before a second black player, Bob Gibson, won the coveted pitching award. Black National League sluggers dominated the homerun charts, and by the mid-1970s, of the top ten lifetime homerun hitters, five were from the group integrating baseball in the mid-1950s.

In contrast, Elston Howard was the American League's first Most Valuable Player in 1963, and Tommie Agee was the league's first black Rookie of the Year in 1966. Vida Blue was the first black American League Cy Young winner in 1971. Minnie Minoso was on the inaugural Gold Glove Award list, and Vic Power joined Minoso on subsequent lists (winning ten Gold Gloves between them). If you compare the number of black National Leaguers in the Hall of Fame to black American Leaguers, you get a stark contrast.[6]

Of the ten black players with the highest total baseball rankings who debuted between 1947 and 1959, eight were National Leaguers, including the top seven:

Willie Mays	95.9
Henry Aaron	89.1
Frank Robinson	77.0
Roberto Clemente	42.2
Willie McCovey	37.3

Jackie Robinson	32.0
Ernie Banks	26.9
Minnie Minoso	26.0
Larry Doby	22.7
Roy Campanella	22.5

The National League's advantage in signing top black players continued into the 1960s with Dick Allen, Joe Morgan, Willie Stargell, Billy Williams, and Jim Wynn. The American League's best black debuts included Reggie Smith and, later, Reggie Jackson. National League pitchers such as Bob Gibson, Fergie Jenkins, and Don Newcombe were easily the best black pitchers during the first twenty years of black participation in Major League Baseball.

During 1946–64 the top National League rookies compiled much higher combined total baseball rankings (TBR) than did their American League counterparts. Of the rookies represented in table 2.1, the combined National League TBR was 50 percent greater than that of the American League. American League teams had six of the seven least productive groups of rookie stars during the era.

Despite the wealth of talent available, some Major League teams lagged in canvassing widely for black players. Sportswriter Harold Rosenthal noted in 1953 that some teams were just beginning to scout black players at the sandlot level and not just in the Negro League and other higher-level leagues.[7] Nevertheless, a decade after Rickey's innovation, sportswriter James Murray wrote, "Jackie Robinson, it is my intention to prove, was to the National League what Babe Ruth was to the American. He was a revolution. The sociological aspects of his advent are not germane here—and it is to Rickey's credit that he never claimed he had any in mind."[8] Murray pointed out that the National League appeared stronger than the American League, primarily because the owners in the older league searched for the best black and white talent, whereas the American League owners were not as aggressive in signing top black talent. Sportswriter Al Hirshberg also believed that National League dominance could be traced to the

American League's delay in signing black players.[9] During the 1960 season the National League had "four times as many Negroes as the American has, and certainly all the outstanding ones."[10]

Aside from Cleveland and Chicago, why did the other American League teams haltingly and ineptly seek black talent in their attempt to overtake the Yankees? Chicago and Cleveland were the only two teams to interrupt the Yankees' eighteen-year reign. Were some owners afraid of their fans' reaction to signing blacks? Note, however, that a "southern" team such as the St. Louis Browns signed blacks early on. Unfortunately for the Browns, they signed mediocre talent. Thus, they found themselves in the worst possible situation: possibly antagonizing white fans while reaping little benefit on the field from their black players. Given the Browns' horrendous attendance, perhaps the team did not have many fans to worry about offending. At least the Dodgers and Indians found players who helped them win, regardless of their fans' reactions.[11]

When Jackie Robinson and Roy Campanella transformed Brooklyn into the National League's powerhouse, the other New York teams quickly tried to sign black players. The Giants and Yankees quickly signed five black players, including Monte Irvin. The Yankees announced their signing of Artie Wilson and Louis Marquez in 1949. Unfortunately for the Yankees, Bill Veeck also claimed Wilson. Eventually, the two teams settled their dispute, with Wilson going to the Yankees and Marquez to the Indians. Although each player eventually played in the Major Leagues, neither was even a journeyman; Wilson got only twenty at bats in the Majors, all with the New York Giants. Sportswriter Dan Daniel cited an incentive for the Yankees to sign good black talent: "Acquisition of Negro players became a matter of financial wisdom . . . for the Yankees. In Newark, the Eagles of the Negro National League have gone out of business, leaving the entire Negro clientele open to an invitation from the Bears." In addition, the Black Yankees disbanded, leaving Yankee Stadium without an attraction for blacks.[12] Yet the Yankees would not field a black player for several more years.

While Elston Howard was the first black player to play for the

Yankees, he had competition from Vic Power, a Puerto Rican black. The Yankees, like Brooklyn before them, were cautious in their choice of the first black to wear the pinstripes. Power was a superb fielder who wielded a respectable bat, and he would be on four All-Star teams during his career. Yet he was outspoken and flashy. Even worse from the Yankees management's point of view, Power allegedly dated white women, this at a time when racial discrimination was still prevalent. Indeed, Power was probably everything the Yankees feared in a black player. A New York sports editor unctuously claimed that "the first requisite of a Yankee is that he be a gentleman, something that has nothing to with race, color, or creed." Some of the Yankees' contemporary white players—Whitey Ford, Mickey Mantle, and Billy Martin—were not known for their perfect decorum, although, to be fair to the Yankees, Martin's imbroglios led to his being consigned to baseball's Siberia in Kansas City (apparently Mantle and Ford were too valuable to be exiled).[13] The Yankees claimed when trading Power to the Kansas City Athletics that he had failed to "hustle." Power retorted, "They were just looking for excuses. . . . What did they want me to do? Mow the lawn in the outfield after the game was over?" The initial press reports implied, however, that George Weiss knew Power was a good prospect who had led the American Association in batting average in 1953: "We did not want to lose Power. But the Athletics would not make the deal without him being included. He was the first player they asked for."[14] Conversely, Howard was described as a "clean-cut religious young man who has his sizeable feet planted firmly on the ground. . . . The brown-skinned All-America boy—he skips coffee and says he rarely sips a beer."[15]

According to the *New York Times*, the Yankees had been publicly criticized for not having any black players. Weiss emphasized that "color played no part in the Yankee decision to let Vic go." He defended his trade of Power: "It would be weak to hold Power just because we were afraid of censure. We showed our good faith toward Negro players by bringing up Power and Howard and will bring up others to the Yankees when they merit it." He also stated, "I see no reason why a Negro player should be differentiated from a white, or why a promising deal should be passed up because of fear of criticism." The sportswriter quoting Weiss agreed with him: "No reasonable mind would quarrel with this view. Pressure groups and spurious liberals have been badgering Weiss for some time. That he has refused to be intimidated is to his credit. Weiss is not a social worker. He's a baseball man, his job is to win pennants."[16] The Yankees acquired veteran first baseman Eddie Robinson in the Power trade, although they considered pitcher Harry Byrd as the key acquisition.[17] In addition, the Yankees had rookie Bill "Moose" Skowron ready for the Major Leagues, and Skowron proved a solid, if not spectacular, player.

Howard's path to the Major Leagues took a detour, when the Yankees converted him into a catcher. Given that two-time Most Valuable Player "Yogi" Berra was the Yankees catcher and the team's surfeit of catching talent, including future all-star Gus Triandos, some critics believed that the switch was just a delaying tactic: "For years I defended the Yankees. After watching developments this spring, however, I am convinced they don't want a Negro player; they want a Negro superman."[18] Indeed, the Yankees would initially use Howard in the outfield.[19] Howard, himself, remained patient: "I never had the feeling that the Yankees really didn't want to bring me up [to the Majors]." The switch worked, and, indeed, Howard developed into a Gold Glove catcher as well as a Most Valuable Player. Howard's quiet, uncomplaining attitude eased his way onto the Yankees roster, with later American League president Lee MacPhail (son of former Yankees co-owner and general manager Larry MacPhail) believing that "the Yankees were very anxious that the first black player that they brought up would be somebody with the right type of character. Elston was ideal."

Even after Howard reached the Major Leagues, however, the Yankees management sometimes lapsed into crude behavior, with Casey Stengel complaining (joking?), "When I finally get a nigger, I get the only one that can't run." Howard was more conciliatory. He noted that initially he could not stay in the team's hotel during spring training until owners

Topping and Webb interceded. Casey Stengel stood up for him, too, when Kansas City and Chicago restaurants would not serve him:

> In Kansas City and Chicago they wouldn't serve me in the restaurants until Stengel raised hell. Stengel told the hotel, "We came as a ball club and Elston Howard is part of the ball club. If he can't be accommodated, we'll leave." I never heard anything nasty raised from any of the other ball clubs, because if I had there would have been a fight. I just couldn't have taken what Jackie [Robinson] took. I was born in St. Louis and I came up in the ghetto areas. Any time I heard a man say "nigger" or "black so-and-so," I was ready to fight.[20]

Howard further recalled that Yankee players included him in their leisure-time activities. He later expressed disappointment that the team did not hire him as its manager, even after he had coached for the team for over a decade. His wife commented, "[Elston's] dream was to manage the Yankees. We always thought that since they acted like great white liberals, they might give Elston a chance. Elston wondered why he had to be better than everyone else, why he had to be superman to manage a baseball team. They wanted you to have a Ph.D. to manage if you were black, and about any white guy could manage. To Elston, it was like a slap to the face."[21]

Because of their championship status, the Yankees probably had less need to innovate by integrating. Certainly, the team's owners were not ahead of the changing social mores, but they were not the most reactionary either. Given the relative ease of getting top-flight black players (the Major League teams blithely raided the Negro Leagues, leaving behind little compensation), the Yankees certainly could have obtained even greater talent. For instance, had they been a little more aggressive, the Yankees could have had Ernie Banks. During the early 1950s Banks played for the Negro League Kansas City Monarchs. Three Major League teams bid for Banks's services—the Cubs, White Sox, and Yankees. The Yankees had plenty of opportunity to scout Banks out, given that the Monarchs played in the Yankees' Kansas City Minor League stadium. Moreover, the Yankees knew their current shortstop, Phil Rizzuto, was fading. Finally, Banks wanted to play for the Yankees and, given his friendly disposition, would have been a "good fit" for the Yankees. The Chicago Cubs proved more aggressive, however, and purchased Banks.[22] The Yankees eventually used Tony Kubek at shortstop, but he hit 450 fewer homeruns than Banks. Upon his resignation as Yankees general manager, Weiss claimed that since 1948 the Yankees had spent $500,000 in their search for Negro players; he denied that the Yankees turned down Willie Mays.[23]

Was there an economic incentive influencing the Yankees' hesitancy in playing blacks? In addition to having a black team playing in its Minor League stadium, the Yankees collected rent money from other black teams playing in Yankee Stadium. According to the *Sporting News*, Negro League teams used four of the Yankees' Major and Minor League ballparks. This relationship between the Yankees and Negro League teams dated back to at least the 1920s, as the Yankees' financial records held by the National Baseball Hall of Fame attest. The Yankees got $125,000 just from the rental of their stadium.[24] The Brooklyn Dodgers did not have a lucrative stadium rental agreement with the Negro League, so the Dodgers did not have any reason to hesitate, as did the Yankees, in raiding the Negro League of players. Clearly, the Yankees could not plead ignorance regarding the talent residing on the black teams. One of their tenants, Effa Manley of the Newark Eagles, offered Larry Doby to the Yankees for $100,000 before selling him to Bill Veeck's Cleveland Indians for $10,000 and an additional $5,000 if he remained on Cleveland's roster. Apparently, the Yankees did not believe Doby was as talented as reputed, and in 1949 sportswriter Dan Daniel wrote that "the Yankees . . . are kicking themselves that they let Doby get away from them."[25] Note that although Veeck was a visionary and one of the more liberal owners, he was conscious of the need to drive a hard bargain. According to historian Mark Ribowsky, Manley complained to Veeck, "You know, if Larry Doby were white, and a free agent, you'd give him a hundred thousand dollars to sign as a bonus . . . [but] I'm in no position to be bargaining with you." Manley felt pressured by black-owned newspapers that chided her for delaying Doby's debut.[26]

The Yankees also may not have felt as compelled to sign black players, as their Minor League organization still churned out good prospects. While Yankees rookies did not win as many Rookie of the Year Awards as did Brooklyn/Los Angeles Dodgers rookies, the Yankees still had a disproportionate number of such recipients. Gil McDougald (1951), Bob Grim (1954), Tony Kubek (1957), Tom Tresh (1962), Stan Bahnsen (1968), and Thurman Munson (1970) won Rookie of the Year awards. The Yankees also introduced Johnny Kucks, Bobby Murcer (the "next Mickey Mantle"), Joe Pepitone, Bill Skowron, and Tom Sturdivant as well as the more famous Whitey Ford, Elston Howard, and Mickey Mantle. At one point in the late 1950s the Yankees had introduced the most players into the Major Leagues: 43 of the 318 current Major League regulars were originally Yankees. In addition, the Yankees still had an unmatched ability to purchase or trade for needed talent. Yet the franchise would suffer from the premature fading (due to injuries) of Mickey Mantle and Roger Maris. Ironically, even by 1959, Paul Richards, Baltimore Orioles general manager, said that the Yankee farm system was not producing enough talent.[27] By 1969, for instance, the Yankee infield of Joe Pepitone, Horace Clarke, Gene Michael, and Jerry Kenney proved as mediocre as any the Yankees had ever fielded. Journeymen Jake Gibbs and Ron Woods also played regularly. The Yankees, like most of their American League rivals, sorely missed a star of the caliber of Aaron, Mays, or Frank Robinson.

Franchise Relocation

A second form of innovation tried by owners in an effort to strengthen weaker teams was for the moribund American League franchises to move to better locations. The Philadelphia Athletics, St. Louis Browns, and Washington Senators drew the smallest crowds in the American League. By 1961 all three teams would be relocated: St. Louis to Baltimore, Philadelphia to Kansas City, and Washington to Minneapolis. In the National League the Boston Braves transferred to Milwaukee in 1953. According to 1950 census information, the counties containing Boston, Philadelphia, and St. Louis had the lowest "median income (counting families and unrelated individuals) of any cities with Major League Baseball teams in 1949. Philadelphia, St. Louis, and Washington DC also had the highest proportions of blacks. The teams that relocated between 1953 and 1961 typically did not go to cities with higher median incomes, as Milwaukee and San Francisco were the only cases in which the median incomes in the SMSA were higher than in the original cities. In most of the other cases the median incomes were relatively close to those in the original cities.[28]

How well did the franchise relocations of the 1950s work for the American League? The St. Louis Browns averaged over three hundred thousand fans per season during their last five years. At times many of the teams in the Pacific Coast, International, and American Association Minor Leagues outdrew the Browns. The Browns barely survived by selling off their best players and by receiving loans from other American League owners. During the four years leading up to the team's relocation, the Browns sold forty-eight players for over a $1 million and received $300,000 in loans.[29] According to a February 1949 *Baseball Digest* article, some observers thought that the Browns were divesting themselves of all of their Major League talent before selling the franchise: "The theory is that a major league franchise has a certain minimum value that can't be reduced even if no players of established major league caliber go with it, and, therefore, that the Browns simply are peddling everything salable before getting out of the baseball business."

The writer of the article concluded, however, that "[the Browns] recognize they can't draw much more poorly with no big leaguers in their lineup than they have drawn with a few, and that they may as well take advantage of their rivals' prosperity and cash in while the cash is good. It won't always be that way." Indeed, the writer complimented the team's owners, the DeWitt brothers: "The fabulous price on a player of something less than fabulous ability means simply that the Browns are in the happy position of being the only team in the major leagues with talent for sale in an era of cheap money." Ironically, Browns management blamed fans for not attending games: "Our fans don't seem to realize all the features the Browns have offered them that they don't get in other major league cities. We were the first to flash hits and errors on our big scoreboard. We're the only city in the country where the up-to-the-minute batting averages and pitching records of the players are carried on the scorecards. Besides that, we try to make our customers comfortable by renting them seat cushions, though in cities like Detroit, New York and Washington you don't have such a privilege offered you."[30]

The situation was so dire in St. Louis that both the Cardinals and Browns had previously investigated relocating. The Cardinals wanted to relocate to Detroit and share Navin Field with the Tigers, but naturally, the Tigers were lukewarm to the idea at best.[31] The Browns were planning to relocate to Los Angeles in 1941. The team's president, Donald Barnes, arranged for satisfactory air transportation, negotiated a settlement with Los Angeles Minor League team owner Philip Wrigley (for more money than Wrigley eventually received from Walter O'Malley of the Dodgers), and received guarantees from civic leaders in Los Angeles to subsidize any subpar attendance. Barnes was very thorough in arranging the deal, even securing the promise of $250,000 from Sam Breadon, the St. Louis Cardinals owner, to reward the Browns for leaving St. Louis. In addition, Breadon was to lobby for National League approval of the move.[32] Unfortunately for the Browns, the Japanese attacked Pearl Harbor on December 7, 1941, the day before Barnes could get the owners' approval, and his plan was never implemented. In response to his proposed trespass upon their territory, the Pacific Coast League got a new amendment passed that restricted the Major Leagues' ability to encroach upon Minor League territory.

Bill Veeck purchased the Browns and hoped to drive the Cardinals out of the city. When wealthy August Busch purchased the Cardinals, however, Veeck knew the Browns would be the team leaving St. Louis. Veeck then wanted to move the team to Baltimore but was stymied by his fellow owners, who did not like his iconoclasm. In addition, Baltimore's new stadium would not be available for the 1953 season. Later Veeck was forced out of owning the team, and the new owners moved the franchise to Baltimore.[33] With general manager Paul Richards's aggressive activities, the Orioles began their metamorphosis from the American League franchise with the worst win-loss record to one with the best. While the Orioles became successful on the field, they struggled to become equally successful at the gate. The franchise, with a somewhat less dismal record, averaged over 930,000 fans per season during its first five years in Baltimore. This number was a disappointment, as some observers expected twice as many fans per season during the first years of the relocation.[34] Part of the Orioles' difficulties may have arisen from competition from the resurrected Baltimore Colts football team in 1953.

Moving to Baltimore was a risky move for the Browns. The city's past Major League history had been uneven. The old Baltimore Orioles had won pennants from 1894 to 1896, finished second in 1897–98, and had held the National League's second best winning percentage over the eight-year period, 1892–99, trailing only Boston. Given their sterling record, the Orioles' annual average attendance of slightly more than two hundred thousand was lackluster, and, indeed, the Orioles barely outdrew the weak St. Louis Perfectos (later Cardinals) franchise. The St. Louis franchise possessed the worst record over the eight years, winning only 36 percent of its games. The two cities were similar in size, so Baltimore's poor attendance was puzzling. Regardless of the reasons for the disappointing crowds, the city gained a terrible reputation in the minds of baseball owners. The American League did not hesitate to move its Baltimore franchise to New York when an opportunity arose. Several Major League owners later heaped scorn upon Baltimore's bid for admission several years after the transfer. Charles Comiskey, owner of the Chicago White Sox, responded to the Baltimore Federal League club's application for a Major League franchise: "Baltimore is a minor league city and not a hell of a good one at that." Brooklyn Dodgers owner Charles Ebbet provided an additional explanation for the owners' disdain for the city: "You have too many colored population to start with. They are a cheap population when it gets down to paying their money at the gate."[35]

The modern team's history partially confirmed the owners' fears. The Baltimore Orioles' initial attendance mark of close to 1.07 million matched or surpassed the season attendance marks of the great championship clubs of 1969–71. Even the novelty of winning did not spur attendance. The Orioles became serious contenders as early as the 1960 season. In 1964 the team fought the Yankees for first place. On September 20 Baltimore played a Sunday doubleheader at Memorial Stadium. The team was just a half-game out of first place, but fewer than nine thousand fans showed up. According to Joseph Durso, "Natives explained the lack of interest by pointing out that the Baltimore Colts were playing on TV."[36] The club arranged for Saturday night doubleheaders, hoping to catch fans returning from the beach and also for cooler temperatures. It was not until the 1980s, and then the building of the Camden Yards Stadium in the 1990s, that the club became one of the "wealthy" teams that regularly attracted two million fans per season.

The Philadelphia Athletics, formerly a formidable rival to the Yankees, dismantled their great 1929–31 team by selling the likes of Mickey Cochrane, Jimmie Foxx, Lefty Grove, and Al Simmons. Owner and manager Connie Mack failed to rejuvenate his franchise after these sales, although the team had winning records in four out of six seasons between 1947 and 1952, finishing as high as fourth place in 1948. Thereafter, the team slumped badly, losing 198 games in the final two seasons in Philadelphia.[37] The Athletics, despite having essentially the same win-loss record for the first five years in Kansas City as the last five years in Philadelphia, saw attendance increase by 151 percent to just over a million per season. Unfortunately, the later trend in attendance in Kansas City was downward. From 1961 to 1967 the team struggled to average seven hundred thousand fans per season.

The Washington Senators, known for being "first in peace, first in war, and last in the American League," were actually respectable between 1919 and 1945 and won almost half of their games, including three pennants in ten years between 1924 and 1933. Unfortunately, the team suffered through its worst records during the postwar era. The Senators won exactly one more game than did the St. Louis/Baltimore franchise between 1946 and 1960, and both teams were about fourteen "games back" of the Philadelphia/Kansas City Athletics. Although the Senators had their best attendance since 1949 during their last season in Washington DC in 1960, the team drew 150 percent more fans during its first five seasons in Minnesota than it did during the last five years in Washington. Much of the increased attendance no doubt emanated from the team's far superior performance in Minnesota. The Twins won over half of their games during their first five seasons, capped by a World Series appearance in 1965. In comparison, the Senators won only two-fifths of their games during the final five years in the capital.

Regulars Bob Allison, Earl Battey, Harmon Killebrew, and Camilo Pascual showed promise, however, on that last Washington Senators team. The Twins drew 1.46 million fans during the pennant season of 1965, but this was not much higher than the numbers attracted in 1962 and 1963. Even worse, the 1965 attendance level would not be surpassed until 1984, despite two division titles in 1969 and 1970. The Senators' move was unique in that the team was the first to leave a single-team city. The Athletics, Braves, and Browns, like the Dodgers and Giants, all left multi-team cities. The Twin Cities enticed Calvin Griffith with a larger stadium and adequate parking. The stadium in Bloomington, Minnesota, initially had 3,500 parking spaces, with an opportunity to add another 11,500.[38]

The first National League franchise relocation fared better than did the American League's. Echoing the Major Leagues' complaints regarding Baltimore, the Boston Braves had a winning record over their final five seasons in Boston (although the team slumped badly in its last two seasons) but drew just over eight hundred thousand fans per season. Indeed, after the pennant-winning season of 1948, the team's attendance for the last four seasons declined precipitously, as fewer than three hundred thousand fans showed up in 1952. The Braves, usually less popular than the Red Sox, vacated the city and moved to Milwaukee in 1953. The team's success at the gate astounded the baseball world and got other owners dreaming of more lucrative venues. In addition, fellow National League owners shared $425,000 more in gate-sharing revenue in 1953 than in 1952 from the Braves. The team was spectacularly successful during its first five seasons in Milwaukee; having a pennant winner in 1957 and finishing second, just one game behind the Dodgers, in 1956 helped make the franchise's honeymoon a sweet one. The Braves' five-year attendance from 1953–57 rivaled the Los Angeles Dodgers' attendance during their first five years. Clearly, a smaller market with a successful team could rack up impressive attendance figures. Indeed, Walter O'Malley claimed that he could not compete with the Braves, given his situation in Brooklyn, as he feared that the Braves' greater income would enable them to field the largest and best farm system, gaining them a permanent advantage.[39]

Although Bill Veeck admitted his guilt in baseball's franchise relocation frenzy—in particular, the move by the Braves—he noted a key difference between the first three relocations and the subsequent ones: "The [earlier] moves were logical and probably inevitable. The later moves were more opportunistic and detrimental to the game's image." He added, "The picture of the traveling carnival and the floating crap game has come unmistakably into focus. Sweep into town, bleed it dry, fold your tent and beat the cops to the nearest freight yard."[40]

Although Baltimore, Kansas City, and Minnesota were improvements over their former venues, the Browns/Orioles, Athletics, and Senators/Twins may have bungled their chances for even better opportunities. During the controversy surrounding the sale and potential relocation of the Philadelphia Athletics, much comment was made concerning the possibility of preempting any National League shift to the potentially lucrative West Coast. American League owners coveted the Los Angeles and San Francisco markets, but they wanted two teams to relocate west in order to save on travel expenses. With the Orioles ensconced in Baltimore in 1954, the American League owners were less enthusiastic about relocating the Athletics to the West Coast, and the team temporarily moved to the smaller city of Kansas City. The *New York Times* commented on the move: "A year ago the American League might have done something since it had two weak franchises in St. Louis and Philadelphia. But the Brownies became the Baltimore Orioles. . . . That leaves the Athletics all alone. The National League, which would love to tap the rich Coast territory, is practically embarrassed to discover that it has no weak franchises."[41]

The American League owners also were worried about the lack of a large stadium on the West Coast. They were concerned, too, about the added travel expense.[42] Regardless of the Orioles' on-the-field success, the league probably would have been stronger if, say, the Browns and Athletics had co-opted the Los Angeles and San Francisco areas. Bill Veeck went on a fact-finding trip to California in the summer of 1953, but he was unable to move the Browns there.[43] According to sportswriter Edgar Williams, Yankees owner Del Webb wanted the Browns to relocate to Los Angeles but could not pull it off, perhaps because of the other owners' animosity toward Veeck.[44] By relocating the Browns to Baltimore, the league may have further imperiled the already tottering Washington Senators franchise. When the American League moved into California during the 1960s, the National League Dodgers were entrenched in Los Angeles and the Giants were in San Francisco.

Given Congress's clamor for Major League Baseball in the burgeoning cities of the West and South and legislators' willingness to threaten baseball's antitrust exemption, an expansion out of the Midwest also promised to generate political goodwill. The American League owners chose not to make the more dramatic shift to the West Coast until the 1961 expansion to California, however, while replacing the Senators in Washington DC; neither move stemmed the Yankees juggernaut, nor did the moves dramatically improve attendance.

The American League expansion team in Los Angeles, the Angels, drew only 604,000 fans in its inaugural season. Although a surprise third-place finish in 1962 almost doubled attendance, the franchise faltered at the gate and averaged only 716,000 fans during its final three seasons in Los Angeles. Thereafter, the franchise shifted to Anaheim, where it eventually attracted over two million fans per season on a consistent basis. Still, the American League's southern California franchise was second-rate compared with the Dodgers.

All in all, then, the franchise relocations of the weaker teams during the 1950s, as well as those of the Dodgers and Giants, benefited, to varying degrees, the teams that moved and eliminated five cities that potentially could have been included in a new Major League. Surprisingly, the departure of one franchise in multi-franchise cities did not herald an era of prosperity for the remaining team. The Philadelphia Phillies attendance increased by only forty thousand per season in the five years after the Athletics left, compared with the five seasons leading up to the move. While the increase in attendance was probably dampened by the Phillies' inferior performance, about ten wins fewer per season post-Athletics, the Phillies did not become prosperous upon the departure of the Athletics. The St. Louis Cardinals also declined after the Browns left the city, both on the field and in the stands. The Cardinals won an average of ten fewer games per season in the first five post-Browns seasons, compared with the last five seasons of the Browns' residency, and the attendance fell off by thirty-three thousand per season. While the attendance decline might have been greater had the Browns remained, clearly the team's departure did not usher in good times for the Cardinals.

The Boston Red Sox suffered the worst of the now single-franchise cities. The Red Sox had been pennant contenders in 1948–50 with strong attendance. The team tailed off by 1952 but never became truly awful and still drew more than a million fans. The Red Sox were the favorite team in Boston, even outdrawing the pennant-winning Braves in 1948, when the Red Sox finished second after a one-game playoff. After the Braves left, the Red Sox won eight more games in 1953 than in 1952 but drew one hundred thousand fewer fans. For the five-year period after the Braves left, the Red Sox averaged almost three hundred thousand fewer fans per season. While a poorer record hurt attendance (nine fewer wins per season), the Red Sox fared badly by any standard. Finally, the Yankees had New York to themselves for four seasons until the Mets began playing in 1962. The Yankees won eight pennants between 1953 and 1962 (four in the first five-year period and four in the second five-year period). The Yankees drew an average of seventy thousand more fans in the absence of the Dodgers and Giants, so there is little evidence that National League fans in New York fled to Yankee Stadium in the Bronx to assuage their loss.[45]

Did the holdover teams take advantage of their monopoly status by hiking ticket prices? The Boston Red Sox did not raise ticket prices in 1953, but the team did increase prices in 1954. The ticket prices had remained steady since 1946, however, so the increase might have occurred even if the Braves had remained in Boston. The Cardinals hiked ticket prices for some box seats after the Browns left the city, but they reduced general admission and bleacher prices at the same time. The Phillies only increased their general admission ticket prices in the wake of the Athletics' move. The team did not raise prices in 1956. In some of these cases the remaining team may not have had time to change ticket prices, as the Braves relocated shortly before the season. The New York Yankees and Baltimore Orioles did not change their prices after the Dodgers, Giants, and Senators left the vicinity. The Yankees did raise box and reserved prices in 1959, but such prices had been constant since 1955. The Orioles did not raise prices in 1961. Thus, the holdover teams did not appear very opportunistic when they had a city or region to themselves. Sports economists have suggested that the owners of the Cardinals, Phillies, Red Sox, and Yankees found that fans of the dearly departed franchises did not immediately switch their loyalty to the remaining team.[46]

The Amateur Draft

Weaker teams could lobby to change the rules in hopes of promoting competitive parity. Player control was a controversial issue throughout the postwar era. As some teams created large farm systems, controlling hundreds of players, critics charged the talent-rich teams, such as the

Cardinals, Dodgers, and Yankees of signing a disproportionate share of and hoarding good prospects. The Yankees, for instance, at various times had Elston Howard, Sherm Lollar, and Gus Triandos behind Yogi Berra at catcher. The charge was damaging because the weaker teams lacked good talent and the players stagnating on the farms lost potential earnings.[47] The critics were rarely able to demonstrate, however, that many talented players languished an inordinate length of time in the Minors. Indeed, the Yankees found it advantageous to trade Lollar and Triandos rather than maintain their surfeit of catchers.

The Yankees and Dodgers sold or traded many of their promising Minor League players throughout the postwar period. Still, the charge that a team such as the Yankees controlled vast legions of potential Major League stars rankled fans and pundits alike and, worse, attracted congressional attention. Other baseball officials believed that competitive parity might have been better served if Major League teams had a limit on how long they could control such players.[48]

The Yankees appeared to sign a disproportionate number of talented kids during the 1950s. While opponents bemoaned New York's ability to sign amateur players, the Yankees were quick to exploit their advantage. The Yankees provided a "little green book designed to sell big green kids on a career in the Bronx. 'Play Ball with the Yankees' points out that the Mighty Magnets have landed in seventeen World Series in the past thirty years." Not leaving anything to chance, the Yankees also featured a photo of Joe DiMaggio "getting a Cadillac from his adulators: 'Thank the Good Lord for making me a Yankee.'"[49] Yet the Yankees did not rely solely upon slick brochures. Paul Richards cited not only the Yankees' vast farm system but the team's dedication to superior scouting, teaching, and esprit.[50] Conversely, other teams tried to lure youngsters away from the Yankees by pointing out the club's surfeit of talent, as presumably a youngster might fear the greater competition and sign with a weaker club, where advancement was more likely. Yankees scout Paul Kritchell responded by telling young players, "No club ever has enough really good ballplayers."[51] In addition, the Yankees were the first Major League team to set up a spring training instructional school, where Minor League players received coaching from Casey Stengel and his coaching staff; thus, Stengel could see talented prospects for himself, while the kids gained valuable training in the ways of being a New York Yankee. Yankees veteran Jerry Coleman believed that the Yankees were adept at creating an esprit de corps, which he compared with his experience in the United States Marine Corps. Other teams quickly imitated the Yankees and started their own instructional schools.[52]

The Yankees were not one of the most aggressive employers of large bonuses. The largest bonuses paid by the Yankees during the 1950s went to pitcher Ed Cereghino ($70,000) and Andy Carey ($65,000). Marv Throneberry received $50,000, Bobby Brown got $60,000, and Tommy Carroll got $40,000.[53] The reader should note that none of these bonus babies were African-American. Then again, few African-American players received large bonuses from any team. By 1960, however, the club changed its thinking. With the ouster of George Weiss, new general manager Roy Hamey resorted to paying high bonuses, which the team could afford. He signed Howard Kitt in 1960 for $80,000: "We are convinced that in order to keep our roster stocked for the achievement of pennants, we must adopt a more combative role in the nationwide fight for fine prospects. We have to meet and overcome the rugged competition in this field which is offered by Los Angeles and Milwaukee of the National [League] in particular."[54]

Some baseball executives favored an unrestricted draft of Minor League players compared with the existing system. Organized baseball held a draft of Minor League players once a year. Indeed, this draft, beginning with Major League teams selecting unprotected Minor Leaguers, created a reaction that percolated down through the layers of Minor League Baseball. A Major League club could draft two Minor Leaguers, and its Minor League clubs in turn could make their draft picks later. Each team paid a specific amount for each draftee.[55]

This draft of Minor League players did little, however, to redress competitive imbalance, as most of the players available were mediocre at best. Moreover, George Trautman claimed that over "the last few years the so-called second division clubs are the clubs that do not draft."[56] Yet the facts dispute Trautman's recollections. During a four-year period, 1956–59, a total of forty-six Minor League players were drafted. The Dodgers and Yankees did not draft any players, while Kansas City and Washington combined to draft seven players. The Cubs, Phillies, Pirates, and Reds drafted twelve players between them. Most were nonentities, but a few, such as Gary Geiger, Jerry Lynch, Claude Raymond, and Tony Taylor had lengthy, if undistinguished, Major League careers.[57]

Baltimore general manager and manager Paul Richards argued for an unrestricted, reverse-order draft of Minor League players not protected on the forty-player rosters. Such a draft could have eroded the Yankees' stockpile of Minor League talent.[58] Frank Lane also pressed for exposing all Minor Leaguers not on the forty-player roster to a draft each year. The owners approved a compromise plan in late 1958 whereby all first-year Minor League players would be exposed to a draft but would be protected thereafter under the existing rules; this approach became known as the first-year rule.[59] The Yankees, via general manager George Weiss, opposed the plan, as did fellow World Series participant Milwaukee. Weiss said piously, "If baseball legislation is to be based on such selfish reasoning and not what is good for the game, the National Pastime as we have known it is indeed on perilous ground."[60]

Although the first-year player rule was designed to help the weaker teams sign players and thereby promote competitive balance, several teams argued that these weaker teams could not protect enough players to build rapidly. Possibly buttressing this argument was Yankee general manager Ralph Houk's (perhaps Machiavellian) statement: "I think the present first-year rule definitely helps the weaker clubs, and specifically the expansion clubs. As of now, I'm for the rule until somebody can suggest something better."[61]

Some owners also favored a restriction on signing amateur players, perhaps via a reverse-order draft; under such a draft the team with the worst win-loss record the previous season drafted first. Such a system held two attractions: helping promote competitive balance and curbing payments to the youngsters. Despite the ostensible potential of fostering competitive balance, the Major Leagues were hesitant to imitate other professional sports by implementing such a draft. Initially, seven American League teams voted against the measure, with one club abstaining.[62]

Why did the teams oppose a draft of amateur players? First, some of them preferred the status quo, despite the rising bonuses. The wealthier teams typically used their advantages in revenue to outbid their less wealthy peers. Walter O'Malley feared the Milwaukee Braves precisely because the large crowds flocking to Braves games made Milwaukee a fierce competitor for amateur players. Thus, the stronger teams were against "socialism" in signing amateur players. Second, some baseball officials opposed the amateur draft because they worried about the legal ramifications of drafting seventeen-year-old players.

Whatever their legal fears, owners eventually implemented a reverse-order draft in 1965. Some observers attributed part of the Yankees' decline to their inability to sign a preponderance of amateur talent because of the draft. Baseball economists are dubious about the effects of a reverse-order draft upon competitive balance. Recall the previous story of the Browns signing Mickey Mantle. Suppose, instead, that the Browns, having finished last, selected Mickey Mantle as the number one pick in the draft. If Mantle became a star, the same impetus to trade him to the Yankees would still exist (ignoring the possible adverse fan reaction in St. Louis). The draft, then, provides a windfall to the last-place team (which can sell its talented youngsters) without affecting competitive balance. Yet the seemingly plausible effect on competitive balance provided camouflage for the owners' real reason for promoting the amateur draft: to curb bonuses. A *New York Times* sportswriter appeared to understand the draft's effect upon competitive balance: "A secondary purpose, at least theoretically, is to produce a more even distribution of talent over a period of time." The writer had earlier stated, however, that "the motivating force is clear": "Competitive bidding for young prospects has pushed bonus payments as high as $200,000 for one untried player in recent years. . . . By 'drafting' exclusive negotiating rights to a player, each club will be freed of the necessity of matching some other club's offer."[63]

Baseball researcher David Thomas presents evidence that the reverse-order aspect of the draft is less powerful than one might expect because of the difficulty of predicting stardom. Unlike football and basketball, in which most of the players have played in college and are older, many baseball draftees are selected right out of high school (although the college teams do provide a significant proportion of the amateur draftees). Major League teams with good scouting and good luck could transcend a lowly draft status. In the very first draft the Cincinnati Reds, who had finished second in 1964 and therefore had a late position in the draft order, selected future Hall of Fame catcher Johnny Bench as well as longtime players Bernie Carbo and Hal McRae. Certainly, the last place Athletics and Mets of 1964 did well in the 1965 draft: Sal Bando, Jim McAndrew, Rick Monday, Nolan Ryan, and Gene Tenace.

Thomas's numbers show, however, that even other strong teams, such as the 1967 American League champions Boston Red Sox, could do well in the draft. In the 1968 draft the Red Sox landed Cecil Cooper, Jack Curtis, Bill Lee, Lynn McGlothen, and Ben Oglivie, all solid players. According to Thomas's research, the Yankees tied for thirteenth in most productive drafts of 1965–69. These drafts were the results of the 1964–68 seasons, which included one Yankee pennant and one last-place finish. The Yankees draft record, then, is not surprising. The Yankees did better in the drafts of 1970–79, finishing sixth. Their nemesis, the Los Angeles Dodgers, finished first, however, in drafting during 1965–69, despite having slightly poorer drafting positions than did the Yankees, and fourth during the 1970s. The Cincinnati Reds had the second best drafting record for 1965–69, despite generally winning records and mediocre drafting positions during that period. Therefore, the amateur draft did not necessarily consign the dregs of the talent pool to the Yankees. Given that the American League fared relatively poorly compared to the National League in the amateur draft over 1965–89, blaming the amateur draft for the Yankees' skid of the late 1960s may be erroneous.[64]

What was the distribution of new playing talent, and how did the amateur draft affect the distribution? Did teams in the larger cities introduce the most and best new players? Thorn, Palmer, and their colleagues listed the five hundred hitters and three hundred pitchers with the highest career total baseball rankings. Table 7.1 shows the distribution of players who began their careers in 1903 or later, thereby reducing the pool of talent to 638 players, among the teams on which they made their Major League debuts (see appendix). These players represent the top 15–25 percent of the regular players in any given year. Because some of these players may have been purchased or acquired just prior to their Major League debuts, table 7.1 gives a rough approximation of the "initial" distribution of top talent across Major League teams and the productivity of each team's scouting and Minor League system. Some franchises languished in the cellar of their league because they did not develop good young talent or employ astute scouts, while other franchises continually fielded winning teams because they were adept at developing or scouting (and buying) good Minor League and amateur talent. The original sixteen franchises introduced an average of 33.5 star players between 1903 and the mid-1990s, an average of a new productive player every second or third year. These franchises introduced star players with a combined average lifetime TBR's of 691.9.

The relationship between city size and team output of talent was not perfect. The large-city teams Brooklyn/Los Angeles and both Chicago clubs have not fared well in talent creation, while the smaller or shared-city teams such as the Cardinals, Pirates, and Red Sox have been adept.

Using the players with the highest TBR's, shown in table 7.1, table 7.2 shows that the distribution of top young talent converged between the 1919–45 and 1965–95 periods (see appendix). The amateur draft was not the sole driving force between the narrowing differences in talent disparity, as the 1946–64 era saw a significant dwindling. During the

1919–45 era the Cardinals and Yankees developed farm systems that led to parades of talented players. The gaps between the Yankees and the Browns, Reds, Senators were huge. Although other teams began to improve their farm productivity, the absolute level of dominance by the top producers would not change much in the 1946–64 era, but the least-productive teams improved. By the 1965–95 period the teams in the top quartile produced only 35.9 percent of the overall TBR's, while the teams in the bottom quartile produced 17 percent.[65] The amateur draft coincided, at least, with a further diminishing of the disparity.

Major League Baseball's chronic competitive imbalance worried owners throughout the postwar period. By the end of the era, however, five different National League teams appeared in the World Series between 1960 and 1964, and the Phillies came close in 1964. In the American League the Yankees' superiority appeared endless. To borrow from Bob Dylan, however, "The times, they were a-changin'."

During the immediate post–amateur draft era (1965–74), the Yankees plunged from winning 60.9 percent of their games against the other original franchises to just 46.4 percent. The White Sox and Indians also suffered major declines in win-loss records.[66] Indeed, over this ten-year period these two teams had the worst records among the original American League franchises. The standard deviation of win-loss records shrank further from the 1955–64 standard deviation, implying greater competitiveness between the original eight franchises. Baltimore, Kansas City/Oakland, Minnesota experienced dramatic improvements in their ten-year win-loss records. The standard deviation for win-loss records between the original eight franchises during the 1965–74 period was the lowest of the 1946–84 era. The standard deviation rebounded slightly during the initial decade of free agency (1975–84) but remained lower than in the 1946–64 period.

Why did some teams in the American League experience such reversals of fortune? In some cases teams acted individually (but with their fellow owners' blessings) by relocating to cities with potentially larger fan bases. Note that the Athletics, Browns/Orioles, and Senators/Twins relocated between 1953 and 1961 and, in the case of the Athletics, again in 1968. Relocation proved to be quite effective in promoting competitive balance, as the greener pastures afforded greater financial resources to develop farm systems and sign top amateur players.

The increased competitive balance coincided with the amateur draft, but the Orioles and Twins did not attain superiority via the amateur draft, as their biggest stars predated the draft. The collective action regarding amateur players was a response by owners primarily to curb spending on bonuses, and the pro-competitive balance aspects of the reverse-order draft, if any, were arguably only a secondary consideration. An examination of baseball teams' relative strength in the postwar era suggests that competitive balance was more likely to be achieved when all the franchises had the means to hire top players, which meant being located in cities with potential to generate sufficient revenue.

8

The Major League Cartel

Keeping Out the Interlopers

The events of 1946–64 occurred within the context of a Major League Baseball cartel. While the Yankees and the other teams acted independently in most contexts, they banded together under joint league frameworks. In most businesses a dominant firm such as the Yankees would desire to drive out rivals. Of course, the Yankees had a symbiotic relationship with the Kansas City Athletics and St. Louis Browns. The greatness of the Yankees meant that other teams would sport losing records. Literally, it took two teams to tangle. The teams therefore needed to cooperate, at least in some regards, and professional sports teams usually formed leagues. Leagues, however, often acted as cartels.

The Major Leagues' cartel agreement is of interest to economists. How did the teams arrange to divide profits, monitor and punish cheaters, and prevent other teams' entry? In one way baseball cartels differ from other cartels in that individual firms within the league, the teams, could openly attempt to compete for the best talent and set their own prices; within the cartel organization, then, competition could still persist. A few team owners, however, occasionally proposed a more rigid cartel organization in which the interests of individual teams would be more fully subordinated to the interests of the cartel.

The cartel faced several challenges during the postwar era. Successful cartels must withstand attacks from within (e.g., the cartel members' tendency to cheat on the collusive agreement and to encroach upon territory occupied by existing cartel members) and from without (e.g., the threat of entry by envious firms). Major League Baseball offers a good opportunity to study the effectiveness of measures to prevent entry.

The National League is the most enduring baseball cartel, although it faced competition by at least five rival leagues, of which only one survives today. Throughout its first quarter-century the National League repeatedly used certain tactics to deter teams from entering the league and also learned several new ones. When peace was declared with the American League, the combined Major Leagues proved strong enough to squelch the Federal League after only two seasons; thereafter, the Major Leagues were not seriously threatened until the postwar era. The National League's main weapons in deterring entry have included using political influence, controlling the supply of a key input (labor), and, in later years, practicing spatial preemption. The league also used advertising, tough talk, and avoiding disclosure of profit data to deter entry. Conversely, the cartel faced challenges from within with respect to franchise relocation and to curbing spending on amateur players. Similar tensions persist today, with owners seeking ways to curb spending on free agents collectively and legally and to relocate moribund franchises to more lucrative cities.

With the shift of the Baltimore Orioles to New York in 1903, the American League was set to compete with the established National League. The two leagues reached a truce in 1903, and the subsequent fifty seasons of stability reflected the success of the agreement between them. Between 1903 and 1952 no franchise relocated, and no franchises were added to the sixteen teams. Before 1903 baseball franchise changes occurred almost annually. Although the National League survived from 1876, other leagues, aside from the American League, came and went. A third "Major League," the Federal League, existed during World War I, but it quickly fell apart. No other professional sports league came close to the fifty-year era of stability that Major

League Baseball experienced. Professional basketball, football, and hockey underwent the usual winnowing process, typically in which franchises folded or were shifted from smaller towns to larger cities; as these leagues became established, they also expanded to double or triple the number of original teams.

After 1952 five of the sixteen teams had switched cities by opening day of the 1958 season. After 1960 the Major Leagues almost doubled to their present thirty teams. Why did Major League Baseball's stability crumble after 1952? Although attendance at Major League games stagnated during the 1950s, real appreciation in franchise values and the generally favorable results from relocating franchises encouraged prospective owners and large cities to dream of acquiring a Major League franchise, whether by buying an existing team or forming a new league. What did the incumbent owners do in response to these interlopers?

In their responses to demands for more teams or new leagues, Major League owners had reason to tread carefully. Since the 1922 Supreme Court ruling allowing baseball's asserted exemption to antitrust legislation, the owners had guarded their special rights as though they were sacred. Throughout the various congressional hearings of the 1950s and 1960s, legislators sometimes implied that the antitrust exemption could be rescinded and used such an implication as a threat to entice the Major League owners to expand, to curb wayward owners, or to stop blacking out telecasts of Major League games. The legislators recognized the value of the antitrust exemption, with Senator Karl Mundt of South Dakota making his beliefs quite explicit:

> We should do it with our eyes open that we are thereby expanding tremendously the financial value of a baseball franchise. We are giving to the fortunate owner an exclusive right which increases vastly his economic investment, and his economic opportunity, and increases vastly the resale value of the investment that he already has. Now I ask you, sir, whether in good conscience we can, by legislative fiat, make dollar bills out of 50-cent pieces for the people who own these

baseball clubs without assuming some responsibility to be sure that public service is considered by the owners of the club.[1]

Sportswriter Red Smith's article was placed in the 1959 Senate hearings. He wrote, "[Major League owners] are keenly aware that there are men in Washington ready to slam them with antitrust legislation—a vastly more frightful ogre than Khrushchev—if they attempt openly to protect their monopoly."[2] Rather than waiting for a Khrushchevian "shoe" to drop upon them, the owners often acceded to the legislators' requests.

Economic Theories of Deterring Entry

According to economists F. M. Scherer and David Ross, the rate of entry is higher when "pre-entry profits are ample, when demand is growing rapidly, and when barriers associated with scale economies [lower per-unit cost as output increases, i.e., 'bigger is better' in terms of average cost] and product differentiation are low."[3] In addition, a new team or league offering an innovation may also be encouraged to enter. Because a cartel has better opportunities to earn economic profits (which differ from accounting profits primarily by adjusting for the forgone interest on owners' invested capital; owners' forgone salaries, if any; and basing depreciation upon changes in the market value of the stadium and other equipment) than a purely competitive industry, the cartel will probably repeatedly face envious potential entrants.

What tactics can a cartel use to deter entry? Economist Robert Smiley investigated tactics used by incumbent firms to prevent entry. He surveyed managers and executives of firms in manufacturing and service industries and found that most of the managers and executives resorted, at least occasionally, to some of these anticompetitive tactics: advertising, talking tough, introducing new product lines or expanding capacity, and not revealing profitability.[4]

Baseball owners could place franchises in most of the viable cities to forestall their entry into the league. They often used tough talk and went to absurd lengths to camouflage their profitability. The owners of the postwar period were similar to their modern counterparts in being loathe to provide information regarding profits. At times they even hesitated to provide attendance figures to the public. Baseball researcher Peter Craig described how reticent Major League officials were in response to queries for his research around 1950. In one instance Craig found a New York Yankees financial report in a used bookstore, but at the time he did not have sufficient funds to purchase it. When he returned to purchase the item, he was informed that a Yankees official had purchased the report.[5] The Yankees declined Craig's request to view the report. In addition, owners attempted to control the key input: players.

Smiley did not ask his respondents whether they had enlisted government intervention to create barriers to entry. Incumbent firms might enlist political support for legislation directly benefiting the incumbents or stymieing potential entrants. Smiley's survey also did not include predatory pricing. Although the public likes to think that firms frequently engage in predatory pricing, the evidence suggests that such tactics as setting prices below profitable levels, as suggested by Phillip Areeda and Donald F. Turner, are not pervasive, and Major League owners usually did not threaten to cut ticket prices in the face of encroachment by upstart leagues.[6]

Tactics Used by Major League Team Owners to Combat Entry

The Major Leagues employed a number of barriers to keep out new teams. Some of the barriers to entry arose naturally as the industry evolved (such as large concrete and steel stadiums), while other barriers were designed specifically to deter entry (such as local political intervention on behalf of a favored franchise, the reserve clause, and league alliances). Although economist Lance Davis argues that the Major League cartel failed to maximize collective profits, the attempts after 1903 to prevent entry, at least, appear astute and successful.[7] The National League alone proved less successful in preventing entry, facing competition by the American Association, the Union Association, the Players' League, and, finally and most enduringly, the American League. The addition of the American League and having a combined total of sixteen relatively stable franchises provided enough strength, however, for the National League to combat the Federal League and any other potential entrant for over fifty years. The cartel, albeit expanded by almost double the sixteen teams and facing significantly altered labor rules, has now persisted for more than a century.

Control of a Key Input

Economist Smiley did not identify another barrier to entry: the control of a key input such as labor. Early baseball owners sought ways to control labor. The early days of professional baseball were marked by contract jumping and player "revolving" (i.e., players moving from team to team by their own volition, sometimes honoring their contract and then moving or sometimes jumping out of a current contract). Clearly, such a chaotic situation reduced the attractiveness of trying to develop talent. Most leagues enacted sanctions against teams that induced contract jumping. The National League owners pledged to defend each others' property rights through a system of fines and blacklists. A player or team owner who violated the agreements could be blacklisted. With league sanctions such rules might reduce bidding within, say, the National League, but teams in other leagues had little to fear from attempting to raid players from the National League. National League owners attempted to form "alliances" with other leagues whereby sanctions would be levied against teams that violated the agreements. The owners also sought to reduce bidding for players by introducing a "grace" period for an owner to resign his current players without competition from other owners. Of course, the grace period was an imperfect form of labor control, and owners sought stronger measures.

By 1879 National League owners had enacted an embryonic reserve clause. Each owner could designate five of his players as "reserved," and other National League teams could not attempt to sign these players. Eventually, the reserve clause was extended to the entire roster.[8]

Again, the reserve clause did not eliminate competition from teams in rival leagues. Within a league, with each team firmly controlling its players, the owners' property rights were strengthened. Yet their property rights to their labor input still had one major flaw: such rights lacked transferability.

In 1884 the St. Louis Browns of the American Association wished to trade pitcher Tony Mullane to Toledo. Technically, the Browns would have had to release Mullane from his contract, and Toledo would have had to sign him. Both teams clearly feared that a release would induce bidding from not only other clubs in the American Association but also from the two rival leagues. The American Association president suggested a way out of the conundrum: "There can be no such thing under the national agreement as a qualified release. The effect of a release is plainly stated: thereby the player becomes eligible to contract with any club. . . . There is a way, of course, by which . . . the clubs of any association party to the national agreement might be debarred from competition with Toledo for Mullane's services, viz: before releasing him [to get a gentleman's agreement from the other clubs not to contract with Mullane]. . . . I know of no other way in which it can be covered."[9] While St. Louis and Toledo succeeded in getting such a gentlemen's agreement from their fellow American Association owners, such a mechanism was unwieldy and risky. The two teams later attempted to trade Mullane back to St. Louis, but this time the Cincinnati club bid for and won Mullane's services.

On other occasions owners covetous of particular players would take the "safer" but costlier method of purchasing the team currently possessing those players. Detroit bought Buffalo in 1885 in order to get Dan Brouthers, among others. Clearly, this imperfection in the owners' property rights to their players needed a remedy. Eventually, the leagues created agreements by which owners could transfer players from one club to another: "Crude practices such as these finally led to agreements which permitted the direct assignment of player contracts or reservation rights from one club to another. This forged the last link in the reserve rule and created in the player an asset which clubs could transfer for cash or other consideration."[10]

The stronger definition of the owners' rights to their players raised the value of their player assets because teams in smaller cities with star players could now sell or trade these players to teams in the larger cities. The Coase Theorem's prediction of efficient allocation of assets required such well-defined property rights as well as low transaction costs. If owners possessed the rights to players' labor as under the reserve clause, the owners would transfer players to where they were most valuable. If players owned the rights to their labor, as under free agency, they would move to where their services were the most valuable. Without well-defined property rights, owners and players would expend resources in acquiring such property rights. With property rights well defined, the main transaction cost would now be that of negotiating a deal in person or by telephone, telegraph, or mail, yet fan displeasure over losing star players, aside from any changes in the team's win-loss record, might prove a deterrent to player movement.

By 1903, then, the two Major Leagues had essentially established their cartel and erected adequately protected property rights over baseball labor. With stable property rights Major League teams could concentrate on developing new young talent and acquiring or selling proven veterans. These property rights withstood the threats of the Federal League in 1914–15 and the Mexican League in 1946–47.

When World War II ended, there were many former Major Leaguers returning to the game. Indeed, there seemed to be a surfeit of players. While many of the players were rusty, they still retained their "Major League" cachet. Thus, the time appeared propitious for a new Major League. The wealthy Pasquel brothers bankrolled a new league in Mexico. The Major Leagues quickly labeled the Mexican League an "outlaw league." In other words, any player who signed with or any American team that played against a Mexican League team would face sanctions. New York Giant player Danny Gardella felt that the team's management treated him "pretty shabbily."[11] A team in the nascent Mexican League offered him a five-year contract, and Gardella signed.

Some Major League players such as Vern "Junior" Stephens found the Mexican offers tempting enough to sign up. Other players used the Mexican League to get better offers from the American teams. Unfortunately for the players signing with the Mexican League, conditions were difficult to adjust to. In addition, the league foundered quickly.

Gardella wanted to return to Major League Baseball but found himself blacklisted. He filed suit against Major League Baseball, claiming that he was "unlawfully deprived of earning a living in retaliation for his acceptance of an offer from the Mexican League" and that "baseball is a monopoly, operates across state lines, via the farm systems and the use of radio and television, and that Organized Ball comes under the jurisdiction of the Sherman Anti-Trust Act."[12] St. Louis Cardinals pitcher Max Lanier also jumped to the Mexican League, and he, too, filed a lawsuit against baseball when he was blacklisted. Cardinals owner Fred Saigh intervened, however, to help get Lanier back, so the player dropped his suit. Lanier later testified that baseball needed the reserve clause. To avoid a potentially damaging court case, Major League Baseball decided to negotiate. Gardella settled his suit before trial, and he signed with the St. Louis Cardinals.[13]

Moreover, maintaining a blacklist against a large number of players was liable to backfire against the two leagues, as potential upstart leagues could use the pool of blacklisted players to gain "Major League" status. The Major Leagues' later threats to blacklist players who signed with outlaw teams were often hollow, as players who signed with the Federal or Mexican leagues were, after a time, allowed back into organized baseball.

Because the Major Leagues relied heavily upon the Minor Leagues for new players, close ties between these teams also precluded entry of new Major League teams. By a form of vertical integration Major League teams often owned or controlled a number of Minor League clubs. The first baseball commissioner, Judge Kenesaw Mountain Landis, disapproved of farm systems, and while he occasionally "freed" farm hands, he proved unable to stymie the trend. His executive assistant,

Leslie O'Connor, gathered evidence that led to the abrogation of the Minor League contracts of ninety-two Detroit Tigers Minor League players. In O'Connor's later capacity as general manager of the Chicago White Sox, he capitulated to reality and reluctantly developed their modest farm system during the 1950s.[14] He still maintained his disapproval of a farm system's ability to keep players in the Minors for up to seven years before a player could seek employment and advancement with another Major League team. Landis and O'Connor wanted an unrestricted draft of Minor League players, cooperative baseball schools and tryout camps, and direct subsidy of the Minor Leagues by the Majors as a whole.

While the American Basketball Association and American Football League might hope to gain favorable widespread publicity and credibility by signing top college players, such avenues were almost nonexistent for potential baseball entrants. Because Minor League players did not attain the national recognition of, say, a top collegiate football or basketball player, a fledgling Major League could not hope to gain much by signing even the best Minor League players. In addition, such players would be vulnerable to any reserve clause or blacklist edicts passed by the Major Leagues.[15]

The Major Leagues' ability to "draft" promising players from the Minor Leagues also helped deter Minor League teams in larger cities from aspiring to Major League status. Some of the Minor Leagues, such as the Pacific Coast League (PCL), attempted to reduce the loss of players in order to stockpile sufficient talent to attain Major League status. A few independent Minor League teams were able to protect impressive amounts of talent, such as Jack Dunn's Baltimore Orioles of the 1920s, with Lefty Grove and George Earnshaw. In return for the Major Leagues' ability to draft promising Minor League players, the Minor Leagues received protection of territorial rights. Sometimes, however, the Major Leagues felt free to abrogate these rights.

The Pacific Coast League attempted to get Major League status after World War II. Although Los Angeles and San Francisco were obvious candidates for Major League teams, Oakland, Portland, Sacramento,

San Diego, and Seattle were still too small. Nevertheless, the league attained a special category: open. The category was above AAA and afforded the league some protection against having players drafted with limited compensation by Major League teams.[16] Some of the PCL owners put a great deal of effort and expense into running their clubs. Paul Fagan, owner of the San Francisco Seals, maintained Seals Stadium as one of the best ballparks in the country. His players often flew to games, years before Major League teams did. The team sold many players to the Major Leagues, often for $50,000 or more.[17]

By the mid-1950s Congress was looking askance at the Major Leagues' monopolization of players, especially in conjunction with expansion. Some legislators even had the temerity to examine the reserve clause. Baseball officials defended the system by attributing to it remarkable powers, such as maintaining competitive balance and integrity (a potential free agent might "throw" a game to a potential new employer's team).

During the 1958 Senate hearings Paul Dixon, counsel for the Senate, pierced the veil surrounding the reserve clause, asking Calvin Griffith, owner of the woebegone Washington Senators, "Does not the reserve clause, and the unlimited number of ballplayers that the other major league teams can get, make it harder for you to get good ballplayers?" Griffith replied, "Well, we are not in financial position to go out and bid $100,000 to get ballplayers."[18] Dixon was more aggressive with commissioner Ford Frick.

> DIXON: But isn't it also true that even with this reserve clause that you have had so long in baseball, the wealthier clubs are presently out-bidding the poorer clubs by the use of the bonus rule that we have talked about?
>
> FRICK: The reserve clause only keeps clubs from raiding each other.
>
> DIXON: But you say you do not want anybody to legislate mediocrity. God save us from mediocrity. But hasn't baseball, by the handling of its own house, in effect legislated mediocrity? A good exam-

ple is the comparison of the New York Yankees and the Washington Senators.[19]

Wyoming senator Joseph O'Mahoney continued the inquisition, asking, "The fact is you have the reserve clause in the American League, but you do not have the equalization of competitive strength?" Frick replied, "Senator, that is true as of the year of our Lord 1958."[20]

Although the senators were skeptical about the reserve clause, they never rescinded baseball's exemption, thereby maintaining a Damoclean threat. Interestingly, economist Simon Rottenberg wrote a seminal paper in 1956 suggesting that player distribution might be similar under either a reserve clause or free agent regime.[21] His paper, however, did not receive the attention of the legislators.

The players themselves were not too aggressive in loosening the owners' control over them. After World War II a few baseball players attempted to form a union. Previous attempts had always ended in failure. They engaged labor relations authority Robert Murphy to help them. Some contemporary observers felt that the effort was futile, as players had vastly different skills: "No two ball players are of precisely the same ability, therefore it is impossible to set a maximum wage scale, although a minimum would be feasible."[22] Murphy's efforts were largely futile, although he succeeded in getting small gains for the players, including an increase in per-diem expense money for spring training, promptly dubbed "Murphy money." Despite Murphy's failure to get a union going, the owners granted some concessions in 1946, including a minimum salary of $5,000 and a pension. By 1957 Major League players won a minimum salary of $7,000, up from $6,000.[23]

Major League owners boasted about the players' pension plan. Former Yankees owner Larry MacPhail persuaded his fellow owners to implement the pension in 1947. Revenue from the All-Star games and national television contracts funded the pension. The pension became a selling point for inducing talented athletes to choose baseball. The pension also improved relations between owners and players.[24] At the same time, however, it provided another deterrent against Major League players considering joining an outlaw league.

Thus, in the postwar years Major League players still needed to have their collective consciousness raised. During the 1958 Senate hearings Mickey Mantle, Stan Musial, Robin Roberts, Ted Williams, and Ed Yost all testified to the need for the reserve clause. No journeyman Major League or disgruntled Minor League players testified.[25] While some Senators might have wondered about the skewed sample of player witnesses, most seemed content to trade pleasantries with the big stars.

Players, of course, had to be wary of criticizing the reserve clause in a public forum. A "prominent" professional football player requested anonymity when criticizing the proposed exemption for football's version of the reserve clause: "If you give football 100 percent exemption from the antitrust laws you people will be betraying 420 men thereby giving them absolutely no recourse by law."[26] Conversely, Bob Friend, National League player representative, asserted that the players backed the reserve clause as essential for the game's survival. According to him, baseball players were not ready for a union. He viewed a union as divisive: "You immediately make a sharp cleavage between the players and the club executives . . . we immediately will begin antagonizing the owners. . . . It would tend to destroy the image of the baseball star for the youngsters because of the haggling between the players and the owners."[27] Meanwhile, Judge Robert Cannon, legal advisor to the players, testified before the Senate by quoting outfielder Gene Woodling's observation about the relationship between players and owners: "We have it so good we don't know what to ask for next." Cannon added, "I think this sums up the thinking of the average major league ballplayer today."[28]

Marvin Miller and historian Robert Burk describe Cannon's ludicrous position: the owners financed the union and recommended, if not directly paid, the judge to the players.[29] Miller wrote that such an arrangement was illegal. Moreover, such attitudes as held by Chicago White Sox owner A. C. Allyn Jr. augured ill for future labor-management relations. Allyn defended the reserve clause by telling the Senate, "The players, it is true, either have to sign a contract with us or not at all, but they do have *the privilege of not at all*, and we are not permitted to cut their salaries more than a nominal amount at any time. And normally we do nothing but raise salaries in this business."[30]

Defeating the Continental League

The leagues could also discourage other teams' entry by practicing spatial preemption; just as dry cereal manufacturers could develop a wide range of cereals to deter new entrants into their industry, the Major Leagues could keep franchises in almost all of the large cities to prevent either the entry of an aspiring third Major League or the feasibility of a second team being profitable in those cities. St. Louis was a classic example of a city barely able to sustain two teams, but the Major Leagues sometimes hesitated moving one of the franchises in fear that a potential rival league might move in. Despite the league's resistance, however, St. Louis Cardinal owner Sam Breadon wanted to relocate to Detroit and share, via rental payments, Briggs Stadium. But the Detroit franchise refused to share its stadium. One historian believes that such a sharing arrangement, while collectively beneficial, was opposed by the rest of the Major League owners.[31] The St. Louis Browns and, later, the Philadelphia Phillies tried to relocate to Los Angeles before Walter O'Malley succeeded in moving the Brooklyn Dodgers there.[32] Of course, spatial preemption touches upon the question of whether the Major Leagues were of an optimal size and located in the optimal cities. While spatial preemption often meant expanding, some Major League owners, at times, advocated consolidation.[33]

When the reshuffling of franchises belonging to the American and National leagues ended in 1903, were the sixteen teams optimally located to preclude others' entry? The sixteen teams were in ten of the fifteen largest cities in the country. Baltimore (6), Buffalo (8), San Francisco (9), New Orleans (12), and Milwaukee (14) were not represented.[34] The Baltimore Orioles, once a National League team, moved to New York and became the Yankees in 1903. Buffalo's last Major League team, which was in the Federal League, disappeared in 1915, and the other Major League owners thought that Buffalo was too close to New York City to support a team. San Francisco's distance from the other Major League teams precluded its inclusion into either league, while New Orleans suffered both from distance and relative poverty. Per capita income in Louisiana remained well below the United States average throughout the twentieth century, while, according to 1929 figures, most of the Major League cities were in states possessing above-average per capita incomes. Only Missouri residents had less than the national per capita income in 1929.[35] Milwaukee might have suffered from its proximity to Chicago, although the first franchise relocation in 1953 was by the Boston Braves to Milwaukee. Of the five cities with multiple franchises—New York, Chicago, Philadelphia, St. Louis, and Boston—the latter two were each less than half the size of Philadelphia and barely one-sixth the size of New York. These two cities were the first to lose franchises, while Philadelphia became the third. Even New York lost two franchises after the 1957 season, although the city regained a National League franchise for the 1962 season.

With rapid urban growth in the West and South and improved air transportation, many cities were becoming viable Major League sites, with presumably healthy demand for big league baseball. Congressional investigations throughout the 1950s cited the desire for more Major League franchises, and the franchise relocations of the 1950s only whetted many cities' thirst for big league baseball. Senators and representatives urged, if not threatened, baseball to expand, thereby making the big leagues truly national in scope.[36]

By the 1950 census the ten cities with Major League Baseball held similar positions in the population rankings. Cincinnati's population ranking fell to eighteenth, however, while Pittsburgh's was twelfth. The largest cities without Major League Baseball included Los Angeles (4), Baltimore again (6), San Francisco (11), Milwaukee (13), Houston (14), Buffalo (15), New Orleans (16), and Minneapolis (17). Using metropolitan areas instead of simple city populations would have changed the rankings: Baltimore would have fallen to twelfth, while San Francisco–Oakland would have moved to seventh, and Kansas City would have replaced New Orleans.[37] The other cities would have held similar rankings regardless of definition. Baltimore, Kansas City, Los Angeles, Milwaukee, and San Francisco would get franchises in the turbulent mid-1950s, while Houston and Minneapolis–St. Paul would get franchises in 1961 and 1962. Buffalo and New Orleans remain outside of Major League Baseball to the present day.

In 1960 Houston, especially, loomed as an attractive site for a team. Yankees owner, Del Webb, who was the chairman of the American League's realignment committee, gave the city a strong endorsement. The city was the largest without a Major League team at the start of the new decade. In addition, St. Louis Cardinals owner August Busch was willing to sell his Houston Minor League franchise, and he pledged to cooperate with Houston interests in getting a National League franchise for the city.[38]

Although economist James Quirk believes that "self-interest of league members argues for expansion of membership in a league until all cities capable of supporting a franchise in the sport are absorbed in the league, allowing for the added transport and other costs incurred in such expansion," Major League owners appear to have held a different view.[39] Owners recognized the disadvantages of having more teams: it diluted the level of playing talent, increased demand for players, reduced shares of national radio and television contracts, reduced the number of games with established teams, and decreased each owner's voting power. While allowing too many viable sites to remain without franchises invited potential upstarts such as the Continental League, there is little reason to believe that the optimum required the absorption of "all cities capable of supporting a franchise."

There was one potentially disastrous, to the Major League cartel, result of the franchise movements of the 1950s. When the Dodgers and Giants left the New York area, they left Major League Baseball vulnerable to a new league. Certainly, the National League may have erred in letting the two teams vacate New York without having a replacement team ready. Indeed, the National League might have been better off if the Braves, Cards, or Phillies had shifted to the West Coast in 1953 rather than the wealthier Dodgers and Giants.

There was a historical precedent illustrating the folly of leaving New York open to possible interlopers. After the first National League season in 1876, the league owners voted to expel the Philadelphia and New York franchises for failing to make their final western road trips. Apparently, the New York and Philadelphia teams did not want to undertake the financially unattractive trip, so William Hulbert, leader of the National League, decided to enforce the league edict on having teams play the entire schedule instead of following it haphazardly. Such discretion had been the bane of the National Association.[40] While the league edict undoubtedly caught the attention of the remaining teams and instilled a measure of discipline, the failure of the league to replace the Philadelphia and New York teams with other area ball clubs is a mystery. The American Association quickly entered these two cities. The American Association was, until the formation of the American League, the longest-lived rival to the National League.

With New York vacated by the National League after 1957, the New York Yankees naturally sought to maintain their newfound monopoly. Sportswriter Harold Rosenthal described their position in *Sporting News* that year: "The Dodgers and Giants are pulling out without anybody pushing them and without—at least in the case of the Dodgers—any financial pressure. In other words they are saying to us, 'We don't want this territory. We're leaving it to you.' The American League is saying, 'Thank you, and we're taking it.'"[41] The existing baseball rules allowed the National League fifteen days after the Dodgers and Giants had left to place another team in the city; otherwise, the New York Yankees would have exclusive rights.[42]

While the Philadelphia Phillies discouraged talk of a rival National League team in New York City, other National League teams looked enviously at it. At times rumors swirled that Cincinnati, Philadelphia, and Pittsburgh might play games in New York. The Cincinnati Reds and Pittsburgh Pirates expressed interest in relocating, although the former team's interest may have been an attempt to coerce the city of Cincinnati into building a new stadium. Reds owner Powell Crosley cited parking problems at Crosley Field and stated that he was, "very

discouraged with the city's complacency in solving the parking problem
. . . a sufficient amount of discouragement on my part—and bang!
I'm liable to move."[43] Crosley wanted eight thousand parking spaces,
but the city had only purchased thirty-five small parcels of land. Of
course, O'Malley and Stoneham had complained about parking in
Brooklyn and at the Polo Grounds, so Crosley's threat might have
seemed a little silly.

In 1959 former Major League general manager Branch Rickey and
New York attorney William Shea saw an opportunity, sensing the time
was propitious to start a third Major League. Certainly, the growth
of cities throughout the United States created more sites capable of
sustaining a Major League team. Rickey and Shea outlined their plans
on June 18, 1959. The Continental League would play in eight cities
to be selected from Buffalo, Dallas/Fort Worth, Denver, Houston,
Indianapolis, Los Angeles, Miami, Montreal, New York, San Diego,
and Toronto. On July 27 Shea announced that he had backers for
teams in Denver, Houston, Minneapolis–St. Paul, New York, and
Toronto.[44]

By 1960 Shea listed the eight prospective teams as being Atlanta,
Buffalo, Dallas–Fort Worth, Denver, Houston, Minneapolis–St. Paul,
New York, and Toronto.[45] Several of these cities, including New York,
indicated a willingness to build Major League–size stadiums. Yet the
league faced another formidable barrier: getting players. As Rickey put
it, "I only know that 20 great cities cannot be permanently branded as
minor league by the arbitrary and capricious methods of the controlling number of 16 clubs."[46] He recognized the Major Leagues' ability
to thwart any new league: "So long as the major leagues are able to
maintain their existing absolute monopoly of players and territories
and further continue their tactics patently employed for the purpose
of defeating any organization of a third major league, we, alone,
find ourselves unable to complete the formation of the Continental
League."[47]

Sportswriter Herbert Simons summarized the obstacles facing the
Continental League: getting Major League players and television

contracts, providing pension benefits commensurate with the Major Leagues' plan, paying reparations, and getting stadiums. Conversely, any expansion team would have an advantage because established Major League teams would play them, whereas established Major League teams would not play Continental League teams.[48] He neglected one crucial obstacle—the implacable unwillingness of Major League owners to countenance a new league. While these owners would employ more genteel and nuanced tactics than sliding hard with sharpened spikes, their ruthlessness and cunning rivaled that of such worthies as Ty Cobb and John McGraw.

The Major Leagues dominated the field of organized baseball. Through a series of interlocking agreements all Minor Leagues subordinated themselves to the whims of the Major League owners. An upstart league such as the Continental League had to apply to become a member of organized baseball; otherwise, it could be labeled an outlaw league. If the Continental League did not become a member of organized baseball, then getting players would be extremely difficult, as players would be risking their professional careers by playing for a new, uncertain league. The existing Major Leagues could thus set the requirements for entry into organized baseball, and they did.

Shea and Rickey claimed that Minor League realignment in the wake of eight new Major League teams would provide a source of young talent. Teams in formerly AAA and open leagues had plenty of young players. Rickey exuberantly said, "Why there are players all over the world."[49] In addition, Rickey believed the Majors' first-year draft rule, which exposed talented Minor Leaguers to draft by Major League teams, could provide players for the Continental League. In addition, the league anticipated buying players from Minor League clubs. Ford Frick agreed with Rickey that these were avenues available to the nascent Continental League.[50] Despite these bland assertions, however, tension lurked.

Having such a baseball legend as Branch Rickey involved undoubtedly helped give the Continental League credibility. Yet the existing Major Leagues, having recently disposed of the Mexican League and denying the Pacific Coast League Major League status, were loathe to see any upstarts. Nor did the Major Leagues savor the idea of increased demand for the existing pool of players. The Major League owners, cognizant of congressional pressure for more Major League teams, issued unctuous statements, such as one on August 18, 1959, in which they reported that their committee unanimously approved of a third league, if it adhered to "regulations": "The most important requirement is that the new league will have to satisfy the owners of any franchises it takes and any league from which it appropriates territory."[51] Baseball commissioner Ford Frick reminded the Continental League that it would have to meet the requirements of any potential "expansion" team in Major League Baseball (keeping in mind that there had not been an expansion team in over fifty years): a population base of at least six hundred thousand, a stadium capacity of twenty-five thousand, a schedule of 154 games, a minimum players' salary of $7,500, and uniform Major League players' contracts.[52]

According to one estimate, the eight new teams might need a combined $60 million to meet these requirements, mostly for constructing new stadiums or refurbishing existing Minor League stadiums.[53] By stating these requirements, Major League Baseball attempted to present a reasonable face to the public; after all, what could be fairer than to insist that the nascent league meet existing standards?[54] Of course, allowing the existing leagues to set the requirements for entry may well be a blatant violation of most people's conception of antitrust rules. An analogous situation would be for two existing grocery store chains to dictate terms of entry for a third grocery chain. Congress, with its rules constraining new political parties, was hardly in a moral position to accuse professional sports leagues. Conversely, while Bill Shea complained about the indemnities demanded by the American Association ($1 million), citing the International League's demand for only $48,000 when the Browns moved into Baltimore, he conveniently forgot about other indemnities that had been paid.[55] Walter O'Malley and Horace Stoneham, for example, had paid the Pacific Coast League large indemnities for their invasion of Los Angeles and San Francisco.

Frick also stated that the Continental League would have to establish a pension system similar to that operated by the Major Leagues. "The existing major league players benefit plan is far more than a retirement program," he explained. "It covers health, welfare, group life and widow's benefits, as well as retirement. It will be impossible to transfer players between leagues unless the pension plans are equal in all essential respects."[56] While the demand seemed reasonable, a skeptic might observe that the pension plan represented a barrier to entry. Finally, the Major Leagues held a trump card: they could forestall the formation of a third league by expanding themselves, which was, ultimately, their tactic. In addition, after some hesitation, the American League approved Washington's relocation to Minneapolis–St. Paul, thereby knocking out one of the original five teams in the Continental League.[57]

The Continental League agreed to the requirement of having no salary ceiling. George Weiss of the New York Yankees, a man known for his constant bleats that salaries were spiraling out of control, stated, "We of the major leagues would like to see quite a few $100,000-a-season players. They would merit this pay on performance, and on impact on the gate, and would indicate a very healthy state in the game. The more $100,000 players we have, the more prosperous would baseball be, and the more intrigued would our fans be."[58] One is entitled to view Weiss's statement as ironic, given that in 1960 former MVP's Mickey Mantle and Yogi Berra were paid well below $100,000.

Acquiring large stadiums was another barrier to entry into the Major Leagues. The Yankees, although at best lukewarm about having another team in New York, offered to sell their lease on Yankee Stadium to the city of New York, thereby allowing for the possibility of having a Continental League team playing there. Branch Rickey and Bill Shea blasted the offer, disdaining to play in such an "antique." They were undoubtedly hoping the city would build a new stadium, which their team would occupy.[59] Weiss angrily criticized the Continental League's disdain of a Yankee Stadium lease: "It's damned unfair for a stadium financed by public funds to operate against a private corporation that pays the city $200,000 a year in taxes. Anyone who says the [new] park will pay for itself is crazy. Every municipal stadium in the country is a white elephant. . . . The city won't lift a finger to help us get the parking space we need desperately at Yankee Stadium, but it's ready to pour money down the drain to accommodate the Continental League."[60] These views would have made Weiss a pariah among today's owners. Years later his new team, the New York Mets, would play in a "white elephant," Shea Stadium. Other prospective cities offered to build a stadium, contingent upon the guarantee of a team agreeing to play there. The mutual contingency between city officials and team officials raised the question "Which came first, the team or the stadium?"

Both the Major Leagues and the Continental League looked to Congress for support. The Continental League hoped that Congress would force Major League Baseball to enact stricter limits on the number of players controlled by any one club. Former Colorado Senator Edwin Johnson had suggested in 1958 limiting the number of players a Major League team could control. He believed the limit would also reduce the attractiveness of paying high bonuses, which, in turn, would enable Minor League owners to sign more amateur players and then be able to sell them; although Rickey disliked the player control limit, he, too, thought the rule would curb bonus payments. Tennessee senator Estes Kefauver's 1959 bill proposed limiting the number of players controlled to one hundred, with forty being on the parent team's roster. In addition, within two years of the bill's enactment the Major Leagues would have to hold an open draft of all players not on the forty-player parent roster. Any league meeting the standards of baseball, specifically the Continental League, would be eligible to participate in the open draft.[61]

Congress and baseball owners recognized the importance of this legislation. Shea claimed that a law validating the reserve clause while not limiting the number of players controlled by any team "would prohibit forever the formation of any other Major League—not just the Continental League—except by consent of the 16 major league club owners": "Rumors, apparently inspired [by Major League Baseball], appeared in the press, that both major leagues were planning to expand into 10-club circuits. . . . Nothing ever came of this, of course."[62] Senator Phil Hart of Michigan asked Shea, "If this bill does not become law, does it mean the end of the Continental League?" Shea responded, "We have several alternatives. We could operate outside Organized Baseball, without benefit of the draft, conduct war and raids on Organized Baseball. That would not be illegal because I contend the reserve clause binding a player to a major league club is illegal anyhow. We would have to raid because there are no players anywhere else. . . . It looks like they're pushing us to it, particularly because of the time element." Senator Carroll asked, "Couldn't you develop your own market of players?" "It would take years and years to get started" was Shea's reply.[63] The senator then blustered, "If [Major League owners] would take that position [preventing Continental League teams from getting players] . . . it would be crystal clear that these 16 clubs control . . . some 4,000 players and therefore they have a franchise veto coupled with a strong player control, and I think the Congress would be forced to take action to break it up."[64]

Edwin Johnson was pessimistic about the Continental League's prospects if Congress did not enact the player control limit did not get passed: "The Continental League will be a dead duck and it isn't likely that anyone again will try to organize another major league."[65] Conversely, Major League Baseball officials testified to the deleterious effects of the bill's rules, and surprisingly, even Rickey thought the player control limit was harmful, especially because he believed the limit would hurt the Minor Leagues.[66] Ford Frick claimed that the limits would "leave over 100 of the 150 minor league clubs without major league assistance."[67] He also argued that most Minor League teams were unable to conduct the requisite scouting for new players and were thus dependent upon the Major League teams to supply players. Even if the Minor League teams succeeded in scouting and developing players without Major League subsidies, player sales could never make up the shortfall. Frick claimed, probably erroneously, that only eleven new players made the Majors each year.[68] Senator Kenneth Keating of

New York opposed the limits for two reasons. First, he thought they would hurt the Minor Leagues by inducing Major League teams to cut the subsidies. Second, he believed "that a third major league will be held up interminably if legislation is enacted which sets arbitrary Federal limits on the number of players a team may control."[69]

In the event opponents of the limit were persuasive enough that the legislation pertaining to the draft did not make it out of the subcommittee. Many observers saw the failure to get the legislation passed as being fatal to Continental League interests. Indeed, Shea stated, "It was a severe blow, but we are not finished." Meanwhile, Ford Frick claimed, "It was a bad piece of legislation, which would have hurt the Continental as well as the American and National Leagues."[70] Conversely, sportswriter Herbert Simons did not think the Kefauver bill limiting player control to one hundred or even forty would have helped the Continental League much in any case.[71]

The Continental League staggered forward. Although not stated publicly, apparently the league's backers hoped that Congress would also eliminate the need to reimburse the Minor Leagues for loss of territory.[72] With the collapse of their hopes of congressional help, the league announced that it had a plan to compensate the Minor League teams and leagues for its trespass of their territories, thereby meeting one of the Major Leagues' requirements. The league offered to pay forty cents per admission as reparations in the year in which it gained Major League status.[73]

The American League's Untoward Expansion

The Major Leagues' expansion plans were closely intertwined with the Continental League threat. *Plans* may be too formal a word for what actually transpired. Ford Frick wanted expansion to be orderly. "I do not want anyone to move so fast that mistakes will be made," he declared. "Any fast operation would harm baseball."[74] Yet he was unable to stop the two leagues' stampede to get the most desirable locations.

Because the leagues had not grown in over fifty years, and the National

League's last "expansion" consisted of absorbing some teams from the defunct American Association, there were few precedents to guide the Major Leagues. The Major Leagues were concerned about expanding to ten teams.[75] Previous attempts to field ten teams had floundered, as too many teams fell out of contention. Splitting a ten-team league into two five-team divisions did not gain favor either. Some Major League officials believed that eventually the leagues would need to expand to twelve teams, with two six-team divisions, and this was in fact what happened in 1969. The key problem was finding an additional eight teams.

The Major Leagues formed a "Territorial Definition Committee" at its annual meetings. The committee suggested that a two million population figure be the threshold for having two teams in a city, which made Los Angeles eligible for a second team and Detroit just short. Of course, given Detroit's eventual population decline, the city probably would not have been able to sustain two teams. Nevertheless, at the time the Tigers worried about the possibility of another team moving into the city. A writer for the *Sporting News* outlined the team's concern in a February 1958 article: "The Tigers' high command . . . pointed out that only recently it had undergone nearly $5,500,000 expense for purchase of the Detroit club with the knowledge and understanding that the Motor City was a one-team town."[76]

With the makings of a quid pro quo, New York Yankees owner Dan Topping raised the question of whether the American League could place a team in Los Angeles: "If New York is open, then we must regard Los Angeles as open. I asked the commissioner for an official opinion." In other words, was that city "open territory" for the American League? Frick answered by declaring both cities open.[77] Of course, the Yankees and Dodgers were lukewarm, as were the Philadelphia Phillies, who enjoyed being the only National League team in the region. The Yankees later stated that they would acquiesce to having a National League team in the city.[78] Although the owners were divided regarding New York's status as open territory, commissioner Frick made it clear that he favored having another National League team in New York. In a sense the eventual solution was to set up a compromise: the American League could place a team in the Los Angeles area, while the National League could reclaim Brooklyn or Queens.[79]

Meanwhile, New York public officials wasted no time in trying to get another National League team. By the summer of 1958 Mayor Robert Wagner and William Shea offered a stadium site at Flushing Meadows: "The city is ready to borrow money to build a suitable and modern ball park. We can do that without increasing the city's debt as this would be a self-liquidating project."[80] Shea suggested that the city join a "third Major League" in order to get another team.[81]

The American League owners felt that the National League had "stolen a march" on them in the race for California. The American League owners coveted California. The World Series of 1959 and the ninety-thousand-plus attendance at each of the three games played in the Los Angeles Coliseum only reinforced the realization of their blunder.[82] When the American League initially discussed expanding to Minneapolis–St. Paul and Los Angeles, the National League was lukewarm. According to an anonymous official, "Well, fine for the American League, which is running second and is kicking itself from Boston to Kansas City because it let us grab Los Angeles and San Francisco. But for us, why expansion? We are happy. We have what we want, a solid circuit from the Atlantic to the Pacific. Sure, New York wants us back. But we have not missed New York."[83] In addition, Milwaukee was proving to be a far better location than Baltimore or Kansas City.

While grappling with expansion, American League officials made some bizarre proposals. One suggested expanding into Minnesota and forming a second American League team in New York. While the proposal was undoubtedly doomed to be dead on arrival, as the Yankees were highly unlikely to approve it, there was an added twist. The expansion New York club would then be traded to the National League for Philadelphia or Pittsburgh.[84] Adding to the confusion was the dire situation in Washington DC, where Senators owner Calvin Griffith wanted to relocate.

Although Major League owners eventually favored expansion on its merit, there was a strong political aspect to the situation. As the *Sporting News* pointed out, Washington DC was strategically important in placating members of Congress who might too closely examine the subtleties of baseball's antitrust exemption: "Organized Baseball must have some countering move in Washington. Even if the Continental League does get started it may not succeed. Then O.B. must have something to offer in the way of expansion."[85] When Griffith finally moved his team, the American League promptly replaced it with an even worse ball club, the new, not improved, Senators. For the American League's finances reestablishing a club in Washington DC was a detriment.

The American League briefly considered expanding by only one team in 1961. In order to do so, the National League would have to add a team that year too. After approving Griffith's shift of his Senators to Minnesota, the league faced a tough decision. The league awarded the new Washington Senators franchise to a group headed by General Elwood "Pete" Quesada. The National League would either add a team in Houston or New York. By expanding by only one team, the American League deferred the contentious Los Angeles issue for a season. To accommodate the odd number of teams, the two leagues would introduce interleague games, accounting for 54 games of a proposed 166-game schedule.[86]

American League president Joe Cronin's interleague play proposal excited fans, but the two leagues had previously disagreed about its desirability. Interleague play usually failed in the face of one league or the other having a significant attendance advantage over the other. When the American League was drawing larger crowds than the National League, it eschewed interleague play. After the mid-1950s, when the National League began to outdraw the American League, the senior circuit disdained the concept.

During the 1962 summer meetings owners again discussed interleague play. Most of the National League teams opposed the proposal, although the Cincinnati Reds favored it. The Los Angeles Dodgers were vociferous foes. To the surprise of many, the New York Yankees now favored interleague play. When he was the general manager of the Yankees, George Weiss had been a staunch foe, claiming that it would "take the zip" from the World Series, which he probably viewed as the Yankees' private preserve. He also stated that interleague play might raise "grave questions about the honesty of baseball competition." A National League pennant winner playing two American League title contenders during the waning days of a season, for instance, might have an incentive to lose to the weaker contender in order to improve its chances of winning the World Series. The *Sporting News* conducted a small, nationwide poll of two hundred readers concerning interleague play. About 70 percent of the readers favored the idea.[87]

The issue continued to surface as late as 1963, when Frick, hoping to end the 162-game schedule, drew up a 154-game schedule for 1963 that included interleague play. With attendance faltering in the Major Leagues during 1963, American League owners expressed renewed interest in the concept, but National League owners once again shunned the idea.[88]

By finally agreeing to expand, the Major Leagues made the Continental League redundant. On August 1, 1960, Bill Shea and Branch Rickey agreed to halt Continental League activities contingent upon the Major Leagues' promise to expand to ten clubs each by 1961 or 1962. Milwaukee Braves owner Lou Perini suggested that the Major Leagues might absorb a few of the Continental League franchises. Although most observers believed that the Continental League was dead as of August 1, the league's officials still maintained that the organization would continue until irrevocable Major League expansion plans were finalized.[89]

Aside from the New York and Los Angeles opportunities and the perceived need to replace the Washington Senators in the capital, Dallas–Fort Worth and Houston loomed as the most attractive candidates. The American League was loath to let the National League get into Texas first. By mid-October the National League virtually guaranteed Houston an expansion franchise, and observers believed that the American League would counter with a team in Dallas–Fort

Worth. Indeed, some observers felt that Dallas–Fort Worth was the more attractive site. Civic leaders in both areas pledged that their cities would build stadiums upon inclusion into the Major Leagues. As early as 1960, Houston officials boasted of a domed stadium with parking for twenty-five thousand cars, while Dallas–Fort Worth touted a thirty-one thousand–seat, domed stadium that would be expandable to sixty thousand or more seats, with parking for twenty thousand cars.[90]

On August 30, 1960, American League president Joe Cronin announced that the American League would expand to ten teams, although he did not announce which cities would get ball clubs. He also supported rapid American League expansion in order to thwart the National League from getting the best locations, and he cited the American League's failure to move promptly into California. Dan Topping of the Yankees pushed for an American League expansion team in Los Angeles by 1962.[91] The National League once again stole a march on its rival league, however, when on October 17 the league voted to expand into Houston and New York. Sportswriter Ed Prell noted that once again the National League had co-opted a lucrative territory—Texas—ahead of the fumbling American League. National League president Warren Giles even announced that the American League could not stop the expansion New York team, as he had a foolproof (well, assuming that Ford Frick did not change his mind) procedural rule: "The National League could propose an amendment making New York an exception to the rule [against violating another team's territory]. The unit system is in effect in joint meetings. Each league has a vote and so does Frick. If the American League votes against the amendment, Frick will cast the deciding vote." Because Frick had earlier declared New York open territory, he was committed to voting with the National League. The American League could use a similar procedure in placing a team in Los Angeles.[92] The status of the new National League franchise in New York depended partly on whether the city built a new ballpark. In hopes of forestalling a new stadium, the Yankees offered a long-term lease to any prospective National League team, while Horace Stoneham offered the empty Polo

Grounds as a temporary playing field. On October 26 the American League surprised everyone by announcing that it was expanding to ten teams in 1961, not 1962, as expected. The league chose Los Angeles and Washington for its new cities. Afterward Frick pleaded for both leagues to avoid such haphazard actions and to meet jointly for any future expansion decisions, but the owners had made it clear that he was just a cipher.[93]

The American League's expansion into Los Angeles came with some stipulations. Shortly after the American League had announced its nine-team plan, the two leagues arranged a compromise about Los Angeles. The owners of the expansion team, however, had to compensate Walter O'Malley $450,000, half the sum total of his reported outlays, in order to get the Los Angeles territory for the Dodgers. The new team also had to play in the city's Wrigley Field and not the Los Angeles Coliseum. Once Chavez Ravine opened, the new team could lease the stadium from the Dodgers for $200,000 rental and no concessions revenue. Wrigley Field was a Minor League stadium with only twenty-two thousand seats and limited parking. No surprise, but O'Malley owned Wrigley Field. He used Rule 1(c) of the updated baseball code, which required unanimous approval of violating someone's territory to force the compromise. The owners amended Rule 1(c) by stipulating that any future incident would be adjusted by the new team paying to the existing Major League team whose territory was being violated $100,000 plus half of any indemnity paid to a Minor League team.[94]

According to Bill Veeck, O'Malley had bullied the American League into accepting these stipulations, claiming that any American League expansion into Los Angeles had to gain his assent. O'Malley could point out, with justice, that he had incurred substantial legal fees and other expenses to get the Chavez Ravine site and to compensate the Pacific Coast League for moving into that league's territory. In addition, he had paid the Los Angeles Coliseum to convert the stadium for baseball. Thus, any American League franchise would be free riding upon the Dodgers' efforts. Frick agreed and stated that all sixteen owners had to approve of having an expansion team in Los Angeles. Del Webb of the Yankees acquiesced to O'Malley's bullying, possibly because Webb hoped to build the Angels' new stadium. Veeck disagreed with O'Malley and claimed that the Dodgers owner had forced the Angels to play in Los Angeles's Wrigley Field for a season before sharing Chavez Ravine as a tenant. Playing in the former Minor League stadium reduced the Angels' attendance, and Veeck estimated that the other American League teams lost $500,000 when they played the Angels instead of other rivals. Webb, at least, got a contract to refurbish Wrigley Field.[95] Another American League owner, Calvin Griffith, also complained about the new team in Los Angeles: "That trip to Los Angeles is murder. There has to be another team in the state of California to build up a rivalry for the Angels in the American League like the Dodgers and the Giants have in the National. It costs too much to go to the Coast for one game."[96]

The "marriage" between the Angels and the Dodgers was not blissful. The teams squabbled over seemingly trivial matters The Dodgers, for example, assessed the Angels for half the cost of toilet paper at Chavez Ravine, even though Dodger fans constituted three-quarters of the total attendance. Eventually, the Dodgers adjusted the bill. Because the Angels were a poor gate attraction at both Wrigley Field and Chavez Ravine, the club wanted to move, even to what was then still the small town of Anaheim. Even O'Malley suggested that the American League would be wise to approve the move: "You must realize that the Yankees are just about the only team in the American League that can draw enough in Los Angeles to cover hotel and travel expenses. The others are probably willing to try anything to take in more money."[97]

A perceived dearth of talent had been one of the barriers facing the Continental League. The *Sporting News* cited the case in which the Boston Red Sox had to call up a Minor League outfielder who was hitting .211 in the Minors as evidence of the paucity of talent, and even as late as 1965, sportswriter Francis Stann cited a lack of quality players that was stymieing a second round of expansion.[98] Conversely, contradicting their claims that there simply were not enough "Major League" players to man a new eight-team league, some officials wanted to expand beyond the proposed ten-team leagues. Bill DeWitt espoused a twelve-team league by 1963.[99] With expansion Major League owners suddenly downplayed the player shortage issue. In response to the perceived lack of big-league talent, Chicago Cubs owner P. K. Wrigley brushed aside the concern: "There will be players available as soon as the youngsters learn that there is greater opportunity in the game. The fact that there will be more room at the top is the only incentive we need for development of more playing material."[100] J. G. Taylor Spink, editor of the *Sporting News*, suggested that the Major Leagues make peace with the colleges in order to bolster their pool of talent. Major League teams often did not wait for college players to graduate before offering talented youngsters large bonuses.[101]

After pleading that there were not enough Major League players to share with the Continental League, how did the Major Leagues find players for their expansion teams? To stock the two American League expansion teams, Cronin proposed a plan in which the existing eight teams would each submit a list of fifteen players, including seven on their active twenty-five man roster as of September 1, 1960. Each existing team would lose seven players. Each new team would select twenty-eight players and had to select ten pitchers, two catchers, six infielders, and four outfielders. The remaining six players could play any position. The new teams would pay $75,000 for each player selected to his original franchise, a total of $2.1 million for each incumbent team. Notice that rather than charge a direct fee for joining the American League, the league "sold" players to the new teams. The distinction generated favorable tax treatment for the new franchises.[102]

Although the American League owners thought the expansion pool a generous one, Frick told reporters that a new club might win [only] fifty games. Not surprisingly, there were no pitchers offered in the expansion pool who had won as many as ten games in 1960. The two American League expansion teams expressed "delight" over the players they nabbed in the expansion draft, although there really was not much to gain by denigrating the available players. "We are very happy about the players we obtained," said Fred Haney of the Angels.[103]

The Yankees supposedly lost the most in the expansion draft. The team lost the first two pitchers selected: Eli Grba and Bobby Shantz. In addition, the club lost pitcher Duke Maas, outfielders Bob Cerv and Ken Hunt, and first basemen Dale Long and Bud Zipfel. Other Major League players, seeing that the price of expansion players was $75,000, were determined to get pay increases. Mickey Mantle wanted $75,000 for 1961 instead of the $65,000 he had received in 1960. Roger Maris wanted to double his salary from $20,000 to $40,000.[104]

Before settling on its policy for providing expansion teams with players, the National League briefly considered trimming rosters to twenty-three players. The expansion teams could then choose from among the twenty-fourth and twenty-fifth players on the existing eight teams. One National League official said, "We think these eight men on each side will form the nucleus of a sound club for each of the new entries."[105] Apparently, fantasy baseball began long ago.

Because the National League delayed expanding until the 1962 season—although the New York Mets and Houston Colt .45s started organizing in 1960—the owners of existing teams could rig the expansion player draft to their advantage. Conversely, the two new teams could organize their Minor League systems and start signing players. Although the National League owners criticized their American League brethren, their expansion pool plan was quite similar. The main difference was that the NL created a "premium class" of players. Each premium player cost $125,000, instead of the $75,000 charged for all other players in the expansion pool. Each existing team would offer two premium players, and each expansion team could select up to four such players from all of the existing teams; the rules stipulated that each existing team would lose only one of its two premium players. In addition, the expansion team could select an additional player from each existing club for $50,000. Otherwise, the National League teams would offer fifteen players, including seven from their August 31, twenty-five-man roster. Houston and New York could each buy a maximum of twenty-eight players, for a total of $2.1 million, but each team was compelled to take at least twenty players for $1.7 million. Each established team received at least $425,000 (four players at $75,000 each and the premium player) from the two expansion teams, up to $525,000. No existing club would lose more than seven players.[106] Theoretically, every existing team would lose at least three players from its twenty-five-player roster.

There was a crucial difference, however, between the leagues' separate plans. The American League teams had no opportunity to manipulate their twenty-five-and forty-player rosters because it was retroactive to August 31, 1960, while the National League teams had months to prepare for their August 31, 1961, roster.[107] The American League teams complained when Ford Frick approved the National League plan, but NL owners claimed their plan would provide just as much talent as the American League pool did. When the National League expansion draft ended, Mets and Colt .45s officials expressed the almost obligatory satisfaction with the pool, but both would struggle to field solid teams.[108] After the 1963 season the other Major League owners recognized that these new teams needed help. The owners voted to let the expansion teams option four first-year players without restriction instead of the usual one player, but American League owners rejected a similar measure the following year.[109]

Major League Baseball's cartel succeeded in repelling invaders such as the Continental League, primarily by controlling players and by expanding into potential Continental League cities. In addition, by appearing to be "reasonable" in requesting that outside teams meet certain minimum standards, the cartel erected significant barriers to entry. But incumbent owners usually reacted to rather than anticipated events. When the Dodgers and Giants abandoned New York City, tempting Shea and Rickey to form a new league, the owners had to scramble to meet the new threat. Fortunately, their near-ironclad control of players gave them an almost insurmountable advantage—insurmountable, that is, unless Congress meddled. Eventually, the owners resorted to preempting the CL by placing expansion teams in potential cities, thereby dousing the invasion threat and placating nosy legislators. The hurried scramble for desirable locations, however, caused the process to be less than optimal.

The Major Leagues' first wave of expansion in 1961 and 1962 produced mixed results. The American League appears to have bungled the effort, and its credo might have been, "Expand in haste, repent at leisure." The four new teams were not artistic successes on the field, although the Angels had two winning seasons during their first five years (see table 8.1 in the appendix). Because the incumbent National League owners had an extra year to manipulate their rosters, the Mets and Colt .45s expansion draft pickings were slimmer than the pickings offered to their American League counterparts, which was reflected in their records. Despite the inferior records on the field, the two National League teams drew a combined 13.8 million fans between 1962 and 1966, in part due to their new stadiums. The two American League teams struggled to draw seven million fans between 1961 and 1965. The new Senators lasted eleven terrible seasons, interrupted only by Frank Howard's tape measure homeruns. The team had one winning season and never drew even a million fans in any season; twice it drew over eight hundred thousand fans. For the American League's finances the reestablishment of a club in Washington was more likely subtraction by expansion. The Angels would eventually shift to Anaheim, and the Senators would move to Dallas–Fort Worth.

After the first wave of expansion, some Major League officials expressed optimism that further growth was imminent, citing such cities as possible candidates as Buffalo, Dallas–Fort Worth, Montreal, San Diego, and Toronto. Indeed, Yankees owner Del Webb wanted the American League to expand to twelve teams in 1961, but his proposal was defeated.[110] Maybe he hoped that there would be more stadiums for him to build.

The Sixteen-Headed Hydra

The Cartel Faces the Enmity Within

The Major League Baseball cartel consisted of sixteen (and later twenty) independent, often strong-willed owners. Sometimes owners had to band together to prevent a maverick owner's self-interest from injuring the group. On other occasions owners acted jointly to curb the injurious effects of too much competition within the group. Hence, the cartel curbed the individual owners' self-interest in order to enhance the collective interest.

Carpetbaggers and Major League Baseball's Image

The First Wave of Relocations

Major League owners reserved the right to prohibit franchise relocations. There were sound reasons for this arrangement. In analyzing the territorial restraints exercised by sports leagues, law professor Jeffrey Glick cited justifications of such restraints in order to avoid creating "serious hardships for the other league members both in terms of travel schedules and costs . . . by balancing the interests of all teams in site selection, a legitimate restraint can promote on-field competition in locations acceptable to both participants, create a marketable product and thereby promote economic competition."[1] Owners believed that having a stable group of teams promoted fan loyalty, so the movement of six of the original sixteen franchises raised the issue of whether fans would become disenchanted. In addition, ball club owners were concerned about the adverse publicity of an owner's seemingly too opportunistic peregrinations. To protect such loyalty, the leagues had created stringent rules against franchise movements, originally requiring unanimity within a league and near unanimity from all of the Major League teams. Moreover, the leagues occasionally helped ailing franchises with cash or players in order to keep them from going out of business or moving.

Such conservatism against franchise movements broke down in the aftermath of the 1951 House subcommittee meetings, which detailed the demand for baseball by the rapidly growing cities of the West and South and growing awareness of the inability of Boston, Philadelphia, and St. Louis to support two teams. Subsequently, the requirement of unanimity was loosened to require only three-fourths approval within the league and an even lesser role for the other league.

All of these moves created underlying tension. The move by the Athletics to Kansas City, for example, raised travel costs for the league as a whole. The franchise relocation caused teams to have to travel an additional twenty thousand miles, and travel costs averaged 6.4 cents per mile per person. Many teams had an entourage of forty people, so the total higher cost to the league was roughly $50,000. The Athletics, of course, bore the largest share of the increase, some $20,500. Of course, movement to the West Coast promised to escalate travel expenses by even larger amounts. A Major League study suggested that mileage would double from its 1954 level of 138,000 to 301,000 miles, and Dodgers and Giants owners O'Malley and Stoneham may have offered to reimburse their fellow National League owners for any extra transportation expense.[2]

By 1960 six of the original sixteen franchises had relocated or were about to. Although the moves by the Boston Braves, Philadelphia Athletics, and St. Louis Browns to Milwaukee, Kansas City, and Baltimore, respectively, seemed justified to most observers, the subsequent moves seemed less so. The Brooklyn Dodgers were a most profitable franchise until the very end, while the New York Giants were not in as dire straits as the first three teams to relocate. The Giants had been considering relocating for several years. As early as the mid-1950s, Minneapolis public officials courted the team.[3] Certainly, the Dodger's move from Brooklyn left enduring bitterness.

O'Malley's and Stoneham's teams played in old stadiums with inadequate parking, so both owners sought new stadiums with ample parking. Stoneham explained, "People have moved out of the city. You used to be able—at least over in Brooklyn they could—go out and get a crowd from within walking distance of the park and fill the stands. You can't do that any more. Nowadays people have to drive in from the suburbs. We have a transportation problem, and we have a parking problem. It takes people too long to get through the traffic close to the Polo Grounds, and too long to get away."[4] To help facilitate franchise moves, the National League changed its rules from requiring unanimous approval for such a shift to only a two-thirds majority.[5] Because the Dodgers and Giants were invading the Pacific Coast League's territory, they agreed to pay $900,000 over three years to the remaining Pacific Coast League teams. The two teams planned to generate the costs by levying a ten- or fifteen-cent surcharge on their tickets.[6]

While O'Malley planned to build a new stadium with private funds, the Dodgers would use the Los Angeles Coliseum until Chavez Ravine was built. The Coliseum Commission granted the team revenue from concessions for all but eleven games; the Dodgers agreed to pay $200,000 flat rental for 1958 and 1959. For eleven games with San Francisco the Dodgers would pay 10 percent of gate receipts as rent and relinquish all concession revenues. The San Francisco Giants received a generous stadium deal from the city. San Francisco's mayor outlined the arrangement: a new stadium seating forty-five thousand; parking for at least ten thousand cars, with the city retaining parking revenue; all concession revenue going to the ball club; and rental of the stadium at 5 percent of the gross receipts after first deducting taxes, visiting club's shares, and the league's share, although the club guaranteed a rental payment of $125,000.[7] Not everyone was overjoyed with the mayor's largesse. An editorial in *Barron's* argued that the deal "seems to play hob with the precepts of sound municipal finance, as well as those of free enterprise. The blunt fact is that in order to break into the big leagues the Bay City has agreed to underwrite the construction and operation of a ball park and related facilities. Thereby, in effect, it has placed the public credit behind a private venture. The deal may represent a smashing victory on the West Coast for better baseball and civic pride. But it also stands for the triumph, in a great U.S. metropolis, of expediency over principle."[8] The editorial cited the heavy burden on taxpayers. Of course, public financing of professional sports venues has persisted in the decades since San Francisco underwrote the stadium.

There were perceived risks in moving to California. During the postwar boom the Pacific Coast League considered requesting Major League status in the late 1940s, but nothing came of this movement.[9] Although the Pacific Coast League had lobbied for Major League status for over a decade, that league's attendance levels did not provide overwhelming proof of the West Coast cities' ability to support such status. The Pacific Coast League's players were somewhere between AAA and Major League quality, but the Los Angeles Angels and Hollywood Stars rarely drew over three thousand fans per game, hardly encouraging to baseball moguls.[10] According to the *New York Times*, the consensus of the owners was that "evidence is lacking that Los Angeles is a good baseball town; the Pacific Coast League would fight invasion bitterly; and it might take two years to place a team in Los Angeles. The Washington Senators, however, preferred to have the A's shifted to Los Angeles where . . . Wrigley Field probably could be obtained for the 1955 season on a major league level."[11]

When New York and Brooklyn announced their plans to go west, some owners thought that San Francisco would prove a better baseball town. Chicago Cubs owner Philip Wrigley told O'Malley that "San Francisco is more closely knit and has more civic pride, and this will be reflected in its support of baseball. Los Angeles is like a Newfoundland puppy, suddenly grown up and sprawled out all over."[12] By allowing both the Giants and Dodgers to move, the National League hoped not only to mitigate increases in travel expenses but also to maintain a key rivalry. The Dodgers and Giants preferred to move in tandem, to maintain the rivalry found in New York. Indeed, Major League executives, such as Wrigley, had frequently commented on the desirability of fostering rivalries between cities in close proximity.[13] Certainly, an American League shift of, say, the Browns and Athletics would have been less of a hallowed rivalry to transfer.

The Dodgers and Giants received early confirmation of the sagacity of their West Coast move. The Dodgers drew 167,000 fans to the team's opening three-game set with the San Francisco Giants. San Francisco Giants secretary Eddie Brannick was pleased with his team's share of the revenue (the 27.5 cents per admission share to the visiting team): $45,982.47. "It's the largest check I ever took out of another team's ball park," he said.[14] The Dodgers did well at the concessions stands too. The team kept 30 percent of the gross from foodstuffs, and observers estimated that the team cleared $100,000 in concessions revenue during the three-game series.

Preseason sales presaged the huge crowds. By late January the Dodgers had sold almost eight thousand season box seats at $250 each. The team also sold a thousand season reserved seats. The Giants were also well ahead of their best advance ticket sales. With the absence of the Dodgers and Giants, the Yankees also did well with advance sales; in fact, that team had a 98.5 percent renewal rate of their box seats. In addition, the team was doing well with other advance sales. Indeed, the 1958 preseason sales were brisk across the Major Leagues.[15] The Dodgers hoped to break the single-game attendance record and to come close to breaking the 1948 Cleveland Indians single-season attendance record.[16]

The Dodgers did even better in 1959. In addition to their stellar paid attendance during the 1959 season of over two million, the team also distributed a half-million tickets to its Knothole club for youngsters, armed forces personnel, and other promotions. Sportswriter James Murray estimated that the Dodgers made $3.3 million in profits before taxes—"more money in a single season than any other franchise holder in the history of baseball."[17]

Five months before the 1962 season and the opening of the new Chavez Ravine stadium, the Dodgers had already sold over $3 million worth of seats, including 11,786 season box seats and 1,919 reserved seats. Thus, if the team did not sell another ticket, it would have one million in attendance. The season ticket total exceeded by four thousand that for the 1960 season, the previous best attendance in Los Angeles. Dodger fans renewed all but 175 season tickets out of 7,716. When the Giants visited the Dodgers for a Monday-Tuesday two-game set during May 1962, attendance totaled 91,828.[18]

The Dodgers were thus extremely successful in their move from Brooklyn to Los Angeles. Despite three pennants in their last five years in Brooklyn, attendance stagnated at about 1.1 million per season. Attendance almost doubled in Los Angeles. While the Brooklyn franchise was hardly as troubled as those of the Athletics, Braves, and Browns, O'Malley astutely recognized the gains to be found in California. Bill Veeck has suggested that O'Malley was mainly motivated by real estate—the promise of free land in Los Angeles.[19] O'Malley's partner in the West Coast shift, Horace Stoneham, was not as fortunate. The Giants had fallen into mediocrity during the final three years in New York, and their attendance had dwindled to 650,000 in 1957. The move to San Francisco succeeded in raising attendance by five-sixths during the first five seasons compared to the last five in New York, but San Francisco's attendance badly lagged behind that of the Dodgers. During the tight pennant race between the Giants and the Dodgers in 1962, the Los Angeles franchise drew over one million more fans than did the Giants. In any event baseball historian G. Edward White believes that the Major Leagues made a mistake in taking so long to expand to the West Coast.

At about the same time that the Dodgers and Giants relocated, the perennial "sick man of the American League," the Washington Senators, was considering moving to Minneapolis–St. Paul. Minneapolis officials contacted Calvin Griffith in 1957 about relocating and gave generous guarantees. Testifying before Estes Kefauver's Senate subcommittee, Frick said he opposed the transfer of the Senators but that if the team moved, the National League would expand to ten teams by planting a city team in Washington DC and in New York.[20] He had reason to tread carefully before the Senate committee. New York representative Emanuel Celler warned baseball against any "irresponsible franchise shifts while Congress' back is turned in adjournment. . . . The National Pastime belongs in the National Capital and I deplore these attempts to move it without regard for fan loyalties . . . [such shifts were] more evidence of money-grabbing."[21] He had long opposed organized baseball's antitrust exemption. Senator Karl Mundt vociferously opposed the Washington Senators moving from the capital: "I simply say they do not have the right to run out of town, to evacuate the city, to leave the National capital without the national support, to ignore their responsibilities to the international situation, to the fight against juvenile delinquency, to the maintenance of a spirit of Americanism which reflects itself throughout baseball that they cannot permit cupidity to that extent, to take them from the city." He offered Major League owners a threatening quid pro quo: "Once they decide to leave Washington DC, without representation in either of the two major baseball leagues, by such action, they automatically repeal the protective legislation which we pass."[22]

Despite these congressional rumblings, Griffith was sorely tempted. Minneapolis–St. Paul was offering to expand its existing baseball stadium, if Major League Baseball would guarantee a team. The Washington Senators were the obvious candidate, but the Cleveland Indians also took notice. The city council approved a $5.75 million bond to expand Metropolitan Stadium from twenty-one thousand seats to forty-one thousand, with parking for up to fifteen thousand cars. The Minnesotans cast their nets across the Major Leagues, sending invitations to Baltimore, Cleveland, Kansas City, and even the Dodgers. In September 1958 a writer for the *Sporting News* speculated, "The Dodgers are in park trouble and with that lawsuit [revolving around the team's acquisition of property in Chavez Ravine] they may be looking for a home."[23] There were two potential drawbacks. The Minneapolis Minor League team was a disappointment at the gate, drawing just 135,000 for sixty-two home dates, despite having a second-place team. In addition, the remaining American Association teams were waiting to demand the same $900,000 indemnity that the Pacific Coast League had received for the invasion of California by the Dodgers and Giants.

Although the evidence is mixed that Baltimore drew fans from and weakened Washington, the situation facing the Senators was bleak. Griffith Stadium was small and was located in a deteriorating neighborhood. Calvin Griffith was also worried about the city's changing racial makeup: "The trend in Washington is getting to be all colored." By 1960 the city would be predominantly black. Interestingly, he did not blame the Baltimore Orioles for his attendance woes, as he claimed that his clientele came from the District of Columbia and neighboring suburbs in Virginia. He was not even enthused about the proposed new stadium for Washington DC because it would be built near the Maryland state line.[24] While the proposed move also had the attraction of hurting the fledgling Continental League by occupying one of its proposed cities, the owners' fears about the adverse political fallout stymied the move.

Few things were simple within Major League Baseball. Griffith's hopes to move to Minnesota for the 1960 season failed without even going to vote. One American League official told the *Sporting News*, "There was no personal disaffection for Griffith. We respect him as a club owner. But our opposition to the move stands as notice that we will not sanction any frivolous or impractical franchise shifts. There has to be merit and a solid justification for moving franchises." New York Yankees owner Dan Topping was publicly opposed to the shift, while Chicago and Cleveland were apparently also against it.[25]

Griffith tried again and barely received approval to shift his Senators to Minneapolis–St. Paul in late 1960. Cleveland and Detroit opposed the move, but the other owners decided it could be beneficial. Griffith received a guarantee of one million a year in attendance for the first five years and much higher radio and television revenues than he earned in Washington DC.[26] He found Minnesota to be much more profitable than Washington DC. There were, however, moments of doubt. Residents of the two cities reputedly feuded, as described in a story in *Sports Illustrated* in 1961: "No self-respecting St. Paul citizen would watch a Minneapolis team play baseball, or vice versa. Deciding that neither city could support a major league team without help from the other, Griffith hedged by renaming his club the Minnesota Twins and announcing it would play its home games in Metropolitan Stadium in suburban Bloomington, a spot equidistant from both downtown areas. This, Griffith hoped, would win over citizens of both towns."[27]

Such concerns were well founded. Indeed, the franchise set a record for the lowest attendance for its opening three-game series of any of the relocated franchises. However, Griffith was pleased that almost half of his advance sales came from the area beyond the two cities.[28] Observers wondered whether Twins attendance would hold up once fishing season opened. As one writer described the scene:

> Round One is over and the walleyes won. The weekend of May 13–14, the walleye fishing season opened, and there was noticeable decrease in the "big exodus" to the northland. While the Twins were drawing 10,103 fans at Metropolitan Stadium in Bloomington, highways on the opposite side of town were clogged with cars loaded with fisherman. . . . Minnesota state officials and resort and travel observers estimated there were about a half-million fishermen in action over the weekend. That's a pretty big chunk of the whole Minnesota population of slightly over 3,000,000. It is even bigger when one considers that the fisherman and the baseball fan usually are of the same age group and the same general social and economic level. . . . A poll conducted by the Minneapolis *Star* and *Tribune* indicated that about 70 percent of the adult males in Minnesota go fishing.[29]

In addition, Minnesota residents had the highest home ownership rates in the country; the reporter believed they were therefore more likely to stay at home puttering around their homes (unlike apartment dwellers) than attending ballgames.

As the golden age of Major League Baseball waned and after the Continental League disappeared in the wake of expansion, some Major League owners coveted such rapidly growing cities as Atlanta, Dallas–Fort Worth, Seattle, and even Oakland. Civic leaders in these towns sought "Major League status" by promising to build new stadiums with public money, which they would lease at generous terms. In a reversal of the famous movie line, these cities promised, "If you come, we will build it." The turmoil affected the Minor Leagues, too, leading them to come together in order to realign their leagues.[30]

The Second Wave of Relocations

Organized baseball was generally supportive of its members, although self-interested efforts by individual team owners regularly put pressure on the alliance. The members usually countenanced a fellow owner's desire to move to greener playing fields. Some owners grew disenchanted, however, with even their team's new home and developed wanderlust.

Although Athletics owner Arnold Johnson had been excoriated throughout the American League for allegedly being the Yankees' lackey, Kansas City fans soon had reason to rue his death in 1960. Initially, fans wondered whether Johnson's widow would continue to operate the team.[31] When she put the team up for sale, some residents hoped the city would purchase the club. Such a purchase, however, was not allowed by the Missouri state constitution. To help entice a new owner to keep the team in Kansas City, fans in the city participated in an attendance drive to push the season attendance past the 850,000 level. The drive was successful, and almost one hundred thousand attended a three-game set with the New York Yankees. As sportswriter Ernest Mehl pointed out, "In 1955, when the Athletics were labeled the worst outfit ever to perform in the league, they finished sixth. . . . The fact is the city wants to keep the club; the fans are convinced that with local ownership and an aggressive operation the team can be improved. This belief is so strong that everyone is willing to gamble on it."[32]

New owner Charles Finley provided early hope that he would change things for the better. Early on he announced, "We will have no alliances with any other club in the American League. There will be no such trades as have been made in the past. When we develop stars, we are going to keep them."[33] He claimed to have spent $400,000 for promotion and park improvement, but this sum would soon haunt Kansas City officials and fans.[34] Nor was his determination to keep the team in Kansas City sincere; indeed, like a groom ogling the bridesmaids, he was chronically dissatisfied with the situation there and cast covetous glances around the country. Ostensibly, he chafed at the stadium lease with the city, especially after the new Kansas City Chiefs football team received an allegedly better lease. By the middle of the 1962 season his eyes were roving, and he made no pretense to hide it. He started with Dallas–Fort Worth then continued with Atlanta, Louisville, and Oakland. The American League thought Dallas–Fort Worth a good choice for relocation but hesitated to approve the move for fear of displaying "callous disregard" of the fans in Kansas City, which might hurt the game's image.[35] In a letter the Kansas City Chamber of Commerce pointed out that "the news story is disquieting and obviously unfair to the people of the central states area who have given such remarkable support to the Athletics and to the American League since 1955."[36] Attendance in Kansas City averaged almost a million during the first five years, despite a terrible club that only once finished as high as sixth place. Finley countered that he lost $1.55 million during 1962, although half of the loss was due to depreciation of players. He claimed that he had lost about $1 million the year before, again mostly due to depreciation. His depreciation allowance, however, was ending shortly.[37]

In order to retain the club, Kansas City's mayor and city council offered lease terms that they characterized as "the most generous" in baseball. To avoid the yearly fear that Finley would shift the franchise, the city wanted all attendance provisions removed from the cancellation clause. An earlier lease with Arnold Johnson contained a provision that if attendance fell below 850,000 in a season, the pact could be canceled. Finley also received such a clause, but the city wanted to remove it. Finley added to the complexity by saying he had spent over $400,000 in stadium improvements, a claim the city thought too high. The current lease charged the Athletics $1,000 in basic rent (later reduced to $1) and 5 percent of the paid admissions. The city also received 7.5 percent of the concessions. Finley had the Missouri Sportservice operate concessions at the stadium, and he received 29 percent of the total concession revenue. The city offered the Chiefs a $1 basic annual rental fee and charged 5 percent of paid admissions after the first two years if receipts topped $1.1 million. The city and the Chiefs would split the concessions equally.

Finley's lease appeared favorable when compared with other Major League teams. The Milwaukee Braves paid no basic rent but instead paid 5 percent of paid admissions on the first million in attendance, 7 percent on the next 500,000 in attendance, and 10 percent for attendance over 1.5 million. In addition, the club shared 10 to 16 percent of concessions with the county. Baltimore, Cleveland, and Washington all paid basic rents of at least $60,000 as well as 7 percent of paid admissions, if they were greater than base rent. Each club paid at least 10 percent of concessions, with Cleveland sharing 45 percent. Minnesota paid a flat 7 percent of paid admissions and one-tenth of concessions. While the football lease appeared more generous, the Chiefs were willing to sign for many more years than the Athletics. Throughout the remainder of 1963 Finley and the city argued about the lease. Finley kept insisting that the city owed him $400,000 (later reduced to $300,000) for stadium improvements. Kansas City fans quickly tired of Finley's annual threats to go elsewhere. Some fans were willing to bid him adieu and try for another Major League team, which is what eventually happened. All through the summer and fall of 1963 Finley and the city bickered. At one point Finley went to city hall and presented his check for $2 to cover the next two years' basic rent on the stadium. He denied he was negotiating with Oakland.[38]

Finley's antics in trying to move the team to Oakland incurred the wrath of Missouri and Kansas legislators. Senator Edward Long of

Missouri supported a bill bringing professional team sports under the federal antitrust laws, with certain exceptions, because, he said, Finley's "attitude toward the fans of the Athletics and people of Kansas City and his resultant actions offer clear proof that the baseball leagues must be able to protect the game of baseball against irresponsible club owners. This bill would ensure that sports leagues could continue to work as leagues in protecting their particular sport from the abuses of renegades."[39] Long also echoed Emanuel Celler's dislike of mixing sports with profits; he wanted to know "whether or not the average franchise owner makes his decisions solely on the basis of business or does he consider the fact that baseball is a sport and a game."[40] Long's colleague Missouri senator Stuart Symington testified before the Senate committee on professional sports: "I am just interested in the fans of Kansas City."[41] Long and Symington blustered about Finley's proposed move, but, ultimately, nothing concrete was done.

Finley eventually proposed a four-year contract in which the Athletics would pay $50,000 rental payments while keeping all of the concession revenue. The concession clause would repay him for his now $300,000 in stadium improvement. In addition, however, he wanted two option periods that could be exercised by the Athletics if the attendance fell short of 950,000; if attendance fell below 950,000, the Athletics would pay no rent. The city declined. Finley immediately signed a two-year contract to play in Louisville, Kentucky, pending a permanent move to Oakland. He signed the contract without the approval of his fellow owners, many of whom opposed it. The American League eventually issued him an ultimatum to settle with Kansas City or else, using a clause in the league's constitution entitled "Involuntary Termination of Membership." The other owners could force out any owner whose actions threatened them or were not in the best interests of baseball.[42] Finally, on February 26, 1964, Finley capitulated and signed a four-year lease. The lease's crucial clauses included an annual rental of 5 percent of paid admissions and 7.5 percent of the concession income, the first $50,000 of said rent to be paid to the city, and the excess to be applied against the $300,000 stadium improvement tab. If attendance did not reach 575,000, no rent would be paid, except the amount due for concessions.[43]

Oakland offered Finley similar terms as Kansas City had: $50,000 rent, two years in advance, and he could have the parking concession for $300,000. When the new stadium was complete, he would pay 5 percent of the paid admission up to one million attendees and 10 percent above that number; in addition, he would share the concessions income. The city offered a twenty-year lease. Throughout the situation the American League owners had mixed feelings. Finley's fellow owners quietly hoped that the team would eventually move to Oakland, thereby mitigating the transportation costs of having only one team on the West Coast. Apparently, league officials had introduced Finley to the Oakland interests. The American League even concocted a schedule that would include Oakland for the 1964 season. San Francisco Giant's owner Horace Stoneham revealed Finley's Oakland plans in 1963, when Finley approached him about leasing Candlestick for a couple of seasons until the Oakland park was completed.[44]

Of course, the saga did not end with Finley's signing a short-term lease with Kansas City. Indeed, his fellow owners hoped he would sell the team, but he placed an $8 million price tag on it, thereby discouraging potential bidders. After the 1964 season sportswriters mulled Finley's next move, but the situation was relatively quiet at year's end.[45]

Paralleling Finley's squabbles with Kansas City, the Milwaukee Braves ownership disliked the relatively small losses they incurred in the early 1960s, after years of great profitability. Attendance in Milwaukee astounded baseball people. After setting a National League record for home attendance in 1953, Braves owner Lou Perini chortled, "You are the finest fans in baseball. You have restored their pride to members of the entire Braves organization." In addition to the large crowds, Perini boasted that his team had "the highest per capita concessions sales in the major leagues" that year: "I see the most influential and wealthy people eating three and four hot dogs and drinking beer or Coke in preference to going out and having a restaurant meal. They do it because they enjoy it." He went so far as to disdain the potential gains in California: "I don't believe that California would duplicate the same enthusiastic response. They are more of the blase type."[46]

Because of the huge attendance, the Braves were able to shun televising home games for many years. Some sports promoters, however, urged caution about interpreting the fabulous attendance figures. Basketball owner Ben Kerner (who eventually moved his Hawks from the Tri-Cities in Iowa and Illinois—now called the Quad Cities—to Milwaukee to St. Louis and later to Atlanta) stated, "Baseball is bleeding [Milwaukee] putting nothing in and taking everything out. Milwaukee is a strange place. When the Braves begin to lose and the novelty wears off, the absolute bottom will fall out." An anonymous baseball official claimed, "Beware those towns where baseball emotions get too high because they also get too low. Give me a town with St. Louis' stability."[47] Despite retaining the core of the team in future Hall of Fame players Hank Aaron, Eddie Mathews, and Warren Spahn, the Braves slowly deteriorated throughout the 1960s. Attendance also fell. Although the 1960 gate was near two million and the team reported over $500,000 in gross profits, the decline became marked in subsequent years.

Some observers attributed part of the Braves' troubles to the re-location of the Washington Senators to Minneapolis–St. Paul. The American League team allegedly siphoned off baseball fans living in the upper Midwest and western Wisconsin, thereby limiting the Braves' drawing power to only eastern Wisconsin.[48] Braves officials did not use the Minnesota Twins as an excuse for the club's poor showing in 1961. The owner, Lou Perini, attributed the fall-off in attendance to several factors—a natural reduction in enthusiasm now that the "honeymoon" was over, bad weather, the difficulty in climbing stairs to the upper decks, and construction around the stadium that created traffic tie-ups. Perini promised that an escalator to the upper deck would be operable for the 1962 season.[49] He announced to Braves stockholders that the team might have been slow in developing new stars, thereby leading to its fall in the standings. In addition, the presence of aging stars such as Mathews and Spahn kept the payroll high; indeed, some observers thought the Braves might have had the highest payroll in all of baseball. The Braves trimmed the payroll by selling Johnny Antonelli and Frank Thomas to the Mets; the two veterans earned a combined $75,000 in 1961.

Another observer attributed part of the decline in attendance to the increase in ticket and parking prices as well as a new rule prohibiting fans from bringing their own beer into the park: "The law, now repealed, was a master stroke of public relations ineptitude in a town that likes to think that it invented beer."[50] The Braves raised ticket prices for the 1961 season, after having raised them in 1958. In 1962 they upped them again. Perini reported a loss of just under $80,000 for 1961, the team's first deficit figure since moving to Milwaukee. Indeed, season ticket sales for 1962 were only six thousand, or roughly half of the record number sold in 1959.[51] Perini decided to sell the club to a group of Chicago businessmen in late 1962 for a reported $5.5 million; he claimed to have purchased the club for $500,000 in 1944, plus assuming debts. The new owners quickly sought to lift the ban on telecasts of home games in hopes of raising revenue. Despite his success in Milwaukee, Perini could not resist firing a shot at the city and its fans: "If the Braves aren't on top within two or three years, the fans can throw us out of the town. If the fans desert us, this is not a major league city."[52]

As early as 1963, the new owners of the Braves were rumored to be considering transferring the franchise to Atlanta. That city was planning to build a new stadium, pending a commitment from a Major League team. The closest teams to Atlanta were the Cincinnati Reds, St. Louis Cardinals, and Washington Senators—the closest nearly five hundred miles away. Clearly, Atlanta could capture a very large area, not only for actual attendance at games but for television and radio audiences. The city was growing, whereas Cincinnati, St. Louis, and Washington were stagnating. The Braves were not the only team considering Atlanta. Charles Finley considered the city in 1963, but his fellow American League owners persuaded him to desist, as they preferred to hold the city open for another team, perhaps Cleveland. Ironically, a Kansas City sportswriter concluded that while Atlanta's biggest asset was its potential television market, Kansas City had potentially as large a TV market. That team could draw from the Plains states and into Colorado, including Denver.[53]

To entice a Major League team, the Atlanta and Fulton County Recreation Authority scrambled to get a stadium built in time for the 1964 season and to issue invitations to Major League teams to relocate. The city wanted to build a stadium seating forty-five thousand, later increased to fifty-seven thousand, for baseball. With the new realities of attracting fans, the mayor touted the fact that thirty-two lanes of expressways converged upon the stadium site from every direction, and these expressways ensured that three-fourths of the population of Georgia were within ninety minutes driving time of the stadium.[54] Because the stadium would not be ready in time for the 1964 season and Milwaukee civic leaders promised to help with ticket sales, the Braves decided against moving. Later civic officials threatened legal action based on the stadium lease. Braves president John McHale said, "The Braves will be in Milwaukee, today, tomorrow, next year and as long as we are welcome. . . . It is quite natural for cities seeking major league franchises to solicit the interest of those clubs whose attendance has declined, just as Milwaukee did in 1953."[55] His remarks, similar to George Wallace's contemporaneous boasts regarding segregation, proved as ephemeral.

The Braves announced an operating loss for the year ending October 31, 1963, of about $60,000, slightly smaller than the previous years' loss. Bill Veeck characterized this loss as a "bookkeeping loss," as the club undoubtedly had earned a profit on operations. Within six months of McHale's statement Atlanta came wooing again. Mayor Allen of Atlanta claimed, "I have the verbal commitment of a major league baseball club to move its franchise to Atlanta, if we have a stadium ready by 1965." Although Allen initially was coy about which team had made the promise, by the fall he indicated that Atlanta coveted the Braves, even in the face of threatened litigation by Milwaukee officials.[56]

The Braves did not fare well in 1964, either on the field or at the gate. As the 1964 season opened, hopes were high that the team might draw a million fans, instead of the 773,000 it had attracted during 1963. One Braves official stated that the turnstiles would accelerate once school ended. He pointed out other advantages such as cheap parking and cheap concession prices, which he claimed to be 15 percent below the average for other parks, and a clean stadium. The team had bad luck at its home opener. The crowd was the largest in four years, but an outbreak of rowdiness, largely attributed to college and high school students, marred the game.[57] The team estimated its operating losses for the year at $500,000. John McHale stated, "We had hoped to be able to stay in Milwaukee but events of 1964 have made that impossible." The Braves also made it clear that they were "well able to pay the $175,000 which the plaintiff's [Milwaukee County] proposed 1965 budget estimates prospective rental payments on the stadium for the year [1965]."[58] By mid-season even the editor of the *Sporting News*, C. C. Johnson Spink, assumed the relocation was a fait accompli. Spink attributed part of the Braves' difficulties to the Minnesota Twins: "With the arrival of the Twins, the Braves were completely boxed in, drastically reducing their drawing territory. . . . The Braves had only Wisconsin for patronage." He lauded Atlanta's charms: virgin territory and more media revenue. "With the move, the N.L. again will steal a march on the A.L."[59]

The hope that the Braves would move to Atlanta hiked the demand for Braves stock. When the team initially offered 115,000 shares to residents of Wisconsin in March 1963, the price was close to $11.38 a share; the team was unable to sell more than 13,500 shares, and the price dropped to $3.50. With the rumored shift to Atlanta, the share price moved up to $15.50.[60]

Of course, Braves fans were upset at the rumored shift. While there was an irony in that Milwaukee had courted the team when it was in Boston, Milwaukee fans could point to greater support of the team than that given in Boston. One local politician, John Doyne, expressed the general feeling: "If the Braves pull up stakes for Atlanta, it could be the worst mark against baseball since the Black Sox scandal. . . .

How a ball club is permitted to come into a city like this, milk it for a dozen years and then jump elsewhere, I can't understand."[61] Naturally, Milwaukee residents wrote their congressman. Representative Henry Reuss wrote to Ford Frick and Warren Giles, requesting them to help keep the Braves in Milwaukee, but he received only vague assurances that "every effort" would be made to consider all the angles of any proposed shift. Eventually, the Milwaukee County Board served the club with a restraining order, based on breach of contract, as there was still a year to go on the stadium lease. Bill Veeck described the pivotal clause in the lease: play "all their home games on its National League schedule" in Milwaukee. Instead of being able to pay a reasonable approximation of the expected rent and satisfying the lease contract, the Braves were committed to playing at County Stadium.[62] This last step worked. The National League voted to keep the Braves in Milwaukee for one last season to honor the lease; concurrently, the league also voted that the Braves moving to Atlanta in 1966 was "in the league's best interest."

The team's desire to go south was easily understandable. After all, the Braves reportedly could hope to clear $750,000 to $1.5 million a year for five years from television revenue alone in Atlanta, instead of the $400,000 the organization earned in Milwaukee.[63] As usual, a Senate subcommittee was considering yet another sports antitrust bill during the summer of 1965. Wisconsin senator William Proxmire wanted to attach an amendment requiring all television and radio revenue to be put into a common pool and shared equally among all of the Major League clubs. He believed that such a policy would dampen the allure of cities such as Atlanta that promised big television contracts: "I can assure you that it was not lack of local support, but the lure of a television bonanza that prompted the Chicago businessmen, who bought the [Braves] . . . to make the decision to move. . . . [Sharing television money] would remove the incentive for teams to switch franchises merely to gain additional radio and television revenue."[64] Proxmire cited football's Green Bay Packers as an example of the beneficial effects of revenue sharing.

In one last, almost gratuitous, gesture Braves official John Quinn suggested to Milwaukee fans that they would be better off releasing the Braves from the last year of the stadium lease: "I feel that more friends would be won, not only in the National League itself but among fans everywhere, if the Braves were to be released. What can be achieved by [forcing them to remain in Milwaukee]? The Braves are gone, committed to Atlanta. Why hold them against their will?" Although he admitted that expansion and the hopes of obtaining another franchise were years away, he suggested that the city settle for a Minor League team for the time being.[65] The American League briefly considered placing a franchise in Milwaukee if the Braves relocated. Although Minnesota Twins president Calvin Griffith thought his team might benefit by as much as two hundred thousand in increased attendance per season in the absence of the Braves, he also hoped an American League team in Milwaukee might jump the gate because of the intercity rivalry.[66]

The lingering ill will triggered by the transfers of the Athletics and the Braves ended in an ironic twist. The American League dutifully replaced the Athletics with the Kansas City Royals. After the expansion Seattle Pilots floundered in 1969, the league shipped the team to Milwaukee for the 1970 season. The league habitually replaced failed teams with new ones, as even Seattle earned another club in 1977. Each time the American League expanded by two teams, one of the new teams was a replacement for one that had vacated a city.

Cleveland was becoming a struggling franchise during the 1960s. After Bill Veeck sold the club, attendance dwindled. Even the record-setting 1954 team faced a much diminished gate. According to sportswriter Robert Creamer, although the Indians were usually second or third in the American League, Cleveland fans grew weary of the team's perennial "bridesmaid" role: "Sad is the bleat of the Cleveland baseball fan . . . he spends as much time jeering his favorites as he does cheering them." Creamer suggested that a hypothetical Indians fan might reply to the club's overall excellent showing (ninety-five wins a season for the past eight seasons, up until 1956): "Second. That's right. Second to the Yankees. They're always second. They can't beat the Yankees." Of course, when the team failed even to reach that lofty perch, attendance skidded even more. Veeck created an atmosphere of fun during the 1948 pennant, and fans flocked to the games—2.62 million of them paid full admission. The new owners eschewed his flamboyant antics and assumed that a winning team would draw sufficiently: "The financiers . . . managed somehow in just a few short years to change the atmosphere in Municipal Stadium from carnival to lecture on dried prunes, from raw, emotional excitement which permeated all Cleveland to an irritating dullness which is permeating all Cleveland too."[67]

One observer also attributed the fans' apathy to the new owners raising ticket prices for the better seats after 1949. A check of Cleveland's scorecards reveals that the team maintained its reserved seating price through 1950, although prices of box, reserved, and general admission seats increased in 1952.[68] There was also resentment against general manager Frank Lane, who reportedly had a five cents per head attendance bonus during 1958–60. Lane, known as "Trader Frank," dealt Roger Maris to the Athletics, en route to the Yankees. Even worse, he traded Rocky Colavito to the Tigers on April 17, 1960, giving rise to the "Curse of Rocky Colavito," a scaled-down version of the Red Sox's "Curse of the Bambino."[69]

The Indians claimed a loss of $800,000 by mid-September of the 1964 season, partly because season ticket sales were only 2,800. Gabe Paul, part owner, believed the eventual loss would eclipse the $1.2 million loss incurred in 1963. Paul reiterated his desire to continue owning the team and keeping it in Cleveland. Some observers also felt that the American League would hesitate to approve a plan to relocate from Cleveland, given that it had forced Finley to remain in Kansas City.[70] In any case Cleveland civic leaders fought to keep the Indians from wandering.

Seattle loomed as a potential new home for the Indians. A franchise in Seattle would have a large, albeit sparsely populated, territory to monopolize. Seattle worked hard to make itself presentable. During

1964 the chamber of commerce helped lead a drive to sell eight thousand season tickets for the 1965 season. Eventually, the campaign sold more than $500,000 worth of tickets. A prospective team would begin playing in the Minor League Sicks' Stadium, which would be expanded to 24,500 seats until a larger, permanent Major League stadium was constructed. Exemplifying the musical chairs nature of Major League Baseball, another rumor swirled that if the Indians moved to Seattle, the Cincinnati Reds would leave their "small park which sits in a blighted area" for the charms of Cleveland's Municipal Stadium.[71] The era thus ended with the formerly stable roster of teams shattered, although the relocations were beneficial at the gate.

Competition for Amateur Talent

During the postwar era baseball officials and players often referred to free agents. Unlike the free agents of our era, however, these were generally talented amateur players. Indeed, amateur high school and college players represented the last vestige of a free market for baseball labor during the postwar era. Unlike professional football and basketball, Major League Baseball did not conduct a draft of amateur players during the postwar years. Instead of one team possessing the exclusive right to negotiate with an amateur player, all teams could deal with any youngster. Major League owners would be collectively better off by creating "single-buyer" bidding for amateurs, via a draft. A few teams, however, pursuing self-interest, opposed any draft. Thus, there was internal tension within the cartel.

Major League teams often offered large signing bonuses to these seventeen-and eighteen-year-old players as well as their college-age brothers. Major League Baseball attempted to respect college baseball programs by not signing players until their class graduated. Anticipating the seemingly endless escalation of bidding for free agents in the last decades of the twentieth century, the "bonus babies" reaped ever greater bonuses throughout the postwar period.

The owners quickly realized that this free market for labor could be costly. Baseball officials and the press often exaggerated the bonuses paid to callow youths, but whatever the true figures, baseball people bemoaned the expenditures. Even by the late 1940s, some youngsters received bonuses of nearly $100,000, more than the top Major League players received in any given season. Indeed, $100,000 was probably more than many regular players made in four or five seasons. In an effort to curb the spending, owners repeatedly passed legislation. Before the 1946 season they enacted a rule whereby any boy signed for more than $6,000 would forever be known as a bonus player; he could not be optioned, and waivers made on him were not withdrawable.[72] Robin Roberts was one such player. Teams apparently finessed the rule by offering bonuses in excess of $6,000 but payable over a number of years. Thus, in 1948 the rule was amended to define a bonus player as any player receiving a total of $6,000 or more, regardless of the timing of the payments. If another team acquired the bonus player from the original team, the new team could option the player once. The rules failed to curb bonus payments, and in 1949 thirty-eight boys received bonuses.

By the early 1950s young players had received an estimated $4.5 million in bonuses. Tom Yawkey of the Red Sox, tired of buying established Major Leaguers, plunged heavily into the bonus market, signing such baseball nonentities as Frank Baumann, Marty Keough, Ed Urness, and Jerry Zimmerman. Because the owners seemingly could not help themselves, they passed a new rule stipulating that any player signed for more than $4,000 had to remain on the Major League roster for two years, unless he were open to unrestricted selection after one year if left in the Minors. Waivers on bonus men were not revocable, and the waiver price was a dollar. The hope was that forcing bonus players to clog up Major League rosters would discourage wild bidding. In 1955 some owners proposed limiting the number of bonus men to two players per team, but the proposal failed. By 1957, with allegations of chicanery running rampant, the owners rescinded the existing rules on bonus players.[73] Curiously, if you were an owner thinking of signing a bonus baby, your best bet was someone whose surname began with *K*, as some of the bonus babies that became top-notch players included Al Kaline, Harmon Killebrew, Sandy Koufax, and Harvey Kuenn. Koufax signed for $20,000, as he related in his autobiography (author Brent Kelley lists the bonus as $24,000).[74] Predicting baseball stardom is difficult, however, and many of these bonus babies did not fulfill their promise, including other players with *K* surnames such as Ted Kazanski and Marty Keough. Overall, "one out of ten" made a large impact.[75]

Allegations of cheating led to distrust among the owners. Several called not for new rules but for effective enforcement of the existing rules. Because effective enforcement required Major League owners to reveal their finances fully to the commissioner's office, such calls for enforcement usually met defeat. George Weiss, of the Yankees, disliked the first-year rule enacted in the late 1950s; instead, he wanted baseball to hire a bonus administrator to monitor activity: "The first-year draft rule is a menace. It threatens baseball. It discourages the signing of many precocious young men. When you face that, you are undermining the game. . . . You are forced to rush [the bonus player] onto your major roster. This creates injustice to older players."[76] A second problem with the rule requiring placing bonus babies on the Major League roster had to do with the ill effects upon the young players. These youngsters typically did not play much in the Major Leagues and missed the seasoning they would have received in the Minor Leagues. Thus, bonus players were arguably held back in their development.

General manager Frank Lane disliked the bonus system, arguing that it was "a curse to too many of the young players": "It destroys their incentive. With all that money in their pockets, they feel so secure that they're not keenly interested in learning how to play baseball." Branch Rickey, too, preached against the demoralizing aspects of large bonuses: "The bonus is unfair to the older players, and, in general, hurts team morale. It is unearned and undeserved by its recipient and, in many cases, corrupts the boy morally and economically."[77] Major League officials advocating for the amateur draft in the hopes of curbing large bonuses were essentially saying, "We'll exploit you, and it will be good for your soul." St Louis general manager Bing Devine pointed out, however, that the large bonuses encouraged youngsters to choose Major League Baseball over the other professional sports. In addition, he cited the Major Leagues' pension program as an inducement for talented young athletes.[78] To help curb spending on untried players, owners again implemented a rule whereby some bonus babies had to be retained on the Major League roster for two years; Sandy Koufax was one of these players.

Why would Major League teams pay so much for untested youngsters? One sportswriter claimed, "With farm, scouting, school and coaching costs as high as they are these days, it costs about $200,000 to develop a ballplayer from the time he enters a club system in the lower Minors until he is ready for the majors—if he ever is. Accordingly, if a bonus player makes good his first season or two, he will have been a bargain even at $100,000."[79]

Although most independent Minor League teams folded during the 1950s, the logic of signing with an independent team appealed to some amateur players who did not get large bonuses. As sportswriter Bob Stevens pointed out, "They [amateur players] could see where it was more intelligent to sign with an independent and become draftable by, or saleable to, sixteen big league outfits, than to become a chattel of one particular club and wait for the incumbent to wear out or die."[80]

The revised bonus rules did not appreciably curb bonus payments in 1959, but the new rules forced Major League teams to place more bonus players on their twenty-five-man active roster. These moves, of course, prevented the youngsters from getting playing time in the Minors and crowded out veterans.[81]

Owners devised yet another new rule. Any bonus baby not left on the Major League roster after his first year was available to be drafted by another Major League team. The St. Louis Cardinals, for instance, canceled their options on four high-price bonus players rather than promote them to the Major League roster. Bing Devine liked the first-year draft rule, believing that it would prove an effective deterrent to reckless bonuses, not because of the fear of losing players but because, he explained, "you have no place to put them, I think most clubs will let them alone."[82]

Not all of the teams approved of the first-year draft, even after it had been in effect for a couple of years. The Yankees and Braves especially disliked the rule. Even the *Sporting News* expressed its reservations about the new regulation, as previous rules had created subterfuges that should not have been part of the game. One solution was for the commissioner's office to examine each team's financial records, which the commissioner had the right to do.[83] Still, the rule was having an effect. Some thirty-nine bonus players sat on Major League rosters during the 1959 season instead of being exposed to the draft; in 1960 the number jumped to sixty-five. In addition, twenty-six players from the 1959 class remained on Major League rosters. Several of these players were worth protecting: Dick Allen, Pat Dobson, Jim Fregosi, Randy Hundley, Sam McDowell, Ken Sanders, Joe Torre, and Wilbur Wood.[84] Dodgers director of scouting Al Campanis believed, however, that bonuses would increase again in 1961 because most teams had money to spend, and the addition of four teams to the Major Leagues exacerbated the competition for amateur talent. Even George Weiss, now general manager of the Mets, was willing to splurge in the free agent market: "It is quite true that when I was in the Yankee office I was not known as a spender. The situation did not demand spending because we always had a player surplus and could offer a package for any man who might be available and who could help us. . . . We are giving bonuses now . . . but not as lavishly as reported. . . . We are not likely to establish ourselves with green free agents."[85] Weiss's successor on the Yankees, Roy Hamey, planned to spend liberally on youngsters because the team was flush with cash from the 1960 World Series and the expansion draft.[86] The Yankees could no longer rely on their prestige to sign players for minimal bonuses: "Kids today are investment-minded and do not quite understand how they can cut in on AT&T with a brochure relating the glories of the 'home of champions.' They want Yankee dollars."[87]

At the 1961 Major League meetings the owners decided to tinker with the first-year player rule. First, owners reduced the draft price on first-year players from $12,000 to $8,000. Second, teams could protect only one first-year player. Third, teams wishing to send first-year bonus players to the Minors had to expose such players to irrevocable waivers. Fourth, the owners eliminated the privilege of reacquiring such players until they went through the $8,000 unrestricted draft. All of these rules raised the risk of signing bonus players. The Dodgers led the opposition to this plan.[88]

The player draft held in December 1961 included fifteen first-year players. Overall, Major League teams paid $680,000 for all draft picks. Most of these players never became stars, although Bo Belinsky and Moe Drabowsky are recognizable names. A similar result occurred during the December 1962 draft. Teams selected thirty first-year players at $8,000 each. Brant Alyea, Glenn Beckert, and Rich Reese were the best-known players selected. In the 1963 draft teams drafted eventual stars Bobby Knoop, Rudy May, Reggie Smith, Bobby Tolan, and Luke Walker. Teams selected fifty-nine first-year players during the 1964 draft, including Ed Herrmann, Sparky Lyle, and Felix Millan.[89] According to St. Louis Cardinal business manager Art Routzong, there was a benefit from drafting first-year players: "We understand that Senator Kefauver was very pleased with the number of players moved up in the first-year draft." Thus, the draft helped boost legislative goodwill toward baseball.[90]

Sportswriter Oscar Kahan believed that the new amendments for the first-year player draft rule would reduce the number but not the top amount of the big payments. After talking with several Major League officials, he believed that total bonus payments would fall by 40 percent. Commissioner Ford Frick agreed: "The beauty of the rule is that it has teeth and is self-enforcing [because it keeps teams from 'loading up' on bonus signees]. It wasn't the violations of the old bonus rules that I found most objectionable, it was the mistrust in the minds of everyone. It created a bad atmosphere of suspicion and doubt."[91] In fact, signings fell between 1958 and 1963. Owners signed 935 players in 1958 but only 602 in 1963, despite there being four additional teams.[92]

Dodgers vice president Fresco Thompson claimed that the rules pertaining to bonus players were having a pernicious effect. He claimed that teams signed only 270 amateurs in 1962, compared to 500 at a similar time in 1961. Instead of signing as many youngsters as possible, Thompson stated, "we are going to lose many boys to pro football, pro basketball and to business in general because they will not accept contracts for comparatively nominal sums."[93] A Major League report issued in 1963 indicated that the teams had spent over $45 million in bonuses during the past seven years, but the report also showed that the recent changes in the bonus system had slowed the growth of bonus payments.[94]

At the December 1962 meetings three proposals to replace the first-year player draft failed. The proposals included limiting the salary of all organized baseball newcomers to $500 per month, except when on a Major League roster; prohibiting a club from signing a first-year player to a contract for the following season until after the draft; and making any first-year player signed before August 1 for the succeeding season draft eligible both the year he signed and the following year. The proposals would purportedly eliminate loopholes in the current rules.[95]

About this time that paragon of free enterprise, Walter O'Malley, weighed in with his opinion regarding the bonus system in a piece in the *Sporting News*. In a case of life imitating cliché the accompanying photo of the avuncular O'Malley showed him puffing on a big cigar. He disliked both an unrestricted draft and a free agent draft: "These are good, old socialistic ideas. I don't believe such ideas have any place in baseball. The inevitable effect of all socialistic experiments is bad. . . . Those who are willing to spend their money should be permitted to do so. Those who aren't willing must accept the consequences."[96] Ironically, O'Malley's Dodgers typically received the largest net gain from the National League's revenue-sharing plan. As the character Chico Escuela, the ballplayer from the Dominican Republic on *Saturday Night Live*, might say, "Baseball [socialism] been 'berra berra' good to me." Aside from the surreal image of socialists conducting a draft

("The Politburo is pleased to select Vladimir Lenin as its number one pick"), one wonders how well O'Malley's attitude would work in that bastion of socialism, the National Football League. O'Malley's sentiments resounded across the continent, and Johnny Johnson, the Yankees farm director, labeled the incipient amateur draft "communistic."[97]

O'Malley believed that the bonus system merely required better enforcement. He claimed that the nation's tax structure could ensure enforcement. With an anachronistic faith in accountants, he said, "Every club employs a national firm of accountants. They wouldn't run the risk of permitting any skullduggery. The clubs' books would clearly show what was paid to each player."[98]

In retrospect a draft of amateur players was an obvious solution to the escalating bonuses. The *Sporting News* contained many articles examining the amateur free agent problem. As early as 1959, Paul Richards, a prominent baseball manager and official, called for an unrestricted free agent draft before a Senate hearing. During 1959 twenty-three amateur players shared $1.2 million in large bonuses (bonuses above $8,000), including such eventual longtime pitchers as Ray Culp and Jim Maloney. In an early version of an NFL/NBA-style free agent draft, proponents urged setting minimum bonuses for boys selected in the draft, perhaps as much as $20,000 in bonus and first-year salary. Setting the level of the bonus was fraught with risks. Too high a level, and baseball would fail to curb its bonus payments by much; too low a level, and talented youngsters might eschew baseball for other sports or, in the case of college graduates, jobs in business. Each team would get one pick, but there would be three drafts throughout the year. Although the plan was promising, Major League owners voted against it during their December 1959 meetings.[99]

By 1961 the American League recommended to Ford Frick that the Major Leagues institute a free agent draft. Teams would pay a specified amount for players, directly implying that the draft's real purpose was to curb spending on untried players. The owners were slowly resolving to confront any legal challenges. One of the chief legal points was baseball's reserve clause. While pro football, for instance, did not have a formal reserve clause, that sport's policy of signing players for two years, with the second year being an option year, was essentially an informal reserve clause. The distinction was enough, in any case, to raise concerns about the legality of combining a free agent draft with a reserve clause. In addition, baseball signed many youngsters right out of high school, before they had reached majority age. Finally, the free agent draft would continue to reduce the Minor Leagues' incentives to find talented youngsters. According to sportswriter Dan Daniel, sixteen of the twenty teams favored a free agent draft, but four teams did not. He did not name the dissenters, although the Milwaukee Braves, New York Yankees, Los Angeles Dodgers, and San Francisco Giants were likely candidates. Frick supported a congressional bill making the free agent draft legal for football, and some senators agreed that baseball could have a similar draft.[100]

Growing dissatisfaction with the first-year player rule again led Major League owners to agree in January 1964 to investigate implementing a free agent draft as a solution to the bonus problem. The Los Angeles Angels signed Rick Reichardt for a $200,000 bonus during the summer. The bonus was enough to purchase twenty-five first-year players in the draft.[101] At the Major Leagues' summer meetings of August 10 and 11, 1964, the teams split evenly on the proposed free-agent draft. The dissenters expressed a desire to toughen the first-year rule. Some of them claimed to be afraid of the legal ramifications of implementing such a draft, but agreed to reconsider the proposal in December.[102]

Walter O'Malley continued to oppose the draft, ostensibly because he feared the legal repercussions: "Is the thing going to leave us open to restraint of trade and/or antitrust litigation?" Conversely, baseball attorney Lou Carroll expressed his opinion that "the U.S. Supreme Court decided in the Toolson case that the business of baseball is not subject to federal antitrust laws. I would regard a free-agent player draft as a rule or regulation of the business of baseball."[103] The *Sporting News* quoted an anonymous "prominent expert on federal law and the anti-trust code" about the legality of a free agent draft. The attorney cited the *Toolson* case, suggesting that because several of the justices who ruled on *Toolson* were still on the bench, the result would be similar for a ruling on the free agent draft. In addition, he did not believe there would be much sympathy for any potential plaintiff: "From a practical point of view, the 17-year-old high school boy who no longer would be able to get a Pontiac convertible for each member of his family, plus a big bonus for himself, is not a particularly appealing plaintiff. There is no backlog of young plaintiffs waiting to sue for past misdeeds." He discounted O'Malley's fears of legal damages.[104]

Leslie O'Connor opposed the free agent draft because he believed it deprived the amateur player his constitutional right of personal freedom in choosing which team to play for.[105] He provided a lengthy and, at times, eloquent argument against the draft in the Senate hearings of 1964. His arguments are no less pertinent today: "If S. 2391 be enacted, its proponents ought to be congratulated or condemned, as the viewpoint may be, for an atavistic achievement. For that will be a denial of human rights, of labor's rights, and a throw-back of over six hundred years to the despotic first labor laws of England—the *Ordinance of Laborers* and the *Statute of Laborers*."[106] He continued,

> The "free-agent draft" is unconstitutional and otherwise illegal (for example, as a common-law conspiracy), in that—
>
> (1) It denies due process of law to the players affected.
>
> (2) It confiscates from those players, and delivers over to the drafting clubs, *to an undefinable degree of loss to the players*, the exclusive property rights the players legally have in their athletic skills and in securing what otherwise would be the market price for their labor;
>
> (3) It deprives those players of their constitutional freedom of contracts; and
>
> (4) Members of the leagues involved are coerced by monopolistic agreements to surrender their constitutional freedom of contract. Thereby they are prohibited from negotiating with players "selected" by other clubs of their league (or a combination of leagues,

such as organized baseball, and the American football leagues if they hereafter agree to "respect" each other's so-called "draft rights," just as they presently "respect" each other's contracts).[107]

Even Charlie Finley recognized the wrongs involved in the draft: "[Major League owners] adapted a free agent draft to eliminate the excessive bonus bidding, thereby solving its own problem at the expense of the prospective player."[108] Bill Veeck pointed out a potentially devastating legal problem with signing eighteen-year-olds to contracts involving the reserve clause: "If he develops quickly enough, he is *legally entitled to disaffirm*. When you sign an eighteen-year-old kid, you have to get his father's signature. By the nature of the baseball contract, the father is signing the boy's bargaining rights away in perpetuity. It happens not to be legal. A man is perfectly entitled to sign away his own rights for a consideration, but nobody is entitled to sign away anybody else's rights for him." He suggested that the player, upon turning twenty-one, could repudiate the contract. If owners refused to sign the promising player, they could be accused of collusion. "They'd sign him all right," he reasoned, "or the baseball contract would face a court test under the worst set of circumstances that could possibly be found."[109]

Leo DeOrsey, an attorney who had been a director of the Washington Senators, had raised the "infant" question before a Senate committee in 1958:

> That bill gives the big-league club owners exemption from antitrust with the following limitation: "That a person who signs a contract when he is a minor shall be entitled to the protection granted him by the laws applicable to infants." And you will notice that in the hearings before the House Mr. Frick testified about infants, and the gist of his testimony was that if an infant signs a contract, and when he reaches the age of 21, if he does not want to agree to continue playing with that team, entering into a new contract, he is placed on a restrictive list, which means he cannot play for anyone until he comes to terms with that club.[110]

And aside from its legal aspects, there were other reasons for owners to be skeptical about the new draft proposal. Not everyone believed that a reverse-order draft would significantly reduce bonuses. Sportswriter Bill Bryson believes that the new amateur free agent draft was unlikely to curtail spending on young talent or to equalize competition, citing the ten-to-one odds against any bonus player "making good in the Majors."[111] Economists are also dubious about a reverse-order draft's ostensible virtue: promoting competitive balance.

Major League owners continued to tinker with the proposed free agent draft. The revised plan included three drafts per year. The main draft would take place in June, when high school and college graduates were available. A second draft in the winter would cover players graduating in mid-year. The third draft in September would cover players in American Legion baseball. The plan would also be accompanied by an unrestricted draft of all players left on Minor League rosters. Players who did not sign with the team that drafted them would go into a special draft the following year. To forestall chicanery the special draft had a random order, so a player would not know which team would get his rights on the second round. The special draft was designed to protect the players. Initially, the plan prohibited teams from swapping draft picks, although the owners left open the possibility. Finally, Latin players were not subjected to the draft, partially because the owners claimed it was difficult to ascertain some players' date of birth. Lee MacPhail expressed the hope that "the big bonuses—the top 20 or so—might be cut down and the rule probably would put an end to six figure bonuses, but the average boy wouldn't be affected."[112]

Accounts differed on who voted against the free agent draft. Sportswriter Russell Schneider listed five teams voting against the free agent draft: the A's, Colt .45s, Dodgers, Mets, and Senators. Three of the teams were expansion clubs. The reporter Cliff Kachline claimed, however, that the Angels, A's, Cardinals, Dodgers, Mets, Senators, and Yankees were against the proposal. The Dodgers wanted to return to the bonus system, with a $10,000 ceiling and strong enforcement measures. Yet when the Dodgers realized that there were not enough teams against the draft, they voted to approve it. Apparently, the Cardinals were the only dissenting voice on the final vote.[113] The New York Yankees management also fought hard to prevent a reverse-order draft of amateur players, although they eventually approved it. As one baseball sportswriter observed, "The untold millions of CBS will not help them. Neither will the skills of the scouts gathered in the years of their glory."[114]

The owners scheduled the first draft for June 1965. Rick Monday was the first player selected. Sportswriter Leonard Koppett speculated that Monday's bonus would be roughly half of Rick Reichardt's $200,000.[115] Some proponents eventually became disillusioned with the rule. According to Philadelphia Phillies farm director Paul Owens, "You still have to go high to sign your No. 1 choice and the value of building a sound organization and scouting system are canceled out."[116]

Major League Baseball owners during the 1950s resembled a sixteen-headed hydra. Each head recognized the many benefits provided by being a part of the cartel, yet each head retained an individual agenda. The hydra was powerful enough to keep out new leagues, but preventing destructive competition within the organization, such as the search for new locations and talent, proved more difficult. Nevertheless, the owners reached 1965 with their hallowed antitrust exemption and reserve clause intact. Despite their increased abuse of players via the amateur draft, the players remained docile, at least for a few more seasons. Unfortunately for the hydra, the overtly opportunistic maverick Charlie Finley would eventually make an administrative mistake that would create the seminal, modern free agent in Jim "Catfish" Hunter, future Hall of Fame pitcher. The hydra would have reason to rue its inability to run Finley out of the game during the 1960s.

The Yankees' Dynasty

Did Success Spoil the Team and Its Fans?

For most of the era New York towered over its rivals, especially at the gate. American League attendance shrank overall after 1949. Part of the decline in attendance certainly did not result from the monotony of Yankee pennants, as even the more competitive National League suffered an attendance decline during the 1950s. Yet the 1949–53 Yankees saw attendance at the stadium fall by almost one-third, however, despite stable ticket prices. The Yankees maintained the same ticket prices between 1949 and 1954, with the exception of a fifteen-cent increase in the price of bleacher seats. The team raised the prices of box seats, reserved, and unreserved grandstand seats only in 1955.[1] By the mid-1950s the New York Yankees' domination of the American League was clearly harming the league's profits.

Challenges and Benefits of Having Stronger Rivals

Would the Yankees have benefited by facing stronger rivals? While the team could not play the strong Indians or White Sox every home date, would less inept Athletics, Browns, or Senators teams have boosted the crowds at Yankee Stadium? Attendance at Yankee Stadium was diminished by games with the hapless Athletics and Browns, as the final two months of the 1953 campaign illustrate. The Athletics and

Browns both finished forty games behind the Yankees. Five games (including a doubleheader) with the Browns at the beginning of August and middle of September netted fewer than thirty-one thousand in attendance. When the Yankees traveled to St. Louis, attendance was not much better. Two games there in the beginning of September attracted fewer than eleven thousand patrons. While the Yankees and Athletics played to respectable crowds during August, a Philadelphia visit to Yankee Stadium drew only 13,300 fans for two games in late September, after the Yankees had clinched the title. The Detroit Tigers, the other faltering team in 1953, failed to draw many fans to Yankee Stadium during a two-game set in mid-September, about eighteen thousand fans total. Clearly, the absence of a tight pennant race mixed with a trio of truly mediocre teams hurt attendance at Yankee Stadium.

Although the American League crowned a different champion in 1954, the novelty of a non-Yankee champion did not hike the gate as much as was hoped. The pennant-winning Cleveland Indians increased their attendance from 1953, but the 1954 pennant winners had barely half the attendance of the 1948 champions. A spectacular double-header in September that killed the Yankees' slender chances drew almost eighty-five thousand paying fans into Cleveland's Municipal Stadium. An earlier three-game set between the two teams at Yankee Stadium before the Labor Day weekend had attracted 140,000 fans. Nevertheless, the Yankees saw the dire consequences of failing to win: after the crucial doubleheader the Yankees played in front of fewer than twenty-six thousand fans total during the next nine games with Detroit, Philadelphia, and Washington. The Yankees could only conclude that playing second-rate teams while not winning a pennant was poison at the gate. Similarly, Cleveland drew only nineteen thousand customers for two games with the third-place White Sox immediately after clinching the pennant, before concluding with thirty thousand in attendance for a three-game set with Detroit.

As shown earlier, although some observers believe that a more "equitable" gate-sharing policy would have helped the teams in smaller cities, the American League's experience of the 1950s confounds the notion. The Yankees were usually the best draw for the Philadelphia, St. Louis, and Washington franchises. These teams got relatively large gates when the Yankees visited, but when they went to Yankee Stadium, they killed the gate. If the St. Louis Browns had started to draw more fans, the Yankees would have been a prime beneficiary under even a fifty-fifty split of the gate. There was truth to the idea that the wealthier teams carried the weaker teams. In most businesses, of course, the strong entities would desire the demise of the weaker entities, but professional team sports differ. What the Yankees needed was not to drive the Athletics, Browns, and Senators out of business but to get the weaker franchises to relocate to better venues or to improve their performances. Yet even the relocation of Philadelphia and St. Louis to Kansas City and Baltimore did not improve league attendance much during the rest of the 1950s. The 1955–58 Yankee clubs averaged fewer than 1.48 million in attendance, while the 1960–64 clubs averaged 20,000 more fans per season than the 1955–58 teams.

What was troubling about the latter era was the lack of National League competition in 1958–61. Because they were the only team in New York, Yankee players felt they could demand more money. New York Transit Authority officials hoped for increased subway traffic to Yankee Stadium to offset the loss of riders going to the Polo Grounds or Ebbets Field. The players, fans, and sportswriters expected the team to draw at least two million fans in 1958 with the Dodgers and Giants in California.[2] The Yankees quickly learned, however, that any such gate enhancement was a mirage. Mantle and Maris's chase of Babe Ruth's homerun record did not restore the gate to the postwar highs of the late 1940s. Although the Yankees attracted about a quarter-million more fans in 1961 than the average during 1955–58, this was a temporary jump. Even a tight pennant race in 1964 could not turn the numbers around. The Yankees experienced a 20 percent decline in attendance between 1960 and 1964.

The Yankees' consecutive pennants dampened attendance in the American League. While the 1949–53 skid in attendance might be attributed to the general decline in attendance at Major League Baseball games, as witnessed by the National League's similar difficulties, the events of 1954–65 belie a general trend. Attendance at National League games rebounded strongly during the rest of the decade. In the American League attendance had a more rhythmic pattern: surges in 1954–55 and 1959, interspersed by declines. By 1964, however, the league attendance was almost exactly the same as it had been in 1960, despite two more teams and a relocated original Senators team. Because National League attendance was growing during the period, except for 1961, one is hard-pressed to indict general demographic trends or television for the decline.

Clearly, franchise shifts muted the stagnation in attendance, so another way to view the situation is to examine attendance for the five American League franchises that did not relocate: Boston, Chicago, Cleveland, Detroit, and New York. In 1949 these teams collectively drew almost nine million fans. By 1953 they had only 5.7 million at the gate. Their attendance figures rose to above six million in both 1954 and 1955. By 1958 these stable franchises were down to just over five million attendees, despite the fact that the Yankees and Red Sox now monopolized their cities. The numbers jumped to 6.68 and 6.52 million in 1959 and 1960 but fell below 5 million in both 1964 and 1965. Although Boston performed terribly in 1965, Cleveland, Chicago, and Detroit finished second, fourth, and fifth in the now ten-team league, and all had winning records. These five teams would collectively have a resurgence in attendance in 1967 and 1968, despite poor teams in Cleveland and New York.

Not Alone Again, Naturally

After 1961 the Yankees faced competition from the National League's new team in the city, the Mets. The National League's absence from the nation's largest metropolis was perhaps inevitably brief. The American League apparently never seriously considered the possibility of placing a second team in the city, in hopes of creating a Dodgers-Giants type of rivalry. While monopolizing New York City did not bring the attendance and revenue boom the Yankees had hoped for, did renewed competition for Major League Baseball spur the team to improve?

At first the Mets provided little competition in terms of the quality of the organization's on-the-field performance, as the team finished last during its first five seasons. But the Mets aggressively marketed their tickets. The team opened ticket offices at Grand Central Station, Pennsylvania Station, and at Macy's on Long Island. The Howard's clothing store chain also handled telephone ticket sales. The team sold luxury boxes for $2,000 for four seats. Included in the luxury box was a free parking space and four memberships in the team's "Diamond Club."[3] By 1964, the Yankees' last pennant-winning year for twelve seasons, the Mets outdrew the incumbent team by over four hundred thousand fans. The Mets hired George Weiss as general manager, and he promptly returned Casey Stengel as field manager.

The Mets' attendance was bolstered of course, by the club's new stadium. Weiss spent considerable time poring over the Flushing Meadows stadium plans. He insisted, for instance, that the original plans had far too few toilets. The new stadium, located in Queens, was conveniently situated for the rapidly growing borough as well as Nassau County. In addition, people living in the county comprising the borough had median incomes of $6,932, well above the median incomes of residents of the other boroughs, which may have been an unstated attraction. Residents of Kings and New York counties had median incomes of $5,837 and $5,423. Queens County also had a lower percentage of blacks than the other boroughs.[4] The new stadium featured unobstructed views and escalators. "But of more interest to the average Met fan," claimed a writer in *Sports Illustrated*, "will be the series of attractive concession stands serving decent food instead of the tired fare that New York sports crowds have been held captive by for so long."[5] Indeed, even the Yankees ended their relationship with the Stevens brothers concessionaires in the early 1960s. The one potential drawback for the new stadium was traffic, especially in 1964, with the World's Fair. Traffic commissioner Henry Barnes joked, "I suspect the first man to start home from the [World's] fair in 1964 may well pass the last man on his way to the fair in 1965."[6]

Even before the 1964 season, observers thought the Mets had a good chance at overtaking the Yankees at the gate. After all, the Mets were moving into their new stadium in 1964. The proximity of the World's Fair also promised to boost attendance at Mets games. The team hoped to sell five thousand season tickets and to generate $2 million in revenues before the season started. George Weiss hoped to draw 1.5 million to the new stadium.[7]

The Yankees had difficulty understanding the Mets phenomenon. Bill Veeck described the response as "a protest against the continued cold, machinelike excellence of the Yankees. It is difficult for fans to find human frailties on the Yankees to identify with."[8] The expansion team was perhaps the most inept team ever, although the 1952 Pittsburgh Pirates and the 1954 Philadelphia Athletics would probably offer stiff competition for the title. Columnist Jimmy Breslin sarcastically analyzed the appeal of the new New York franchise: "The Mets also opened their season with a team which is so bad at playing baseball that it has stepped out of sports and has become, along with the Guggenheim Museum, a driving force in the city's culture." Woe be the Mets if they started winning: "If the Mets ever started to win any games, it would spoil everything. Their followers, living in a city which is a success by itself, and which is filled with people who are successes and others who are in search of success, demand absolute incompetence in their ball club. Anybody can root for a winner. But to be with a loser calls for a special flair, and the New York Mets have put together a following which goes beyond anything that old Ebbets Field ever had."[9]

The two teams charged the same prices for box and reserved seats in 1964, although the Yankees charged twenty cents more for general admission. The Mets did not have bleacher seats.[10] The Mets continued to attract more fans throughout the 1960s and well into the 1970s. In 1970 the Mets drew 1.5 million more fans than the Yankees. The Mets phenomenon continued to inspire some pundits to ask whether fans reveled in the team's ineptitude, an extreme case of rooting for the underdog, and "antihero" status. One writer sarcastically compared the 1966 Yankees with the Mets, who were so successful at wooing fans from Yankee Stadium: "That this can be taken chiefly as a tribute to the Mets' assiduous application of baseball's new merchandising techniques is evident from the way the Yankees have tried to imitate them. In desperation in 1966, the Yankees, possibly in an effort to borrow what they considered the Mets' most effective ploy of all, finished in last place. There can be no doubt that, particularly in the melting pot of New York City's population, underdogs have a way of being more popular than overlords."[11]

In addition to the competition from the Mets, the Yankees were not well-liked by many fans. Sportswriter Robert Shaplen attributed some of the animosity toward the Yankees to George Weiss, who had insisted on decorum during his reign as Yankees general manager. Like his predecessor Ed Barrow, he insisted that the players behave properly on and off the field and punished some players who violated his standards. He traded Billy Martin, for example, after that pugnacious player was involved in several altercations.[12] But Weiss's approach appeared to squeeze the "color" out of the Yankees. "The cold, impersonal method in his treatment, or some unsentimental variation of it, is patently part of Weiss's success," Shaplen explained. "It has also been reflected, many fans think, in Weiss's handling of the ticket problem, with what they consider an attitude of contempt shown them in contrast to the solicitude extended big executives and celebrities, who always seem to get the best seats in the house." Shaplen compared Weiss with contemporary Branch Rickey: "Weiss . . . gives the impression that he's carrying an IBM machine around with him. Which may be why Rickey is imaginatively capable of introducing a Jackie Robinson . . . whereas last spring Weiss traded Vic Power. . . . Weiss denies any bias, says he has tried in the past to obtain Negroes, and defends the trade by saying the Yanks needed pitching more than Power."[13]

After the 1960 season the Yankees owners fired Casey Stengel and replaced him with Ralph Houk. Weiss resigned on November 2, and Roy Hamey became the new general manager. Weiss was the last link to the regime of Ruppert and Barrow. With the Mets' success, some observers felt that the Yankees needed to play up Yogi Berra's comic image as a foil to Casey Stengel (now manager of the "Amazin' Mets"), but the catcher-turned-manager was not really a clown; he would have difficulty enough establishing himself as a rookie manager in 1964.[14] Amusingly, it was Weiss who unwittingly presided over the Mets' success, but whether he gleaned the irony is unlikely.

That master of promotion Bill Veeck criticized the Yankees for their stodgy promotional efforts: "The Yankees do one of the worst promotional job in the majors." He cited the team's impressive advantages: a huge population base and large number of tourists.

> Somehow, the Yankees don't appeal to the average guy; their appeal is to the corporation president. A good percentage of their attendance represents season boxes bought up by companies to entertain guests. Much of the time the seats aren't even occupied. . . . The accepted picture of the Yankee fan is a staid, solid, conservative citizen who latches on to a sure winner because he is used to playing everything safe. . . . The average baseball fan, my beer-drinking, shirt-sleeved guy in the bleachers, is used to enjoying himself. He expects to have a good time when he goes out.[15]

In addition, because many New York residents were transplanted from other Major League cities, they often brought their original loyalty with them.

After Weiss's departure, the Yankees reacted aggressively, as Dan Topping Jr. stated, "We are no longer sitting back and waiting for customers. We're going out to get them. We want family groups, business groups, things like that. And when we get them into the ball park we're going to take care of them. We want to make going to Yankee Stadium seem like a wonderful thing to do."[16] The Yankees promptly improved the stadium's concessions stands and restrooms, hired female ushers, and promised polite service. Yet these improvements failed to reinvigorate attendance.

The Yankees Try to Loosen Up

One lesson the Mets offered was that fans might respond to ineptitude, if it was endearing. Not even George Weiss could wring the color from the Amazin' Mets. The Yankees had tried to curb the youthful indiscretions of Ford, Mantle, and Martin. The team's emphasis, if not obsession, with "professional" behavior on and off the field dated back to Ed Barrow and Joe McCarthy, although Babe Ruth and Bob Meusel's carousing caused friction between Jacob Ruppert and his original partner, Tillinghast L'Hommedieu Huston. When the Yankees won, fans appeared to perceive them as insufferable. Unfortunately, when the Yankees lost, they were not lovable or colorful, unlike the Mets.

The Yankees, however, were not the only team trying to purge its players of color. Officials such as Veeck lamented the growing dearth of exciting players:

> We don't have the colorful, bigger-than-life character in our society any more, and I find that a worrisome thing. . . . Today, you have the corporate lawyer and the team player, both of whom serve a necessary purpose and both of whom are rather dull. . . . Color is the thing they [baseball management] have done everything in their power to get rid of. As soon as a boy is signed, a carefully planned program of brainwashing sets in. There are rules of behavior for the new boy as soon as he reports to his first minor-league team.[17]

Roy Hamey immediately established a different environment, a more informal one. Even so, the Yankees remained a stiff, colorless bunch. During the waning days of the dynasty Phil Linz, a reserve outfielder, proved a little slow in stopping his harmonica playing on the team bus after a loss. Rookie manager Yogi Berra, worrying that the Yankees were in danger of losing the pennant, lost his temper and later fined Linz. As sportswriter Arthur Daley suggested, "It's probably too late for anything to save the Yankees and yet the blowup by the normally over-considerate Berra could prove beneficial to the club."[18]

The Yankees ownership actively sought to revamp the club's image. In the words of New York writer Til Ferdenzi, "War has been declared on stuffiness. The Yankees are still hepped on winning, but they appear to be embarked on a program of finding ways to throw their weight around so the public won't consider them as the bad guys of baseball getting fat and prosperous at the expense of the less fortunate." The Yankees instituted "Suburban Nights" on Thursday nights. Instead of starting at 8:00 p.m., the games started at 6:00 p.m. "The idea behind them is to entice the working man into the Bronx ball yard on his way home one night a week if he knows he's going to get home early enough after the game to spend a little time with the family before the kiddies go to bed." In addition, the team replaced the Stevens brothers as concessionaire, hiring the Automatic Canteen Company of America. The team decided to let fans select players to be honored on Old-Timers' Day. Finally, the club publicized its hiring of a sales promotion manager. Before the 1964 season general manager Ralph Houk predicted that team would draw at least 1.5 million. "The perfect box-office formula is a Yankees lineup which has Mantle and Maris in the lineup every day plus a good race." Unfortunately for the team, advance sales did not improve in 1964. The team continued Suburban Nights in 1965, albeit on Wednesday nights with a 7:00 p.m. starting time, despite the lukewarm response to the concept. When attendance failed to rise, management scheduled a record number of night games for 1965.[19]

Although New York did not draw well during 1964, despite a tight pennant race, a strange phenomenon occurred at Yankee Stadium. Apparently, Yankee players believed that typical crowds at the stadium were heavily anti-Yankee. "Go to a ball game in the Yankee's little green acre and chances are you wonder which club was the home team. Cheers for the opposition, in fact, oftentimes were louder than the hosannahs for the legal tenants of the place. It would appear that the old custom of booing the Yankees while yelling for the enemy has become old hat." Now the fans cheered mostly for the Yankees. Yankee management attempted to help the trend by allowing, for the first time, fans to carry signs (as long as the signs were not supported by poles). Sportswriter Ferdenzi thought that the players' valiant efforts in the face of numerous injuries to Maris and Mantle inspired the fans: "The fans also appreciate the triumph over human frailties. These Yankees are not the most overpowering edition in their history, but they are among the more exciting."[20] Given that attendance continued its downward trend, a cynic might argue that rather than support for the Yankees being on the rise, Yankee haters simply were not showing up in their former numbers.

Nevertheless, sportswriters commented on the "new-style" Yankees. The 1964 team had several new players, including Jim Bouton, Phil Linz, Joe Pepitone, and Mel Stottlemyre. From buttoning the top button on their uniform (in defiance of Yankee tradition) to talking with the press after a loss to writing a racy exposé of life as a Yankee, these newcomers were altering the fans' perception of the team.[21] Could or would the Yankees become rebels or antiheroes and appeal to a growing generation of baby boomers?

Ominous Trends Facing the Yankees

If the Mets phenomenon perplexed the Yankees, their management certainly could not remain oblivious to the ominous trends in attendance. Even drawing two million fans in New York would not have been impressive. Another way to view the weakness of the Yankee fan base is to examine the team's "per capita" attendance. Although New York consistently drew the most fans of any city in the Major Leagues, the city also consistently ranked near the bottom of the attendance-to-population ratio, the per capita attendance. Table 10.1 demonstrates the lackluster attendance at New York area baseball games when compared with other cities (see appendix).

From the Yankees' viewpoint the 1950 per capita attendance was especially troubling. All of the other nine cities in Major League Baseball, except Chicago, had higher per capita figures in 1950 than in 1920, but New York City had the same figure. By 1960 New York's per capita attendance fell to only two-fifths of the 1950 mark. While the other formerly multi-team cities (Boston, Philadelphia, and St. Louis) experienced drops in per capita attendance between 1950 and 1960, none dropped as fast as New York. New York's 0.21 ratio was the lowest figure recorded between 1910 and 1960, and even its higher ticket prices did not fully redress the situation. The Yankees appeared to face an indifferent market, or at least a highly competitive market for leisure activities. The low ratio was not due to a capacity constraint at Yankee Stadium. Throughout the postwar era Yankee Stadium had a capacity of sixty-seven thousand, so the attendance capacity exceeded five million per season.

Did the Yankees compensate for the tepid attendance of the 1955–64 era by lucrative radio and television contracts? While the team received the most revenue from radio and television of any American League franchise (with the exception of 1956, when Cleveland reaped more), it did not immediately increase its broadcasting revenue after the Dodgers and Giants left New York. The Yankees earned $900,000 in broadcasting revenue in both 1956 and 1960.[22]

Years earlier Connie Mack, owner-manager of the Philadelphia Athletics and the architect of the Yankees' main rivals during the late 1920s and early 1930s, stated the conundrum of a successful franchise: "Well, [the fans] lost interest when I had the best club, and now they're kicking because I've got the worst one. What's a fellow to do?"[23] Mack twice dismantled "dynastic" teams. The Yankees at least avoided Mack's fate and earned an after-tax profit of $450,000 per season for 1946, 1950, and 1952–56. The team's after-tax profits peaked in 1947 at $846,737. The general decline in American League prosperity contributed to their $346,806 in after-tax profits during the hotly contested pennant race of 1949, the first of five. While profits rose and fell during this five-year run, plunging in 1952, the fifth year of the Yankee pennant skein of 1949–53 did not bring a diminution in profits. The franchise earned its greatest after-tax profit of the period during 1953 (although after-tax profit figures are not available for 1951). The Yankees saw profits plummet from 1954 to 1956, with the three-year total falling short of the 1953 after-tax profits. Rising payrolls cannot explain all of the sharp decline in profits, as players' salaries only rose by $100,000 between 1952 and 1955 and actually fell in 1956. A stronger explanation for the falling profits was the sharp $800,000 increase between 1953 and 1954 in so-called other expenses, mostly due to a $500,000 increase in spending on the ballpark and large increase in spending on "other miscellaneous expenses."[24] Finally, the rising subsidization of its farm system also reduced the team's profits. The mid-1950s do not appear to have been a particularly profitable period for the Yankees. Unfortunately, subsequent congressional hearings did not request profit data, so the team's earnings numbers during the late 1950s are unknown. Given that attendance and revenue from radio and television broadcasting stagnated between 1956 and 1960, however, the franchise may not have been able to increase revenues significantly. Conversely, with Berra, Ford, and Mantle reaching their peaks, salaries may have shot up dramatically; after all, Mantle was the Most Valuable Player in 1956. Indeed, the Yankee management hoped that the team's swoon during the last third of the 1958 pennant race would douse the players' leverage for salary increases.[25] A return of the profits to the levels of the early 1950s, much less the late 1940s, was therefore unlikely.

Another indicator of profitability, franchise sales prices, implies profitability during 1946–64. Larry MacPhail, Dan Topping, and Del Webb bought the Yankees and Yankee Stadium for $2.8 million in nominal dollars in 1945. Although some press accounts claimed that the heirs of Jacob Ruppert had needed to sell the team because they were "broke," this claim was not substantiated in the *Sporting News*. The newspaper did confirm that estate taxes may have motivated the sale.[26] Given that Ruppert bought out his partner's 50 percent share for $1.5 million in 1922, the 1945 price implies a real depreciation in the franchise's value, especially given that Ruppert had paid $2.5 million to build Yankee Stadium in 1923. After buying out MacPhail's one-third interest for $2.2 million in 1948, Topping and Webb sold Yankee Stadium and the Kansas City Minor League stadium to Arnold Johnson for $6.5 million (with a lease agreement). The two owners then sold four-fifths of the franchise to CBS in 1964 for $11.2 million, and they sold the remaining one-fifth for an additional $2.8 million in 1965 and 1967. Leaving aside Yankee Stadium, the franchise appreciated by at least 8 percent per annum in nominal terms (from $2.8 million to $14 million between 1945 and 1965). While this was not a trivial rate of appreciation, it was not exceptionally high.[27]

Adding to the team's gate stagnation was the problem of a deteriorating roster of players and ballpark. Nearly coincidental with the introduction of the amateur draft, the New York Yankees fell on hard times during the mid-1960s. Sportswriter Leonard Koppett analyzed the decline of the Yankees and suggested four causes: the Major Leagues' tighter rules on the number of players that a team could control; the presence of financially stronger opponents; a diluted talent pool of players, thanks to expansion and to rival sports; and the inexperience of the Yankee front office, especially after CBS purchased the team in the mid-1960s. He also attributed part of their attendance woes to the "overriding blemish: Yankee Stadium itself." The city's other Major League ballpark, the new Shea Stadium, presented a stark contrast with the elderly Yankee Stadium, which would, indeed, be refurbished during the 1970s. Koppett predicted that the Yankee dynasty was over, although ten years later the team started a three-year reign as American League champions.[28]

Lawyer and author Henry Fetter argues that the Yankees' managerial success was based upon a rational, unsentimental approach, although their attitude toward black players may contradict his argument.[29] The team's hesitancy to sign and promote black players in the 1950s deprived the franchise of the services of the wave of great black players—Henry Aaron, Ernie Banks, Willie Mays, and Frank Robinson. The Yankees introduced Elston Howard, but despite the fact that he won a Most Valuable Player Award, he was never as consistently productive as the great National League black stars. George Weiss repeatedly denied that the Yankees purposely eschewed black players. In 1961 he stated, "We may have been slow in coming up with the kind of Negro ballplayer we wanted, but there was never any question of bias. As a matter of fact, with the exception of Jackie Robinson, we were interested from the start in just about every Negro ballplayer who has come up to the majors."[30] Regardless of his disclaimers, the fact remains that after Mickey Mantle, the Yankee farm system did not develop a supremely productive player, black or white, for decades. Thurman Munson, Bobby Murcer, Joe Pepitone, and Mel Stottlemyre were good players, but they never attained the productivity of DiMaggio, Gehrig, and Mantle. The Yankees' precipitous decline might not be attributable to the amateur draft because the team had high draft choices in the 1967 and 1968 drafts—the first and fourth picks, respectively. The franchise's lackluster record in developing players might be attributed both to the deaths of key scouts, including Bill Essick and Paul Kritchell, and to the reduction in the number of affiliated Minor League teams.[31]

While the team continued to draw in excess of a million fans and turn a profit, the low per capita attendance figures may have been an indication that the team was not fulfilling its gate potential. The apparent prosperity, as well as their American League rivals' general inability or unwillingness to sign top black players, may have also masked the team's mistake in failing to sign top black talent.

CBS Buys an Impending Collapse

After their World Series appearance in 1964, the Yankees appeared to be if not at the pinnacle of success, then certainly well placed to continue winning American League pennants. The team had acquired a sugar daddy owner in the well-heeled Columbia Broadcasting System. Yet, instead, the team plunged into turmoil. Yankee management fired rookie manager Yogi Berra and hired World Series rival St. Louis's manager, Johnny Keane, in one of the most bizarre post-Series moves ever. Many observers thought that Keane was an extremely fortunate fellow, as the Yankees still had Whitey Ford, Elston Howard, Mickey Mantle, Roger Maris, rookie star Mel Stottlemyre, and several promising younger players. Yet Howard, Ford, Mantle, and Maris were showing wear and tear, even in 1964. The double play combination of Tony Kubek and Bobby Richardson was nearly at an end, and of course, Yogi Berra was a manager because he no longer played.

When the National Broadcasting Corporation news commentator Chet Huntley reported the Columbia Broadcasting System's purchase of the New York Yankees, he said, "Just one more reason to hate the Yankees."[32] Huntley's remark undoubtedly resonated throughout the baseball world. Houston Colt .45s president Judge Roy Hofheinz added, "The day CBS finally purchases the Yankees will be the blackest day for baseball since the Black Sox scandal." Sports columnist Arthur Daley perhaps summed it up best for the fans: "CBS is so irrevocably identified with feeding the bottomless maw of its television screens that the reaction has to be different. What keeps suspicion alive is that most forms of sport are sure-fire video attractions and that some offerings have such magnetic appeal that they draw fantastically high ratings." He continued by warning about how television could be a cruel, Janus-faced master, paying well but also having used boxing, killed Minor League Baseball, and altered many rules of the games. "The tail was beginning to wag the dog before it even owned a little piece of poor Rover. Through CBS, it now owns a piece. Since it's the Yankees who are involved, the piece might be considered the head." Finally, he bemoaned the shift from sportsmen (and sportswoman, Mrs. Charles Shipman Payson of the Mets) owners to "carpetbaggers and quick-buck men" and corporate bureaucrats.[33]

CBS's purchase of the Yankees during the 1964 season triggered fears of an unholy and unfair alliance. In fact, some of the other owners feared that the anticompetitive aspect of the deal, especially with regard to bidding for network television rights, would renew scrutiny of the reserve clause. As usual, New York congressman Emanuel Celler sensed businessmen seeking profits, and Senator Philip Hart of Michigan opened the Senate hearings of 1965 by stating, "It [the CBS-Yankee acquisition] killed any hopes of passage of the [Professional Sports Antitrust Bill] at the last session of Congress."[34] Indeed, much of the 1965 hearings centered on the acquisition. In addition, CBS and the National Football League had a contract for the 1965 and 1966 seasons; the broadcasting company dropped out of the bidding for baseball's proposed Monday night game. CBS President Dr. Frank Stanton denied any anticompetitive potential and referred to that will-of-the-wisp, synergy—although he called it an "affinity of management skills"—and drew the comparison to both industries' need to draw large audiences. He denied that the network would move local telecasts of Yankee games to its WCBS-TV affiliate; the television schedule was already set. Ironically, Dan Topping, in denying that television already adversely affected baseball attendance, stated, "I don't think the competition is there, particularly in the American League."[35]

The $11.2 million price surprised many observers, as Lou Perini had sold the Braves for $5.5 million in 1962. Yet CBS had acquired much larger businesses than the Yankees. The purchase price represented less than 2 percent of the broadcasting company's revenues in 1960. Indeed, the company could have purchased the Yankees with the profits from its Broadway interest in *My Fair Lady*.[36] Legend claims that Harry Frazee sold Babe Ruth to the Yankees to get funding for *No, No Nanette*, so a CBS purchase of the Yankees out of its *My Fair Lady* profits would have been some sort of irony. Meanwhile, NBC was concurrently considering purchasing the New York Giants football team. Nor was CBS the first serious suitor for the club. According to Dan Topping, the New York investment bankers Lehman Brothers had negotiated a sale for the club in 1962, but the two parties were unable to work out tax questions, so the sale fell apart a few days before the CBS purchase.[37]

The ever-suspicious Emanuel Celler immediately scented something rotten: "I don't think CBS would be interested in the Yankees purely from an entertainment standpoint. CBS must feel there is a huge potential profit from the transaction. This deal confirms my belief that baseball is big business. I think the Department of Justice should examine this sale." Others believed that CBS hoped the purchase would enable the company to enter the pay TV business successfully. CBS piously responded, "Our association with the Yankees is another step in our response to the growing public interest in sports." The network was already paying the Yankees $600,000 per year for the ball club's appearances on the *Game of the Week*.[38]

Some of the other American League owners particularly disliked the fait accompli aspect of the deal. They had little prior notification of the sale and felt that the Yankees had simply railroaded the issue.[39] Senators and baseball owners also wondered whether CBS would keep the Yankees from joining John Fetzer's Major League television plan. S. Jerry Cohen, chief counsel for the Senate subcommittee, asked Fetzer, "What would be the incentive for the Yankees or for CBS to give up a $500,000 contract to participate in a $325,000 deal?" Fetzer replied, "Ultimately we can increase the price [of the national package] to the extent that all ball clubs will be receiving more money, including the Yankees." Fetzer based his optimism on the fact that including the Yankees in the national package would make it more attractive to a network, in addition to his continued hope for a Monday night time slot.[40]

Despite the disclaimers put forth by CBS and Yankees officials, some senators remained unconvinced and believed that the network's purchase would further tilt the playing field in the New York club's favor. Senator Hart undoubtedly spoke for millions of baseball fans when he stated, "I am sure that the Yankees are not going to be weakened as a consequence of the investment by CBS." Ford Frick equivocated about the competitive aspects of the deal: "I suppose the outfit that has the most money theoretically at least could have the greatest chance of getting ball players." Hoping to allay the senators' concerns, Frick lauded the new reverse-order, amateur draft as counterbalance to the Yankees' enhanced purchasing power.[41]

Ball club owners Charles Finley and Art Allyn were outspoken critics of the deal. Because owners could not have interests in more than one club, CBS's purchase of the Yankees created potential violations of the rule. American League president Joe Cronin asked owners to provide information on whether they owned any CBS stock. Baltimore chairman J. A. W. Inglehart resigned as a director of CBS after disclosing that he owned 39,500 shares of stock in the company.[42] A Soviet Union newspaper, *Izvestia*, even weighed in: "In the best tradition of trade in human bodies, the New York Yankees were not even told about the deal. . . . The sensational sale of the New York Yankees is another proof that some sports are being turned into an appendix of commercial television. . . . At the foot of that pyramid made of dollars showing off their skill and might, sweating and often maiming each other, there runs [the players] . . . bought and sold by businessmen."[43]

Other Major League owners had ties with television. Gene Autry, John Fetzer, and Judge Roy Hofheinz all owned stations. Fetzer did not think the purchase hurt his plan for Monday night baseball, seeing as CBS had never been interested in it anyway. In addition, the Yankees were legally committed to joining the package deal in the future.[44]

CBS and the Yankees emphasized that current management would remain in place. Topping emphasized the rising costs associated with the team, claiming that the team's payroll now almost doubled that of any of its rivals. Some observers felt that Topping and Webb sold the 80 percent share because they feared competition from the Mets. General manager Ralph Houk thought CBS might be better positioned to promote the club.[45]

Ironically, White Sox co-owner John Allyn gave an at least symbolic hint that the Yankee club's power in the American League was waning when he responded to a question regarding the team's influence in American League councils: "I think the owners have blown the whistle on this domination. . . . I point to you the recent changes in membership in the executive council, for example. It was unheard of before that the Yankees were not members of the executive council of baseball."[46]

Moreover, CBS had bought a figuratively lame horse. Howard got hurt during the exhibition season. Kubek, Mantle, and Maris also got injured. The team's hitting fell apart, with the team's batting average ranking ninth in the ten-team league. In the end the Yankees finished sixth. Going into spring training in 1966, Yankees general manager Ralph Houk declared to the *Sporting News* that "the only 'clear-cut edge' the American League champions [Minnesota Twins] will have over the sixth-place Yankees in 1966 is at shortstop."[47] Houk was encouraged by Whitey Ford's rehabilitation and the pitching staff in general. His enthusiasm aside, the team started with thirteen losses in their first fifteen games and staggered to a last-place finish. In the post-mortem the *Sporting News Baseball Guide* paid tribute to the Yanks: "Many observers felt the Yankees were the best tenth-place team in major league annals."[48] The team had one of the best win-loss records for a last-place finish and came very close to outscoring its rivals. The team fared badly in games decided by one run, but overall there was reason for management to hope for a Yankee comeback in 1967, especially if Ford, Mantle, and Maris could regain their effectiveness. One can thus understand management's reticence to make drastic changes.

With the team's collapse in 1965 and 1966, what steps did the new owner, CBS, take to restore the team? After the 1965 season the Yankees traded for shortstop Ruben Amaro and pitcher Bob Friend. Friend had seen some good years with the Pittsburgh Pirates, while Amaro had been the starting shortstop for the Philadelphia Phillies. Neither player helped the Yankees. Just before the 1966 season, the Yankees traded for outfielder Lu Clinton, pitcher Al Closter, and shortstop Dick Schofield, acquiring the latter two for cash. Over the next two years the team added many players, but the list is a tribute to journeymen: Len Boehmer, Bobby Cox, Dick Howser, Jack Kralick, Gene Michael, Charley Smith, Thad Tillotson, and John Wyatt. (Interestingly enough, three of the acquired players—Cox, Howser, and Michael—later became managers; two of them eventually managed the Yankees.) Shortstop Michael was probably the best acquisition, starting at shortstop for four years, but he was the proverbial "good field, no hit" infielder. The team was clearly unsuccessful in obtaining frontline players. Ironically, attendance at Yankee Stadium, already tailing off from 1.75 million in 1961 to 1.3 million in 1964, only decreased to 1.1 million during the 1966 season, when the team finished last. Local radio and television broadcast revenues bounced from $1.2 million for 1964 and 1965 to $1.5 million in 1966 and back to $1.25 million in 1967.[49]

There were a number of prominent players traded between July 1, 1965, and April 30, 1967, when it was becoming apparent that the

Yankees needed an infusion of talent. The Yankees acquired none of the most prominent players available: Frank Robinson was the biggest star traded during that interval, although Orlando Cepeda was another slugger in his prime. Robinson won the American League Most Valuable Player Award in 1966, while Cepeda won the National League Most Valuable Player Award in 1967. Other notable players who were available to be traded at the time included Ferguson Jenkins, a future Hall of Fame pitcher, and Ted Abernathy, who would lead the National League in games saved in 1967. Former All-Stars Bill White and Maury Wills were also traded during that period. It is interesting to note that most of these players were black or Latin.

Because the team's performance slumped badly during the late 1960s, CBS did not fare well with its purchase of the Yankees. In 1973 the network sold the team to a group headed by George Steinbrenner for only $10 million, a sharply negative rate of return given the increase in the consumer price index between 1964 and 1973.[50] As economists James Quirk and Rodney Fort have noted, the Steinbrenner purchase price was on a par with the defunct Seattle Pilots and inept Washington Senators/Texas Rangers teams. The crown jewel of baseball had tarnished under CBS's watch. According to Quirk and Fort, the Yankees ranked fourth in the American League in total revenues in 1972. Although the franchise led the league in broadcasting revenues, the Detroit Tigers, Boston Red Sox, and Chicago White Sox all earned more revenue because of sharply higher gate receipts. The Yankees trailed Detroit by over $2 million in revenue. Eight of the National League teams also earned higher revenues than the Yankees in 1972.

The loss of general manager George Weiss and his replacement by an inexperienced general manager may have also hindered the Yankees. Weiss had developed a reputation as a tightfisted, puritanical official. Yet his aggressive negotiation tactics may have had positive consequences for the effort on the field. Years after he retired, Yankee mainstay Tommy Henrich was questioned by former Boston Red Sox second baseman Bobby Doerr. The Red Sox of 1946–50 were a talented group of players led by Ted Williams. For the era the Red Sox's star players were well paid by owner Tom Yawkey, who preferred to maintain a friendly relationship with his players. The Red Sox typically finished just behind the Yankees, and Doerr wanted to know why he and his talented teammates rarely bested the Yankees for the pennant. Henrich explained, "Because you didn't have to and we had to. We needed the extra money from the World Series check. That was our extra salary. You guys were all making more money than us because of Yawkey."[51] Reports in the *Sporting News* also attributed the Red Sox's 1949 "collapse" to "overpaid" players with the long-winded headline "Millionaires' Failure Laid to Too Many Bucks: Highly-Paid Players Weren't 'Hungry Enough' for All-Out Pennant Effort—Scribe Says the Gold [Red] Sox Were Too Self-Satisfied."[52] Henrich's explanation is intriguing, but the Yankees' reported payroll typically ran higher than Boston's, at least from 1950 on.

The Yankees earned the largest profits in the American League during the 1946–64 era. Given the relatively high value of the franchise, the implicit capital costs of the team were higher and, had they been made explicit, might have significantly eroded the team's profits in comparison with those of other teams. Moreover, given their stellar performance on the field, monopolization of the New York market for four seasons, and opportunities to purchase top-flight black talent, one is entitled to ask whether they could have done better at the gate or whether they could have extended their excellence on the field. Indeed, it is fair to ask whether these were incompatible goals, given the events of the 1950s and early 1960s, during which time the monotony of the Yankees' supremacy clearly alienated fans. Would the franchise have been more profitable if the other American League teams had been stronger? Did the staid Yankees face an increasingly alienated fan base—fans who wanted colorful antiheroes?

By 1964 the Yankees were consistently outdrawn by the Los Angeles Dodgers and New York Mets. Even such small-city teams as Boston and St. Louis began to pull in larger crowds than the Yankees. Not only were the Yankees stagnating at the gate, but their American League rivals did not match the National League in attendance. Although Baltimore, Kansas City/Oakland, and Minnesota proved to be better venues for the woebegone Browns, Athletics, and Senators than their former cities, one wonders whether the Yankees and the league would have been better served by having beaten the National League to the West Coast cities and Houston instead of encouraging Arnold Johnson to occupy Kansas City and driving out Bill Veeck before he could figure out how to move the Browns to Los Angeles. As Senators owner Clark Griffith predicted in 1954, "I think there are bigger towns [than Kansas City] with more population that would give our league better balance."[53] Having American League rivals that approximated the drawing power of the Los Angeles Dodgers and San Francisco Giants might have threatened the Yankees' dominance on the field, but it is reasonable to speculate that such lucrative franchises would have helped New York's revenues by increased gate-sharing revenue and possibly more competitive pennant races. In other words, rather than be Snow White to the other American League teams' Seven Dwarves, might the Yankees have been better off being first among (relative) equals?

While the team's superiority hurt the American League at the gate, for the Yankees fielding mediocre teams eventually eroded even the stagnating attendance at Yankee Stadium. The team's farm system produced some decent players but failed to unearth any Hall of Fame–caliber players for decades after 1951. The team had high hopes that Bobby Murcer would be the "next Mickey Mantle." He was not, although he was a solid player. According to the player ratings established by Thorn, Palmer, and others, Roy White would be the most productive African-American player introduced by the team until the 1990s. Reggie Jackson was the team's first black Hall of Fame player, and the Yankees signed him as a free agent in the prime of his career.

The CBS reign proved to be the most disappointing in franchise history since the acquisition of Babe Ruth. While the team would deteriorate during George Steinbrenner's exile from baseball during the late 1980s, the 1965–73 era was one that Yankee fans would just as soon forget. The period of small-city champions arose between 1965 and 1975, just before widespread free agency began. Although the big-city Dodgers and Mets would appear in five of the eleven World Series matches, Cincinnati, Minnesota, Oakland, Pittsburgh, and St. Louis all appeared there too. The descendants of the Athletics, Browns, and Senators dominated the World Series with a combined eight appearances. The Kansas City Royals would later win six division titles in ten seasons and appear in two World Series. The American League's other marquee teams of the 1950s—Chicago and Cleveland—slid into mediocrity for most of the eleven seasons. In the National League even the Cubs would have their longest sustained period of winning baseball since 1945; between 1967 and 1972 the team finished above .500 every season. Since then, the team has had difficulty completing back-to-back winning seasons. During these eleven years nine of the original sixteen franchises won pennants. Two teams that did not, the Braves and the Giants, at least won division titles. For proponents of competitive balance one might argue that these years were very good indeed.

The question of how to return the Yankees to the championship level vexed its management and fans. Did the Yankees simply need a new owner willing to meet the challenge of having strong rivals by spending large amounts of money to acquire the best players? George Steinbrenner eventually answered that question. The advent of free agency raised fears that the rich teams, especially the New York Yankees, could "buy pennants." Certainly, Steinbrenner's signings of free agents Catfish Hunter and Reggie Jackson gave such fears credence. The Yankees snapped out of their unaccustomed mediocrity in 1976 to win four of the next five East Division titles. They added a fifth, somewhat dubious, divisional title during the strike-marred 1981 season. The team also appeared in four of the six World Series championships between 1976 and 1981. But then the team regressed to being merely a strong contender, sometimes not even that, and did not appear in another World Series until 1996, the franchise's longest gap in World Series participation since its initial 1921 appearance.

Many baseball fans today, perhaps still awed by the Yankees' record-setting 1998 campaign and repeated appearances in the World Series, fear a return to the "not-so-good, old days." In 1999 Kansas City Royals fans protested the growing market disparity with signs reading SHARE THE WEALTH before a Royals-Yankees game. According to the *New York Times*, the fans were particularly enraged that Yankee player Bernie Williams's 1999 salary was roughly double that of the entire Kansas City starting lineup's salaries.[54] Since then, the Yankees have demonstrated an ability to afford the largest payrolls, with salaries that would give George Weiss the creeps, but also their share of disappointing performances and several unsuccessful World Series bids. The Yankees may continue to win a disproportionate share of titles, but past experience suggests that it may not be in their interest to overdo it.

Epilogue

What If the Golden Age Ended and Nobody Cared?

By 1966 the Braves were ensconced in Atlanta, and Charlie Finley was eagerly awaiting the opportunity to transfer to the greener fields of Oakland. Los Angeles and San Francisco baseball fans were ecstatic with their Major League teams. Whatever golden age the New York Yankees had experienced, in 1966 the glow was gone, with attendance drooping and a general sense of ennui setting in among traditional fans of the Bronx Bombers.

The Yankees opened the season against Detroit at Yankee Stadium with a seemingly formidable lineup: Bobby Richardson at second base; Tom Tresh in left field; Roger Maris and Mickey Mantle in right and center field; Clete Boyer at third base; Joe Pepitone at first base; Elston Howard behind the plate; and Ruben Amaro at shortstop. Whitey Ford was the starting pitcher. Six of these players had come up through the Yankee farm system. Tresh and Pepitone would show promise by hitting fifty-eight homeruns between them in 1966. In the event the Yankees lost the opening game 2–1, as the Tigers scored the winning run in the top of the ninth on a Norm Cash two-out single.[1] Over forty thousand fans attended the game, which was the best attendance at a Yankee home opener since 1951.

Contrast the opening day starting lineup with that of the final game on October 2: Mike Hegan at first base; Bobby Murcer at shortstop; Bobby Richardson at second base (batting third!); Lu Clinton, John Miller, and Steve Whitaker in the outfield; Billy Bryan behind the plate; Mike Ferraro at third base; and Al Downing starting on the mound. Presumably, many readers of this book are knowledgeable baseball fans, but most of these names would tax anyone's memory. Indeed, the outfield of Clinton, Miller, and Whitaker might have been the worst outfield ever to start a game for the team. At least the Yankees beat the Chicago White Sox 2–0. Indeed, after clinching last place by losing to Chicago on Friday, September 30, the Yankees won the final two games against the White Sox.

In between the opener and the finale the Yankees stumbled early and often. Cleveland won ten straight games to open the season. By April 28 the Yankees were already nine and a half games out of first place, even though they'd only played thirteen games (losing eleven). The Yankee bats were quiet, and the players' fielding was shoddy. After the first eight games sportswriter Leonard Koppett commented that four of the first seven losses came from defensive lapses in the late innings. In six of the first eight games the Bronx Bombers scored two or fewer runs.[2]

While previous Yankee squads had celebrated the holidays in first place, the 1966 vintage was soured early. The Yanks split a Memorial Day doubleheader with the Senators before 31,764 fans in Washington DC The Senators ended the day one game ahead of the Yankees, though Boston and Kansas City were behind New York in the standings. The Yankees' 18-22 record kept them eight and a half games behind the Cleveland Indians. The Yankees split a doubleheader with Chicago on the Fourth of July. The team was now in seventh place, ahead of Kansas City, Washington, and Boston. The team's win-loss record, however, remained a mediocre 31-41, eighteen games behind the Baltimore Orioles. Finally, the Labor Day doubleheader with the Orioles in Baltimore ended the Yankees' pennant aspirations. The Orioles won both games and eliminated the Yankees, who were now twenty-six and a half games behind. The Yankees were in a tight race for last place. After the Labor Day defeats, the Yankees were tied with Kansas

City in eighth place. The Washington Senators were in seventh place, a game ahead of the A's and Yanks. The Red Sox were in last place, a game and a half behind the A's and the Yanks.

Thus, the 1966 Yankees' last-pace finish was hotly disputed. The expansion Senators finished twenty-five and a half games back of the pennant-winning Baltimore Orioles, while the Boston Red Sox finished twenty-six games back. The Red Sox completed the "Impossible Dream" by winning the pennant the next season. The Yankees continued to be mired in the depths of the American League.

Ralph Houk fired Johnny Keane, formerly the luckiest manager on the face of the earth, after the twentieth game. The Yankees were 4-16 at the time. Houk took over managing the team, and the club responded by going 66-73 the rest of the way. Keane was not the last casualty. On September 23 the *New York Times* headline sarcastically read, "Meanwhile, Back at the Stadium, 413 See Last-Place Yanks Lose 87th Game."[3] No, the typesetter did not leave off a couple of digits and a comma. The crowd was the smallest in the American League for the season. The Yankee front office was unable to say whether the attendance was the lowest ever for the franchise. Yankees radio and television announcer Red Barber told his audience of the puny crowd and urged the reluctant cameraman to pan the stadium, showing the empty seats. Three days later Mike Burke fired Barber, claiming that "the decision was made two weeks ago by the Yankee organization before I took over."[4] The next day reporter Val Adams wrote that Barber's actions during the September 22 game was "believed to be one of the incidents contributing to Mr. Barber's departure from the Yankees."[5] In his book *The Broadcasters* Barber made it clear that he believed his reporting the sparseness of the crowd at the September 22 game had cost him his job.[6] Yankee management believed that "the truth shall get you fired."

All in all, the tawdry finish to the 1966 season confirmed the end of the postwar golden era for even the putative beneficiaries: the New York Yankees and their fans. The dynasty ended with nary a whimper from its fans.

Appendix

Table 1.1

Statistical Summary of the New York Yankees' Championship Runs (on a Per–Season Basis)

	Win-loss	Pct.[a]	GA[b]	Attendance[c]	Runs[d]	OpRuns[e]
1921–23	97-56	.632	7.2	1,087,965	843	649
1926–28	101-53	.654	8.2	1,087,747	905	666
1936–39	102-50	.670	14.8	951,441	994	667
1941–43	101-53	.654	13.2	865,993	767	560
1949–53	97-56	.635	3.9	1,896,128	814	611
1955–58	96-58	.622	7.5	1,476,874	775	578
1960–64	101-59	.630	6.5	1,496,641	767	609
1976–78	99-62	.614	4.7	2,150,466	765	603
1998–2001	99-63	.611	11.5	3,183,726	885	729

Sources: *Macmillan Baseball Encyclopedia*, 9th ed.; Sporting News, *The Sporting News Complete Baseball Record Book—1998*, 247–48; Sporting News, *The Sporting News Complete Baseball Record Book—2003*, 257; Thorn, Palmer, and Gershman, *Total Baseball*.

Note: The Yankees also won pennants in 1932 and 1947.

[a] Pct.: wins/(wins + losses).

[b] GA: games ahead of second-place team.

[c] Attendance: home attendance.

[d] Runs: runs scored per season by the Yankees.

[e] OpRuns: runs allowed per season by Yankees.

Table 1.2
Attendance in the Major Leagues, 1946–64
(in Thousands)[a]

American League

	BOS	CHI	CLE	DET	NY	PHI/KC	STL/BAL	WAS/MIN	Total
1946	1,417*	983	1,057	1,723	2,266	622	526	1,027	9,621
1947	1,427	877	1,522	1,398	2,179*	912	320	851	9,486
1948	1,559	778	2,621	1,743*	2,374	945	336	795	11,150
1949	1,597	937	2,234	1,821	2,284*	817	271	771	10,731
1950	1,344	781	1,727	1,951	2,081*	310	247	700	9,142
1951	1,312	1,328	1,705	1,133	1,950*	465	294	695	8,883
1952	1,116	1,232	1,445	1,027	1,630*	627	519	699	8,294
1953	1,026	1,191	1,069	885	1,538*	362	297	596	6,964
1954	931	1,232	1,335*	1,080	1,475	305	1,060	503	7,922
1955	1,203	1,176	1,222	1,182	1,490*	1,393	852	425	8,943
1956	1,137	1,000	865	1,051	1,492*	1,015	901	432	7,894
1957	1,181	1,136	722	1,272	1,497*	901	1,030	457	8,196
1958	1,077	797	664	1,099	1,428*	925	830	475	7,296
1959	984	1,423*	1,498	1,221	1,552	964	892	615	9,149
1960	1,130	1,644	951	1,168	1,627*	775	1,188	743	9,227

1961	851	1,146	725	1,601	1,748*	684	951	1,257	10,163
1962	733	1,132	716	1,208	1,494*	636	790	1,433	10,015
1963	943	1,159	563	822	1,309*	762	774	1,407	9,095
1964	883	1,250	653	816	1,306*	642	1,116	1,208	9,235

National League

	BKN/LA	BOS/MIL	CHI	CIN	NY/SF	PHI	PIT	STL	Total
1946	1,797	970	1,343	716	1,220	1,045	750	1,062*	8,902
1947	1,808*	1,277	1,364	900	1,601	907	1,284	1,248	10,388
1948	1,399	1,455*	1,238	823	1,459	767	1,517	1,111	9,771
1949	1,634*	1,082	1,143	708	1,218	820	1,449	1,431	9,485
1950	1,186	944	1,166	539	1,009	1,217*	1,166	1,093	8,321
1951	1,283	487	894	588	1,060*	938	981	1,013	7,244
1952	1,089*	281	1,025	604	985	755	687	913	6,339
1953	1,163*	1,827	764	548	812	854	573	880	7,420
1954	1,021	2,131	748	704	1,155*	739	475	1,040	8,014
1955	1,034*	2,006	876	694	824	923	469	849	7,674
1956	1,214*	2,046	720	1,126	629	935	950	1,030	8,650
1957	1,028	2,215*	671	1,071	654	1,146	851	1,184	8,820
1958	1,846	1,971*	980	789	1,273	931	1,312	1,064	10,165
1959	2,071*	1,749	858	801	1,422	803	1,360	930	9,995

continued

Table 1.2 National League *continued*

	BKN/LA	BOS/MIL.	CHI	CIN	NY/SF	PHI	PIT	STL	Total
1960	2,254	1,498	810	663	1,795	862	1,706*	1,097	10,685
1961	1,804	1,101	673	1,118*	1,391	590	1,199	855	8,732
1962	2,755	767	610	982	1,593*	762	1,091	954	11,360
1963	2,539*	773	980	859	1,571	907	784	1,171	11,382
1964	2,229	911	752	862	1,504	1,426	759	1,143*	12,045

Source: Thorn, Palmer, and Gershman, *Total Baseball*, 76–77.

Notes:

American League:

St. Louis moved to Baltimore for the 1954 season.

Philadelphia moved to Kansas City for the 1955 season.

Washington moved to Minnesota for the 1961 season.

For 1961–64 attendance of expansion teams, Los Angeles Angels and Washington Senators are included in total but not shown.

National League:

Boston moved to Milwaukee for the 1953 season.

Brooklyn moved to Los Angeles for the 1958 season.

New York moved to San Francisco for the 1958 season.

For 1962–64 attendance of expansion teams, Houston Astros and New York Mets are included in total but not shown.

[a] Asterisks denote pennant winners.

Table 1.3
Win-Loss Records of American League Baseball Teams[a]

Records against only the original eight franchises

Franchise	1946–54	1955–64	1965–74	1975–84
Boston	.569	.487	.506	.549
Chicago	.479	.563	.457	.477
Cleveland	.588	.514	.457	.456
Detroit	.496	.506	.525	.489
New York	.628	.609	.464	.579
Philadelphia/Kansas City/Oakland	.435	.393	.487	.441
St. Louis/Baltimore	.375	.494	.572	.561
Washington/Minnesota	.430	.434	.530	.439
Standard deviation	.088	.068	.041	.056

Records against all franchises

Franchise	1946–54	1955–64	1965–74	1975–84
Boston	.569	.490	.514	.551
California (1961)	—	.477	.472	.484
Chicago	.479	.567	.485	.486
Cleveland	.588	.519	.463	.475
Detroit	.496	.518	.542	.512
Kansas City (1969)	—	—	.478	.551
New York	.628	.616	.500	.570
Philadelphia/Kansas City/Oakland	.435	.404	.517	.471
Seattle (1977)	—	—	—	.403
Seattle/Milwaukee (1969)	—	—	.428	.503
St. Louis/Baltimore	.375	.506	.588	.581
Toronto (1977)	—	—	—	.425
Washington/Minnesota	.430	.443	.540	.467
Washington/Texas (1961)	—	.370	.434	.488

Sources: Sporting News, *Sporting News Official Baseball Guide* (various years).

Note: Using 1965–75 and 1976–84 would not have created much difference. Oakland would have had a significantly worse record in the latter period, while Detroit would have improved.

[a] Years in parentheses indicate a team's first year in the league.

Table 1.4
Baseball Statistics for the Postwar Era

National League

Year	Batting average	On-base percentage	Slugging average	Per-game (both teams)			
				Runs	Homeruns	Walks	Stolen bases
1946	.256	.329	.356	7.92	0.90	7.08	0.77
1947	.266	.339	.391	9.14	1.43	7.22	0.58
1948	.261	.333	.383	8.86	1.37	7.12	0.73
1949	.263	.335	.390	9.08	1.50	7.08	0.59
1950	.262	.336	.402	9.32	1.78	7.34	0.60
1951	.260	.332	.390	8.93	1.65	7.01	0.73
1952	.253	.324	.374	8.35	1.47	6.71	0.64
1953	.267	.336	.412	9.51	1.92	6.78	0.55
1954	.266	.339	.408	9.13	1.81	7.17	0.55
1955	.259	.331	.407	9.06	2.05	6.88	0.61
1956	.257	.324	.401	8.49	1.96	6.41	0.60
1957	.261	.325	.400	8.77	1.90	6.25	0.64
1958	.262	.331	.406	8.80	1.92	6.60	0.63
1959	.261	.328	.400	8.81	1.87	6.41	0.71
1960	.255	.322	.388	8.48	1.68	6.36	0.81
1961	.262	.330	.406	9.05	1.93	6.45	0.76
1962	.261	.329	.393	8.96	1.78	6.48	0.97
1963	.246	.308	.364	7.62	1.50	5.62	0.84
1964	.254	.313	.375	8.03	1.49	5.41	0.78
1998	.262	.334	.411	9.19	1.98	6.71	1.24
1999	.269	.345	.430	10.01	2.23	7.41	1.51
2000	.266	.345	.432	10.01	2.32	7.51	1.26

American League

Year	Batting average	On-base percentage	Slugging average	Per-game (both teams)			
				Runs	Homeruns	Walks	Stolen bases
1946	.256	.328	.365	8.11	1.05	7.09	0.65
1947	.256	.334	.365	8.28	1.09	7.62	0.64
1948	.266	.350	.382	9.45	1.15	8.46	0.59
1949	.264	.354	.379	9.35	1.24	9.11	0.59
1950	.271	.357	.403	10.09	1.60	8.74	0.45
1951	.263	.342	.382	9.26	1.36	7.92	0.67
1952	.253	.330	.366	8.36	1.28	7.46	0.60
1953	.263	.337	.384	8.92	1.42	7.23	0.53
1954	.257	.334	.374	8.38	1.33	7.44	0.58
1955	.259	.339	.382	8.89	1.56	7.78	0.51
1956	.261	.344	.394	9.31	1.74	8.12	0.56
1957	.255	.329	.383	8.46	1.66	7.00	0.60
1958	.255	.325	.384	8.33	1.71	6.56	0.57
1959	.254	.326	.385	8.72	1.77	6.81	0.67
1960	.256	.331	.388	8.77	1.76	7.21	0.68
1961	.256	.332	.395	9.05	1.89	7.28	0.71
1962	.255	.328	.394	8.88	1.92	7.01	0.69
1963	.248	.315	.380	8.17	1.84	6.23	0.68
1964	.248	.317	.382	8.12	1.91	6.42	0.66

Source: Thone, Palmer, and Gershman, *Total Baseball*.

Table 2.1
Franchise Players Introduced by American League Teams, 1946–64

American League

Franchise	Players[a]	TBR/TPI[b]	Career[c]	Last two[d]	Total[e]
Boston	7	122.7	3	1	4
Chicago	8	102.7	0	0	0
Cleveland	13	229.8	2	1	3
Detroit	5	94.7	2	1	3
New York	6	194.4	4	1	5
Philadelphia/ Kansas City	5	71.8	0	0	0
St. Louis/Baltimore	8	115.4	1	0	1
Washington/Minnesota	5	95.5	2	1	3

National League

Franchise	Players	TBR/TPI	Career	Last two	Total
Boston/Milwaukee	10	279.0	0	2	2
Brooklyn/Los Angeles	12	224.2	4	1	5
Chicago	6	130.6	1	2	3
Cincinnati	7	141.6	0	1	1
New York/ San Francisco	12	313.7	1	4	5
Philadelphia	5	111.9	0	0	0
Pittsburgh	6	172.1	4	1	5
St. Louis	9	150.1	1	0	1

Source: Thorn, Palmer, Gershman, and Pietrusza, *Total Baseball*.

[a] Players: players who are in the top five hundred batters and three hundred pitchers by total baseball rankings (TBRS) and who began their careers in 1903 or later. Babe Ruth was initially included both as a batter and as a pitcher.

[b] TBR: career total baseball rating. TPI: career total pitching index.

[c] Career: players who spent their entire career with one Major League team.

[d] Last two: players who spent all but their final season or final two seasons with the Major League team with which they made their debut.

[e] Total: entire career plus all but last two years.

Table 2.2
Number of Players Involved in Cash Transactions, 1946–60
(by Team)

Team	Obtained				Lost				Overall		
	Number[e]	Average age	Previous year TBR[f]	Career TBR[g]	Number	Average age	Previous year TBR	Career TBR	Net[h]	Previous year TBR	Career TBR
Small[a]	216	30.3	−82.5	−229.9	223	30.5	−82.9	−28.5	−7	0.4	−201.4
Average[b]			−13.8	−38.3			−13.8	−4.8		0.1	−33.6
Medium[c]	149	30.9	−44.5	−54.4	118	30.9	−47.5	−117.2	31	3.0	62.8
Average			−11.1	−13.6			−11.9	−29.3		0.8	15.7
Large[d]	181	30.6	−49.9	103.5	205	30.3	−46.5	−35.1	−24	−3.4	138.6
Average			−8.3	17.3			−7.8	−5.9		−0.6	23.1
Total	546	30.5	−176.9	−180.8	546	30.5	−176.9	−180.8	0	0	0

Source: Thorn, Palmer, Gershman, and Pietrusza, *Total Baseball*.

a Small, six teams: Boston (AL), Boston/Milwaukee (NL), Cincinnati, Philadelphia/Kansas City (AL), St. Louis (NL), St. Louis/Baltimore (AL).

b Average: each row divided by number of teams in the size category.

c Medium, four teams: Cleveland, Philadelphia (NL), Pittsburgh, and Washington.

d Large, six teams: Brooklyn/Los Angeles (NL), Chicago (AL), Chicago (NL), Detroit, New York (AL), and New York/San Francisco (NL).

e Number: number of players obtained or traded away. Does not correspond with the actual number of cash trades because of multiplayer transactions.

f Previous year TBR: traded players' combined total baseball ranking from full season prior to being traded (rookies assigned TBR of 0.0).

g Career TBR: traded players' combined lifetime total baseball ranking.

h Net: number of players obtained − number of players lost.

Table 3.1

Average Ticket Prices in the American League, 1946, 1950, and 1952–56[a]

Team	1946	1950	1952	1953	1954	1955	1956	% Change
Boston	1.19	1.37	1.41	1.41	1.67	1.64	1.71	0.44
	(1.19)	(1.11)	(1.04)	(1.03)	(1.21)	(1.20)	(1.23)	(0.03)
Chicago	1.12	1.23	1.21	1.40	1.51	1.52	1.60	0.43
	(1.12)	(1.00)	(0.89)	(1.02)	(1.10)	(1.11)	(1.15)	(0.03)
Cleveland	1.14	1.13	1.54	1.63	1.61	1.67	1.82	0.60
	(1.14)	(0.92)	(1.13)	(1.19)	(1.17)	(1.22)	(1.31)	(0.15)
Detroit	1.11	1.25	1.45	1.54	1.49	1.61	1.65	0.49
	(1.11)	(1.01)	(1.07)	(1.12)	(1.08)	(1.17)	(1.19)	(0.07)
New York	1.29	1.50	1.65	1.68	2.00	1.99	2.04	0.58
	(1.29)	(1.22)	(1.21)	(1.23)	(1.45)	(1.45)	(1.47)	(0.14)
Philadelphia/Kansas City	1.07	1.30	1.32	1.36	1.42	1.88	1.97	0.84
	(1.07)	(1.05)	(0.97)	(0.99)	(1.03)	(1.37)	(1.42)	(0.32)
St. Louis/Baltimore	1.12	1.39	1.33	1.50	1.77	1.79	1.71	1.53
	(1.12)	(1.13)	(0.98)	(1.10)	(1.29)	(1.31)	(1.23)	(0.10)
Washington	1.08	1.17	1.20	1.24	1.57	1.55	1.60	0.48
	(1.08)	(0.95)	(0.88)	(0.91)	(1.14)	(1.13)	(1.15)	(0.06)

Sources: U.S. Congress, *Organized Baseball: Hearings*, 1604–5; and U.S. Congress, *Organized Professional Team Sports*, 2048–52. Nominal figures deflated by consumer price index (all items, 1946 = 100) taken from U.S. Department of Commerce, *Historical Statistics*, 210.

[a]Nominal prices derived from: (home gate/home attendance) + .29. Real values in parentheses (with 1946 = 100).

Table 3.2
Nominal Major League Ticket Prices, 1946–64
(in Dollars)[a]

American League

Team	Years[b]	Bleachers	General admission	Reserved	Box seats
Boston	1946–64	0.60–1.00	1.20–1.50	1.80–2.25	2.40–3.00
Chicago	1946–64	0.60–0.75	1.25–1.50*	1.25–2.00	1.80–3.00
Cleveland	1947–64	0.60–0.75	1.20–1.50	1.50–2.50	2.00–3.00
Detroit	1948–64	0.60–1.00	1.20–1.50	1.50–2.00	2.00–3.00
Los Angeles	1961–64	1.50–n/a[c]	1.50–1.50	2.50–2.50	3.50–3.50
New York	1949–64	0.60–0.75	1.25–1.50	2.00–2.50	3.00–3.50
Philadelphia/ Kansas City	1949–64	n/a	1.25–1.50*	2.00–2.50	2.50–3.00
St. Louis/ Baltimore	1950–64	0.75–0.75	1.35–1.25	1.85–2.25	2.25–3.00
Washington	1961–64	0.75–n/a	1.50–1.50	2.50–2.50	3.00–3.00
Washington/ Minnesota	1950–64	0.60–n/a	1.25–1.50	1.50–2.50	2.00–3.00

National League

Team	Years	Bleachers	General admission	Reserved	Box seats
Boston/ Milwaukee	1946–64	0.60–0.75	1.20–1.55	1.80–2.30	2.40–3.10
Brooklyn/ Los Angeles	1950–64	0.60–n/a	1.25–1.50	1.75–2.50	3.00–3.50
Chicago	1946–64	0.60–0.75	1.25–1.51	n/a	1.80–3.00
Cincinnati	1946–64	0.65–1.00	1.20–1.50	1.90–2.25	2.20–3.00
Houston	1962–64	1.50–n/a	1.50–1.50	2.50–2.50	3.50–3.50
New York	1962–64	0.75–n/a	1.30–1.30	2.50–2.50	3.50–3.50
New York/ San Francisco	1946–64	0.75–0.90*	1.30–1.50*	1.75–2.50	2.50–3.50

continued

Table 3.2 National League *continued*

Team	Years	Bleachers	General admission	Reserved	Box seats
Philadelphia	1949–64	0.75–1.00	1.30–1.50	2.00–2.25	2.50–3.25
Pittsburgh	1949–64	1.00–1.00	1.40–1.50	2.20–2.50	2.75–3.00
St. Louis	1950–64	0.75–1.00	1.35–1.50	1.85–2.25	2.25–3.50

Sources: American League, *American League Red Book* (1955–64); Sporting News, *Sporting News Official Baseball Guide* (1950–62); and various team scorecards and newsletters for the years 1946–54.

[a] For ticket prices, the first number indicates the first price listed; the second number is the ticket price in 1964. Asterisks denote first year for general admission: Chicago (AL) (1953) and Philadelphia/Kansas City (1955); general admission and bleachers: San Francisco/New York (1955); bleachers: Pittsburgh (1946).

[b] Years: years data is available.

[c] n/a: not available (typically meant team did not have this class of tickets).

Table 3.3
Ticket Prices after Pennant-Winning Season, 1946–64

Year[a]	American League	Prices	National League	Prices
1946	Boston	Same	St. Louis	Unknown
1947	New York	Unknown	Brooklyn	Unknown
1948	Cleveland	Same[b]	Boston	Same
1949	New York	Same	Brooklyn	Unknown
1950	New York	Same	Philadelphia	Same
1951	New York	Same	New York	Same
1952	New York	Same	Brooklyn	Same
1953	New York	Raised[c]	Brooklyn	Same[d]
1954	Cleveland	Same	New York	Raised[e]
1955	New York	Same	Brooklyn	Same
1956	New York	Same	Brooklyn	Same
1957	New York	Same	Milwaukee	Raised[f]
1958	New York	Raised[g]	Milwaukee	Same
1959	Chicago	Raised[h]	Los Angeles	Same
1960	New York	Same	Pittsburgh	Same
1961	New York	Same	Cincinnati	Same[i]
1962	New York	Same	San Francisco	Same
1963	New York	Same	Los Angeles	Same
1964	New York	Same	St. Louis	Same

Sources: For both leagues: Sporting News, *Sporting News Official Baseball Guide* (1950–62). For American League: American League, *American League Red Book* (1963–64); and various team scorecards. For National League: Sporting News, *Sporting News Dope Book* (1964).

[a] Year: year the team won a pennant.
[b] Known prices same, but some prices unknown.
[c] Raised bleacher prices; box and reserved no longer have lower split prices.
[d] Bleacher prices actually dropped.
[e] General admission and bleacher prices unknown.
[f] All prices raised except bleacher.
[g] General admission and bleacher prices the same.
[h] Box seats only price raised.
[i] Bleacher seats raised, but all others the same.

Table 3.4
Real Gross Operating Income/Total Income, 1946, 1950, and 1952–56
(in Thousands of Dollars)

American League	1946	1950	1952	1953	1954	1955	1956
Boston	2,249	1,912	1,694	1,524	1,700	2,074	2,012
Chicago	1,509	1,217	1,625	1,865	2,087	2,208	1,942
Cleveland	1,418	1,817	2,181	1,904	2,386	2,158	2,153
Detroit	2,154	2,309	1,660	1,575	1,766	2,122	1,855
New York	3,455	3,417	2,941	3,013	3,274	3,573	3,606
Philadelphia/Kansas City	989	975	1,131	963	873	2,189	1,795
St. Louis/Baltimore	819	598	736	545	1,753	1,534	1,518
Washington	1,405	1,011	1,025	988	1,071	1,009	1,015
Total	13,999	13,257	12,992	12,378	14,909	16,868	15,895

National League	1946	1950	1952	1953	1954	1955	1956
Boston/Milwaukee	1,425	1,384	687	2,245	2,551	2,597	2,657
Brooklyn	2,680	2,119	2,085	2,198	2,047	2,554	2,789
Chicago	1,890	1,594	1,345	1,094	1,143	1,306	1,184
Cincinnati	1,177	910	827	850	1,048	1,138	1,736
New York	2,056	1,633	1,774	1,683	2,276	2,093	1,776

Philadelphia	1,258	1,652	1,033	1,213	1,169	1,532	1,638
Pittsburgh	1,207	1,759	1,038	933	887	1,013	1,490
St. Louis	1,818	1,685	1,233	1,227	1,675	1,462	1,621
Total	13,510	12,736	10,023	11,443	12,795	13,695	14,890

Sources: U.S. Congress, *Organized Baseball: Hearings*, 1610; U.S. Congress, *Organized Professional Team Sports*, 1604–5, 1608–9. Deflated by CPI (all items, 1953 = 100), U.S. Department of Commerce, *Historical Statistics*, 210.

Notes: Gross operating income (games at home; games away; exhibition games; radio and television; and concessions [net]) reported for 1946 and 1950.
Total income (games at home; games away; exhibition games; radio and television; concessions [net]; and other income) reported for 1952–56.

Table 3.5a

Concessions Income (Net), 1952–56

(in Nominal Dollars)

Team	1952	1953	1954	1955	1956	Total
American League						
Boston	176,673	164,844	162,814	205,855	215,477	925,663
Chicago	287,844	316,331	325,841	349,381	287,690	1,567,087
Cleveland	139,981	104,386	125,581	127,486	90,491	587,925
Detroit	203,335	188,832	239,099	350,856	297,472	1,279,594
New York	441,512	470,756	397,843	487,081	495,557	2,242,749
Philadelphia/Kansas City	235,696	232,776	191,117	242,589	200,233	1,102,411
St. Louis/Baltimore	93,034	64,274	242,568	234,876	239,132	873,884
Washington	142,554	111,162	97,994	94,385	115,617	561,712
National League						
Boston/ Milwaukee	43,338	425,549	548,005	510,948	542,406	2,070,246
Brooklyn	239,121	272,712	240,135	272,812	315,407	1,340,187
Chicago	302,836	242,962	308,715	336,349	283,444	1,474,306
Cincinnati	104,761	107,351	144,354	141,638	234,599	732,703
New York	262,909	236,542	309,353	245,769	196,141	1,250,714

Philadelphia	70,047	79,031	69,525	162,822	188,961	570,386
Pittsburgh	117,959	129,984	119,268	115,333	193,518	676,062
St. Louis	255,407	225,427	225,389	210,253	266,449	2,283,936

Source: U.S. Congress, *Organized Professional Team Sports*, 354–63, 2048–52.
Note: Prices changed by 2.5 percent total over the period.

Table 3.5b

Concessions Income (Net) per Home Attendee, 1952–56
(in Nominal Dollars)

Team	1952	1953	1954	1955	1956	Total
American League						
Boston	0.16	0.16	0.17	0.17	0.19	0.17
Chicago	0.23	0.27	0.26	0.30	0.29	0.27
Cleveland	0.10	0.10	0.09	0.10	0.10	0.10
Detroit	0.20	0.21	0.22	0.30	0.28	0.24
New York	0.27	0.27	0.27	0.33	0.33	0.29
Philadelphia/Kansas City	0.38	0.64	0.63	0.17	0.20	0.30
St. Louis/Baltimore	0.18	0.22	0.23	0.28	0.27	0.24
Washington	0.20	0.19	0.19	0.22	0.27	0.21
National League						
Boston/Milwaukee	0.15	0.23	0.26	0.25	0.27	0.25
Brooklyn	0.22	0.23	0.24	0.26	0.26	0.24
Chicago	0.30	0.32	0.41	0.38	0.39	0.36
Cincinnati	0.17	0.20	0.21	0.20	0.21	0.20
New York	0.27	0.29	0.27	0.30	0.31	0.28
Philadelphia	0.09	0.09	0.09	0.18	0.20	0.13
Pittsburgh	0.17	0.23	0.25	0.25	0.20	0.21
St. Louis	0.28	0.26	0.22	0.25	0.26	0.25
Total average						0.22

Source: U.S. Congress, *Organized Professional Team Sports*, 354–63, 2048–52.

Note: Figures derived by dividing information in table 3.5a by the home attendance. Prices changed by
2.5 percent total over the period.

Table 3.6
Nominal Concessions Prices at Major League Ballparks, 1946–64
(in Dollars)[a]

Team	Years[b]	Soft drinks	Hot dogs	Beer
American League				
Boston		n/a[c]	n/a	n/a
Chicago	1946–60	0.10–0.15	0.15–0.30	0.25–0.40
Cleveland	1951–64	0.10–0.10	0.20–0.30	0.25–0.40
Detroit	1960–64	0.15–0.15	0.30–0.30	0.35–0.40
Los Angeles	1961	0.25	0.30	0.40
New York		n/a	n/a	n/a
Philadelphia/Kansas City	1946–64	0.10–0.15	0.15–0.30	0.35–0.40[d]
St. Louis/Baltimore	1950–64	0.10–0.15	0.15–0.25	0.25–0.40
Washington	1961–64	0.15–0.15	0.25–0.30	0.35–0.40
Washington/Minnesota	1957–64	0.10–0.15	0.25–0.25	0.35–0.40[e]
National League				
Chicago	1946–64	0.10–0.15	0.15–0.30	0.25–0.40
Cincinnati	1946–55	0.10–0.10	0.15–0.25	0.20–0.25
Houston	1962–63	0.15–0.15	0.30–0.30	0.35–0.35
Los Angeles/Brooklyn		n/a	n/a	n/a
Milwaukee/Boston	1951–56	0.10–0.10	0.20–0.20	0.30–0.30
New York		n/a	n/a	n/a
Philadelphia	1954–64	0.15–0.15	0.25–0.30	0.40–0.40[f]
Pittsburgh	1948–64	0.10–0.15	0.15–0.30	n/a[g]
San Francisco/New York	1963	0.15	0.30	0.40
St. Louis		n/a	n/a	n/a

Sources: Various team scorecards and newsletters for years 1946–64 (some gaps in reporting
concessions prices).

[a] The first number is first price listed; the second number is the last price listed.

[b] Years: years for which data is available.

[c] n/a: not available. Boston, New York (AL), Los Angeles/Brooklyn, St. Louis, and New York (NL)
never listed prices.

[d] First year Kansas City sold beer was 1960.

[e] First year Washington/Minnesota sold beer was 1959.

[f] First year Philadelphia sold beer was 1962.

[g] Pittsburgh never sold beer.

Table 3.7
Radio and Television Revenue, 1946, 1950, and 1952–56
(in Thousands of Dollars)[a]

Franchise	1946	1950	1952	1953	1954	1955	1956
Boston	49 (67)	204 (227)	367 (369)	370 (370)	361 (359)	477 (476)	477 (470)
Chicago	41 (56)	186 (207)	261 (263)	356 (356)	434 (432)	522 (522)	519 (511)
Cleveland	3 (5)	256 (284)	453 (456)	615 (615)	636 (633)	568 (567)	1,053 (1,036)
Detroit	75 (103)	194 (216)	320 (323)	316 (316)	327 (326)	348 (348)	403 (397)
New York	120 (164)	416 (462)	475 (479)	625 (625)	675 (672)	725 (724)	900 (886)
Philadelphia/Kansas City	25 (34)	185 (205)	169 (170)	293 (293)	300 (299)	210 (210)	210 (207)
St. Louis/Baltimore	34 (47)	87 (97)	9 (9)	56 (56)	313 (311)	301 (301)	302 (297)
Washington	26 (36)	128 (142)	170 (171)	283 (283)	341 (339)	317 (316)	317 (312)
League	375 (514)	1,659 (1,843)	2,225 (2,242)	2,914 (2,914)	3,390 (3,373)	3,470 (3,466)	4,183 (4,116)

Standard deviation[b]	.096	0.59	0.71	0.64	0.44	0.49	0.72
Top/bottom quartile[c]	6.87	3.12	5.23	3.67	2.14	2.53	3.82

Sources: U.S. Congress, *Organized Baseball: Hearings*, 1604–5; and U.S. Congress, *Organized Professional Team Sports*, 2048–52. Consumer price index (1953 = 100) taken from U.S. Department of Commerce, *Historical Statistics*, 211.

Note: St. Louis transferred to Baltimore in 1954, and Philadelphia transferred to Kansas City in 1955.

[a] Real revenue in parentheses.

[b] Standard deviation: the standard deviation of the team's individual share of total league estimated home revenue (without gate sharing) with mean = .125.

[c] Top/bottom quartile: the two teams with the largest home revenues/the two teams with the smallest home revenues.

Table 3.8
Major League Payrolls, 1952–56
(in Nominal Dollars)

Team	1952	1953	1954	1955	1956
American League					
Boston	413,029	410,854	450,796	435,220	428,822
Chicago	324,464	374,342	427,659	482,135	496,061
Cleveland	523,934	555,915	592,660	648,218	557,172
Detroit	549,980	478,654	425,501	463,947	494,393
New York	561,420	617,144	674,622	629,995	680,679
Philadelphia/Kansas City	387,758	392,097	357,329	375,457	345,257
St. Louis/Baltimore	350,810	396,510	386,216	472,193	475,276
Washington	341,974	339,267	376,971	387,282	316,975
National League					
Brooklyn	505,139	526,660	570,707	559,097	598,666
Chicago	331,109	425,072	449,024	398,119	380,752
Cincinnati	312,010	293,841	325,318	382,074	441,355
Milwaukee/Boston	333,251	372,998	401,505	448,466	469,924
New York	565,644	573,624	518,208	588,429	530,540
Philadelphia	353,320	353,463	375,677	406,819	448,220
Pittsburgh	400,760	352,099	350,849	364,858	346,822
St. Louis	417,688	408,422	417,105	360,979	412,094

Source: U.S. Congress, *Organized Professional Team Sports*, 2048–52.

Notes: The consumer price index rose by 2.5 percent over the period.

Figures for Washington and Chicago Cubs include coaches' salaries; Brooklyn, manager's, coaches', trainers', and clubhouse salaries; Cincinnati, coaches' and manager's salaries and bonuses; and Pittsburgh, manager's and coaches' salaries. Figures for New York Giants represent "team salary expense."

Table 3.9
Nominal Total Expenses, 1946, 1950, and 1952–56
(in Thousands of Dollars)

Team	1946	1950	1952	1953	1954	1955	1956
American League							
Boston	1,526	2,287	2,484	2,359	2,212	2,417	2,524
Chicago	1,016	1,295	1,855	1,959	2,271	2,445	2,244
Cleveland	1,103	1,389	2,621	2,238	2,256	2,377	3,121
Detroit	1,400	2,269	2,282	2,113	2,315	2,379	2,413
New York	2,343	3,126	3,066	3,146	3,750	3,900	3,913
Philadelphia/Kansas City	849	1,316	1,548	1,390	1,291	2,974	2,495
St. Louis/Baltimore	637	689	1,274	1,388	1,697	2,105	1,913
Washington	825	1,026	1,112	1,104	1,257	1,251	1,245
National League							
Boston/St. Louis	1,287	1,582	1,174	2,339	2,327	2,292	2,448
Brooklyn	1,664	2,253	1,859	2,232	2,040	2,216	2,384
Chicago	1,181	1,681	1,606	1,700	1,589	1,713	1,758
Cincinnati	881	1,202	1,159	1,199	1,331	1,460	1,922
New York	2,159	2,148	2,600	2,363	2,475	2,656	2,413
Philadelphia	1,110	1,448	1,265	1,519	1,725	2,179	2,156
Pittsburgh	1,065	1,707	2,056	1,652	1,425	1,920	2,064
St. Louis	557	1,377	1,415	1,737	2,279	1,727	1,658
Total	19,604	26,794	29,378	30,441	32,240	36,012	36,673

Sources: U.S. Congress, *Organized Baseball: Hearings*, 1604–5, 1608–9; and U.S. Congress, *Organized Professional Team Sports*, 354–63, 2034–44.

Note: Figures for 1946 and 1950 represent operating expense plus player contracts.

Table 3.10
Nominal Other Expenses, 1946, 1950, and 1952–56
(in Thousands of Dollars)[a]

Team	1952	1953	1954	1955	1956	1956/1952[b]
American League						
Baltimore/St. Louis	930	946	1,109	1,435	1,217	1.31
Boston	1,920	1,920	1,752	1,906	1,932	1.01
Chicago	1,151	1,223	1,405	1,444	1,486	1.29
Cleveland	1,619	1,346	1,392	1,501	2,180	1.35
Detroit	1,164	1,199	1,335	1,423	1,384	1.19
Kansas City/Philadelphia	1,039	936	891	2,106	1,893	1.82
New York	2,107	2,244	3,031	3,101	2,968	1.41
Washington	658	699	741	806	852	1.30
National League						
Brooklyn	1,265	1,669	1,531	1,535	1,677	1.33
Chicago	1,069	1,004	983	1,074	1,085	1.01
Cincinnati	816	892	1,024	1,023	1,238	1.52
Milwaukee/Boston	899	1,430	1,583	1,684	1,696	1.89
New York	1,786	1,646	1,829	1,792	1,769	0.99
Philadelphia	932	1,047	1,108	1,665	1,627	1.75
Pittsburgh	1,435	1,270	1,190	1,330	1,473	1.03
St. Louis	943	1,071	1,227	1,141	1,131	1.20
Total	19,730	20,541	22,133	24,966	25,609	1.30

Source: U.S. Congress, *Organized Professional Team Sports*, 354–63, 2034–44.

Note: "Other expenses" not shown for 1946 and 1950.

[a] Other expenses: all expenses except players' salaries, players' bonuses, players' contracts purchased and sold, and officers' salaries.

[b] 1956/1952: ratio of 1956 to 1952 other expenses.

Table 3.11
Nominal Players' Salaries, Players' Bonuses, and
Players' Contracts Purchased (Sold), 1946, 1950, and 1952–56
(in Thousands of Dollars)[a]

Team	1952	1953	1954	1955	1956	1956/1952
American League						
Baltimore/St. Louis	267	372	571	642	683	2.56
Boston	515	389	409	461	542	1.05
Chicago	621	656	670	816	618	1.00
Cleveland	834	741	693	718	798	0.96
Detroit	1,046	845	892	870	932	0.89
Kansas City/Philadelphia	439	384	335	805	535	1.22
New York	689	644	592	656	802	1.16
Washington	387	336	430	356	319	0.82
National League						
Brooklyn	574	481	407	570	596	1.04
Chicago	450	657	567	594	617	1.37
Cincinnati	304	269	258	392	590	1.94
Milwaukee/Boston	244	855	690	541	658	2.70
New York	703	608	528	724	502	0.71
Philadelphia	319	458	578	501	479	1.50
Pittsburgh	484	245	98	453	479	0.99
St. Louis	418	608	992	531	454	1.09
Total	8,295	8,549	8,709	9,631	9,603	1.16

Source: U.S. Congress, *Organized Professional Team Sports*, 354–63, 2034–44.
Note: "Other expenses" not shown for 1946 and 1950. St. Louis's and Pittsburgh's numbers are the result of player purchases and sales.
[a] Players' contracts purchased (sold) is the net amount.

Table 4.1

Real Personal Consumption Expenditures on Recreation, Selected Years (in Millions of Dollars)

Year	Toys[a]	Radio/TV[b]	Movies[c]	Sports[d]	Private[e]	Total	% Private
1945	1,034	469	1,574	126	3,525	6,663	52.9
1946	1,633	1,231	1,692	200	4,968	8,539	58.2
1947	1,628	1,345	1,394	194	4,911	8,088	60.7
1950	1,836	2,194	1,116	180	6,161	9,044	68.1
1953	2,033	2,207	867	161	6,542	9,290	70.4
1960	2,983	2,779	627	191	8,481	12,066	70.4

Source: U.S. Department of Commerce, *Historical Statistics*, 1:401. Deflated by consumer price index (all items, 1800–1970), with 1946 = 100, in U.S. Department of Commerce, *Historical Statistics*, 1:210.

[a] Toys: nondurable toys and sport supplies; and wheel goods, durable toys, sport equipment, boats, and pleasure aircraft.

[b] Radio/TV: radio and television receivers, records, and musical instruments; and radio and television repair.

[c] Movies: motion picture theaters.

[d] Sports: spectator sports.

[e] Private: toys + radio/TV + books and maps + magazines, newspapers, and sheet music + flowers, seeds, and potted plants.

Table 4.2
Number of Night Games in the American League, 1947–64

Year	BOS	CHI	CLE	DET	LA	NY	PHI/KC	ST.L/BAL	WAS	WAS/MIN
1947	14	17	26	n/a[a]	0	14	24	32	0	39
1948	14	20	26	14	0	14	26	39	0	35
1949	14	22	28	14	0	14	30	32	0	39
1950	15	20	29	14	0	14	27	34	0	40
1951	13	19	30	14	0	14	31	32	0	42
1952	14	20	28	14	0	17	34	41	0	37
1953	15	22	30	14	0	16	35	41	0	45
1954	17	21	30	14	0	17	33	39	0	42
1955	17	19	29	14	0	16	38	32	0	35
1956	17	24	29	14	0	17	43	42	0	40
1957	19	21	30	21	0	18	39	43	0	34
1958	19	24	28	21	0	22	46	45	0	36
1959	25	26	35	21	0	22	53	46	0	44
1960	29	35	36	23	0	25	52	56	0	43
1961	28	37	41	29	57	29	46	62	43	31
1962	24	37	36	27	53	24	53	59	55	32
1963	34	41	41	27	59	29	56	57	57	38
1964	32	39	50	34	66	35	51	61	47	35
	360	464	582	329	235	357	717	793	202	687

Source: American League, *American League Red Book* (1948–65).

[a] n/a: not available but may be 0.

Table 4.3

Attendance at American League Night Games, 1947–64
(in Thousands)

Team	Night games	Night attendance	Total attendance	Night total (by percentage)	Night average
Boston	360	7,477	20,434	36.6	20,769
Chicago	464	10,315	20,219	51.0	22,230
Cleveland	582	10,963	22,238	49.3	18,837
Detroit	329	8,749	22,478	38.9	26,593
Los Angeles	235	2,469	3,329	74.1	10,507
New York	357	10,246	30,453	33.6	28,700
Philadelphia/Kansas City	717	7,745	13,440	57.6	10,802
St. Louis/Baltimore	793	8,407	12,669	66.4	10,601
Washington	202	1,516	2,463	61.4	7,485
Washington/Minnesota	687	7,399	14,062	52.6	10,770
League	4,726	75,282	161,785	46.5	15,929

Source: American League, *American League Red Book* (1948–1965).

Table 4.4
Characteristics of Major League Cities, 1950

Team	Black (%)[a]	Median income ($)[b]	SMSA median income ($)[c]	Black median income ($)[d]
Baltimore	23.7	2,817	2,399	1,345
Boston Braves/Red Sox	4.5	2,677	2,191	1,587
Brooklyn Dodgers	7.6	3,151	2,554	1,696
Chicago Cubs/White Sox	11.6	3,479	2,695	1,919
Cincinnati Reds	12.4	2,899	2,297	1,357
Cleveland Indians	10.9	3,451	2,611	1,743
Detroit Tigers	13.8	3,536	2,902	2,290
Kansas City	10.5	2,840	2,383	1,407
Los Angeles	5.2	3,118	2,297	1,627
Milwaukee	2.5	3,476	2,535	2,032
Minneapolis	1.0	3,202	2,254	1,652
New York Giants	19.6	2,347	2,554	1,696
New York Yankees	6.7	3,297	2,554	1,696
Philadelphia Phillies/Athletics	18.2	2,869	2,429	1,548
Pittsburgh Pirates	7.5	3,144	2,359	1,608
San Francisco	5.6	3,009	2,557	1,865
St. Louis Cardinals/Browns	17.9	2,718	2,403	1,402
St. Paul	1.6	3,265	2,254	1,652
Washington Senators	35.0	3,355	2,892	1,843

Source: U.S. Department of Commerce, *Census of Housing: 1950*, vol. 2.

[a] Black (%): based on county population, except for Baltimore, St. Louis, and Washington DC (city population).

[b] Median income ($): families and unrelated individuals, county data (census table 45), except for St. Louis and Washington DC (city data).

[c] SMSA median income ($): individuals, SMSA data (census table 87).

[d] Black median income ($): individuals, SMSA data (census table 87).

Table 5.1
Households with Television Versus
Baseball Attendance, 1946–64
(in Thousands)

	TVs[a]	AL[b]	NL[c]
1946	8	9,621	8,902
1947	14	9,486	10,388
1948	172	11,150	9,771
1949	940	10,731	9,485
1950	3,875	9,142	8,321
1951	10,320	8,883	7,244
1952	15,300	8,294	6,339
1953	20,400	6,964	7,420
1954	26,000	7,922	8,014
1955	30,700	8,943	7,674
1956	34,900	7,894	8,650
1957	38,900	8,196	8,820
1958	41,924	7,296	10,165
1959	43,950	9,149	9,995
1960	45,750	9,227	10,685
1961	47,200	10,163	8,732
1962	48,855	10,015	11,360
1963	50,300	9,095	11,382
1964	51,600	9,235	12,045

Sources: U.S. Department of Commerce, *Historical Statistics*, 796 (series 93-105); and Thorn, Palmer, and Gershman, *Total Baseball*, 76–77.

Note: The American League expanded to ten teams in 1961; the National League expanded to ten teams in 1962.

[a] TVs: households with television sets.

[b] AL: attendance in the American League.

[c] NL: attendance in the National League.

Table 5.2
Major League Television Broadcasts, Selected Years, 1946–64

American League

Team	1949 H[a]	1949 A[b]	1953 H	1953 A	1958 H	1958 A	1959 H	1959 A	1963 H	1963 A	1965 H	1965 A
Boston	77	0	66	0	35	20	27	24	33	22	30	26
Chicago	77	0	**c	0	53	0	53	0	43	13	52	13
Cleveland	U[d]	0	66	0	*e	0	13	42	24	28	19	27
Detroit	35	0	**c	0	11	28	12	29	10	31	11	29
Los Angeles	—	—	—	—	—	—	—	—	0	20	0	20
New York	77	0	77	0	77	63	77	46	81	46	76	47
Philadelphia/Kansas City	77	0	**c	0	0	0	0	10	1	40	5	35
St. Louis/Baltimore	U	0	**c	0	21	32	21	33	6	44	8	39
Washington	—	—	—	—	—	—	—	—	11	19	11	24
Washington/Minnesota	77	0	**c	0	24	24	8	5	4	46	4	46

continued

Table **5.2** Major League Television Broadcasts *continued*

National League

Team	1949		1953		1958		1959		1963		1965	
	H	A	H	A	H	A	H	A	H	A	H	A
Boston/Milwaukee	77	0	**[f]	0	0	0	0	0	5	20	*[g]	*[g]
Brooklyn/Los Angeles	77	0	77	0	0	0	0	11	0	9	0	9
Chicago	77	0	77	0	77	0	77	0	77	5	81	5
Cincinnati	77	0	**[f]	0	23	30	23	30	17	30	10	28
Houston	—	—	—	—	—	—	—	—	0	14	0	13
New York	—	—	—	—	0	0	0	0	76	52	81	41
New York/San Francisco	77	0	77	0	0	0	0	0	0	9	0	9
Philadelphia	77	0	**[f]	0	30	40	21	33	24	30	21	30
Pittsburgh	0	0	0	0	0	25	0	27	0	33	0	34
St. Louis	30	0	**[f]	0	0	30	0	41	0	21	0	24

Sources: Turkin, *Radio and TV Baseball*; "Log of Play-by-Play Broadcasts and Telecasts," *Sporting News*, April 20, 1949, 27; "Log of Play-by-Play Broadcasts and Telecasts," *Sporting News*, April 16, 1958, 31; "Log of Play-by-Play Broadcasts and Telecasts," *Sporting News*, April 8, 1959, 27;

"Log of Play-by-Play Broadcasts and Telecasts," *Sporting News*, April 13, 1963, 28; "Log of Play-by-Play Broadcasts and Telecasts," *Sporting News*, April 17, 1965, 32.

a H: home games

b A: away games

c Chicago (all but night games); Detroit (about half); Philadelphia (weekend afternoon, ten night, Opening Day, and first game of holiday doubleheaders); St. Louis (small number); and Washington (few dozen).

d U: unknown

e All weekend games and six night games.

f Boston (limited number may be telecast); Cincinnati (all but Sundays, holidays, and night); Philadelphia (weekend afternoon, ten night, Opening Day, and first game of holiday doubleheaders); St. Louis (small number).

g "Seventeen selected games."

Table 5.3

Number of Minor League Teams, Selected Years, 1946–60

Year	Classification						Total	Affiliated[a]	Percentage
	AAA/Open	AA	A	B	C	D			
1946	24	16	16	58	78	124	316	193	61.1
1947	24	16	22	68	109	150	389	227	58.4
1949	24	16	28	84	106	190	448	235	52.5
1950	24	16	32	76	120	180	448	214	47.8
1951	24	16	30	68	98	133	369	181	49.1
1952	24	16	24	62	80	102	308	175	56.8
1953	24	16	34	52	74	92	292	160	54.8
1955	24	22	22	51	58	66	243	161	66.3
1960	30	14	14	20	20	54	152	128	84.2

Sources: For number of teams, see Johnson and Wolff, *Encyclopedia*, 220–302. For Minor League teams affiliated with Major League teams, see Sumner, *Minor League Baseball Standings*, 611–14.

Note: Figures for 1952, 1953, and 1955 differ slightly from data supplied to Congress during the 1957 hearings (U.S. Congress, *Organized Professional Team Sports*, 371, 373, 376, 378, 380).

[a] Affiliated: affiliated with a Major League team.

Table 5.4
Minor League Profitability: Average Team
in Each Classification, Selected Years, 1946–53
(in Thousands of Dollars)

Class	1946	1947	1948	1949	1950	1952	1953	1955	1956
Open	n/aª	n/a	n/a	n/a	n/a	−54.5	−36.4	−6.3	−27.1
AAA	36.9	33.6	20.2	19.6	−47.8	−44.8	−56.4	−17.9	−30.3
AA	13.8	43.2	21.6	13.0	6.5	−7.4	−30.5	−6.9	−22.7
A	4.5	−4.0	−0.9	5.8	−18.9	−21.2	−25.7	−14.4	−28.6
B	2.4	2.4	−2.4	−1.4	−14.0	−22.3	−21.3	−15.0	−18.2
C	3.8	1.3	−0.3	−3.2	−8.7	−7.4	−7.8	−5.3	−4.7
D	2.6	−1.1	−2.3	−3.6	−6.6	−8.4	−11.4	−5.6	−6.0
Total	13.0	11.6	4.7	3.4	−14.4	−16.8	−21.4	−9.3	−15.6

Sources: U.S. Congress, *Organized Baseball: Hearings*, 1625; and U.S. Congress, *Organized Professional Team Sports*, 370. Nominal figures deflated by consumer price index (all items, 1946 = 100) taken from U.S. Department of Commerce, *Historical Statisics*, 210.

Note: No data available for 1951 and 1954. Not all teams reported, so the data is a sample.

ª n/a: not applicable (open class began after 1950).

Table 5.5
Population of Cities with Minor League Teams

Year	Teams in United States	With population[a]	Population	Average
1946	300	296	26,788,122	90,500
1949	435	427	31,804,794	74,484
1953	273	270	25,058,240	92,808
1960	136	136	14,758,493	108,518

Teams that folded

Years	Teams in United States	With population	Population	Average
1946–49	15	14	294,916	21,065
1949–53	197	191	7,740,834	40,528
1953–60	162	159	12,263,719	77,130

New teams

Years	Teams in United States	With population	Population	Average
1946–49	150	145	5,311,588	36,632
1949–53	35	34	994,280	29,244
1953–60	25	25	1,963,972	78,559

Sources: For teams, see Johnson and Wolff, *Encyclopedia*, 220–302; and U.S. Department of
   Commerce, *Census of Population: 1960*, 1:69–99.
Note: Population figures are from the 1950 census. Some towns were not listed in 1950.
[a] With population: teams whose town's population was listed in the 1950 census.

Table 6.1

Nominal and Real Reported Net Income before Taxes, American League, 1946, 1950, and 1952–56 (in Thousands of Dollars)[a]

Franchise	1946	1950	1952	1953	1954	1955	1956
Boston	723	70	–342	–421	3	243	122
	(990)	(78)	(–345)	(–421)	(3)	(243)	(120)
Chicago	493	206	162	462	450	441	331
	(675)	(228)	(163)	(462)	(448)	(441)	(326)
Cleveland	315	851	368	355	1,144	412	–167
	(432)	(945)	(371)	(355)	(1,138)	(412)	(–164)
Detroit	754	577	–26	44	115	530	190
	(1,032)	(641)	(–26)	(44)	(114)	(529)	(187)
New York	1,113	1,086	686	987	501	803	863
	(1,523)	(1,207)	(692)	(987)	(499)	(802)	(850)
Philadelphia/	141	–115	–51	–102	–218	37	2
Kansas City	(193)	(–128)	(–52)	(–102)	(–217)	(37)	(2)
St. Louis/	182	48	–330	–707	654	–87	74
Baltimore	(249)	(53)	(–332)	(–707)	(651)	(–87)	(73)
Washington	580	220	110	44	90	6	36
	(794)	(244)	(111)	(44)	(90)	(6)	(36)
League	4,300	2,942	577	661	2,739	2,386	1,452
	(5,888)	(3,269)	(582)	(661)	(2,726)	(2,383)	(1,429)

Sources: U.S. Congress, *Organized Baseball: Hearings*, 1064–65; and U.S. Congress, *Organized Professional Team Sports*, 2048–52. Consumer price index taken from U.S. Department of Commerce, *Historical Statistics*, 211. Using 1953 = 100: 1946, 73.0; 1950, 90.0; 1952, 99.3; 1953, 100.0; 1954, 100.5; 1955, 100.1; 1956, 101.6.

Note: Boston won pennant in 1946; Cleveland won in 1954; New York won all other years.

[a] Real income in parentheses.

Table 6.2
Distribution of Total Gate Revenue in the American League, 1946, 1950, and 1952–56 (in Millions of Dollars)

Actual (after gate sharing)

	1946	1950	1952	1953	1954	1955	1956
Top[a]	3.61	3.30	2.66	2.53	2.99	3.02	3.06
Bottom[b]	0.99	0.56	0.80	0.53	0.53	0.77	0.76
Standard deviation[c]	0.058	0.076	0.056	0.065	0.058	0.043	0.046
Top/bottom quartile[d]	3.04	4.87	2.88	3.83	3.77	2.42	2.24

Estimated (without gate sharing)

	1946	1950	1952	1953	1954	1955	1956
Top	4.02	3.48	2.71	2.59	2.94	2.96	2.99
Bottom	0.81	0.38	0.70	0.44	0.43	0.66	0.68
Standard deviation	0.068	0.085	0.060	0.069	0.059	0.045	0.046
Top/bottom quartile	3.86	7.47	3.23	4.62	4.18	2.55	2.26

Sources: U.S. Congress, *Organized Baseball: Hearings*, 1064–65; and U.S. Congress, *Organized Professional Team Sports*, 2048–52. Consumer price index (1953 = 100) taken from U.S. Department of Commerce, *Historical Statistics*, 211.

[a] Top: team with the largest real total gate revenue (after or without gate sharing). New York Yankees for all seasons.

[b] Bottom: team with the smallest real total gate revenue (after or without gate sharing). St. Louis in 1946, 1950, 1952–53; Philadelphia in 1954; Washington in 1955–56.

[c] Standard deviation: the standard deviation of the teams' individual shares of total league estimated home revenue (after or without gate sharing) with mean = 0.125.

[d] Top/bottom quartile: the two teams with the largest home revenue/the two teams with the smallest home revenues.

Table 6.3
Estimated Net Gate-Sharing Revenue, 1946, 1950, and 1952–56 (in Thousands of Dollars)[a]

Franchise	1946	1950	1952	1953	1954	1955	1956
Boston	105	36	3	–60	37	4	–10
	(144)	(40)	(3)	(–60)	(37)	(4)	(–10)
Chicago	–6	22	–109	–52	–54	30	16
	(–8)	(25)	(–110)	(–52)	(–54)	(30)	(16)
Cleveland	78	–111	–21	38	40	83	84
	(107)	(–124)	(–21)	(38)	(40)	(82)	(83)
Detroit	–105	–156	–55	–80	–97	–26	–63
	(–144)	(–173)	(–56)	(–80)	(–97)	(–26)	(–62)
New York	–285	–149	–45	–56	47	56	65
	(–390)	(–165)	(–45)	(–56)	(46)	(56)	(64)
Philadelphia/	72	178	72	98	100	–204	–110
Kansas City	(99)	(197)	(73)	(98)	(100)	(–204)	(–108)
St. Louis/	137	156	103	91	–129	–59	–65
Baltimore	(188)	(173)	(104)	(91)	(–129)	(–59)	(–64)
Washington	2	23	50	21	57	116	83
	(3)	(26)	(50)	(21)	(56)	(116)	(81)

Sources: U.S. Congress, *Organized Baseball: Hearings*, 1604–5; U.S. Congress, *Organized Professional Team Sports*, 2048–52; and Sporting News, *Sporting News Official Baseball Guide* (1951, 1953–57). Consumer price index (1953 = 100) taken from U.S. Department of Commerce, *Historical Statistics*, 211.

Notes: Figures may not add up to zero due to rounding.

Boston won pennant in 1946; Cleveland won in 1954; New York won all other years.

St. Louis transferred to Baltimore in 1954, and Philadelphia transferred to Kansas City in 1955.

[a]Estimated by multiplying (road attendance – home attendance) by .29. Real revenue in parentheses.

Table 6.4
Team Revenues Under Different Gate-Sharing Plans 1953 and 1956
(in Millions of Dollars)

1953

Franchise	Home revenue[a]	%	Actual revenue[b]	%	50-50% revenue[c]	%	50% tax revenue[d]	%
Boston	1.45	.138	1.39	.133	1.35	.129	1.38	.132
Cleveland	1.74	.166	1.78	.169	1.76	.168	1.52	.145
Chicago	1.67	.159	1.61	.154	1.61	.153	1.49	.142
Detroit	1.37	.130	1.29	.123	1.14	.109	1.34	.128
New York	2.59	.247	2.53	.242	2.27	.217	1.95	.186
Philadelphia	0.49	.047	0.59	.056	0.77	.074	0.90	.086
St. Louis	0.44	.042	0.53	.051	0.68	.065	0.88	.084
Washington	0.74	.070	0.76	.072	0.88	.084	1.02	.097
Standard deviation[e]		.070		.065		.052		.035
Top/bottom quartile[f]	4.64		3.83		2.78		1.95	

1956

Franchise	Home revenue	%	Actual revenue	%	50–50% revenue	%	50% tax revenue	%
Baltimore	1.54	.109	1.47	.104	1.38	0.98	1.65	.117
Boston	1.94	.137	1.93	.137	1.96	.139	1.85	.131
Chicago	1.60	.113	1.61	.114	1.76	.125	1.68	.119
Cleveland	1.58	.112	1.66	.118	1.82	.129	1.67	.118
Detroit	1.74	.123	1.68	.119	1.62	.115	1.75	.124
Kansas City	2.00	.142	1.89	.134	1.56	.111	1.88	.133
New York	3.04	.215	3.11	.220	3.00	.213	2.40	.170
Washington	0.69	.049	0.77	.055	0.99	.070	1.23	.087
Standard deviation	.046		.046		.041		.023	
Top/bottom quartile	2.26		2.24		2.10		1.49	

Sources: U.S. Congress, *Organized Baseball: Hearings*, 1604–5; U.S. Congress, *Organized Professional Team Sports*, 2048–52; and Sporting News, *Sporting News Official Baseball Guide* (1951, 1953–57). Consumer price index (1953 = 100) taken from U.S. Department of Commerce, *Historical Statistics*, 211.

Note: Dollar amounts in current dollars (1956 prices 1.6 percent greater than 1953 prices).

[a] Home revenue: estimated home revenue before any gate sharing.

[b] Actual revenue: home and away revenue under actual gate sharing.

[c] 50–50% revenue: estimated home and away revenue under a fifty-fifty split of the gate.

[d] 50% tax revenue: estimated revenue under system where 50 percent of home revenue is "taxed" and then divided evenly between all of the teams in the league.

[e] Standard deviation: the standard deviation of the team's individual share of total league estimated home revenue (without gate sharing) with mean = .125.

[f] Top/bottom quartile: the two teams with the largest home revenues/the two teams with the smallest home revenues.

Table 7.1
Distribution of Players with the Highest Career Total Baseball Rankings, by Team of Major League Debut

Original sixteen franchises

Franchise[a]	Number[b]	Total TBR[c]	Entire career[d]	All but last two years[e]	Total[f]	Total/ number[g]
BKN/LA (NL)	36	614.3	8	4	12	0.333
BOS (AL)	40	1,018.0	12	1	13	0.325
BOS/MIL (NL)	30	632.5	3	6	9	0.300
CHI (AL)	33	574.2	9	4	13	0.394
CHI (NL)	28	554.3	3	3	6	0.214
CIN (NL)	30	493.9	4	2	6	0.200
CLE (AL)	41	711.7	7	4	11	0.268
DET (AL)	32	708.2	9	9	18	0.563
NY (AL)	43	847.0	18	5	23	0.535
NY/SF (NL)	45	966.7	8	11	19	0.422
PHI (NL)	25	589.3	2	2	4	0.160
PHI/KC/OAK (AL)	34	843.9	1	2	3	0.088
PIT (NL)	32	765.2	5	2	7	0.219
STL (NL)	38	812.6	5	2	7	0.184
STL/BAL (AL)	31	532.4	5	1	6	0.194
WAS/MIN (AL)	18	406.0	5	3	8	0.444
Average	33.5	691.9	6.5	3.8	10.3	0.308

Expansion franchises

HOU (NL)	13	297.5	2	2	4	0.308
LA/CAL (AL)	12	169.8	3	0	3	0.250
NY (NL)	17	317.8	0	0	0	0.000
WAS/TEX (AL)	12	159.1	2	1	3	0.250
Others[h]	48	985.6	10	5	15	0.313
Total	638	13,000.0	121	69	190	0.298

Source: Thorn, Palmer, Gershman, and Pietrusza, *Total Baseball*.

[a] Franchise: (AL) represents American League and (NL) represents National League.

[b] Number: players who are in the sixth edition top five hundred batters and three hundred pitchers by

total baseball rankings (TBRs) and who began their careers in 1903 or later. Babe Ruth was initially included both as a batter and as a pitcher.

^c Total TBR: career total baseball ranking.

^d Entire career: players who spent entire career with the same Major League team.

^e All but last two years: players who spent all but their final season or final two seasons with the Major League team with which they made their debut.

^f Total: entire career + all but last two years.

^g Total/number: proportion of players who spent all or all but the last two years with their original Major League team.

^h Others: Buffalo (Federal League), Florida Marlins, Kansas City Royals, Seattle Pilots/Milwaukee Brewers, Montreal Expos, San Diego Padres, Seattle Mariners, and Toronto Blue Jays.

Table 7.2
Distribution of Top Players by Quartile

1919–1945	Number[a]	Percentage	Total TBR[b]	Percentage
Top quartile	62	43.1	1,293.1	42.0
Second quartile	38	26.4	996.6	32.3
Third quartile	26	18.1	502.0	16.3
Bottom quartile	18	12.5	290.4	9.4
Normalized standard deviation[c]		.518		.555
1946–1964				
Top quartile	47	37.9	1,046.7	41.0
Second quartile	32	25.8	658.2	25.8
Third quartile	25	20.2	480.6	18.8
Bottom quartile	20	16.1	364.7	14.3
Normalized standard deviation		.351		.442
1965–1995				
Top quartile	78	34.2	1,512.5	35.9
Second quartile	60	26.3	1,072.1	25.4
Third quartile	48	21.1	912.9	21.7
Bottom quartile	42	18.4	716.8	17.0
Normalized standard deviation		.269		.305

Source: Thorn, Palmer, Gershman, and Pietrusza, *Total Baseball*.

Note: The 1919–64 era consists only of the original sixteen franchises. The 1965–95 era consists only of the original sixteen franchises and four expansion teams of 1961 and 1962.

[a] Number: number of players introduced by teams within that quartile.

[b] Total TBR: combined career TBRs of players introduced by teams within that quartile.

[c] Normalized standard deviation: standard deviation of normalized number/mean and TBR/mean.

Table 8.1

Records of Expansion Teams' First Five Seasons, 1961–66

Win-loss						
Team	1961	1962	1963	1964	1965	1966
Houston	—	64-96	66-96	66-96	65-97	72-90
Los Angeles	70-91	86-76	70-91	82-80	75-87	—
New York	—	40-120	51-111	53-109	50-112	66-95
Washington	61-100	60-101	56-106	62-100	70-92	—
Attendance (in thousands)						
Team	1961	1962	1963	1964	1965	1966
Houston	—	924	720	726	2,151	1,872
Los Angeles	604	1,144	821	760	567	—
New York	—	923	1,080	1,733	1,768	1,933
Washington	597	730	536	600	560	—

Source: Sporting News, *Sporting News Complete Baseball Record Book—1998*, 211, 276, 305, 321–22.

Note: Los Angeles and Washington debuted in 1961, Houston and New York in 1962. Shea Stadium opened in 1964, Houston Astrodome in 1965, and RFK Stadium in 1962. The Los Angeles teams shared Dodger Stadium.

Table 10.1
Per Capita Attendance at Major League Baseball Games

City	1910	1920	1930	1940	1950	1960
Baltimore	—	—	—	—	—	1.26
Boston	1.09	0.76	1.16	1.24	2.86	1.62
Chicago	0.49	0.49	0.55	0.35	0.54	0.69
Cincinnati	1.05	1.42	0.86	1.87	1.07	1.32
Cleveland	0.52	1.15	0.59	1.03	1.89	1.09
Detroit	0.84	0.58	0.41	0.69	1.06	0.70
Kansas City	—	—	—	—	—	1.63
Los Angeles	—	—	—	—	—	0.91
Milwaukee	—	—	—	—	—	2.02
New York	0.24	0.54	0.45	0.36	0.54	0.21
Philadelphia	0.57	0.34	0.52	0.33	0.74	0.43
Pittsburgh	0.82	0.73	0.53	0.76	1.72	2.82
San Francisco	—	—	—	—	—	2.43
St. Louis	0.88	0.97	0.80	0.69	1.56	1.46
Washington	0.77	0.82	1.26	0.57	0.87	0.97
Major Leagues	0.51	0.61	0.56	0.53	0.87	0.81

Sources: Sporting News, *Sporting News Complete Baseball Record Book—1998*; and U.S. Department of Commerce, *Census of Population: 1960*, 1:1–66 (table 28).

Note: SMSA data did not significantly affect New York's ranking but did push Boston, Philadelphia, and Pittsburgh closer to New York's per capita figures.

Notes

Introduction

1. U.S. Senate, *Organized Professional Team Sports* (1959), 313. Baseball's relationship with Congress is chronicled in Lowe, *Kid on the Sandlot*.

2. U.S. Senate, *Organized Professional Team Sports* (1960), 30.

3. "Russians Say U.S. Stole 'Beizbol,' Made It a Game of Bloody Murder," *New York Times* (hereafter cited as NYT), September 16, 1952, 1, 6.

4. "U.S. 'Beizbol' Is a Bloody, Beastly Game, Say Russians," *Chicago Tribune* (hereafter cited as CT), September 16, 1952, sec. F, 2; Paul Kennedy, "Small Plants Curb Denied by Lovett," NYT, September 17, 1952, 16; Harry Schwartz, "Soviet's 'Beizbol' Bitter Jest Here," NYT, September 21, 1952, sec. 4, 6; and "New Soviet Envoy to U.S. Plans to Witness 'Beizbol,'" NYT, September 19, 1952, 19.

5. "Robinson Charges Yankee Race Bias," NYT, December 1, 1952, 31; Dan Daniel, "Jackie Off Base in TV Rap, Say Yankees," *Sporting News* (hereafter cited as SN), December 10, 1952, 3; and "Robinson Should Be Player—Not Crusader," SN, December 10, 1952, 12.

1. Those Damn Yankees

1. New York Yankees Baseball Club, General Ledger and Cash Books, 1913–44.

2. *Macmillan Baseball Encyclopedia*, 10th ed.

3. Halberstam, *Summer of '49*, 304–5.

4. "Philadelphia Soap Opera," *Sports Illustrated* (hereafter cited as SI), November 8, 1954, 15.

5. Gordon Cobbledick, "No High Cost," *Baseball Digest* (hereafter cited as BD), May 1951, 35–36.

6. Robert H. Boyle, "Yes: It's Livelier," SI, August 28, 1961, 17.

7. Tom Brody, "Is the Ball Deader?" SI, August 12, 1963, 13.

8. Tom Brody, "Is the Ball Deader?" SI, August 12, 1963, 13.

9. Til Ferdenzi, "Yank Road Show Box-Office Boffo in Cronin Circuit," SN, September 15, 1962, 6.

10. Dan Daniel, "Bomber Brass Set for Sizzling Battle over Champs' Pay," SN, November 5, 1958, 4.

11. Hugh Trader, "Paul Richards Says Yanks," BD, December–January 1960, 5, 7. See also Earl Flora, "Majors Still Doubt," BD, June 1960, 67–68.

12. Stanley Frank, "Boss of the Yankees," *Saturday Evening Post*, April 16, 1960, 112.

13. Dan Daniel, "Yank Fizzle Leaves '60 Outlook Fuzzy," SN, September 23, 1959, 1–2, 8.

14. Dan Daniel, "Yankee-Haters Cheer, Predict Continued Flop," SN, September 30, 1959, 15.

15. Stanley Frank, "Boss of the Yankees," *Saturday Evening Post*, April 16, 1960, 111.

16. Dan Daniel, "Yankee-Haters Cheer, Predict Continued Flop," SN, September 30, 1959, 15.

17. Edgar Munzel, "Chisox, Who Murder 'Em at Night, Hike Arc Slate," SN, January 11, 1961, 7.

18. Because there were some fifty new, presumably weaker, pitchers and players in the American League, the variance in performances should have increased. By looking at batters with three hundred or more at bats and pitchers with one hundred or more innings pitched, we can determine the standard deviations in batting average, slugging average, and earned run average for 1960 and 1961:

	Standard deviation batting average	Standard deviation slugging average	Standard deviation ERA
1960	.023	.072	0.63
1961	.028	.084	0.87

American League batters hit .256 in both seasons. The league slugging average rose from .388 to .395 between the two seasons, while the ERA rose from 3.88 to 4.03.

Although the original National League teams devised a draft plan that better protected their rosters, one would expect an increase in the standard deviation similar to that found in the American League expansion episode, as yet another fifty players were now Major League caliber. Only the standard deviation of pitchers' ERA, however, conformed to this theory.

	Standard deviation batting average	Standard deviation slugging average	Standard deviation ERA
1961	.029	.085	0.72
1962	.028	.075	0.74

National League hitters batted .262 in 1961 and .261 in 1962; their slugging averages fell from .406 to .393. Reflecting the lower batting and slugging averages, pitchers' ERA dropped from 4.04 to 3.95.

19. "Ruth's Record Can Be Broken Only in 154 Games, Frick Rules," NYT, July 18, 1961, 20.

20. "No * Will Mar Homer Records, Says Frick with !! for Critics," NYT, September 22, 1961, 38.

21. Richard J. H. Johnston, "Homer Record after 154 Games Won't Count with Fans on Street," *NYT*, September 21, 1961, 42.

22. C. C. Johnson Spink, "Writers Back Frick's Homer Decision," *SN*, August 9, 1961, 1, 4.

23. Hy Hurwitz, "Mick Wouldn't Want Mark if It Was Set in 155 Games," *SN*, August 9, 1961, 4.

24. James Reston, "The Asterisk That Shook the Baseball World," *NYT*, October 1, 1961, sec. 4, 8.

25. Veeck, *Veeck as in Wreck*, 241.

26. Jack Olsen, "Try to Catch the Babe," *SI*, September 11, 1961, 20.

27. John Drebinger, "Maris Fails to Hit No. 61, Gets Last Chance Today," *NYT*, October 1, 1961, sec. 5, 1.

28. John Drebinger, "Maris Hits 61st in Final Game," *NYT*, October 2, 1961, 1.

29. Joe King, "Majors Feeling First Symptoms of Jitters at Gate," *SN*, June 9, 1962, 4.

30. Tom Briere, "Fans Snap Up Twins' Tickets—600,000 Advance Sale Likely," *SN*, April 6, 1963, 2.

31. Bob Burnes, "Majors Pray for a Miracle to Block Rout," *SN*, August 3, 1963, 1, 6; and Joe King, "King Cites 3 Factors in A.L.'s Ticket Lab," *SN*, March 7, 1964, 1, 4, 14.

32. American League, *American League Red Book* (1963), 3.

33. C.C. Johnson Spink, "Ticket Smiles in N.L., Frowns in A.L.," *SN*, February 29, 1964, 1–2, 14.

2. Player Movement and Building the Yankees

1. Coase, "Problem of Social Cost."

2. Knowles, Sherony, and Haupert, "Demand for Major League Baseball"; Surdam, "Tale of Two Gate-Sharing Plans"; and Surdam, "Non-Price Determinants."

3. George M. Weiss and Robert Shaplen, "Best Decision," *SI*, March 13, 1961, 31–32.

4. U.S. Congress, *Organized Professional Team Sports*, 2048–52.

5. Hal Middlesworth, "Every Rookie Costs," *BD*, June 1959, 30.

6. "Baseball Businessman," *Forbes*, August 1, 1951, 12–17.

7. U.S. Congress, *Organized Professional Team Sports*, 374, 378.

8. Robert Shaplen, "The Yankees' Real Boss," *SI*, September 20, 1954, 35.

9. Sam Levy, "Braves' Farm Bill," *BD*, July 1948, 67–68.

10. Harold Rosenthal, "Dodgers Bargain Club—Cost Only $90,000," *SN*, September 28, 1955, 1.

11. Jack McDonald, "Giants' Gems Bargain Counter Pickups," *SN*, August 19, 1959, 1, 6; and "Giants Building N.L. Powerhouse," *SN*, April 18, 1962, 3–4, 8.

12. Bill Bryson, "One-Third of Big League Talent Discovered by Three Clubs!" *BD*, May 1958, 67–76.

13. *Macmillan Baseball Encyclopedia*, 9th ed., 2505–2730.

14. Bill Bryson, "One-Third of Big League Talent Discovered by Three Clubs!" *BD*, May 1958, 71.

15. Shirley Povich, "Red Sox Off Gold Standard," *BD*, March 1949, 27.

16. H. G. Salsinger, "News for Baltimore," *BD*, March 1954, 55–56.

17. Surdam, "Coase Theorem and Player Movement."

18. Frederick Lieb, "90 Former Cardinals Flood Big Time," *SN*, May 2, 1946, 3.

19. Les Biederman, "Deals with Pirates Brought Dodgers $700,000," *SN*, November 9, 1949, 5.

20. Alexander, *Our Game*, 229; and Macht, "Philadelphia Athletics–Kansas City Athletics–Oakland A's," 329.

21. U.S. Congress, *Organized Professional Team Sports*, 347–49, 1345–47, 2082–2105, 2132–34, 2149–52, 2491–92.

22. Arch Ward, "Senator Official Challenges A's Shift," *CT*, October 14, 1954, sec. F, 1.

23. "Johnson Acquires Athletics for $3,500,000 for Transfer to Kansas City," *NYT*, November 5, 1954, 25.

24. John Drebinger, "Athletics Transfer to Kansas City Wins Final Answer," *NYT*, November 9, 1954, 33.

25. "Connie Mack Charges League Is Forcing Athletics to Shift to Kansas City," *NYT*, October 30, 1954, pt. 1, 21.

26. "Connie Mack Charges League Is Forcing Athletics to Shift to Kansas City," *NYT*, October 30, 1954, pt. 1, 21.

27. Roscoe McGowen, "Fate of Athletics is Awaited Today," *NYT*, October 28, 1954, 49.

28. Arch Ward, "Senator Official Challenges A's Shift," *CT*, October 14, 1954, sec. F, 1; "League Votes A's Transfer to Kansas City," *NYT*, October 13, 1954, pt. 3, 1; and Roscoe McGowen, "Fate of Athletics is Awaited Today," *NYT*, October 28, 1954, 49.

29. Ernest Mehl, "Johnson Testified to Spike Reports of Yankee 'Tieup,'" *SN*, August 7, 1957, 11.

30. "American League Scouting Reports," *BD*, March 1957, 7–26; Arthur Daley, "The Maris the Yankees Got," *BD*, March 1960, 41–42; Ernest Mehl, "Cooler Pat on Kaycee's Attack by Mauler Maris," *SN*, June 3, 1959, 10; Ernest Mehl, "A's Lashed, Lauded for Swapping Maris," *SN*, December 23, 1959, 5–7; and Dan Daniel, "Dan's Verdict—A's ahead in N.Y. Deals," *SN*, December 23, 1959, 5. According to Donald Dewey and Nicholas Acocella, Maris would have been a Yankee sooner but for the American League office. When Kansas City obtained him from Cleveland, some other American League owners worried that the deal

was a setup for the Yankees to obtain the heralded youngster. The league office warned the Athletics and Yankees not to make such a transaction, so the two teams waited a year (*Ball Clubs*, 276). When the Athletics received Maris from Cleveland in 1958, Dan Daniel reported, "George W. Weiss and Casey Stengel also sought an incumbent for the hoo-dooed berth in left field. Maybe they had their hooks out for Maris because, when [Frank] Lane sent Roger to the Athletics, he exacted a promise from Parke Carroll that the flychaser would not be relayed to New York" ("Kaycee Sets Fastest Pace in Trade-Deadline Dashes," *SN*, June 25, 1958, 6). Throughout Maris's season and a half in Kansas City trade rumors swirled around him. The Kansas City beat writer Ernest Mehl, who wrote for *SN*, downplayed such talk and claimed that the Athletics would not trade Maris. The Boston Red Sox accused the Athletics of planning to send Ralph Terry and Maris to the Yankees, with a Red Sox official claiming that Terry might be returning to the Yankees soon because "he is starting to develop into a winning pitcher" (Ernest Mehl, "A's Back Dickerson Deal as 'Sound,'" *SN*, September 3, 1958, 4; "A's Glance Back at Their Trades, Feel They Just about Broke Even," *SN*, October 22, 1958, 19; and "Yanks Level Gaze on A's Jewel, Head Bidders for Basher Maris," *SN*, October 29, 1958, 19). I could not find any evidence in the *Sporting News*, however, that American League officials warned the Yankees and Athletics about exchanging Maris.

31. George M. Weiss and Robert Shaplen, "The Man of Silence Speaks," *SI*, March 6, 1961, 49.

32. "Kansas City Obtains Martin From Yanks," *NYT*, June 16, 1957, sec. 5, 1; and "Braves Obtain Schoendienst; Thomson, O'Connell and Crone Go to Giants; Martin to A's," *CT*, June 16, 1957, pt. 2, 1.

33. John Drebinger, "Yanks Get Lopez, Terry from A's," *NYT*, May 27, 1959, 40. For discussion of the trade, see Ernest Mehl, "Yanks Cut Down to Size, Says A's Carroll," *SN*, June 3, 1959, 2, 9; and Edgar Munzel, "'It's Disgusting,' Fumes Veeck at Yanks-A's Deal," *SN*, June 3, 1959, 2, 9. Two baseball historians allege that Terry was loaned to Kansas City for seasoning and that Clete Boyer experienced a somewhat similar situation, but they do not cite their sources. Supposedly, the Yankees did not want an inexperienced Terry clogging up their roster until he was ready (Dewey and Acocella, *Ball Clubs*, 275). Athletics fans, however, were not necessarily opposed to the trade (Ernest Mehl, "Kaycee Sees Yankee Deal as Big Mound Boost for A's," *SN*, June 10, 1959, 32; and Ernest Mehl, "Spirited Athletics Ripping Label of 'Yank Farm Club,'" *SN*, June 24, 1959, 17).

34. Ernest Mehl and Dan Daniel offer different perspectives in *SN*: Mehl, "Ditmar Seen as Key Player in Yank-A's Deal: 'Needed Men Who Could Do the Job Now'—Johnson," *SN*, February 27, 1957, 5–6; Daniel, "Casey Tabs Ditmar as Great Prospect," *SN*, March 6, 1957, 9.

35. John P. Carmichael, "Why Yankees Took a Shantz," *BD*, May 1957, 49; and Bob Oates, "Why Yanks' Second-Pitching Wins," *BD*, April 1959, 63–64.

36. Clifford Kachline, "Major Scouts Tab Siebern as Top Prospect: Yank Flyhawk Draws Most Votes in Survey," *SN*, February 26, 1958, 7.

37. Charles Dexter, "Are the Yankees Crumbling?" *BD*, February 1958, 11–16; Charles Dexter, "The Yankees' Kustom-Kut Kid," *BD*, October–November 1958, 75–80; and John Drebinger, "Yanks Trade Bauer, Larsen and Get Maris in 7-Player Deal with A's," *NYT*, December 12, 1959, 27.

38. "A's Pay $50,000 for 3 Yankees," *CT*, March 31, 1955, pt. 6, 1.

39. Edward Prell, "Yanks Acquire Athletics' Ditmar in 13 Man Deal," *NYT*, February 20, 1957, pt. 3, 1; William Briordy, "Yankees Obtain Ditmar and Shantz in 13-Player Deal," *NYT*, February 20, 1957, 39; Dan Daniel, "Casey Tabs Ditmar," *SN*, March 6, 1957, 9; and Ernest Mehl, "Kaycee Puzzled by Big Buildup Given Ditmar after Yank Deal," *SN*, March 6, 1957, 9.

40. John Drebinger, "Yanks Get Lopez," *NYT*, May 27, 1959, 40. See also H. G. Salsinger, "Yanks to be Even Stronger!" *BD*, January 1957, 53–54.

41. John Drebinger, "Yanks Get Lopez," *NYT*, May 27, 1959, 40; and John Drebinger, "Yanks Trade Bauer," *NYT*, December 12, 1959, 27.

42. "Yankees Trade Four for A's' Terry, Lopez," *CT*, May 27, 1959, pt. 6, 1.

43. Ed Prell, "Yanks Acquire Athletics' Ditmar," *NYT*, February 20, 1957, pt. 3, 1. Ditmar was considered a good prospect. The *New York Times* reported, "Until this spring both Daley and Ditmar ranked among the top-flight pitchers in the American League. Ditmar, though he won only fifteen games, was the Yanks' top winning pitcher last season and played a strong role in the stretch drive. . . . Daley . . . also has failed to come up to expectations this spring" ("Yanks Get Daley of A's for Ditmar and Johnson," *NYT*, June 15, 1961, 54).

44. Ed Prell, "Yanks Acquire Athletics' Ditmar," *NYT*, February 20, 1957, pt. 3, 1.

45. Ernest Mehl, "Ditmar Seen as Key Player," *SN*, February 27, 1957, 5–6; and Dan Daniel, "Yankee Swaps Bonanzas to Other Clubs, Too: Senators and Orioles Top Gainers from N.Y. Deals," *SN*, March 13, 1957, 5. See also Carl Lundquist, "Borowy, Sain, Hopp and Mize All Helped on New Clubs," *SN*, August 15, 1956, 7–8.

46. Ernest Mehl, "A's Corralled 14 Players—Result of Yankee Deals," *SN*, January 11, 1961, 1, 4; Ernest Mehl, "A's Back Dickerson Deal," *SN*, September 3, 1958, 1, 4; and Dan Daniel, "Dan's Verdict—A's Ahead," *SN*, December 23, 1959, 7.

47. Ernest Mehl, "Spirited Athletics Ripping Label," *SN*, June 24, 1959, 17.

48. Dan Daniel, "Deal with Kaycee Viewed as Scant Help for Yankees," *SN*, June 3, 1959, 10; and Ernest Mehl, "Kaycee Sees Yankee Deal," *SN*, June 10, 1959, 10. See also Ernest Mehl, "Yankees Cut Down," *SN*, June 3, 1959, 2.

49. Dan Daniel, "Dan's Verdict—A's Ahead," *SN*, December 23, 1959, 7.

50. Roy Terrell, "Yankee Secrets?" *SI*, July 22, 1957, 8–13.

51. Ernest Mehl, "A's Boss Raps Critics of His Deal," *SN*, March 20, 1957, 1–2; Ernest Mehl, "A's Rip Rep That They Will 'Trade Only with Yanks,'" *SN*, December

4, 1957, 19; Jack Walsh, "Three's Crowd in N.Y., Says Stoneham," sn, July 24, 1957, 14; Dan Daniel, "Dan's Verdict—A's Ahead," sn, December 23, 1959, 5; "Yanks Trade Four," ct, May 27, 1959, pt. 6, 1; "Yankees, A's Make 15th Deal! Swap 7," ct, December 12, 1959, pt. 2, 3; Ed Prell, "Yanks Acquire Athletics' Ditmar," nyt, February 20, 1957, pt. 3, 1, 3; Edgar Munzel, "'It's Disgusting,' Fumes Veeck at Yanks-A's Deal," sn, June 3, 1959, 9; and John F. Steadman, "Kansas City Finds Daley Deal," bd, October–November 1959, 47–49.

52. Joseph Sheehan, "Yanks Get Byrd and Eddie Robinson in 13-Man Deal," nyt, December 17, 1953, 57; and "American League Meets Here Tomorrow on Sale of Athletics," nyt, October 27, 1954, 36.

53. Edgar Williams, "The Lowdown on Baltimore," bd, September 1954, 62; and "American League Meets Here Tomorrow on Sale of Athletics," nyt, October 27, 1954, 36.

54. Dan Daniel, "Weiss Will Take Rubber off Bankroll for Players," sn, July 19, 1961, 1–2.

55. J. Roy Stockton, "Them Phillies," *Saturday Evening Post*, October 4, 1941, 27–50; and Bill Dooly, "Nugent Rang Up $500,000 in Ten-Year Deals for Phils," sn, February 18, 1943, 1, 7.

56. Harold Burr, "Cape Cod Cards Keep on Buying Birds," sn, April 30, 1947, 5.

57. Ed McAuley, "Veeck Pulls Off Brownie Trade in Self-Defense," sn, November 26, 1947, 14.

58. "Yanks Request Chandler to Probe Brown Deals," sn, November 26, 1947, 10.

59. Dan Daniel, "Weiss Thunders Answer to Critics of Yankee Swaps," sn, January 13, 1960, 23.

60. George M. Weiss and Robert Shaplen, "The Man of Silence Speaks," si, March 6, 1961, 48.

61. Jerome Holtzman, "Finley Rips Kaycee's 'Farm Club' Label," sn, December 28, 1960, 7; and Ernest Mehl, "'A's Will Develop Stars and Keep Them'—Finley," sn, December 28, 1960, 7, 14.

62. Ernest Mehl, "Finley's Face Red; Kaycee, Yanks Swap!" sn, June 21, 1961, 20.

63. Ernest Mehl, "Lane Leaves Door Open for Yank Deal," sn, March 15, 1961, 5.

64. "Yanks Acquire Daley in Deal with A's," ct, June 15, 1961, pt. 6, 1.

3. The Game on the Ledger

1. Chicago Baseball Club, *Probate Court Proceedings*.

2. Sporting News, *Sporting News Dope Book* (1955, 1964).

3. John P. Carmichael, "Minors Decry tv," bd, February 1949, 50; and Frank Graham, "Death of a Ball Club," bd, February 1950, 26.

4. Red Smith, "MacPhail's Turf," *BD*, May 1946, 25–26.

5. "Baseball Businessman," *Forbes*, August 1, 1951, 12–17.

6. Barry Kremenko, "Yankees Build Plush Boxes for Upper Crust," *SN*, April 6, 1960, 17.

7. Bob Addie, "Advance Sales Key to Survival—Ehlers," *SN*, May 4, 1955, 2.

8. "36 Pages of Scouting Reports," *SI*, April 10, 1961, 92.

9. Clifford Kachline, "Yanks Flags Linked to Huge Income Bulge over Rivals," *SN*, November 3, 1962, 10.

10. Veeck, *Veeck as in Wreck*, 121.

11. Craig, *Organized Baseball*, 201–2; Woodard, *So You Want to Run*, 24–25; and Washington Senators scorecard, 1961.

12. Bill Fay, "Sports in the Spring," *Collier's*, March 6, 1948, 14.

13. Veeck, *Veeck as in Wreck*, 121.

14. "Big League Baseball," *Fortune*, August 1937, 115.

15. Veeck, *Veeck as in Wreck*, 119.

16. James Murray, "Dodgers after Dark," *SI*, June 15, 1959, 67–68.

17. Robert Coughlan, "Baseball: Nine Men," *SI*, February 27, 1956, 23.

18. Dan Daniel, "Hizzoner, the Hot Dog, Now 70-Year-Old Sizzler," *SN*, May 25, 1962, 40; and Stevens's quote found in Dan Daniel, "Yankee Stadium Club Reflects Game's Posh Era," *SN*, May 23, 1962, 13, 16.

19. Bob Joyce, "Big Time's 1963 TV Take Pegged at $13.1 Million," *SN*, March 16, 1963, 19; Oscar Kahan, "Sponsors to Shell Out Record $83 Million for Major Air Rights," *SN*, March 14, 1962, 24; Oscar Kahan, "Majors Wrapping 'Attractive Package' to Boost Air Income," *SN*, March 14, 1964, 5; and Harold Rosenthal, "Mets Net $1 Million Per Year in TV Pact," *SN*, November 22, 1961, 13.

20. Oscar Kahan, "Free Agent Draft Cards' Solution to Wild Bonuses," *SN*, November 23, 1960, 33; Clifford Kachline, "Majors Study Super Scouting Service," *SN*, November 24, 1962, 2; and Sporting News, *Sporting News Dope Book* (1955, 1964).

21. Robert Coughlan, "Baseball: Nine Men," *SI*, February 27, 1956, 57.

22. Carter, Gartner, Haines, Olmstead, Sutch, and Wright, *Historical Statistics*, 2–281.

23. Levin, Mitchell, Volcker, and Will, *Report*, 61, 65, 69, 73, 77.

24. Shirley Povich, "Red Sox off Gold Standard," *BD*, March 1949, 28.

25. Gordon Cobbledick, "'Free' Players Would Wreck Game," *BD*, July 1946, 15. See also Hy Hurwitz, "Players Warned to Relax Demands or Break Owners," *SN*, March 16, 1955, 8.

26. A simple regression showing payroll as a function of the current season's win-loss record had an $R^2 = 0.411$. There were forty observations of eight teams for each of the five seasons. The win-loss variable was significant at the 0.01 percent level.

Payroll =
160,043.7 + 599,742 (Current Win-Loss)
(2.685)   (5.147)
$R^2 = 0.411$ Adjusted $R^2 = 0.395$. (1)

An equation using a dummy variable for the New York Yankees 1 if New York, 0 otherwise, was an improvement:

Payroll =
244,527.3 + 134,428.7 (NY Dummy)
(4.26)   (3.54)
+ 397,208.2 (Current Win-Loss)
(3.39)
$R^2 = 0.560$ Adjusted $R^2 = 0.536$. (2)

All variables were significant at the 1 percent level.

Some observers cited the Washington Senators as a team unable to pay market salaries. To test this claim, I ran a regression with a dummy variable for Washington as well as the one for the Yankees:

Payroll =
280,929 – 77,364 (Washington Dummy) +
(5.09)   (–2.41)
+ 131,756 (NY Dummy) + 344,424 (Current Win-Loss)
(3.69)   (3.07)
$R^2 = 0.62$ Adjusted $R^2 = 0.589$. (3)

All variables were significant at the 5 percent level.

I also ran a set of regressions using the previous season's win-loss record to test whether Cleveland's pennant-winning season of 1954 affected its 1955 payroll.

Payroll =
210,354.6 + 122,499.9 (NY Dummy)
(3.91)   (3.44)
+ 468,474.6 (Previous Win-Loss)
(4.28)
$R^2 = 0.614$ Adjusted $R^2 = 0.593$. (4)

All variables were significant at the 1 percent level.

I ran a regression with a dummy variable for Washington as well as the one for the Yankees:

Payroll =
243,533 – 75,074 (Washington Dummy)
(4.69)   (–2.52)
+ 119,260 (NY Dummy) + 421,711 (Previous Win-Loss)
(3.58)   (4.05)
$R^2 = 0.67$ Adjusted $R^2 = 0.644$. (5)

All variables were significant at the 1 percent level, except for the Washington dummy variable, which was significant at the 1.63 percent level.

An equation using the previous season's win-loss record and second previous season's win-loss as well the dummy variable for New York had a higher R^2 than equation 4:

Payroll =
171,098 + 259,392 (Previous Win-Loss)
(3.11)   (1.77)
+ 291,050 (Second Previous Win-Loss) + 108,524 (NY Dummy)
(2.04)   (3.11)
$R^2 = 0.65$ Adjusted $R^2 = 0.625$. (6)

All variables were significant at the 5 percent level, except for the previous season's win-loss variable, which was significant at the 10 percent level.

27. U.S. Department of Commerce, *Statistical Abstract*, 357, 359.

28. Robert Shaplen, "Yankees' Real Boss," *SI*, September 20, 1954, 34.

29. Arthur Daley, "Strange Vic Raschi Deal," *BD*, May 1954, 88–91.

30. Dan Daniel, "Weiss Sounds Warning on Pay Spiral," *SN*, March 5, 1958, 4.

31. Dan Daniel, "Looks Like Restful Winter for Weiss—Few Yankees Hikes," *SN*, October 8, 1958, 9.

32. Dan Daniel, "Yankee Payroll to Hit Record 500 Gs," *SN*, January 8, 1958, 1; and Dan Daniel, "Player Payrolls Rocket to Outer Space," *SN*, February 12, 1958, 1–2. The salary information shown in the *Sporting News* typically was lower than information reported to the various congressional committees. Indeed, information provided to the congressional committees sometimes appeared contradictory. The payroll figures for 1952–56 used here represent the total amount for the season; owners also gave the congressional committee salaries as of August 31 of each season, but these figures were almost always lower than the season payroll figures. Apparently, with injuries and players shuttling back and forth, the season payroll represented salaries for more than just the players on the roster as of August 31. Author John Rossi's assertion that teams whose television revenues were larger than their player payrolls guaranteed them a profit is patently false (*Whole New Game*, 58). While several teams did receive more television revenue than the cost of their player payroll, such payrolls constituted a minority of overall expenses.

33. Dan Daniel, "Players' Pay Soars to All-Time High: Majors' Tab for '60 Close to $10 Million," *SN*, January 6, 1960, 9; and Dan Daniel, "Bomber's Payroll Cutback Starts with Comet, Bullet," *SN*, January 27, 1960, 9.

34. Dan Daniel, "Weiss Braced for Yankees' Contract Squawks," *SN*, January 21, 1959, 5, 8; Dan Daniel, "Mantle Tops List of Yanks 'Invited' to Take Pay Cuts," *SN*, January 28, 1959, 8; and Dan Daniel, "Salary War On—Bombers Lead Attack," *SN*, February 18, 1959, 1–2.

35. Dan Daniel, "Salaries Soar to Absolute Limit, Owners Claim," *SN*, March 9, 1960, 1, 4.

36. Dan Daniel, "Spiraling Major Payrolls Near $10 Million," *SN*, March 9, 1955, 2.

37. Lloyd McGowan, "2-Million Tag on Dodgers' Crop," *SN*, March 9, 1955, 1, 6.

38. Dan Daniel, "Yank Gold Rush Sets Major High," *SN*, January 9, 1957, 1; Dan Daniel, "Yankees, Dodgers Battle Pay-Balkers," *SN*, January 23, 1957, 1–2; Dan Daniel, "Player Payrolls Soaring to Record Peaks," *SN*, January 14, 1959, 1–2; and Dan Daniel, "Soaring Salaries Heading for New Highs," *SN*, January 18, 1961, 1–2.

39. Robert Coughlan, "Baseball's Happy Serfs," *SI*, March 5, 1956, 31.

40. Ray Gillespie, "DeWitt Finds Major Payrolls Still Rocketing," *SN*, February 14, 1962, 1, 6.

41. Bob Hunter, "Fast-Stepping Kids Figure to Skyrocket Future L.A. Budget," *SN*, February 1, 1961, 18; and Dan Daniel, "Yankee Front Office Alerted for Sizzling Hassles on Salaries," *SN*, November 8, 1961, 1.

42. Robert Coughlan, "Baseball's Happy Serfs," *SI*, March 5, 1956, 31; and U.S. Congress, *Organized Baseball: Hearings*, 1610. Note that the figures presented to Congress included players, managers, and coaches, while those for 1952–56 were primarily players only.

43. U.S. Congress, *Organized Professional Team Sports*, 2048–52.

44. Levin, Mitchell, Volcker, and Will, *Report*, 61, 65, 69, 73, and 77.

45. Dan Daniel, "Rival Clubs Moan over New Yank Policy of No Salary Cuts," *SN*, January 25, 1961, 14.

46. Dan Daniel, "Yankee Payroll Will Top 800 Grand," *SN*, February 7, 1962, 1, 4; Dan Daniel, "Yankee Front Office Alerted," *SN*, November 8, 1961, 9; Til Ferdenzi, "Hamey Tangles with Yank Heavyweights in Pay Spats," *SN*, January 31, 1962, 9; and Til Ferdenzi, "Maris' 32-Gee Hike Sets Yankee Record," *SN*, March 7, 1962, 3–4.

47. Til Ferdenzi, "Maris Shakes 'Nightmare,' Takes Slash in Yankee Pay," *SN*, January 4, 1964, 6; and Edgar Munzel, "'64 Payrolls Climb: Dodgers Set Tempo," *SN*, January 11, 1964, 1–2, 4.

48. Hy Hurwitz, "Players Warned to Relax Demands or Break Owners," *SN*, March 16, 1955, 8.

49. Edgar Munzel, "'64 Payrolls Climb: Dodgers Set Tempo," 1–2, 4.

50. Dan Daniel, "Salaries to Top Ted's $125,000 Peak?" *SN*, February 4, 1959, 3.

51. Burton Crane, "Athletes Plight Spurs Tax Aid Base," *NYT*, May 8, 1955, 1, 4; and Dan Daniel, "American Bar Association to Aid Players," *SN*, June 8, 1955, 1–2.

52. Regis McAuley, "Feller Predicts Player Tax Help 'within 5 Years,'" *SN*, March 5, 1958, 4.

53. Hollander, *Complete Handbook of Baseball*, 178.

54. Carter, Gartner, Haines, Olmstead, Sutch, and Wright, *Historical Statistics*, 2–281.

55. Hal Lebovitz, "Player-Depreciation Rule Gave Indians 'Book Loss,'" *SN*, August 14, 1957, 17; and Veeck, *Hustler's Handbook*, 33.

56. U.S. Congress, *Organized Professional Team Sports*, 1415.

57. Adding to the confusion, the *Sporting News* reported $3.4 million spent on bonuses during the postwar period (Bob Burnes, "Five Million Bonus Tab Shocks Majors," *SN*, July 23, 1958, 1, 4). The *Sporting News* report had National League teams spending $2.22 million in bonuses, compared with the $1.99 reported in Bryson's story. His figure of $2.33 million spent by the American League roughly doubled the figure reported in *SN*, although the latter report did not include figures for Kansas City and New York. In any event the owners were concerned enough to introduce repeatedly new legislation to curb bonus spending.

58. Bill Bryson, "Only One of Ten Pays Off," *BD*, April 1958, 5–9.

59. For dissenting views, see Dan Daniel, "Players Jittery over Plane Travel, *SN*, May 10, 1961, 1, 4; and Les Biederman, "Players Toss Travel Gripes at Owners," *SN*, December 1, 1962, 1–2, 8.

60. Carl Lundquist, "Fare Hike to Speed Majors Shift to Air," *SN*, August 29, 1956, 1–2.

61. Bob Burnes, "Majors Face Air-Transport Squeeze," *SN*, July 26, 1961, 1–2; Bob Burnes, "Tight Schedules Put Majors Up In Air," *SN*, June 9, 1962, 1–2, 4; and Bob Burnes, "Frick Sees 26-Week Season along with 12-Club Loops," *SN*, April 25, 1964, 26.

62. Joe King, "Wrigley Opens Coast Door to Majors' Entry," *SN*, February 27, 1957, 1–2.

63. Harry Simmons, "Dodger-Giant Shift Boosts NL Travel 90 Pct.," *SN*, September 4, 1957, 1, 6.

64. Jack McDonald, "Harridge Sees No Transfers in AL," *SN*, October 30, 1957, 2.

65. Ray Gillespie, "$85 Million Policies Cover Two Majors," *SN*, March 9, 1960, 1–2, 8.

66. Using 1946, 1950, and 1952–56 data:

Real Total Expense =
886,502 + 1,341,241 (New York Yankees Dummy) +
(3.69)   (6.83)
2,002,155 (Win-Loss Percentage)
(4.18)
$N = 112$ $R^2 = 0.461$ Adjusted $R^2 = 0.452$
Both variables were significant at the 0.001 level.

Using the natural log of real total expenses did not improve the equation. I also employed dummy variables for New York City teams (the Brooklyn Dodgers, New York Giants, and New York Yankees) and relocated teams (the Milwaukee Braves, Baltimore Orioles, and Kansas City Athletics). Both variables were significant, and the equation had similar goodness-of-fit measurements:

Real Total Expense =
834,530 + 1,882,334 (Win-Loss Percentage)
(3.39)   (3.76)
+ 807,447 (New York City Dummy) + 551,502 (Relocation Dummy)
(6.30)   (3.29)
$N = 112$ $R^2 = 0.462$ Adjusted $R^2 = 0.447$

Similar equations hold for using real other expenses as the dependent variable. Equations using real player expenses as the dependent variable, however, had much lower goodness-of-fit.

A set of equations using win-loss record as the dependent variable displayed very low goodness-of-fit measures. The New York Yankees dummy variable and New York City dummy variable had much less explanatory value.

67. Clifford Kachline, "Majors Study Super Scouting," SN, November 24, 1962, 1–2.

68. "Baseball Candor Via Air Vent," SI, September 22, 1958, 21.

69. U.S. Congress, *Organized Baseball: Hearings*, 1599–1600; U.S. Congress, *Organized Professional Team Sports*, 353–63; Gordon Cobbledick, "The Accent's Still on the 'Con,'" BD, August 1954, 65–66; and Garry Hern, "A Warning to AL Owners," BD, November–December 1954, 23–24.

70. Lester Smith, "Red Sox Splashed in Bath of Red Ink; Lost 142 Gs in '58," SN, February 10, 1960, 15.

71. Oscar Kahan, "Anheuser-Busch Reports 8-Year Deficit of $124,064 on Cardinals," SN, March 22, 1961, 19–20.

72. Clifford Kachline, "Dodgers Netted Cool $2 Million in '62," SN, September 14, 1963, 1, 4.

73. Dave Brady, "Griffith Tabs Twins' 428-G Profit Best in Club History," SN, February 21, 1962, 33; and Shirley Povich, "Senators in Red by $250,000 but Increase Budget for 1962," SN, January 10, 1962, 24.

74. Les Biederman, "Bucs Drew over Million, but Took Bath in Red Ink," SN, December 29, 1962, 12.

75. Doug Brown, "Mailman's Pouch Bulging with Fat Pacts for Orioles," SN, January 11, 1961, 7; Doug Brown, "Oriole Stockholders in Jolly Mood: 1964 Profit of $301,092," December 26, 1964, 10; John F. Steadman, "Orioles Beating Drums in Pitch for Record Season-Ticket Sales," SN, November 15, 1961, 18; and "Orioles Show Profit of $99,262 Despite Gate Drop to 774,343," SN, January 25, 1964, 18.

76. Lester Smith, "Giants' 1960 Profit Three Times Greater than in '59," SN,

December 13, 1961, 9; "Shareholders Hear of Giant Pay-TV Plans," SN, November 9, 1963, 11; Curly Grieve, "Wealthy Giants Gathering Golden Nest Eggs," SN, May 2, 1964, 2; Lester Smith, "Watchdog Gilbert Eyes Giant Profit Ledger," SN, August 1, 1964, 7–8; and Lester Smith, "Disappointing Year for Giants—Lower Profit, Defeat of Pay-TV," SN, November 21, 1964, 15.

77. Nick Thimmesch, "Tiger Is Underfed," SI, May 18, 1959, 17–18.

78. Dan Daniel, "'Players Salaries to Stay High'—Stoneham," SN, November 2, 1955, 1.

79. "Larry MacPhail Buys the Yankees," SN, February 1, 1945, 10.

80. Frederick Lieb, "Yank Empire Rated Games' Top Value," SN, February 1, 1945, 3. Note that these are approximations, using year-to-year consumer price index figures to deflate the sales prices.

81. Quirk and Fort, *Pay Dirt*, 49–57.

82. Chicago White Sox scorecards, 1959–61.

83. Veeck, *Hustler's Handbook*, 330.

84. Dave Brady, "IRS Puts Owners' Fears to Rest; No Changes in Depreciation Period," SN, February 29, 1964, 1, 20.

85. Shirley Povich, "Lush TV Fees," BD, March 1965, 34.

4. Changing Demographics

1. U.S. Department of Commerce, *Historical Statistics*, 1:224.

2. U.S. Department of Commerce, *Historical Statistics*, 1:224, 316, 401.

3. U.S. Department of Commerce, *Historical Statistics*, 1:169, 173.

4. U.S. Department of Commerce, *Historical Statistics*, 2:716–18, 721.

5. U.S. Department of Commerce, *Historical Statistics*, 1:396, 398, 404; and 2:718.

6. U.S. Department of Commerce, *Historical Statistics*, 1:210, 401.

7. U.S. Department of Commerce, *Historical Statistics*, 1:210, 400.

8. Seagrave, *Drive-In Theaters*, 235.

9. U.S. Department of Commerce, *Historical Statistics*, 1:385.

10. U.S. Department of Commerce, *Census of Housing: 1960*, 1:28–29.

11. U.S. Department of Commerce, *Historical Statistics*, 1:20.

12. U.S. Department of Commerce, *Historical Statistics*, 1:11.

13. U.S. Department of Commerce, *Historical Statistics*, 1:40.

14. "Big League Baseball," *Fortune*, August 1937, 116.

15. Surdam, "Non-Price Determinants," discusses factors affecting attendance at Yankee Stadium before World War II.

16. "Big League Baseball," *Fortune*, August 1937, 116.

17. Ed Rumill, "Night Ball Is Here to Stay," *Baseball Magazine* (hereafter cited as BM), May 1948, 399.

18. Shirley Povich, "Majors Overdo Arc Ball, Pioneer MacPhail's View," SN, June 1, 1955, 1–2.

19. Joe King, "MacPhail in Dark on Arcs—Stoneham," sn, June 15, 1955, 1–2.

20. Ed Rumill, "Night Ball Is Here to Stay," bm, May 1948, 400.

21. Joe King, "Majors Arc Ball to New High in '56," sn, December 14, 1955, 2.

22. Ed Rumill, "Night Ball Is Here to Stay," bm, May 1948, 399.

23. Red Smith, "Under the Lights," si, August 30, 1954, 32.

24. Boston Braves scorecard, 1946.

25. Chicago Cubs scorecards, various years; and Cleveland Indians scorecard, 1954.

26. Veeck, Veeck as in Wreck, 121, 127.

27. "Big League Baseball," Fortune, August 1937, 116.

28. Veeck, Veeck as in Wreck, 125–27.

29. William Furlong, "Master of the Joyful," si, July 4, 1960, 60.

30. "Beer and Bratwurst," si, September 30, 1957, 18.

31. Dan Daniel, "Gal Execs Could Make Turnstiles Spin," sn, August 31, 1960, 9, 28.

32. Robert Creamer, "Unbarnacled Truth," si, April 14, 1958, 89.

33. Herb Heft, "Orioles Out-of-Town Fans Spent $5,500,000," sn, January 12, 1955, 57; and Baltimore Baseball Club, Survey.

34. Baltimore Baseball Club, Survey; and Herb Heft, "Orioles Out-of-Town Fans Spent $5,500,000," sn, January 12, 1955, 7.

35. Bob Allen, "Braves Bought $75,000,000," bd, March 1966, 80; and Red Thisted, "Braves Worth Five Million to Milwaukee," sn, October 28, 1953, 13.

36. Harold Rosenthal, "Giants' Poll Brings More Parking, Earlier Arc Play," sn, March 2, 1955, 8.

37. Harold Rosenthal, "Fans Helping Selves by Poll," sn, November 25, 1953, 10, 12.

38. Harold Rosenthal, "Giants' Poll Brings More Parking, Earlier Arc Play," 8.

39. New York Giants Baseball Club scorecard, 1954.

40. New York Giants Baseball Club scorecard, 1949.

41. New York Giants Baseball Club scorecards, 1952, 1954, 1956.

42. Harold Rosenthal, "Fans Helping Selves by Poll," sn, November 25, 1953, 10 and 12.

43. "Survey Shows Parking, tv Keeps Fans at Home," sn, August 10, 1955, 5.

44. Carl Lundquist, "'Game to Act on Fans Ideas Revealed in Survey'—Frick," sn, December 14, 1955, 12.

45. James Murray, "The Case for the Suffering Fan," si, August 20, 1956, 35.

46. "Food for Thought in Survey Findings," sn, August 10, 1955, 10.

47. Carl Lundquist, "Game to Act," *sn*, December 14, 1955, 14.

48. "Fans Speak Out as the Game's Best Friend," *sn*, November 30, 1954, 4, 6.

49. J. G. Taylor Spink, "Sharp Date Dip Challenges Big Time," *sn*, October 11, 1961, 1–2.

50. Hugo Autz, "Frick Flashes 'Go' on March 19–26 as Nationwide Boom for Baseball," *sn*, February 2, 1955, 4.

51. Gerald Holland, "Golden Age Is Now," *si*, August 16, 1954, 46–48.

52. Robert H. Boyle, "Help! Does All This Stuff," *si*, October 22, 1962, 31.

53. *Information Please Almanac* (1947), 810; *Information Please Almanac* (1950), 241; *Information Please Almanac* (1954), 252; and *Information Please Almanac* (1959), 470.

54. *Information Please Almanac* (1947), 810; *Information Please Almanac* (1950), 241; *Information Please Almanac* (1954), 252; and *Information Please Almanac* (1959), 470.

55. Ray Keyes, "Million Kids In Fast-Growing Little League," *sn*, June 14, 1961, 11.

56. Kenneth Rudeen, "Little League," *si*, August 19, 1957, 58. See also Robert Creamer, "Unbarnacled Truth," *si*, April 14, 1958, 93.

57. Robert H. Boyle, "Report That Shocked," *si*, August 15, 1955, 30.

58. Hugo Autz, "Kid Ball Yields Record Harvest of Talent," *sn*, October 6, 1962, 1, 4.

59. J. Roy Stockton, "'Bonus Here to Stay'—Bing; 'Destroys Incentive'—Lane," *sn*, March 22, 1961, 19–20.

60. Veeck, *Veeck as in Wreck*, 121.

61. Maher and Gill, *Pro Football Encyclopedia*, 112–27.

62. William Leggett, "Success Is Killing the al," *si*, September 9, 1963, 20.

63. Bob Burnes, "Majors-nfl Stadium Clash Shaping Up," *sn*, February 8, 1961, 1, 4; and Clifford Kachline, "Majors to Challenge Football with Latest Finish in 35 Seasons," *sn*, November 9, 1963, 16.

64. Veeck, *Veeck as in Wreck*, 118–19; and Veeck, *Hustler's Handbook*, 302.

65. Veeck, *Veeck as in Wreck*, 121.

66. Robert Coughlan, "Baseball: Nine Men," *si*, February 27, 1956, 57.

67. Veeck, *Veeck as in Wreck*, 336–38.

68. Dan Daniel, "'Lofty Payrolls Are a Challenge to Game'—Busch," *sn*, March 23, 1955, 4.

69. "32 Pages of Scouting Reports," *si*, April 15, 1957, 45–83; "36 Pages of Scouting Reports," *si*, April 10, 1961, 51–92; Boston Red Sox scorecard, 1946; Cleveland Indians scorecards, 1952–53; Detroit Tigers scorecards, 1956–57; Baltimore Orioles scorecards, 1954; Brooklyn/Los Angeles Dodgers scorecards, 1949 and 1963; Chicago Cubs scorecard, 1946; Boston Braves scorecard, 1946,

New York/San Francisco Giants scorecards, 1947 and 1960; Cincinnati Reds scorecard, 1950; and New York Mets scorecards, 1962 and 1964.

70. Robert Creamer, "Quaint Cult of the Mets," *si*, May 6, 1963, 61–62.

71. James Murray, "Suffering Fan," *si*, August 20, 1956, 34.

72. James Murray, "Suffering Fan," 36.

73. James Murray, "Suffering Fan," 42.

74. "32 Pages of Scouting Reports," *si*, April 15, 1957, 47–83.

75. "36 Pages of Scouting Reports," *si*, April 10, 1961, 63, 73, 77, 92.

76. Jack McDonald, "Giants' Park Dazzling Palace," *sn*, April 6, 1960, 13, 16; and "Beer and Bratwurst," *si*, September 30, 1957, 18.

77. Jack McDonald, "Beer and Bratwurst," *si*, September 30, 1957, 19.

78. Harold Rosenthal, "'49 Series Win Weiss' Big Moment," *sn*, February 8, 1956, 13–14.

79. Robert Coughlan, "Baseball: Nine Men," *si*, February 27, 1956, 22–23.

80. Bob Hunter, "Fast-Stepping Kids Figure to Skyrocket Future LA Budget," *sn*, February 1, 1961, 18, 22; and Bob Hunter, "Lifting Curtain on Dodgers' Dream House in Fantasy Land," *sn*, April 11, 1962, 25–26.

81. Jack McDonald, "Giants' Park Dazzling Palace," *sn*, April 6, 1960, 13, 16.

82. Harold Rosenthal, "Polo Grounds to Get 150-G Face-Lifting," *sn*, July 19, 1961, 25.

83. Dave Brady, "New DC Park Perfect Game Dream Site," *sn*, July 7, 1962, 3–4; Harold Rosenthal, "Flushing Meadow Stadium Work 'Right on Schedule,'" *sn*, November 10, 1962, 17; Carl Lundquist, "Shea Stadium Last World in Color and Class," *sn*, April 18, 1964, 25–26; and Barry Kremenko, "Mets Promise Fans Quick Traffic Flow," *sn*, July 4, 1964, 2.

84. "New Washington Stadium Will Be Ready," *sn*, September 6, 1961, 35; and Dave Brady, "Senators Agree to Play in New Capital Stadium," *sn*, October 4, 1961, 32, 38.

85. Clark Nealon, "Houston Stadium Delayed; Opening Scheduled for '64," *sn*, April 11, 1962, 33; and Clark Nealon, "'Magnificent Dream' Rapidly Coming True," *sn*, December 5, 1964, 9–10.

86. "'Bible' Receives O'Malley Report on NL's Huddle," *sn*, July 27, 1960, 6; Braven Dyer, "Angels to Open '66 Season in Anaheim Park," *sn*, August 22, 1964, 7; and C. C. Johnson Spink, "Angels Closing Deal for Anaheim Leap," *sn*, August 1, 1964, 1, 8.

87. Melvin Durslag, "Call Them Mickey's Mice," *si*, July 20, 1964, 45.

88. Oscar Kahan, "New Sports Stadium Suffers Setback in St. Louis," *sn*, January 31, 1962, 8; Oscar Kahan, "St. Louis Voters Flash 'Go' Signal on New Stadium," *sn*, March 14, 1962, 13; and Les Biederman, "Bucs to Occupy 54,000-Seat, $25 Million Stadium in 1968," *sn*, December 26, 1964, 20.

89. Chicago White Sox scorecard, 1960.

90. Washington Senators scorecards, 1957 and 1959.

91. Boston Braves scorecard, 1946.

92. Houston Colt .45s scorecard, 1962; and New York Mets scorecards, 1962 and 1964.

93. Edgar Munzel, "White Sox Earmark $1 Million for Expansion and Stadium Club," SN, December 22, 1962, 11.

94. "Fans Speak Out," SN, November 30, 1954, 4, 6; Carl Lundquist, "Game to Act," SN, December 14, 1955, 12; and Carl Lundquist, "Games Not Too Long, Just Delays, Survey Shows," SN, August 11, 1962, 1–2.

95. Dan Daniel, "Frick Group Blueprints O.B. Shakeup," SN, May 16, 1962, 1–2.

96. Stanley Frank, "What Ever Happened to Baseball?" SI, August 27, 1962, 20.

97. Oscar Kahan, "Speed-Up Rules Make Hit with Hurlers," SN, January 26, 1963, 1, 6; and Jim Gallagher, "Majors Slash Game Time by Ten Minutes," SN, July 13, 1963, 28.

98. Veeck, Veeck as in Wreck, 124.

99. Frederick Lieb, "Flair for Fun Flits from Major Scene," SN, December 13, 1961, 1–2.

100. Stanley Frank, "What Ever Happened to Baseball?" SI, August 27, 1962, 19.

101. Garry Hern, "'Players' Sidelines Hurting Game'—Cronin," SN, May 18, 1955, 1.

102. Leonard Shecter, "Rational Rebel," SI, May 13, 1963, 81–82.

103. William Whyte, "The Class of '49," Fortune, June 1949; and Whyte, Organization Man.

104. "Big League Baseball," Fortune, August 1937, 112.

105. Brooklyn Dodgers scorecards, 1949–51.

106. Dan Daniel, "Hooting Gotham Fans Ignite Stadium Melee," SN, September 20, 1961, 11.

107. Les Biederman, "Teen-Agers Rip Out Seats, Beat Up Youth, Start Fights in Pirate Park, SN, May 9, 1964, 12.

108. Earl Lawson, "New Tax Law Slows Season Ducat Sales," SN, January 12, 1963, 1–2.

109. Oscar Kahan, "Cronin, Giles Calm Fears over New Tax Law," SN, January 19, 1963, 5.

110. Oscar Kahan, "Soaring Ducat Sales Chasing Tax Fears," SN, April 20, 1963, 1–2, 6.

111. Brooklyn Dodgers scorecards, 1954–57.

112. Cincinnati Reds scorecards, 1950.

113. Sporting News, Sporting News Dope Book (1965), 17, 75.

114. Los Angeles Dodgers scorecards, 1962–64.

115. Milwaukee Braves scorecards, 1955–56.

116. Chicago White Sox scorecard, 1957.

117. Baltimore Orioles scorecard, 1955.

118. Los Angeles Angels scorecards, 1962–64; Detroit Tigers scorecards, 1962–64; and New York Yankees scorecard, 1965.

119. Boston Braves scorecard, 1946.

120. Philadelphia Phillies scorecard, 1949; and Cleveland Indians newsletter, June 1952.

121. U.S. Department of Commerce, *Seventeenth Census*, vol. 2.

122. A. S. "Doc" Young, "The Jackie Robinson Era," *Ebony*, November 1955, 154–55.

123. Huston Horn, "Bravura Battle for the Braves," *SI*, November 2, 1964, 33.

124. Maurice Moore, "Court Dismisses Negro Player's Civil Right Suit," *SN*, September 23, 1953, 11.

125. Shirley Povich, "Can Negro Win Housing Fight in Spring Camp?" *SN*, March 8, 1961, 10; Frederick Lieb, "Florida Airs Housing Plan for Negroes," *SN*, May 3, 1961, 27; "Teams' Help Sought to End Segregation," *NYT*, February 1, 1961, 44; and Dan Daniel, "Negroes Submit Formal Protest on Segregation," *SN*, March 8, 1961, 8.

126. Dan Daniel, "Bias Beef on Negroes in Mag Story Untrue, Scott Says," *SN*, April 6, 1960, 1, 4; and Robert Boyle, "Private World of the Negro Ballplayer," *SI*, March 21, 1960, 17, 80–81.

127. Russ J. Cowans, "Negro Loop Down to Four as Clowns, Clippers Drop Out," *SN*, February 2, 1955, 6.

128. Paul O'Boynick, "K.C. Monarchs Sell 12 Players, Eight to Majors," *SN*, February 1, 1956, 29; and Ernest Mehl, "Negro League Era Fading with Breakup of Monarchs," *SN*, February 8, 1956, 15.

129. For a recent analysis, see Quinn and Surdam, "Case of the Missing Fans." See also Burger and Walters, "Market Size."

5. Television and Baseball

1. U.S. Senate, *Professional Sports Antitrust Bill—1965*, 50.

2. Dan Daniel, "Television Clause Snags Player Contract," *SN*, September 25, 1946, 1–2.

3. Edgar Munzel, "2 Chi Owners Blast Player Bid for TV $s," *SN*, November 26, 1958, 4.

4. "Radio Log of Daily Play-by-Play Broadcasts," *SN*, April 16, 1947, 16.

5. Bill Paddock, "Video's Vital Role in Series Shown by Survey," *SN*, October 19, 1949, 11.

6. Veeck, *Hustler's Handbook*, 303.

7. Dan Parker, "Poor Reception for TV," *BD*, March 1951, 52–53; Tom Swope,

"Chandler Wraps Up $6,000,000 Video Deal," *SN*, January 3, 1951, 4; and Shirley Povich, "But Reception's Good Here," *BD*, March 1951, 53–54.

8. "Saigh Criticizes, Others Praise Video Contract," *SN*, January 3, 1951, 4.

9. Dan Daniel, "Indians, Chisox, A's Join ABC in Saturday TV Chain," *SN*, June 3, 1953, 4; Jack McDonald, "Coast Howls over Major TV Invasion," *SN*, June 10, 1953, 9; Frank Finch, "Major Video Fails to Cut Gate at L.A.," *SN*, June 24, 1953, 10; Sporting News, *Sporting News Official Baseball Guide* (1954), 102; and Oscar Kahan, "Majors' TV Sponsors to Spend Record $26,200,000 This Year," *SN*, March 14, 1956, 25.

10. "Frick Appoints Six to Study Radio-TV," *NYT*, December 31, 1952, 18; Harold Rosenthal, "TV to Demand Top Games," *SN*, March 14, 1964, 5; C. C. Johnson Spink, "Will TV Wind Up as Boss of Baseball?" *SN*, April 4, 1964, 1, 4; and Oscar Kahan, "Sponsors to Shell Out Record $83 Million for Major Air Rights," *SN*, March 14, 1962, 24.

11. Roone Arledge and Gilbert Rogin, "It's Sports," *SI*, April 25, 1966, 100.

12. Roone Arledge and Gilbert Rogin, "It's Sports," *SI*, April 25, 1966, 100.

13. Oscar Kahan, "Sponsors to Shell Out Record $83 Million for Major Air Rights," *SN*, April 13, 1960, 26.

14. Dave Brady, "Cost of Aircasting Majors' Tilts Soar to $75 Million," *SN*, March 15, 1961, 15; and Oscar Kahan, "Sponsors of TV Games to Shell Out $39 Million," *SN*, March 14, 1962, 24.

15. Dan Daniel, "Majors Reap $4 Million Yearly in New Pact with Gillette, NBC," *SN*, March 2, 1960, 9; and Dan Daniel, "Players to Ask Pension Increase," *SN*, June 15, 1960, 4.

16. "ABC to Televise 25 Major League Saturday Games," *SN*, March 30, 1960, 20.

17. Oscar Kahan, "Sponsors of TV Games to Shell Out $39 Million," *SN*, April 13, 1960, 26.

18. Jack Gallagher, "NBC Pre-Pays TV Fee to Pad AFL Bankroll for Talent Fight," *SN*, September 12, 1964, 53.

19. Bob Burnes, "New Television Contract Gives Multi-Millionaire Look to NFL," *SN*, February 8, 1964, 38; James Enright, "Grid TV Gravy Grading Majors to Act," *SN*, February 15, 1964, 1, 6; and Barry Kremenko, "NBC's $36 Million, Five-Year TV Pact Puts AFL in Black," *SN*, February 8, 1964, 38.

20. U.S. Congress, *Telecasting*, 64–66; and Dave Brady, "Frick with Eye to Future, Backs Celler's TV Bill," *SN*, September 6, 1961, 27.

21. Oscar Kahan, "Majors Wrapping 'Attractive Package' to Boost Air Income," *SN*, March 14, 1964, 5.

22. Dave Brady, "Rich Clubs Agree to Divvy TV Pot," *SN*, February 8, 1964, 1, 4.

23. Shirley Povich, "Lush TV Fees," *BD*, March 1965, 34.

24. Dave Brady, "Package Setup Seen for Sports Network," *SN*, May 9, 1964, 10.

25. Carl Lundquist, "Majors Unwrap Video X-Mas Gift," *SN*, December 26, 1964, 17, 26; and "Fetzer Wrapping Up Sales of TV Package," *SN*, December 19, 1964, 4.

26. Roscoe McGowen, "'Pay TV Costly? Bleacher Prices OK'—O'Malley," *SN*, May 18, 1955, 2.

27. Lowell Reidenbaugh, "Eight Pitchers among Ten Drafted by Majors," *SN*, December 7, 1955, 12. For a detailed look at pay-TV and sports in general, see M. R. Werner et al., "$6,000,000 Question," *SI*, December 26, 1960, 80–89.

28. Clifford Kachline, "West Coast Clubs Scan Toll-TV for Multi-Million Cut," *SN*, September 21, 1963, 10.

29. Clifford Kachline, "Pay-TV of Giant, Dodger Games Likely in '64," *SN*, August 31, 1963, 1, 6.

30. U.S. Senate, *Organized Professional Team Sports* (1958), 383.

31. U.S. Senate, *Organized Professional Team Sports* (1958), 139–40.

32. Carl Lundquist, "'Fans Will Never Have to Pay for Series TV' Weaver Says," *SN*, October 31, 1964, 24.

33. Melvin Durslag, "Pay-Video Survey Reveals 52% of 'Fans' Never Attend a Game," *SN*, July 25, 1964, 6.

34. Til Ferdenzi, "Players Seek Share of Pay-Video Gravy," *SN*, April 25, 1964, 17. See also "'Players to Divvy Pay-TV Profits' Asserts Cannon," *SN*, October 3, 1964, 18.

35. Melvin Durslag, "Pay-Video Survey Reveals 52% of 'Fans' Never Attend a Game," *SN*, July 25, 1964, 6; Bob Hunter, "O'Malley Taps New Mother Lode—Fee TV," *SN*, August 1, 1964, 2; and Clifford Kachline, "Dodger and Giant Pay-TV to Start July 7," *SN*, April 4, 1964, 2.

36. Bob Hunter, "O'Malley Taps New Mother Lode—Fee TV," *SN*, August 1, 1964, 2.

37. Melvin Durslag, "The Rise and Fall of Pay TV," *SN*, November 21, 1964, 10. See also Jack McDonald, "Giants Sit Tight, Let STV Carry Fight into Court," *SN*, November 21, 1964, 10, 20; and Bob Hunter, "Pay-TV Encounters Roadblock; LA Debut Delayed to July 17," *SN*, June 27, 1964, 18.

38. Hal Lebovitz, "Everybody's Eyeing O'Malley's Big Test of Subscription TV," *SN*, April 4, 1964, 2, 6; and Bob Hunter, "Pay-TV Boss Mapping Counter-Attack," *SN*, November 21, 1964, 1, 10. Fetzer's plan was unlikely to affect pay-TV significantly, as the Dodgers and Giants each were likely to be in only two or three national games per season (Ralph Ray, "Pay-Video No Threat to Monday Network Show, Fetzer Claims," *SN*, September 5, 1964, 28; and Harold Rosenthal, "Room for Both Pay, Free TV in Baseball," *SN*, April 25, 1964, 17).

39. Dan Daniel, "Television Opens Up," *BM*, May 1948, 411.

40. Milton Richman, "War, Weather Cloud 1951 Outlook," *BD*, February 1951, 24.

41. Edgar Munzel, "Bill Will Push Battle at Next AL Session," *SN*, April 22, 1959, 6; and Veeck, *Veeck as in Wreck*, 275.

42. Dan Daniel, "TV vs. Baseball," *BM*, July 1951, 259.

43. Dan Daniel, "TV Must Go," *BM*, November 1952, 36.

44. Milton Richman, "War, Weather Cloud 1951 Outlook," *BD*, February 1951, 25.

45. Dan Daniel, "Television," *BM*, May 1948, 411–12.

46. U.S. Senate, *Professional Sports Antitrust Bill—1965*, 51.

47. Paul Richards, "Why the American League Is Dying," *Look*, February 17, 1959, 41–47.

48. Dan Daniel, "TV Must Go," *BM*, November 1952, 6; "Yanks' Televising of Game in Philly Part of Survey of Effect on Gate," *SN*, October 1, 1952, 8; and "Yankees Reducing Home Games on TV," *NYT*, January 28, 1953, 35.

49. Dan Daniel, "Yank TV Blackout Pitch Expected to Force Showdown," *SN*, August 31, 1955, 14.

50. American League, *American League Red Book* (1948), 2; and American League, *American League Red Book* (1952), 5.

51. Oscar Ruhl, "From the Ruhl Book," *SN*, March 30, 1949, 15; and Hal Lebovitz, "Indians Plan to Limit TV to Road Title," *SN*, November 25, 1953, 9.

52. Stan Baumgartner, "Crackdown Seen on Major Telecast," *SN*, June 8, 1949, 1–2.

53. Dan Daniel, "TV Must Go," *BM*, November 1952, 6.

54. Craig, *Organized Baseball*, 252; and Jordan, *Long-Range Effect*.

55. Dan Daniel, "Yank TV Blackout Pitch Expected to Force Showdown," *SN*, August 31, 1955, 14.

56. In both cases the variable was not statistically significant at the 5 percent level.

Percentage Change in Attendance between 1947 and 1950 =
1.105 + 2.742 (Change in Win-Loss Percentage)
(6.31) (5.01)
–0.860 (% with TV in 1950)
(–1.40)
$N = 16$ $R^2 = 0.664$

Percentage Change in Attendance between 1947 and 1953 =
2.425 + 2.000 (Change in Win-Loss Percentage)
(2.12) (3.59)
–2.024 (% with TV in 1953)
(–1.50)
$N = 16$ $R^2 = 0.522$

57. Turkin, *Radio and TV Baseball*.

58. "Sponsors Will Spend $31,800,000, New High, on Major Aircasts in '57," *SN*, April 3, 1957, 10; and Lowell Reidenbaugh, "Majors Outside N.Y. to Stand Pat," *SN*, September 14, 1955, 1.

59. "Log of Play-by-Play Broadcasts and Telecasts," *sn*, April 16, 1958, 31; "Log of Play-by-Play Broadcasts and Telecasts," *sn*, April 8, 1959, 27; "Log of Play-by-Play Broadcasts and Telecasts," *sn*, April 13, 1963, 28; and "Log of Play-by-Play Broadcasts and Telecasts," *sn*, April 17, 1965, 32.

60. U.S. Congress, *Organized Baseball: Hearings*, 1604–5; and U.S. Congress, *Organized Professional Team Sports*, 2048–52.

61. U.S. Congress, *Organized Professional Team Sports*, 2048–52.

62. Alexander, *Our Game*, 222.

63. Dan Daniel, "TV vs. Baseball," *BM*, July 1951, 259; and Dan Daniel, "TV Must Go," *BD*, November 1952, 36.

64. Koppett, *Koppett's Concise History*, 232, 235.

65. U.S. Congress, *Organized Baseball: Hearings*, 1616.

66. U.S. Congress, *Organized Baseball: Hearings*, 1625.

67. Edgar Brands, "Clubs Advised to Insist on Long-Term TV Pacts," *sn*, February 2, 1949, 25.

68. U.S. Congress, *Organized Baseball: Hearings*, 168. See also John P. Carmichael, "Will Korea Strike?" *BD*, October 1950, 37; and Milton Richman, "War, Weather Cloud 1951 Outlook," *BD*, February 1951, 24–25.

69. U.S. Congress, *Organized Baseball: Hearings*, 197.

70. U.S. Congress, *Organized Baseball: Hearings*, 198.

71. U.S. Senate, *Organized Professional Team Sports* (1958), 209; and U.S. Senate, *Organized Professional Team Sports* (1960), 139.

72. U.S. Senate, *Professional Sports Antitrust Bill—1964*, 44, 47.

73. Sporting News, *Sporting News Official Baseball Guide* (1951), 108. Apparently, the Major League teams later refused to sell Liberty Broadcasting the rights to their games, and the broadcasting company subsequently went bankrupt; the Liberty Broadcasting System later sued thirteen Major League clubs for continuing conspiracy to monopolize and restrain competition in broadcasting and recreating play-by-play accounts of professional baseball games. Major league baseball settled the case for $200,000 ("$200,000 Settlement Proposed in Anti-Trust Broadcasting Case," *sn*, January 19, 1955, 4; and Tex Maule, "Liberty's O.B. Suit Is Settled for $200,000," *sn*, February 2, 1955, 4).

74. Dan Daniel, "New TV Curbs Likely from Phil-Yank Tussle," *sn*, November 6, 1957, 7.

75. U.S. Congress, *Organized Baseball: Hearings*, 381–82.

76. U.S. Congress, *Organized Baseball: Hearings*, 462.

77. Milton Richman, "War, Weather Cloud 1951 Outlook," *BD*, February 1951, 25.

78. J. Roy Stockton, "Talent Dearth Alarming," *BD*, October 1951, 37.

79. Charles Young, "Minors in Major Difficulty," *BD*, January 1952, 77.

80. Howard Green, "There's LAZINESS in the Minors," *BM*, April 1952, 5, 28.

81. Johnson and Wolff, *Encyclopedia*, 82.

82. Jimmy Jemail, "Television Is Killing the Minors," *SI*, October 4, 1954, 2–3.

83. U.S. Senate, *Organized Professional Team Sports* (1958), 241, 244. For Frick's quote, see U.S. Senate, *Organized Professional Team Sports* (1960), 119.

84. U.S. Senate, *Organized Professional Team Sports* (1959), 61.

85. Jimmy Jemail, "What Should the Major Leagues Do?" *SI*, December 20, 1954, 2–3.

86. Dan Daniel, "Minor Leagues Need Cash Aid, DeWitt Declares," *SN*, August 4, 1954, 2.

87. U.S. Senate, *Organized Professional Team Sports* (1958), 262.

88. U.S. Senate, *Organized Professional Team Sports* (1958), 267.

89. J. G. Taylor Spink, "Limit Radio, Drop Farms, Griff Urges," *SN*, August 4, 1954, 1–2.

90. U.S. Senate, *Organized Professional Team Sports* (1958), 185, 219.

91. Jack Walsh, "'TV Curb Needed to Save Game'—Frick," *SN*, July 23, 1958, 7.

92. U.S. Senate, *Organized Professional Team Sports* (1958), 158–60, 164; and U.S. Senate, *Organized Professional Team Sports* (1959), 57.

93. U.S. Senate, *Organized Professional Team Sports* (1958), 186.

94. Frederick Lieb, "Giles Favors Realignments in Game's Map," *SN*, October 17, 1951, 3.

95. Frank Graham, "Death of a Ballclub," *BD*, February 1950, 26.

96. Willie Klein, "Newark Fans, Yankees, City in Revitalizing Bears," *SN*, February 2, 1949, 10.

97. "Jersey City May Keep Club Despite Loss of TV Station," *SN*, August 10, 1960, 32; and "Come On, Yo-Yo!" *SI*, July 25, 1960, 8.

98. Ward Morehouse, "Minors in Most Wholesome Shape in Five Years," *SN*, February 23, 1955, 21. See also Edgar Munzel, "Minors at Door of Another Boom Era—Lane," *SN*, February 23, 1955, 15; and Harold Rosenthal, "Keep Park Filled with Kids—Harper's Norfolk Success Rule," *SN*, February 23, 1955, 15.

99. "Action Right Now or Minors Will Perish," *SN*, August 17, 1955, 12. See also Dan Daniel, "O'Malley Clears Up Plan to Aid Minors with Cash from TV," *SN*, December 7, 1955, 4; Brad Willson, "Minors Move for 'Fairer' Deal with Majors," *SN*, December 7, 1955, 11; and Brad Willson, "Trautman Urges Majors to Slow Dollar Scramble," *SN*, December 7, 1955, 11–12.

100. U.S. Congress, *Organized Baseball: Hearings*, 1625, 1629, 1633.

101. Surdam, "Television and Minor League Baseball."

102. Finch, "Era of President George M. Trautman," 73.

103. U.S. Senate, *Organized Professional Team Sports* (1958), 264.

104. Surdam, "Television and Minor League Baseball."

105. U.S. Department of Commerce, *Census of Housing: 1950*, 1:9; and U.S. Department of Commerce, *Census of Housing: 1960*, 1:28.

106. U.S. Department of Commerce, *Census of Housing: 1950*, 1:73.

107. U.S. Department of Commerce, *Historical Statistics*, 1:796.

108. "Television in the Tavern," *Newsweek*, June 16, 1947, 64; "Barrooms with a View," *Time*, March 24, 1947, 63–64; and "The Television Set," *Time*, December 15, 1947, 50.

109. U.S. Senate, *Status of UHF and Multiple Ownership*, 172–73.

110. U.S. Department of Commerce, *Census of Housing: 1950*, 1:26–30.

111. U.S. Department of Commerce, *Census of Housing: 1950*, 1:30.

112. U.S. Department of Commerce, *Census of Housing: 1950*, 1:26–30.

113. Surdam, "Television and Minor League Baseball."

114. U.S. Department of Commerce, *Census of Housing: 1950*, 1:66–77; and Johnson and Wolff, *Encyclopedia*, 224, 247.

115. U.S. Senate, *Status of UHF and Multiple Ownership*, 545–47.

116. U.S. Senate, *Status of UHF and Multiple Ownership*, 545–47; U.S. Department of Commerce, *Census of Housing: 1950*, 1:66–77; and Johnson and Wolff, *Encyclopedia*, 224, 247.

117. Fred Russell, "Southern Stumbled on Color Line," *SN*, April 4, 1962, 13–14; and "Why Did Southern Go Under?" *SN*, March 28, 1962, 11–12.

118. Bob Burnes, "Shaky Southern Association Teetering toward Extinction," *SN*, September 20, 1961, 5, 12.

119. Roy Terrell, "Doom around the Corner," *SI*, December 16, 1957, 35.

120. U.S. Senate, *Organized Professional Team Sports* (1960), 140.

121. Roy Terrell, "Doom around the Corner," *SI*, December 16, 1957, 36.

122. Roy Terrell, "Doom around the Corner," *SI*, December 16, 1957, 36.

123. Bob Burnes, "$2,347,000 for Minors-Down Drain?" *SN*, August 3, 1960, 1–2; Clifford Kachline, "$800,000 in Aid Money Sent to 100 Minor Clubs," *SN*, October 26, 1960, 17; "Minors Ask Hike in Handouts from Big Time," *SN*, November 30, 1960, 17–18; and "Minors Veto Proposals for Bigger Handouts," *SN*, December 7, 1960, 11, 16.

124. Chicago Baseball Club, *Probate Court Proceedings*, exhibit 4.

125. Dave Brady, "Frick with Eye to Future, Backs Celler's TV Bill," *SN*, September 6, 1961, 27.

126. Brad Willson, "Aircast Curb Vital to Minor Loops—Trautman," *SN*, November 30, 1955, 5–7.

127. John Holway, "Stop! Killing the Minors," *BM*, October 1956, 28–32.

128. Oscar Kahan, "Minors' Parley Ends Up behind 8 Ball," *SN*, December 7, 1960, 9–10.

129. Clifford Kachline, "Overhaul of Minors Flops; Farm Chiefs Try to Mend Flaws," *SN*, October 6, 1962, 24; and Clifford Kachline, "New Aid Setup for Minors Draws Favorable Response," *SN*, November 10, 1962, 10.

130. Clifford Kachline, "Minors Doomed Unless Majors Act," *SN*, December 8, 1962, 1–2; Clifford Kachline, "Majors Pick Up $10 Million Tab in Minors,"

SN, December 15, 1962, 5, 10; and Edgar Munzel, "Majors Guarantee to Back 100 Minor Clubs," SN, June 2, 1962, 13.

131. Clifford Kachline, "Minors Doomed Unless Majors Act," SN, December 8, 1962, 1–2.

132. U.S. Senate, *Organized Professional Team Sports* (1958), 105; and U.S. Senate, *Professional Sports Antitrust Bill—1964*. See also John Powell's testimony during the same hearings (77–78).

133. Roger Kahn, "Forget Something, Boys?" *SI*, 1954, 12–13.

134. "Television Spreading in Top Minor Loops," SN, April 20, 1949, 26.

135. U.S. Senate, *Organized Professional Team Sports* (1958), 265.

136. Clifford Kachline, "Radio Rights Worth 25 Grand or More to Six Clubs in Minors," SN, January 6, 1960, 7.

137. "Log of Play-by-Play Broadcasts and Telecasts," SN, April 13, 1960, 31; and "Minor League Air Log," April 18, 1962, 39.

6. Where Is Robin Hood When You Need Him?

1. Levin, Mitchell, Volcker, and Will, *Report*, 6–7, 46.

2. U.S. Congress, *Organized Baseball: Hearings*, 1604–5; and U.S. Congress, *Organized Professional Team Sports*, 2048–52.

3. Seymour, *Baseball: The Golden Age*, 8.

4. U.S. Congress, *Organized Baseball: Report*, 36–37.

5. U.S. Congress, *Organized Baseball: Report*, 17.

6. Seymour, *Baseball: The Early Years*, 67–68; and Melville, *Early Baseball*, 58.

7. U.S. Congress, *Organized Baseball: Hearings*, 130–31.

8. Seymour, *Baseball: The Early Years*, 88; and "Sporting: The Professional Base Ball Association—What It Must Do to Be Saved," *CT*, October 24, 1875, 12.

9. U.S. Congress, *Organized Baseball: Report*, 20.

10. Seymour, *Baseball: The Early Years*, 139; and Pietrusza, *Major Leagues*, 66. According to documents in Sullivan, *Early Innings*, 121, the guarantee was $60.

11. Seymour, *Baseball: The Early Years*, 209.

12. Seymour, *Baseball: The Early Years*, 209; U.S. Congress, *Organized Baseball: Report*, 36–37; Sullivan, *Early Innings*, 131; and Pietrusza, *Major Leagues*, 82, 107.

13. U.S. Congress, *Organized Baseball: Hearings*, 1119.

14. Murray Chass, "Reluctant Baseball Owners Approve Pact with Players," NYT, 1996, A1, B13; and Levin, Mitchell, Volcker, and Will, *Report*, 8.

15. Frederick Lieb, "Game Heading for All-Time High at Turnstiles," SN, April 25, 1946, 2.

16. U.S. Congress, *Organized Baseball: Hearings*, 1119.

17. There was only one anomaly: the 1950 Cleveland Indians received only

twenty-three cents per ticket while on the road, which was probably the result of a misstated road revenue figure. The individual components of the team's total revenue do not sum up to the reported total revenue, and making an adjustment to the road revenue would make the per-admission figure more than twenty-eight cents. I adjusted the 1950 estimate to reflect this error. Data pertaining to the twenty-nine-cent estimate are available upon request.

18. "Yanks Set Road Gate Record, Clinch to Top 2,000,000 Mark," SN, September 8, 1962, 7.

19. Veeck, *Veeck as in Wreck*, 274.

20. U.S. Congress, *Organized Baseball: Hearings*, 1107.

21. Scully, *Business of Major League Baseball*, 80; and Quirk and Fort, *Pay Dirt*, 275.

22. As many economists have pointed out, this potential marginal revenue disparity implies that with reasonably free movement of players between teams, whether instigated by owners or by players, teams in larger cities should, on average, attract better players and achieve better records than teams in smaller cities. For empirical support for this assumption, see Bruggink and Eaton, "Rebuilding Attendance," 18–21. Eckard presents evidence that disputes the winning and market size assumption ("Baseball's Blue Ribbon Economic Report," 220–22).

23. Quirk and Fort, *Pay Dirt*, 275.

24. Surdam, "American Not-So-Socialist League," 278–79.

25. Surdam, "Tale of Two Gate-Sharing Plans."

26. "Baseball's Golden Age," SI, April 9, 1956, 55.

27. "Baseball's Golden Age," SI, April 9, 1956, 55.

28. "Yanks Set," SN, September 8, 1962, 7; and day-by-day tally of attendance.

29. Surdam, "Tale of Two Gate-Sharing Plans."

30. Edgar Brands, "Veeck Appeals to Frick in Battle for Television Divvy," SN, February 11, 1953, 5–6.

31. Shirley Povich, "He Saighs over Foes' TV Take," BD, August 1951, 35.

32. John Drebinger, "Veeck Asks Frick End TV 'Coercion' by 3 Bigger Clubs," NYT, February 1, 1953, sec. 5, 1, 8; Veeck, *Veeck as in Wreck*, 276–77; and Turkin, *Radio and TV Baseball*.

33. Edgar Munzel, "Veeck Renews Fight for Road TV Divvy," SN, April 22, 1959, 1, 6. See also Edgar Brands, "Veeck Appeals to Frick in Battle for Television Divvy," SN, February 11, 1953, 5–6.

34. William Leggett, "Success Is Killing the AL," SI, September 9, 1963, 21.

35. C. C. Johnson Spink, "Will TV Wind Up as Boss of Baseball?" SN, April 4, 1964, 1, 4. See also Veeck, *Veeck as in Wreck*, 276.

36. Dick Young, "Hungry 'Have-Nots' Eyeing TV Melon," SN, September 7, 1963, 1–2.

37. Dick Young, "Hungry 'Have-Nots' Eyeing TV Melon," SN, 1–2; and Arno

Gothel, "Griffith to Seek Slice of National Video Pie," *SN*, December 1, 1962, 1, 8.

38. U.S. Senate, *Professional Sports Antitrust Bill—1965*, 55, 120.

39. U.S. Congress, *Organized Baseball: Report*, 85.

40. Francis Stann, "Buy the Browns' Time," *BD*, March 1951, 35–36.

41. U.S. Congress, *Organized Baseball: Report*, 85.

7. Isn't Anybody Going to Help That Game?

1. U.S. Congress, *Organized Baseball: Hearings*, 1600.

2. National League, *National League Green Book* (1959), 35.

3. Veeck, *Veeck as in Wreck*, 171.

4. Shirley Povich, "Can Negro Win Housing Fight In Spring Camp?" *SN*, March 8, 1961, 10.

5. Bryant, *Shut Out*.

6. *Macmillan Baseball Encyclopedia*, 9th ed., 19–22, 41; and Moffi and Kronstadt, *Crossing the Line*, 1994.

7. Harold Rosenthal, "Negro Seen as Majors' Balance Wheel: Colored Stars Possible Key to Big Boom," *SN*, October 28, 1953, 1–2.

8. James Murray, "American League? Phooey!" *SI*, June 11, 1956, 12.

9. Al Hirshberg, "A.L. Pays for Delay," *BD*, September 1966, 33–34.

10. Walter Bingham, "No Joy in Beertown," *SI*, July 25, 1960, 17.

11. Morton Puner, "All-American Lineup," *BD*, August 1950, 84–86.

12. Dan Daniel, "Giants and Yanks Bombarding Dodgers' Lead in Negro Talent," *SN*, February 9, 1949, 2; Dan Daniel, "Feudin' and Fightin' between Bombers, Injuns," February 23, 1949, 2; Wendell Smith, "Inside Story on Signing of Artie Wilson," *SN*, February 23, 1949, 2, 8; and Willie Klein, "Marquez Disappointed over Decision Changing Label from Yank to Indian," *SN*, May 25, 1959, 18.

13. The *New York Times* attributed Martin's trade to, "the fight at the Copacabana . . . while his birthday was being celebrated . . . [he] has been involved in a number of scrapes. . . . It had been whispered that the Yankee front office did not look kindly upon the influence Martin was said to exercise over Mantle" ("Kansas City Obtains Mantel from Yanks," *NYT*, June 16, 1957, sec. 5, 1). Historian Jules Tygiel provides a good discussion of the Yankees' hesitation in putting a black player on the team (*Baseball's Great Experiment*, chap. 15).

14. Joseph Sheehan, "Yanks Get Byrd and Eddie Robinson in 13-Man Deal," *NYT*, December 17, 1953, 57; Moffi and Kronstadt, *Crossing the Line*, 118, 134; Ernest Mehl, "Howard Rated over Power in Attitude and Potential," *SN*, October 28, 1953, 6; Dan Daniel, "What about Vic Power? First Post-Season Poser for Yanks," *SN*, October 7, 1953, 7; and Dan Daniel, "Yankees Carol over Christmas 'Package' Deal," *SN*, December 23, 1953, 9.

15. Bob Broeg, "Howard, Tapped by Yanks, Proves All-American Boy," *SN*, October 28, 1953, 2.

16. Joe Williams, "The Weiss Side, *BD*, March 1954, 12.

17. Shirley Povich, "Yanks' Trade Has 'Deep' Meaning," *BD*, March 1954, 11–13.

18. Clara Jones, "Yanks Want Negro Superman," *SN*, May 19, 1954, 14.

19. Herbert Simons, "Top 50 Rookies," *BD*, March 1955, 6, 9; and Dan Daniel, "Ol' Professor Pegs Howard for Bigger Billing as Bomber," *SN*, February 1, 1956, 19.

20. Moffi and Kronstadt, *Crossing the Line*, 134–35. Stengel's quote is found in Allen, *You Could Look It Up*, 172. Allen also discussed Stengel's racial attitudes. Howard's quotes are from Art Rust's oral history of the Negro Leagues (*Get That Nigger Off the Field*, 128–29). A letter to the editor in the *Sporting News* excoriated the Yankees' hypocrisy in delaying Howard's arrival in the Major Leagues ("Yank Actions Deny Words," *SN*, August 4, 1954, 16).

21. Moffi and Kronstadt, *Crossing the Line*, 135.

22. Moffi and Kronstadt, *Crossing the Line*, 85.

23. Dan Daniel, "Weiss Will Take Rubber Off Bankroll for Players," *SN*, July 19, 1961, 1–2.

24. Dan Parker, "Yanks Have Never Paid Dividend—but Must Now," *SN*, April 25, 1946, 4.

25. Dan Daniel, "Giants and Yanks Bombarding Dodgers' Lead in Negro Talent," *SN*, February 9, 1949, 1, 6; Halberstam, *Summer of '49*, 284; Moffi and Kronstadt, *Crossing the Line*, 85; and Ribowsky, *Complete History of the Negro Leagues*, 299.

26. Ribowsky, *Complete History of the Negro Leagues*, 299.

27. Shirley Povich, "Break Up the Yanks!" *BD*, July 1951, 33–35; Gordon Cobbledick, "Only One Way," *BD*, January 1954, 77–78; Charles Dexter, "Are Yankees Crumbling?" *BD*, February 1958, 11–16; Bill Bryson, "One-Third of Big League Talent Discovered by Three Clubs!" *BD*, May 1958, 67–76; Herbert Simons, "Actual Scouting Reports on 200 Rookies," *BD*, March 1959, 5–14; and Hugh Trader, "Paul Richards Says Yanks Need 5 Pitchers!" *BD*, December–January 1959–60, 5–7. See also Paul Richards, "Why the American League Is Dying," *Look*, February 17, 1959, 41–47. According to Shirley Povich, "Yankee scouts are the most active and also the most discriminating. They don't trifle with good-field, no-hit minor leaguers. They don't trust other farm systems to develop Yankees. . . . Yet, the Yankees know how to patch, too, when their position is desperate" ("Break Up the Yanks!" *BD*, July 1951, 35).

28. U.S. Department of Commerce, *Seventeenth Census*, vol. 2.

29. U.S. Congress, *Organized Baseball: Report*, 85, 95, 194, 197. The *Baseball Digest* ran several articles detailing the Browns' situation: Gordon Cobbledick, "Browns Get Fantastic Prices," *BD*, February 1949, 59–60; J. Roy Stockton, "Cards Decline to Help Browns," *BD*, November 1950, 41–42; Francis Stann, "It's 'Buy the Browns' Time Again," *BD*, March 1951, 35–36; Franklin Lewis, "DeWitts

Proved Shrewd Dealers, BD, September 1951, 99–100; Ben Epstein, "Million Dollar Dealer," BD, April 1956, 43–44; and Hugh Bradley, "He's Traded Three Million in Talent," BD, March 1962, 63–66.

30. Lyall Smith, "What Did the Browns Expect?" BD, September 1948, 51.

31. H. G. Salsinger, "No Chance for N.L. in Detroit," BD, April 1953, 23.

32. J. G. Taylor Spink, "Full Story of Browns' Near-Shift in '41," SN, August 31, 1949, 3–4, 10, 17; Ray Gillespie, "Coast Missed Major Ball by Day in '41," SN, December 4, 1957, 5–6; and U.S. Congress, Organized Baseball: Report, 76, 107, 196. Historian Charles Alexander believes that Barnes was overly optimistic regarding air travel in the early 1940s, believing that convenient air travel only arose in 1957 with the introduction of the Boeing 707 jetliner (Our Game, 293). The Spink article discussed the mechanics of air travel, stating that Barnes and the schedule maker arranged that American League teams would only have to fly out to the coast once per season, with the remaining two coast visits being by train and aided by an open date in the schedule. One of the biggest fears was the risk of an airplane crash; to forestall concern, the teams were to fly out on separate flights, three or four players per flight (J. G. Spink, "Full Story of Browns' Near-Shift," SN, August 31, 1949, 10, 19; and Joe King, "British Air Disaster Stuns N.L., but Won't Halt Season's Flying," SN, February 19, 1958, 9). Sportswriters H. G. Salsinger and Al Wolf described Barnes's potential difficulties in compensating Pacific Coast League owners for the invasion of Los Angeles (H. G. Salsinger, "Post-War Plan: War?" BD, November 1944, 21–22; and Al Wolf, "Coast Deal a Long Way Off," BD, October 1947, 17–18).

33. Gordon Cobbledick, "Three Still Block Veeck," BD, September 1953, 59–60.

34. Joe Williams, "The Weiss Side," BD, May 1954, 58.

35. Seymour, Baseball: The Golden Age, 243.

36. "Things Are Looking Up for the Americans," SI, April 18, 1966, 74; and Joseph Durso, "Baltimore Triumphs, 8–2, after Losing 8–5, in 10," NYT, September 21, 1964, 40.

37. Sporting News, Sporting News Complete Baseball Record Book—1998, 255; Milton Gross, "Mack's Deal No Boon," BD, November 1950, 69–70; and Connie Mack, "Connie Mack Reveals—Why I Broke Up 1932 A's," BD, August 1951, 26–28.

38. Dick Gordon, "Did Twin Cities Double Deal Selves Out of Big League Ball?" BD, March 1958, 19.

39. Sullivan, Dodgers Move West, 43; and Bob Hunter, "Sky's Still Limit for Dodgers' Bonus Babies," SN, January 6, 1960, 2.

40. Veeck, Hustler's Handbook, 303–4, 308.

41. "League to Discuss Athletics' Plight," NYT, October 12, 1954, pt. 3, 32; "Cash Bid Decisive Factor in Authorization of Athletics' Shift to Kansas City," NYT, October 14, 1954, 39; John Drebinger, "Athletics' Transfer to Kansas City

Wins Final Answer," *NYT*, November 9, 1954, 33; and Arch Ward, "Senator Official Challenges A's Shift," *CT*, October 14, 1954, pt. 6, 1.

42. Shirley Povich, "Flirtations Are Over, but Senators' Coast Infatuation Lingers," *SN*, October 31, 1956, 9; and Harry Simmons, "Dodger-Giant Shift Boosts NL Travel 90 Pct," *SN*, September 4, 1957, 1, 6.

43. Frank Finch, "Veeck's Westward Ho! Project Stirs Fans," *SN*, September 2, 1953, 5–6; and Ray Gillespie, "Prospector Veeck Maps His Report on New Homesites," *SN*, September 2, 1953, 6.

44. Edgar Williams, "Lowdown on Baltimore, *BD*, May 1954, 57–62.

45. Sporting News, *Sporting News Complete Baseball Record Book—1998*, 218–335. These facts are similar to attendance information found in Thorn, Palmer, Gershman, *The Official Encyclopedia*, 105–9.

46. Quinn and Surdam, "Case of the Missing Fans."

47. U.S. Senate, *Professional Sports Antitrust Bill—1964*, 33.

48. U.S. Senate, *Organized Professional Team Sports* (1960), 149. Several articles dealt with the various proposals: J. G. Taylor Spink, "Game Moves to End Talent Hoarding," *SN*, July 21, 1954, 1–2; "Unrestricted Draft Seen Almost Certain," *SN*, October 30, 1957, 7; "New Fire Kindled Under Talent-Freeze," *SN*, May 1, 1957, 1–2; Dan Daniel, "'Free Agent Draft' Planned to Aid Minors," *SN*, June 6, 1956, 1–2; and "'Free Draft Directed at Farms'—Weiss," *SN*, November 27, 1957, 1–2.

49. "Baseball Businessman," *Forbes*, August 1, 1951, 12–17.

50. Paul Richards, "Why the American League Is Dying," *Look*, February 17, 1959, 41. See also Til Ferdenzi, "Yanks' Victory Habits Big Sales Point to Kids, Says Scout Boss," *SN*, November 21, 1964, 14; and Hal Lebovitz, "Tribe's 300,000 Gate Drop Blames on Yanks' Runaway," *SN*, September 19, 1956, 9.

51. Roy Terrell, "Yankee Secrets?" *SI*, July 22, 1957, 9.

52. Roy Terrell, "Yankee Secrets?" *SI*, July 22, 1957, 9–10.

53. Dan Daniel, "Hamey Meeting New Challenge Like a Pro," *SN*, November 23, 1960, 5.

54. Dan Daniel, "Hamey Keeps Pledge, Fights Cash with Cash," *SN*, December 7, 1960, 5. See also Dan Daniel, "Yanks Off Bonus Market, Weiss Says, Except If Player Is 'Ready,'" *SN*, August 22, 1956, 2; Gordon Cobbledick, "Only One Way to Overthrow Yankees," *BD*, January 1954, 77–78; Paul Richards, "Why the American League Is Dying," *Look*, February 17, 1959, 37–44; and U.S. Congress, *Organized Professional Team Sports*, 2053.

55. Ernest Mehl, "Carroll Suggest Free-Agent Draft," *SN*, February 18, 1959, 1, 8.

56. U.S. Senate, *Organized Professional Team Sports* (1960), 150.

57. Lowell Reidenbaugh, "Majors Pick Only Nine in Draft Downtrend," *SN*, December 12, 1956, 13; Lowell Reidenbaugh, "Majors Nab Six Hurlers in 11-Player Draft," *SN*, December 11, 1957, 11–12; Oscar Kahan, "Minors Vote Unrestricted

Draft Trial," *SN*, December 10, 1958, 11; and Oscar Kahan, "One Rookie, 13 Others Picked Up in Draft," *SN*, December 9, 1959, 11–12.

58. Paul Richards, "Why the American League Is Dying," *Look*, February 17, 1959, 37–44.

59. Hal Lebovitz, "Draft Rule Change Biggest Step since Farms," *SN*, November 12, 1958, 13; and Clifford Kachline, "Minors Vote Unrestricted Draft Trial," *SN*, December 10, 1958, 9.

60. Dan Daniel, "Weiss Blasts Draft of First-Year Men as 'Radical, Selfish,'" *SN*, December 3, 1958, 10.

61. Oscar Kahan, "Kill First-Year Rule, Ten Clubs Urge," *SN*, April 11, 1964, 1–2, 6; and Barry Kremenko, "Free Agent Draft by Spring of '64—That's Frick's Goal," *SN*, April 4, 1964, 10.

62. Jerome Holtzman, "Majors Split on Free-Agent Draft, Table Plan," *SN*, August 22, 1964, 22.

63. Leonard Koppett, "Baseball's New Draft: Two Views," *NYT*, June 6, 1965, sec. 5, 3.

64. Thomas, "Baseball's Amateur Draft," 92–96.

65. Another way to examine this is to look at the standard deviations of the teams' indexed total baseball ranking (TBR)—that is, each team's TBR divided by the mean TBR. The standard deviation dropped from .555 during 1919–45 to .442 during 1946–64 to .305 between 1965 and 1995. As more Major League teams developed farm systems, the standard deviation fell.

66. See Pluto, *Curse of Colavito*, for an account of Cleveland's version of the Red Sox's "curse of the Bambino." Between Herb Score's eye and arm injuries to Frank Lane trading Rocky Colavito for a prematurely aging Harvey Kuenn, the Indians fell into a thirty-year funk.

8. The Major League Cartel

1. U.S. Senate, *Organized Professional Team Sports* (1958), 315.

2. U.S. Senate, *Organized Professional Team Sports* (1959), 222.

3. Scherer and Ross, *Industrial Market Structure*, 392.

4. Smiley, "Empirical Evidence," 167–80.

5. Craig, *Organized Baseball*, vii.

6. Areeda and Turner, "Predatory Pricing," 697–733; and Koller, "Myth of Predatory Pricing," 105–23.

7. Davis, "Self-Regulation in Baseball."

8. Burk, *Never Just a Game*, 62–64.

9. U.S. Congress, *Organized Baseball: Report*, 29–30.

10. U.S. Congress, *Organized Baseball: Report*, 31. See also Scully, *Business of Major League Baseball*, 2, for a discussion of the evolving property rights.

11. "Gardella, Staking Future in Mexican Loop, Hits Back at Giants for 'Shabby Treatment,'" *SN*, February 28, 1946, 14.

12. A. Van Pelt, "Demand for O.B. Files Withdrawn in Gardella Case," *SN*, August 31, 1949, 13; and Hy Turkin, "Gardella's Counsel to Seek More Data from Chandler," *SN*, September 28, 1949, 2.

13. Bob Broeg, "'Games Need Reserve Clause'—Lanier," *SN*, September 28, 1949, 1–2; and Dan Daniel, "Gardella Drops His Suit, Will Sign with Cardinals," *SN*, October 19, 1949, 2.

14. Herbert Simons, "Farm Foe O'Connor Grabs a Plow," *BD*, March 1946, 17–18.

15. Topkis, "Monopoly in Professional Sports," 702.

16. Bob Stevens, "$900,000 Poultice Soothes Coast Loop," *SN*, December 11, 1957, 13.

17. Al Stump, "Rebel Man of the Minors," *BD*, November 1948, 65–70.

18. U.S. Senate, *Organized Professional Team Sports* (1958), 101.

19. U.S. Senate, *Organized Professional Team Sports* (1958), 183.

20. U.S. Senate, *Organized Professional Team Sports* (1958), 188.

21. Rottenberg, "Baseball Players' Labor Market."

22. H. G. Salsinger, "Contrast in Skill Snag Player Unions," *SN*, April 25, 1946, 3.

23. Dan Daniel, "Television Clause Snags Player Contract," *SN*, September 25, 1946, 1–2; and Dan Daniel, "Executive Council Votes to Hike Players' Minimum Pay to $7,000," *SN*, October 9, 1957, 7.

24. Occasionally, fans thought retired players received munificent benefits from the pension. Frank Scott, chief of the players' central office, clarified that players wanted an increase from $175 to $225 in their monthly pensions. Players with twenty years of service would get $350 per month at age sixty-five (Dan Daniel, "Game's Prestige Growing with Pension Plan," *SN*, July 25, 1962, 7; and Dan Daniel, "Scott Sets Record Straight on Player Pension Demands," *SN*, August 16, 1961, 9).

25. U.S. Senate, *Organized Professional Team Sports* (1958), 24–73.

26. U.S. Senate, *Organized Professional Team Sports* (1958), 711.

27. Dave Brady, "Player Rep Friend Raps Proposal That Athletes Form Labor Union," *SN*, August 3, 1963, 1, 4.

28. U.S. Senate, *Professional Sports Antitrust Bill—1964*, 42.

29. Burk, *Much More than a Game*, 123–24; and Miller, *Whole Different Ball Game*, 6–8.

30. U.S. Senate, *Professional Sports Antitrust Bill—1965*, 144.

31. U.S. Congress, *Organized Baseball: Report*, 76, 196; and Topkis, "Monopoly in Professional Sports," 701.

32. J. G. Taylor Spink, "Full Story of Browns' Near-Shift in '41," *SN* August 31, 1949, 3–4, 10, 17; U.S. Congress, *Organized Baseball: Report*, 76; and White, *Creating the National Pastime*, 321.

33. See Harry Palmer, "Consolidation: A League Official's Views upon the

Subject," *Sporting Life*, June 8, 1887, 2, for consolidation movement in the 1880s. See Levine, *A. G. Spalding*, 55–56; and Seymour, *Baseball: The Golden Age*, 230, for thoughts about expanding and incorporating some Federal League clubs.

34. U.S. Department of Commerce, *Twelfth Census*, 430–32.

35. U.S. Department of Commerce, *Historical Statistics*, 1:244; and Dodd, *Historical Statistics*, 1:243–45.

36. Dan Daniel, "Plans for Expansion Placed on Shelf in New York Sessions," sn, February 9, 1955, 21; Dan Daniel, "'Game Facing Its Most Critical Period'—Frick," sn, July 17, 1957, 5; Dan Daniel, "Yanks Ridicule New York's Third Major Idea," sn, November 26, 1958, 5; Joe King, "'Enough Players to Go Around,' Lane Tells 10-Club Opponents," sn, February 9, 1955, 21; Edgar Munzel, "Realignment Group Tells AL Ten-Club League Is Feasible," sn, March 23, 1955, 17; Carl Lundquist, "'Third Major League Coming,' Says Frick," sn, March 7, 1956, 3; Bill Corum, "Corum Says Majors Could Miss Boat on the Coast by 'Dawdling,'" sn, March 21, 1956, 13; and J. G. Taylor Spink, "'Third Major Must Come Soon'—Rickey," May 21, 1958, 1–2.

37. U.S. Department of Commerce, *Seventeenth Census*, 1:65, 74.

38. Jack Gallagher, "Houston Ready to Join NY in Bid to NL," sn, November 26, 1958, 3; Jack Gallagher, "Houston Well on Way to Majors, Webb Says," sn, December 3, 1958, 7; and J. G. Taylor Spink, "Cards to Sell Houston Franchise: 'Would Co-Operate' in Major Bid," sn, November 26, 1958, 3.

39. Quirk, "Economic Analysis," 47.

40. Voigt, *American Baseball: From Gentleman's Sport*, 69, 121; Spalding, *America's National Game*, 312–13; "The League Championship," *New York Clipper*, September 30, 1876, 211; and "The League Association," *New York Clipper*, September 30, 1876, 213.

41. J. G. Taylor Spink, "Majors Girding for Battle over NY," sn, December 25, 1957, 2.

42. Harold Rosenthal, "Doors Left Ajar for NL Return to New York," sn, February 5, 1958, 13.

43. Earl Lawson, "Parking Lag Spurs Crosley's Warning of Franchise Shift," sn, January 8, 1958, 9; and Dan Daniel, "Third Loop Yelps over Report NL Wants New York," May 11, 1960, 6.

44. Dan Daniel, "3rd Loop Faces 'Name' Player Hurdle," sn, July 1, 1959, 1–2, 10; "Third Leaguers Putting Majors on Spot," sn, August 5, 1959, 7–8; and "11 Other Prospective Cities for New Circuit," sn, August 5, 1959, 7–8.

45. U.S. Senate, *Organized Professional Team Sports* (1960), 14.

46. Oscar Kahan, "Mahatma Dares Majors to Attempt Expansion," sn, December 16, 1959, 9, 12.

47. Oscar Kahan, "Mahatma Dares Majors to Attempt Expansion," sn, December 16, 1959, 9, 12.

48. Herbert Simons, "Continental—or Just Plain con?" BD, October–November

1959, 67–70. See also Gordon Cobbledick, "Accent's Still on the 'Con,'" *BD*, August 1960, 83–84; and Furman Bisher, "Not a Case for Charity," *BD*, August 1960, 85–86.

49. U.S. Senate, *Organized Professional Team Sports* (1959), 161. See also Dan Daniel, "Shea Says Third League Will Recruit Young Talent," *SN*, July 29, 1959, 7; and Dick Young, "Talent No Problem, 'It Will Come from the World,'" *SN*, July 1, 1959, 10.

50. U.S. Senate, *Organized Professional Team Sports* (1959), 73, 78; and U.S. Senate, *Organized Professional Team Sports* (1960), 124.

51. Dan Daniel, "Majors Flash Green Light to Third League," *SN*, August 26, 1959, 2.

52. U.S. Senate, *Organized Professional Team Sports* (1959), 76; and Dan Daniel, "Majors Flash Green Light to Third League," *SN*, August 26, 1959, 2, 8.

53. Dan Daniel, "Gigantic Headache Looms as Promoters Begin Uphill Climb," *SN*, September 2, 1959, 15–17.

54. Shirley Povich, "Continental Sure to Collapse, Says Top Observers," *SN*, December 16, 1959, 10 and 16.

55. U.S. Senate, *Organized Professional Team Sports* (1960), 18.

56. U.S. Senate, *Organized Professional Team Sports* (1960), 102.

57. J. G. Taylor Spink, "Nats Will Shift to Minneapolis," *SN*, October 7, 1959, 1, 4.

58. Dan Daniel, "Owners Hungry for New 100-Grand Stars," *SN*, February 3, 1960, 5.

59. Dan Daniel, "Angry Weiss Puts Up His Dukes for Hot Fight with CL," *SN*, February 24, 1960, 9; and Dan Daniel, "Hot Reactions to NL Bomb on Expansion," *SN*, July 27, 1960, 2, 8.

60. Stanley Frank, "Boss of the Yankees," *Saturday Evening Post*, April 16, 1960, 113.

61. U.S. Senate, *Organized Professional Team Sports* (1958), 239; U.S. Senate, *Organized Professional Team Sports* (1959), 125–29; and U.S. Senate, *Organized Professional Team Sports* (1960), 51, 69.

62. U.S. Senate, *Organized Professional Team Sports* (1960), 15.

63. Dave Brady, "Frick Clears Sacks Testifying against Kefauver Sports Bill," *SN*, May 25, 1960, 9, 14; and Dave Brady, "Rickey, Trautman, Frick Will Testify on Kefauver's Bill," *SN*, May 18, 1960, 7. See also Dan Daniel, "Charges by Rickey Draw Quick Valley from Frick," *SN*, June 22, 1960, 15; and U.S. Senate, *Organized Professional Team Sports* (1960), 39.

64. U.S. Senate, *Organized Professional Team Sports* (1959), 80.

65. U.S. Senate, *Organized Professional Team Sports* (1960), 52.

66. U.S. Senate, *Organized Professional Team Sports* (1959), 161.

67. U.S. Senate, *Organized Professional Team Sports* (1959), 58–61.

68. U.S. Senate, *Organized Professional Team Sports* (1959), 74, 81. For George

Trautman's views, see U.S. Senate, *Organized Professional Team Sports* (1960), 136, 151.

69. U.S. Senate, *Organized Professional Team Sports* (1959), 8, 12.

70. Dave Brady, "C.L. Hopes Fade after Sport Bill's Failure in Senate," sn, July 6, 1960, 8. See also "Changes in Kefauver's Bill Jolts Continental's Chances," sn, June 1, 1960, 13, 16; "C.L. Wins Two Points on Draft Provisions in Kefauver's Bill," sn, June 15, 1960, 4; "Long, Rocky Road ahead for Kefauver Bill; Action Unlikely," sn, June 22, 1960, 15; Bill Paddock, "Frick Blasts Bill Kefauver Claims Would Help C.L.," sn, May 11, 1960, 6, 12; "Kefauver Bill Could Wreck Game," sn, May 18, 1960, 10; and "Continental Hasn't Justified Existence," sn, May 25, 1960, 10.

71. Herbert Simons, "Continental—or Just Plain con?" bd, October–November 1959, 67–70.

72. Dan Daniel, "Frick Warns cl It Must Act in Hurry," sn, July 6, 1960, 8.

73. Dan Daniel, "Frick Warns cl It Must Act in Hurry," 2, 7–8.

74. Bob Hunter, "Frick Fires Expansion Warning in la," sn, November 16, 1960, 1, 4.

75. Jack McDonald, "Harridge Sees No Transfers in al," sn, October 30, 1957, 1–2.

76. Bob Broeg, "Compromise Likely on Territorial Rights," sn, February 5, 1958, 22.

77. Dan Daniel, "Topping Gains New Backers in Coast Pitch," sn, August 24, 1960, 1–2.

78. Dan Daniel, "Yanks Ridicule New York's Third Major Idea," sn, November 26, 1958, 5.

79. Harold Rosenthal, "Doors Left Ajar for nl Return to New York," sn, February 5, 1958, 13; and Joe King, "Los Angeles Tabbed as Two-Team City," sn, January 15, 1958, 1–2.

80. Frederick Lieb, "nl Weighing Expansion to 10 Clubs," sn, July 16, 1958, 1.

81. Dan Daniel, "Yanks Ridicule New York's Third Major Idea," sn, November 26, 1958, 5.

82. Dan Daniel, "al Lays Expansion Groundwork, Will Study Twin-Cities' Request," sn, October 28, 1959, 5–6.

83. Dan Daniel, "al Sets Goal—10-Club Loop for '61—Expansion Out for '60," sn, November 4, 1959, 7.

84. Dan Daniel, "al Sets Goal—10-Club Loop for '61—Expansion Out for '60," sn, November 4, 1960, 7; and Oscar Kahan, "nl Blocks Junior Loop Expansion Plan," sn, December 16, 1959, 5.

85. "First-Year Draft Looks like the Answer," sn, June 1, 1960, 10. For a typical senatorial response, see Senator Joseph O'Mahoney's remarks during the 1958 hearings in U.S. Senate, *Organized Professional Team Sports* (1958), 169, 171.

86. Dan Daniel, "Fans Want Something New, Get It in 9-Club Majors, Inter-Loop Play," sn, November 30, 1960, 1–2; and Shirley Povich, "Now It's Official—Capital's New Nats Open for Business," sn, December 7, 1960, 6.

87. Dan Daniel, "Houston Gets Green Light on Sunday Arc Schedule Next Year," sn, August 11, 1962, 10; George M. Weiss and Robert Shaplen, "Man of Silence Speaks," si, March 6, 1961, 50; and Bob Burnes, "Fan Polls Backs Inter-League Play," sn, February 2, 1963, 1–2.

88. J. G. Taylor Spink, "Majors Must Expand, Writers Concur," sn, November 4, 1959, 1, 14; Clifford Kachline, "Lowdown on Frick Pitch for Inter-Loop Play," sn, September 15, 1962, 2; Frederick Lieb, "Inter-Loop Schedule among Two Proposals Sent to Major Execs," sn, July 21, 1962, 2; Joe King, "al Execs Stir New Demand for Interleague Play," sn, August 17, 1963, 1–2; and Veeck, Veeck as in Wreck, 364–65.

89. Jerome Holtzman, "Big Timers Clearing Decks for Expansion," sn, August 10, 1960, 3–4; and Joe King, "Topping's Pitch for al Club on Coast May Touch Off Row," sn, August 17, 1960, 7.

90. Joe King, "nl Opening Door for Houston-Dallas Likely A. L. Addition," sn, October 19, 1960, 4; Joe King, "al Speeds Expansion—Ten Clubs in '61," sn, November 2, 1960, 3–4; Bill Rives, "Dallas–Ft. Worth Group Picks Site for C.L. Stadium," sn, March 23, 1960, 22; Clark Nealon, "Rich Background Fits Houston for nl Franchise," sn, July 27, 1960, 7, 20; and Clark Nealon and Roy Graham, "Domed All-Weather Parks Planned by Houston, Dallas," sn, August 31, 1960, 13.

91. Dan Daniel, "al Moguls Okay Ten-Club League—Keep Eye on la," sn, September 7, 1960, 4, 9; "Cronin Backed Topping, Webb in Coast Drive," sn, November 9, 1960, 11, 24; and "Webb and Rickey See Peaceful Expansion before '62 Season," sn, September 14, 1960, 9.

92. Ed Prell, "Senior Circuit Grabs New York, Houston," sn, October 26, 1960, 2.

93. Joe King, "Topping's Pitch for nl," sn, August 17, 1960, 7; "al Speeds Expansion," sn, November 2, 1960, 3–4; and "'No More Expansion Surprises,' Says Frick," sn, November 9, 1960, 1, 4.

94. Dan Daniel, "Green Light Reported for al Leap to Coast," sn, December 7, 1960, 1, 6; and Bob Burnes, "Expansion Accord Hailed as Guidepost," sn, December 14, 1960, 1–2. One sportswriter thought that O'Malley might welcome a second team in Los Angeles because a monopoly in a big population center, rather than being an advantage, is a liability (Ed Prell, "Majors to Increase to Ten Each in '62," sn, July 20, 1960, 1–2).

95. Dan Daniel, "Dove of Peace Coos over Expansion Turmoil," sn, November 23, 1960, 11, 32; and Veeck, Veeck as in Wreck, 365–66, 369. For another description of the situation, see Roy Terrell, "Damndest Mess Baseball Has Ever Seen," si, December 19, 1960, 16–19, 60–61.

96. William Leggett, "Success Is Killing the AL," *SI*, September 9, 1963, 20.

97. Melvin Durslag, "Call Them Mickey's Mice," *SI*, July 20, 1964, 45.

98. Carl Felker, "Spink Skeptical of Third Loop; Stresses Scarcity of Top Talent," *SN*, August 5, 1959, 21. See also Francis Stann, "Talent Shortage Delays Majors," *BD*, February 1965, 75–76.

99. Dan Daniel, "'Let's Speed Up Expansion Plan,' DeWitt Tells AL," *SN*, September 21, 1960, 15–16.

100. Edgar Munzel, "NL Expected to Nab Houston and New York," *SN*, July 27, 1960, 1–2.

101. J. G. Taylor Spink, "Talent Supply Plan for 3 Majors Proposed," *SN*, June 1, 1960, 11–12; Oscar Kahan, "Summer Loops for Collegians Proposed," *SN*, December 22, 1962, 1, 4; and Dick Gordon, "30-G Minimum Bonus Urged for Campus Raids," *BD*, 1960, 28–30.

102. Dan Daniel, "Dove of Peace Coos over Expansion Turmoil," *SN*, November 23, 1960, 11, 60.

103. Hy Hurwitz, "'AL Spent Year Laying Expansion Plans,'—O'Connell," *SN*, November 9, 1960, 11; and Joe King, "New Clubs to Find Slab Cupboard Bare," *SN*, December 14, 1960, 11.

104. John Drebinger, "Two American League Clubs Stock Talent in $4,500,000 Draft—3 Yank Pitchers Chosen in Draft," *NYT*, December 15, 1960, 64; and Dan Daniel, "Yanks' Standouts Warming Up for Sizzling Salary Squabbles," *SN*, January 4, 1961, 18.

105. Bob Burnes, "NL Plans Roster Cuts to Stock New Teams," *SN*, January 18, 1961, 2.

106. Donald Janson, "Plan Is Approved for Mets, Colts," *NYT*, June 27, 1961, 36.

107. Dan Daniel, "Majors Hint Move toward Free-Agent Draft," *SN*, July 5, 1961, 5–6; Earl Lawson, "'N.L. Building Solid Base for Two Teams,' Giles Says," *SN*, January 25, 1961, 11; and Donald Janson, "Plan Is Approved for Mets, Colts," *NYT*, June 27, 1961, 36.

108. Clifford Kachline, "NL Brass Backs Player Pool—As Good as AL's," *SN*, October 11, 1961, 4; and Bob Burnes, "Draft Gives Colts, Mets Solid Sendoff," *SN*, October 18, 1961, 7–8.

109. Oscar Kahan, "Big Times Heed Expansion Clubs' Plea, Grant Help," *SN*, December 14, 1963, 1–2; and Clifford Kachline, "Majors Veto Aid Pitch for Expansion Clubs," *SN*, December 19, 1964, 7, 20.

110. Bob Burnes, "Further Expansion Likely for Big Time," *SN*, November 29, 1961, 1, 4; Clifford Kachline, "Frick Calls for Expansion Blueprint," *SN*, December 21, 1963, 1–2; Lloyd McGowan, "Montreal in Majors? 'Could Be, with New Park,' Simmons Says," *SN*, September 7, 1963, 8; and Carl Lundquist, "Summit Meetings Set Up to Air Shifts, Possible 12-Club Loops," *SN*, October 24, 1964, 4.

9. The Sixteen-Headed Hydra

1. Glick, "Professional Sports Franchise Movements," 80.

2. Edgar Munzel, "1955 Chart Adds $52,360 to Traveling Costs in AL," SN, January 19, 1955, 19; Dan Daniel, "Majors Study 'Dry Run' 10-Club Chart," SN, February 2, 1955, 1–2; and Voigt, *American Baseball: From the Commissioners*, 129.

3. U.S. Senate, *Organized Professional Team Sports* (1959), 180.

4. Robert Creamer, "Alas, Poor Giants!" SI, May 20, 1957, 36.

5. SN, as well as other periodicals, amply described the Dodgers and Giants flight to California (Joe King, "Brooks Threaten to 'Go Elsewhere,'" SN, January 9, 1957, 1; Joe King, "Majors' Travel Coasts Soar as Gate Prices Lag," SN, February 27, 1957, 15; Rube Samuelsen, "LA Territory Rights Rich Prize for Bums," SN, February 27, 1957, 15; Dan Daniel, "Giants Put Wheels in Motion for Coast," SN, August 28, 1957, 3; Roscoe McGowen, "Brooklyn Still in NL? Twin Signs Indicate Club Will Stay," SN, September 18, 1957, 9; Roscoe McGowen, "'Next Year' for Dodgers Means California," SN, October 16, 1957, 3–4; Edgar Munzel, "Bargaining over New York Territory Looms," SN, October 9, 1957, 7). The best book on the Dodgers move is Sullivan, *Dodgers Move West*.

6. Bob Stevens, "$900,000 Poultice Soothes Coast Loop," SN, December 11, 1957, 13; and Jack Walsh, "'Don't Expect Dole,' Continental Warned in Sizeup by Frick," SN, January 20, 1960, 7.

7. Frank Finch, "O'Malley Aims at Gate Record in Coliseum," SN, January 29, 1958, 5; and "Mayor's Letter Sealing Deal Spells Out 'Frisco Proposal," SN, August 14, 1957, 4.

8. "Giant Subsidy: It Points Up a Dangerous Trend in Municipal Finance," *Barron's*, August 26, 1957, 1.

9. "Business Side of Baseball," 170; Riess, *Sport in Industrial America*, 168; U.S. Congress, *Organized Baseball: Report*, 75–76, 85, 145, 195, 200–202.

10. U.S. Congress, *Organized Baseball: Hearings*, 1620–24; Henderson, "Los Angeles," 262; and Al Wolf, "P. C. L. Jittery," BD, November 1951, 11–12.

11. "Cash Bid Decisive Factor in Authorization of Athletics' Shift to Kansas," NYT, October 14, 1954, 40. See also Ed Prell, "Harridge Urges Decision Today on Athletics' Future," CT, October 12, 1954, pt. 3, 1. The original Washington Senators considered relocating to California, but owner Calvin Griffith's sentimental ties to Washington DC and pressure from congressmen and President Eisenhower deterred the move.

12. Jack McDonald, "Harridge Sees No Transfer in AL," SN, October 30, 1957, 2.

13. White, *Creating the National Pastime*, 298, 301, 321. Wrigley's quote is in U.S. Congress, *Organized Baseball: Hearings*, 724.

14. Dick Young, "N.L. Finding Rich Gravy in L.A. Bowl," SN, April 30, 1958, 1.

15. C. C. Johnson Spink, "Dodgers Advance Sales Soaring to Record," SN, January 29, 1958, 1–2.

16. Frank Finch, "O'Malley Aims at Gate Record," SN, January 29, 1958, 5.

17. Bob Hunter, "Selling Dodger Ducats—Job for a Magician," SN, October 28, 1959, 7; and James Murray, "The $3,300,000 Smile," SI, February 29, 1960, 54.

18. Bob Hunter, "Dodgers Season Sales of Tickets Top $3 Million," SN, November 22, 1961, 9; and "Dodgers, Giants Stir LA Box-Office Boom," SN, June 2, 1962, 15.

19. Veeck, *Hustler's Handbook*, 306.

20. U.S. Senate, *Organized Professional Team Sports* (1958), 171, 466; and Dan Daniel, "Frick Questioned on Shifts to West and Nat Situation," SN, July 30, 1958, 8.

21. Jack Walsh, "Celler Warns against Washington Exit," SN, September 3, 1958, 5.

22. U.S. Senate, *Organized Professional Team Sports* (1958), 315, 317.

23. Halsey Hall, "Minneapolis Winds Up for Big League Pitch," SN, September 3, 1958, 5; Halsey Hall, "Minneapolis Clears Snag on Majors Bid," SN, September 10, 1958, 9; and Jack Walsh, "Celler Warns against Washington Exit," SN, September 3, 1958, 6.

24. "Baseball Candor via Air Vent," SI, September 22, 1958, 20.

25. Shirley Povich, "Sound Reasons for Rejecting Nat Shift Bid," SN, October 28, 1959, 5–6, 10, 12.

26. Bob Addie, "Nats Barely Made It—Transfer Backed by Minimum of Six Votes," SN, November 2, 1960, 7, 10.

27. Walter Bingham, "No Feud like an Old Feud," SI, May 1, 1961, 50.

28. Walter Bingham, "No Feud like an Old Feud," SI, May 1, 1961, 51.

29. Bob Inserra, "Now It's Fish That Calvin Has to Worry About," SN, May 24, 1961, 7.

30. Roy Gillespie, "54 Clubs Invited to Realignment Meet," SN, November 5, 1958, 1–2.

31. Ernest Mehl, "Johnson Estate Tax May Force Sale of A's," SN, June 29, 1960, 1, 6.

32. Ernest Mehl, "Fans Toss Full Force into A's Turnstile Drive," SN, August 24, 1960, 10. See also Ernest Mehl, "Johnson Estate Tax," SN, June 29, 1960, 1, 6; "Kaycee Preparing for Battle of Bucks to Retain Franchise," SN, July 6, 1960, 27; "Kaycee's Sale Likely before End of Season," SN, August 3, 1960, 17; and "Fans Flock to Back Kaycee's Drive for Hefty Gate Figure," SN, August 17, 1960, 20.

33. Ernest Mehl, "'A's Will Develop Stars and Keep Them'—Finley," SN, December 28, 1960, 7, 14.

34. Ernest Mehl, "Big Spender Finley Offers New Comfort for A's Fans," SN, March 15, 1961, 5.

35. Edgar Munzel, "Majors Guarantee to Back 100 Minor Clubs," *SN*, June 2, 1962, 13.

36. Ernest Mehl, "A's Fans Ask Showdown on Shift," *SN*, June 2, 1962, 1, 4.

37. "Finley Clamps Tight Budget on A's after $1,500,000 Deficit in 1962," *SN*, October 20, 1962, 25.

38. Joe McGuff, "A's Cancellation Clause, Based on Attendance, to Be Challenged," *SN*, June 22, 1963, 19, "Talk of Shift Pitch Angers Kaycee Fans," July 20, 1963, 3, 6; "A's Boss Captures Headlines—Remains Riddle to Kaycee Fans," *SN*, July 27, 1963, 1–2; "A's to Stay if They Get a Suitable Lease," *SN*, October 5, 1963, 14; and "Where's Finley? City Manager Waiting to Talk on A's Lease," *SN*, November 9, 1963, 20; and Ernest Mehl, "'No Plea Made to Shift A's,'—Finley," *SN*, August 31, 1963, 2.

39. U.S. Senate, *Professional Sports Antitrust Bill—1964*, 5. See also U.S. Senate, *Professional Sports Antitrust Bill—1964*, 6, 20, 137–38; Dave Brady, "'Courts Would Back A.L., Not Finley,'—Frick," *SN*, February 15, 1964, 1, 4; C. C. Johnson Spink, "Will US Senators Go to Bat for Kaycee Again?" August 3, 1963, 1–2; and C. C. Johnson Spink, "'A's Stay in Kaycee—if . . . ,' Says Finley," November 2, 1963, 1, 4.

40. U.S. Senate, *Professional Sports Antitrust Bill—1964*, 22.

41. U.S. Senate, *Professional Sports Antitrust Bill—1964*, 25.

42. Clifford Kachline, "AL Ready to Bid Finley Farwell," *SN*, January 18, 1964, 1–2 and 4; and Joe King, "'Ink Kaycee Pact or Lose AL Franchise,' Owners Tell Finley," *SN*, January 25, 1964, 4.

43. Joe McGuff, "Finley Sets Lease Terms for A's Park," *SN*, January 4, 1964, 18; "Kaycee and Finley Play Catch—Wild Pitches Fly All over Lot," *SN*, January 11, 1964, 8; "Kaycee Wonders: Has Charley Gone about as Far as He Can Go?" *SN*, January 18, 1964, 2; "Mayor, Senator, City Manager, Man in Street—They All Hail AL action on K.C.," *SN*, February 1, 1964, 1–2 and 6; "AL Grants Finley 2-Week Extension on Kaycee Deadline," *SN*, February 8, 1964, 6; "Ticket Sales Drag as Finley and K.C. Haggle over Lease," *SN*, February 15, 1964, 4; "Box Score of A's Lease Proposals," *SN*, January 11, 1964, 8; and Ernst Mehl, "White Flag Hoisted by Finley—Can Kaycee Rebuild Fan Faith?" *SN*, March 7, 1964, 8.

44. George Ross, "Oakland Answers 'Yoo-Hoo' by Finley," *SN*, July 20, 1963, 3, 6; "Nod from A.L. Would Unroll Oakland Red Carpet for Finley," *SN*, February 8, 1964, 6; David Condon, "Finley Says A.L. Will Okay A's Shift," *SN*, July 27, 1963, 1 and 4; Rob Holbrook, "A.L. Work Out Sked That Would Include Oakland," *SN*, July 27, 1963, 1–2; Hal Lebovitz, "Horace Let Finley's Cat Out of the Bag," *SN*, July 20, 1963, 3, 6.

45. Joe McGuff, "Kaycee Fans Brace for Yearly Crisis—Finley Eyeing Move," *SN*, October 24, 1964, 20; Joe McGuff, "A's Price Tag Too High," *SN*, October 3, 1964, 20; and C. C. Johnson Spink, "Finley Frets over 'Apathy' in Kaycee," *SN*, December 26, 1964, 1–2. The relocation of the Kansas City Athletics to Oakland

was disappointing in terms of attendance, given that the A's as Finley renamed them were one of the most colorful teams ever. They won five consecutive West Division titles between 1971 and 1975, but the fans failed to respond. Finley struggled to draw even one million fans in any season and finally resorted to Connie Mack's tactic: selling star players. Finley's efforts to sell his stars were stymied by baseball commissioner Bowie Kuhn. Oakland struggled to stay afloat, until Finley sold the team to Walter Haas in 1980. Since then, the A's have had some fine teams, such as the 1988–92 teams, and finally have drawn up to 2.9 million fans in a season. Finley's woes were reflected by the Stoneham family's subsequent troubles in San Francisco. Thus, the Bay Area has had a turbulent history in supporting two Major League teams. At this point Oakland and San Francisco appear to be capable of supporting their teams.

46. "Braves Set National League Attendance Mark," *NYT*, September 21, 1953, 29; and Edgar Munzel, "Braves' Bonanza to Start Trend to Rich Rural Area, Says Giles," *SN*, September 30, 1953, 37.

47. Bob Broeg, "Braves' Doorbell Rings—It's Atlanta," *SN*, August 3, 1963, 7.

48. Bob Broeg, "Braves' Doorbell Rings—It's Atlanta," *SN*, August 3, 1963, 7.

49. Lester Smith, "Yawkey Pulls Tight Curtain on Bosox Financial Figures," *SN*, October 18, 1961, 2; and Bob Wolf, "Braves' Brass Stung by Four-Year Skid," *SN*, October 18, 1961, 1–2.

50. Walter Bingham, "No More Joy in Beertown," *SI*, July 23, 1962, 40.

51. "Log of Play-by-Play Broadcasts and Telecasts," *SN*, April 13, 1960, 27; "Seating Capacities and Price Ranges for Major League Clubs," *SN*, April 12, 1961, 25; Bob Wolf, "Braves' Payroll Bulging—Tabbed as Heaviest in A.L.," *SN*, February 7, 1962, 9; and Lester Smith, "Stockholders Hear Perini and McHale Tell Braves' Plans," *SN*, May 9, 1962, 16.

52. Bob Wolf, "Will Braves Stay in Milwaukee? 'It's Up to Fans,' Perini Declares," *SN*, September 22, 1962, 11; "Last L'il Steam Shovel Chugs into Barn," *SN*, December 1, 1962, 11, 16; "Braves Sizing up Teepee for Teevee," *SN*, December 29, 1962, 9; and Lester Smith, "Atlanta Shift Story Boosts Demand for Braves Stock," *SN*, August 15, 1964, 33. For a description of the economics of the Braves sale, see Veeck, *Hustler's Handbook*, 330–39.

53. Bob Broeg, "Braves' Doorbell Rings—It's Atlanta," *SN*, August 3, 1963, 7; Clifford Kachline, "Atlanta Whiffs, Renews Bid for Big-Time Clubs," *SN*, July 20, 1963, 3, 6; and Ernest Mehl, "K.C. Ranked Right behind Atlanta as Lush Video Market," *SN*, October 24, 1964, 4.

54. John Logue, "Atlanta's Stadium Zooms Off Ground, Heads for Reality," *SN*, June 22, 1963, 4.

55. Bob Wolf, "Civic Leaders Saved Braves for Milwaukee," *SN*, October 5, 1963, 25.

56. Bob Wolf, "Braves Report $43,379 Deficit to Stockholders," *SN*, December 28, 1963, 17, 24; Veeck, *Hustler's Handbook*, 301; Furman Bisher, "Atlanta Votes Speedy Okay on New Park," *SN*, March 21, 1964, 4; Furman Bisher, "'Give Us Braves or Nobody,' Says Mayor, Willing to Wait," *SN*, November 7, 1964, 7; and John Logue, "Atlanta's Mayor Says Lips Are Sealed—until October," *SN*, July 18, 1964, 9–10.

57. Bob Wolf, "Rowdies Run Wild at Braves' Opener," *SN*, May 9, 1964, 17.

58. Quoted in Bill Fleischman, "Braves Will Claim Half a Million Loss in '64 Tax Returns," *SN*, November 14, 1964, 4; Chuck Johnson, "Can Braves Draw One Million? Signs Appear Favorable," *SN*, April 25, 1964, 19; and Bob Wolf, "Quinn's Advice to Milwaukee—'Let the Braves Go to Atlanta Now,'" *SN*, December 26, 1964, 6.

59. C. C. Johnson Spink, "Braves' Shift Needs Only Okay by NL," *SN*, July 11, 1964, 1. National League president Warren Giles also echoed the view that the Twins hurt the Braves ("'Twins Hurt Milwaukee Gate'—Giles," *SN*, July 18, 1964, 10).

60. Veeck, *Hustler's Handbook*, 316; and Lester Smith, "Atlanta Shift Story," *SN*, August 15, 1964, 33.

61. Bob Wolf, "Braves' Fans Bitter, Confused by Short Shrift," *SN*, July 18, 1964, 9.

62. Bob Wolf, "Milwaukee Solon Wants TV Pool, Expansion; Frick Vetoes Idea," *SN*, August 1, 1964, 11; Bob Wolf, "Legal Red Tape Snarls Braves' Moving Plan," *SN*, November 7, 1964, 7; and Veeck, *Hustler's Handbook*, 323–24.

63. Bob Wolf, "'Unpack,' NL Tells Itchy-Footed Braves," *SN*, November 21, 1964, 7–8.

64. U.S. Senate, *Professional Sports Antitrust Bill—1965*, 103, 106. See also U.S. Senate, *Professional Sports Antitrust Bill—1965*, 44.

65. Bob Wolf, "Braves Drop Seven Wisconsin Citizens from Board Posts," *SN*, December 26, 1964, 6.

66. Max Nichols, "A.L. in Milwaukee? Fine Idea, Cal Says," *SN*, November 7, 1964, 2.

67. Robert Creamer, "Indian Summer," *SI*, June 4, 1956, 40.

68. The scorecards did not reveal prices for other seats between 1947 and 1952. Between 1947 and 1952, however, box seats rose from $2.00 to $2.25, and reserved seats increased from $1.50 to $1.65. Unreserved grandstand seats went for $1.20 in 1947 and $1.25 in 1955, the only times the scorecards listed these prices. Bleachers remained $0.60 from 1947 until at least 1957 (Cleveland baseball team scorecards, 1947–57).

69. Bob Broeg, "Braves' Doorbell Rings—It's Atlanta," *SN*, August 3, 1963, 7; and Bob Burnes, "What's Wrong with Cleveland? Nothing a Contender Couldn't Sure," *SN*, August 24, 1963, 26–27.

70. Regis McAuley, "Other Owners Would Block Transfer, Cleveland Says,"

SN, September 12, 1964, 7; "Board Will Meet Soon to Decide Whether Injuns Quit Cleveland," SN, September 19, 1964, 10; and "Mayor of Cleveland Leads All-Out Fight to Save Franchise," SN, September 26, 1964, 10.

71. Hy Zimmerman, "Rich Seattle Lode Lures Majors' Prospectors," SN, September 21, 1963, 1–2; "Season Ticket Sales Already Underway in Northwest City," SN, September 12, 1964, 7; "Seattle 'Secret' Out: City Trying to Land Indians," SN, October 3, 1964, 18; and "Seattle Snags Up Tickets in Drive to Land Indians," SN, October 10, 1964, 23.

72. J. G. Taylor Spink, "Majors Move to Shake Bonus Ills," SN, January 12, 1949, 1, 6.

73. Joe King, "Hamey Cites Twin Target in New Bonus Rule," SN, July 12, 1961, 17, 20. See also Kelley, *Baseball's Biggest Blunder*, for a detailed examination of the bonus rule of 1953–57 and its effects. For chicanery involving bonus babies, see Lyall Smith, "Onus on the Bonus," BD, June 1950, 27–28. For the efficacy of paying bonuses to untried amateurs, see Lyall Smith, "Three Clubs Hit $600,000 Pay," BD, March 1951, 73–74; and Bill Bryson, "Only One of Ten Pays Off!" BD, April 1958, 5–9.

74. Koufax and Linn, *Koufax*, 65–73.

75. Bill Conlin, "Phil's Exec Calls Free Agent," BD, May 1968, 45–46; Dan Daniel, "Yanks Off Bonus Market, Weiss Says, Except if Player Is 'Ready,'" SN, August 22, 1956, 2; Clifford Kachline, "Collectors' Item—Bonus Kids—to Come Up for Grabs in Draft," SN, November 28, 1956, 6; Joe King, "Few Prize Pay-Offs in Bonus Plunges," SN, November 20, 1957, 1–2; and Lowell Reidenbaugh, "Feller Warns of Bonus Spree Dangers," SN, February 5, 1958, 1–2. See also J. G. Taylor Spink, "Majors Moving to Shake," SN, January 12, 1949, 1, 6; Frank Eck, "Bonus Baby Parade to Bushes Due This Season," SN, April 13, 1955, 13; Les Biederman, "Bonuses Ruining the Game, Says Rickey, Must Halt," SN, March 9, 1955, 2; Dan Daniel, "Players Seek Limit on Bonus Kids, Lift of Latin Ball Clubs," SN, July 20, 1955, 13; Dan Daniel, "'Free Draft Direct at Farms'—Weiss," SN, November 27, 1957, 1–2; Edgar Munzel, "Junk Bonus Rule, Briggs Urges," SN, July 27, 1955, 1, 6; Tom Swope, "Minors to Vote on Legislation Aimed at Curbing Bonus Sprees," SN, November 9, 1955, 7; Clifford Kachline, "Bonus and Aircast Curbs against Chief Topics for Minors," SN, November 16, 1955, 9; Oscar Kahan, "Sky Still the Limit under Majors' Plan for New Bonus Rules," SN, November 5, 1958, 2; and Jesse Linthicum, "New Oriole Boss MacPhail Raps 'Spending,'" SN, November 19, 1958, 1, 4.

76. Dan Daniel, "Rickey Still Satisfied by Revised Bill—O.B. Maps Fight," SN, June 15, 1960, 7, 20.

77. U.S. Senate, *Organized Professional Team Sports* (1960), 69.

78. J. Roy Stockton, "'Bonus Here to Stay'—Bing; 'Destroys Incentive'—Lane," SN, March 22, 1961, 19–20.

79. Robert Coughlan, "Baseball's Happy Serf," SI, March 5, 1956, 38.

80. Bob Stevens, "Non-Farms Sell Youths on 16–1 Chance to Rise," BD, September 1948, 75.

81. Clifford Kachline, "Bonus Ogre Continues to Fatten on Major Cash," SN, November 18, 1959, 11, 16.

82. Bob Burnes, "'Draft Curbing Bonus Binge'—Devine," SN, September 28, 1960, 1–2.

83. Bob Inserra, "Majors Stamp Okay on First-Year Draft," SN, June 1, 1960, 1–2; "First Year Draft Looks like the Answer," SN, June 1, 1960, 10.

84. Clifford Kachline, "First-Year Draft Top Convention Topic," SN, November 23, 1960, 13, 16.

85. Dan Daniel, "Weiss Will Take Rubber off Bankroll for Players," SN, July 19, 1961, 1–2.

86. Dan Daniel, "Soaring Salaries Headed for New High," SN, January 18, 1961, 1–2.

87. Joe King, "Bonus Boys Eye Record Lettuce Crop," SN, March 15, 1961, 1–2; "Weiss Loads Brinks Truck with Bucks in Mets' Drive for Kids," SN, April 26, 1961, 26; and "Good Old Days Over, Yankees Plunge into Bonus Binge," SN, June 7, 1960, 1–2.

88. Clifford Kachline, "Owners Will Weigh New Proposal to Put Clamps on Bonuses," SN, November 22, 1961, 6, 8; and Clifford Kachline, "Bonus-Curb Plan Wins Quick Okay at Minors' Confab," SN, December 6, 1961, 21.

89. Oscar Kahan, "Majors Pay Record 680 Gees for Draft Picks," SN, December 6, 1961, 9, 16; "45 First-Year Kids Grabbed in Draft Raids," SN, December 8, 1962, 13, 16; "AL Clubs Outspend NL in Draft Picks," SN, December 14, 1963, 9–10, 14; and "Majors Run Up $572,000 Tab to Draft 63," SN, December 12, 1964, 5–6.

90. Clifford Kachline, "'Rule Slashes $$ Tab, May Lead to Free-Agent Draft,' Routzong," SN, August 17, 1963, 2, 10.

91. Oscar Kahan, "Big Timers See 40 Per Cent Cut in Bonus Spree," SN, December 13, 1961, 5–6.

92. Clifford Kachline, "'Rule Slashes $$ Tab, May Lead to Free-Agent Draft,' Routzong," SN, August 17, 1963, 2, 10.

93. Joe King, "'Game Loses Choice Talent under Bonus Rule,' Says Fresco," SN, July 7, 1962, 10, 14.

94. Clifford Kachline, "$45 Million Major 6—Year Bonus Tab," SN, August 10, 1963, 1–2.

95. Clifford Kachline, "Minors Block Bids to Kill First-Year Draft," SN, December 8, 1962, 5–6.

96. Clifford Kachline, "'Socialism Threatens Game'—O'Malley," SN, December 22, 1962, 1.

97. Leonard Koppett, "Baseball's New Draft: Two Views," NYT, June 6, 1965, sec. 5, 3.

98. Clifford Kachline, "'Socialism Threatens Game'—O'Malley," SN, December 22, 1962, 1–2.

99. Dave Brady, "Richards Suggests 'Free Agent Draft' at Senate Hearings," SN, August 5, 1959, 17, 25; Bob Burnes, "Tyros Tap Major Jackpot for Record $1,200,000 Haul," SN, July 15, 1959, 2; Clifford Kachline, "Free Agent Talent Draft under Study by Game's Bigwigs," SN, October 28, 1959, 4; and Clifford Kachline, "Minors Defeat Free-Agent Draft Motion," SN, December 9, 1959, 5–6.

100. J. G. Taylor Spink, "Uneasy Majors Eye Free-Agent Draft," SN, June 28, 1961, 1–2; Dan Daniel, "NL Execs Okay Grab-Bag Plan in Marathon Huddle," SN, July 5, 1961, 5–6; and Dave Brady, "Senate Bill-Backers to Huddle with Frick," SN, July 5, 1961, 5.

101. Edwin Shrake, "Richest Bonus Baby Ever," SI, July 6, 1964, 16–21.

102. Oscar Kahan, "Majors Run Up $572,000 Tab," SN, December 12, 1964, 5–6; Clifford Kachline, "Free-Agent Draft in Works; Brass Gives 'Go-Ahead,'" SN, January 25, 1964, 4; and Jerome Holtzman, "Majors Split on Free Agent Draft, Table Plan," SN, August 22, 1964, 22.

103. Russell Schneider, "'Dodger Brass Plots against Free-Agent Draft,' Paul Claims," SN, December 5, 1964, 2, 40.

104. C. C. Johnson Spink, "'Free-Agent Draft Legal'—Antitrust Expert," SN, December 12, 1964, 4.

105. Edgar Munzel, "O'Connor No. 1 Foe of Free-Agent Draft," SN, April 11, 1964, 24.

106. U.S. Senate, *Professional Sports Antitrust Bill—1964*, 358.

107. U.S. Senate, *Professional Sports Antitrust Bill—1964*, 370.

108. U.S. Senate, *Professional Sports Antitrust Bill—1965*, 117.

109. Veeck, *Veeck as in Wreck*, 274.

110. U.S. Senate, *Organized Professional Team Sports* (1958), 462–63.

111. Bill Bryson, "It's 10–1 against Draft as Equalizer," BD, April 1965, 11–14.

112. Clifford Kachline, "Path Cleared for Draft of Free Agents," SN, November 21, 1964, 4, 30.

113. Clifford Kachline, "Frick Lauds Great Progress Program," SN, December 19, 1964, 19; and Russell Schneider, "'Dodger Brass Plots against Free-Agent Draft,' Paul Claims," SN, December 5, 1964, 2, 40.

114. Charles Dexter, "The Old Scout's a Bookkeeper Now," BD, August 1967, 67–71.

115. Leonard Koppett, "320 Are Picked in Baseball Draft," NYT, June 9, 1965, 55.

116. Bill Conlin, "Phil's Exec Calls Free Agent," BD, May 1968, 45–46.

10. The Yankees' Dynasty

1. New York Yankees Baseball Club scorecards, 1949–54.

2. Joe Coppage, "Big Spurt by N.L. Paced Majors to 17,460,630 Draw," SN,

November 5, 1958, 18; Ralph Katz, "Subways to Lose by Teams' Moves," NYT, October 9, 1957, 37; Dan Daniel, "Yankees Players Cite 'Monopoly' in Pay Demands," SN, January 15, 1958, 4; Dan Daniel, "Yanks' Golden Egg Slows Down Flow of Inked Contracts," SN, January 29, 1958, 8; and Dan Daniel, "'Bombers Draw Cut by Dodgers,' Giants' Publicity," SN, April 3, 1958, 1, 4.

3. Oscar Kahan, "Ticket Sales Soar—Pre-Season Record," SN, April 24, 1965, 1–2, 4.

4. Robert Shaplen, "How to Build a Ball Club," SI, March 5, 1962, 38; and U.S. Department of Commerce, *Census of Population: 1960*, 1:174–78, 380–84.

5. William Leggett, "Trouble Sprouts for the Yankees," SI, March 2, 1964, 15.

6. William Leggett, "Trouble Sprouts for the Yankees," SI, March 2, 1964, 15.

7. Barry Kremenko, "Mets Threaten Yank Box-Office Reign," SN, January 18, 1964, 1, 8.

8. William Leggett, "Trouble Sprouts for the Yankees," SI, March 2, 1964, 13.

9. Jimmy Breslin, "It's Metsomania," *Saturday Evening Post*, June 13, 1964, 20, 22.

10. Sporting News, *Sporting News Dope Book* (1964).

11. Charles Einstein, "The New Breed of Baseball Fan," *Harper's Magazine*, July 1967, 76.

12. Martin became an equally pugnacious manager, although, according to one interview, he may have inherited this trait from his mother. Under Casey Stengel the Yankees seemingly increased their levity; Yankees who had been broken in under Ed Barrow and Joe McCarthy had been groomed to act like dignified professional men on the field and off: "A calm, cool superciliousness was their trademark and asset" (Charles Dexter, "New Era Yankee," BD, January 1954, 5–9).

13. Robert Shaplen, "The Yankees' Real Boss," SI, September 20, 1954, 35.

14. Dan Daniel, "Cronin Backed Topping, Webb in Coast Drive," SN, November 9, 1960, 3–4; Arthur Daley, "Departure of Weiss Ends an Era," SN, November 16, 1960, 1–2; and William Leggett, "Trouble Sprouts for the Yankees," SI, March 2, 1964, 13.

15. Veeck, *Veeck as in Wreck*, 264.

16. William Leggett, "Trouble Sprouts for the Yankees," SI, March 2, 1964, 14.

17. Veeck, *Veeck as in Wreck*, 122–23.

18. Arthur Daley, "A Fine State of Affairs," NYT, August 25, 1964, 38. See also Leonard Koppett, "A Contrite Linz Draws $200 Fine from Berra," NYT, August 22, 1964, 14; and Murray Olderman, "Hamey Cloaks Yank Tradition in New Tweeds," SN, October 18, 1961, 5–6.

19. Til Ferdenzi, "Stuffy Yankees? Not Anymore—Image Changing," SN,

January 11, 1964, 8; "'Yanks Can't Miss,' Says Houk, Talking about 1,500,000 Gate," April 25, 1964, 13, 24; and "Yanks Act to Hypo Dwindling Crowd," *SN*, December 12, 1964, 15.

20. Til Ferdenzi, "Romance Taking Root in N.Y.—It's with Yanks," *SN*, August 8, 1964, 5–6. See also William Leggett, "Out in Front with a New Look," *SI*, September 28, 1964, 26.

21. William Leggett, "Out in Front with a New Look," *SI*, September 28, 1964, 27–28. On a personal note the author and his friends thought Joe Pepitone a goof for using an electric hair dryer during the late 1960s. A few years later, however, such styling devices were de rigueur for all young men. Joe, you were an unsung pioneer.

22. *Broadcasting* typically listed radio and television revenues in a February or March issue. The 1952–56 figures are also available; see U.S. Congress, *Organized Professional Team Sports*, 359–63.

23. "'Inside' Baseball—From the Owner's View-Point," *Literary Digest*, April 8, 1922, 46.

24. U.S. Congress, *Organized Professional Team Sports*, 2036.

25. U.S. Congress, *Organized Professional Team Sports*, 353, 2056; Lyall Smith, "Three Clubs Hit $600,000 Pay," *BD*, March 1951, 72; Dan Daniel, "Looks like Restful Winter for Weiss—Few Yankee Hikes," *SN*, October 8, 1958, 7; "Bomber Brass Set for Sizzling Battles over Champs' Pay," *SN*, November 5, 1958, 1–2; "Weiss Braced for Yankees' Contract Squawks," *SN*, January 21, 1959, 5, 8; "Mantel Tops List of Yanks 'Invited' to Take Pay Cuts," *SN*, January 28, 1959, 8; and "Salary War On—Bombers Lead Attack," *SN*, February 18, 1959, 1–2, 8.

26. "Larry MacPhail Buys the Yanks," *SN*, February 1, 1945, 10. See also "Big League Baseball," *Fortune*, August 1937, 138.

27. Quirk and Fort, *Pay Dirt*, 405–6.

28. Leonard Koppett, "A Yankee Dynasty Can Never Come Back," *NYT Magazine*, October 2, 1966, 121–22.

29. Fetter, *Taking on the Yankees*, 9.

30. George M. Weiss and Robert Shaplen, "The Best Decision I Ever Made," *SI*, March 13, 1961, 32.

31. Veeck, *Hustler's Handbook*, 136.

32. Val Adams, Big Pitch at Networks Still in Nielsen Curve," *NYT*, August 15, 1964, 14.

33. Arthur Daley, "A Strange Union," *NYT*, August 16, 1964, sec. 5, 2.

34. U.S. Senate, *Professional Sports Antitrust Bill—1965*, 2; and "Celler Is Dubious Over Yankee Deal," *NYT*, August 17, 1964, 31.

35. U.S. Senate, *Professional Sports Antitrust Bill—1965*, 8; and "CBS Bough Yankees," *Broadcasting*, February 22, 1965, 64–65.

36. Richard Rutter, "Big-League Deal Is Minor to CBS," *NYT*, August 15, 1964,

14; and Lester Smith, CBS Deal Pinpoints Soaring Price Tag on Big-Time Clubs," SN, November 28, 1964, 11.

37. Jack Gould, "Yank Deal's TV Rating," NYT, August 15, 1964, 14; U.S. Senate, *Professional Sports Antitrust Bill—1965*, 34; and William Furlong, "A Sad Day for Baseball," SI, September 21, 1964, 26.

38. Joseph Durso, "All Eyes in Sports Seek the Why for New Gleam in CBS's Eye," NYT, August 16, 1964, sec. 5, 2; Joseph Durso, "Yanks' Sale to CBS Stirs Senate Moves for Inquiry," NYT, August 15, 1964, 1, 14; Val Adams, Big Pitch at Networks Still in Nielsen Curve," NYT, August 15, 1964, 14; Jack Gould, "Yank Deal's TV Rating," NYT, August 15, 1964, 14; and Ralph Ray, "Bomber Sale Stirs Bees' Nest of Boos," SN, August 29, 1964, 1–2, 6.

39. William Wallace, "CBS Buys 80% of Stock in Yankee Baseball Team," NYT, August 14, 1964, 1, 18.

40. U.S. Senate, *Professional Sports Antitrust Bill—1965*, 64.

41. U.S. Senate, *Professional Sports Antitrust Bill—1965*, 36, 61.

42. C. C. Johnson Spink, "Finley, Allyn Carry Fight against Yank Sale to Justice Department," October 10, 1964, 6; and Lester Smith, "All AL Owners Asked to Reveal Holdings in CBS," SN, December 5, 1964, 26.

43. "Yankee Serfs Get Soviet Sympathy," NYT, August 16, 1964, sec. 5, 2.

44. Ralph Ray, "Bomber Sale Stirs Bees' Nest of Boos," SN, August 29, 1964, 1–2, 6.

45. U.S. Senate, *Professional Sports Antitrust Bill—1965*, 34; and Til Ferdenzi, "Topping and Webb to Remain in Posts as Bomber Execs," SN, August 29, 1964, 2.

46. U.S. Senate, *Professional Sports Antitrust Bill—1965*, 141.

47. Til Ferdenzi, "Twins Are Good, Yanks Better, Houk Declares in Sizeup for '66," SN, February 5, 1966, 17.

48. Sporting News, *Sporting News Official Baseball Guide* (1967), 39.

49. "Majors Get $25 Million for '65 Rights," *Broadcasting*, March 1, 1965, 45; "Price of Baseball Goes Up, Too," *Broadcasting*, February 28, 1966, 37; and "Baseball's Tab up $2 Million," *Broadcasting*, February 20, 1967, 39.

50. Quirk and Fort, *Pay Dirt*, 405–6; J. G. Taylor Spink, "Looping the Loops," SN, February 8, 1945, 1; and Quirk, "Economic Analysis," 60.

51. Halberstam, *Summer of '49*, 305.

52. John Drohan, "Millionaires' Failure Laid to Too Many Bucks," SN, October 12, 1949, 3. See also Arthur Daley, "That Strange Vic Raschi Deal," BD, May 1954, 88–91.

53. "Johnson Acquires Athletics for $3,500,000 for Transfer to Kansas City," NYT, November 5, 1954, 25.

54. Buster Olney, "Torre Not Yet Ready to Manage Yanks: Zimmer to Stay On," NYT, May 1, 1999, sec. D, 1; and "A Royal Proclamation," *USA Today Baseball Weekly*, May 5, 1999, 3.

Epilogue

1. Leonard Koppett, "Tigers, with Run in 9th, Top Yankees 2–1, before 40,600 at Stadium Opener," *NYT*, April 13, 1966, 48.

2. Leonard Koppett, "Yanks Alone in Last Place after Losing to Indians, 4–2, on Whitfield's Homer," *NYT*, April 21, 1966, 49.

3. Michael Strauss, "Meanwhile, Back at the Stadium, 413 See Last-Place Yanks Lose 87th Game," *NYT*, September 23, 1966, 27.

4. Val Adams, "Red Barber Dismissed after 13 Years as Yankee Broadcaster," *NYT*, September 27, 1966, 94.

5. Val Adams, "Red Barber Says Ex-Athletes Take over Sports Broadcasting," *NYT*, September 30, 1966, 95.

6. Barber, *Broadcasters*, 215–21.

Bibliography

Alexander, Charles C. *Our Game: An American Baseball History*. New York: Henry Holt, 1991.

Allen, Maury. *You Could Look It Up: The Life of Casey Stengel*. New York: Times Books, 1979.

American League. *American League Red Book*. Chicago: American League Service Bureau, 1946–58.

———. *American League Red Book*. Boston: American League, 1959–65.

Areeda, Phillip, and Donald F. Turner. "Predatory Pricing and Related Practices under Section 2 of the Sherman Act." *Harvard Law Review* 88, no. 4 (February 1975): 697–733.

Baltimore Baseball Club. *Survey*. Baltimore: Baltimore Baseball Club, 1954.

Barber, Red. *The Broadcasters*. New York: Dial Press, 1970.

Bjarkman, Peter C., ed. *Encyclopedia of Major League Baseball*. New York: Carroll and Graf, 1991.

Bruggink, Thomas H., and James W. Eaton. "Rebuilding Attendance in Major League Baseball: The Demand for Individual Games." In *Baseball Economics: Current Research*, edited by John Fizel, Elizabeth Gustafson, and Lawrence Hadley, 9–31. Westport CT: Greenwood, 1996.

Bryant, Howard. *Shut Out: A Story of Race and Baseball in Boston*. New York: Routledge, 2002.

Burger, John D., and Stephen J. K. Walters. "Market Size, Pay, and Performance: A General Model and Application to Major League Baseball." *Journal of Sports Economics* 4, no. 2 (2003): 108–25.

Burk, Robert F. *Much More than a Game*. Chapel Hill: University of North Carolina Press, 2001.

———. *Never Just a Game: Players, Owners, and American Baseball to 1920*. Chapel Hill: University of North Carolina Press, 1994.

"The Business Side of Baseball." *Current Literature* 53 (August 1912): 168–72.

Carter, Susan B., Scott S. Gartner, Michael R. Haines, Alan L. Olmstead, Richard Sutch, and Gavin Wright, eds. *Historical Statistics of the United States: Earliest Times to the Present*. Vol. 2, pt. B, *Work and Welfare*. Millennial ed. Cambridge: Cambridge University Press, 2006.

Chicago Baseball Club (American League). *Probate Court Proceedings*. Chicago: Chicago Historical Society, 1958.

Coase, Ronald. "The Problem of Social Cost." *Journal of Law and Economics* 3 (1960): 1–44.

Craig, Peter S. "Organized Baseball: An Industry Study of $100 Spectator Sport." BA thesis, Oberlin College, 1950.

Davis, Lance E. "Self-Regulation in Baseball, 1909–71." In *Government and the Sports Business*, edited by Roger G. Noll, 349–86. Washington DC: Brookings Institution, 1974.

Dewey, Donald, and Nicholas Acocella. *The Ball Clubs: Every Franchise, Past and Present, Officially Recognized by Major League Baseball.* New York: HarperPerennial, 1996.

Dodd, Donald, ed. *Historical Statistics of the States of the United States: Two Centuries of the Census, 1790–1990.* Westport CT: Greenwood Press, 1993.

Eckard, E. Woodward. "Baseball's Blue Ribbon Economic Report: Solutions in Search of a Problem." *Journal of Sports Economics* 2 (2001): 213–27.

Fetter, Henry D. *Taking on the Yankees: Winning and Losing in the Business of Baseball, 1903–2003.* New York: W. W. Norton, 2003.

Finch, Robert L. "The Era of President George M. Trautman." In *The Story of Minor League Baseball*, edited by Robert L. Finch, L. H. Addington, and Ben M. Morgan, 53–86. Columbus OH: National Association of Professional Baseball Leagues, 1953.

Glick, Jeffrey. "Professional Sports Franchise Movements and the Sherman Act: When and Where Teams Should Be Able to Move." *Santa Clara Law Review* 23, no. 1 (Winter 1983): 55–94.

Halberstam, David. *Summer of '49.* New York: William Morrow, 1989.

Henderson, Cary S. "Los Angeles and the Dodger War, 1957–1962." *Southern California Quarterly* 62, no. 3 (Fall 1980): 261–89.

Hollander, Zander, ed. *The Complete Handbook of Baseball.* New York: Lancer Books, 1972.

Information Please Almanac. New York: Macmillan and Doubleday, 1947, 1950, 1954, 1959.

Johnson, Lloyd, and Miles Wolff, eds. *The Encyclopedia of Minor League Baseball.* Durham NC: Baseball America, 1993.

Jordan, Jerry N. "The Long-Range Effect of Television and Other Factors on Sports Attendance." Master's thesis, University of Pennsylvania, 1950.

Kelley, Brent. *Baseball's Biggest Blunder: The Bonus Rule of 1953–1957.* Lanham MD: Scarecrow Press, 1997.

Knowles, Glenn, Keith Sherony, and Michael Haupert. "The Demand for Major League Baseball: A Test of the Uncertainty of Outcome Hypothesis." *American Economist* 36 (Fall 1992): 72–80.

Koller, Roland H., II. "The Myth of Predatory Pricing: An Empirical Study." *Antitrust Law and Economics Review* 4, no. 4 (Summer 1971): 105–23.

Koppett, Leonard. *Koppett's Concise History of Major League Baseball.* Philadelphia: Temple University Press, 1998.

Koufax, Sandy, and Ed Linn. *Koufax.* New York: Viking Press, 1966.

Levin, Richard C., George J. Mitchell, Paul A. Volcker, and George F. Will. *The Report of the Independent Members of the Commissioner's Blue Ribbon Panel on Baseball Economics.* July 2000. www.mlb.com/mlb/downloads/blue_ribbon.pdf.

Levine, Peter. *A. G. Spalding and the Rise of Baseball: The Promise of American Sport.* New York: Oxford University Press, 1985.

Lowe, Stephen R. *The Kid on the Sandlot: Congress and Professional Sports, 1910–1992.* Bowling Green OH: Bowling Green University Press, 1995.

Macht, Norman L. "Philadelphia Athletics–Kansas City Athletics–Oakland A's: Three Families and Three Baseball Epochs." In *Encyclopedia of Major League Baseball—American League,* edited by Peter C. Bjarkman, 293–357. New York: Carroll and Graf, 1991.

The Macmillan Baseball Encyclopedia. 9th ed. New York: Macmillan, 1993.

———. 10th ed. New York: Macmillan, 1996.

Maher, Tod, and Bob Gill. *Pro Football Encyclopedia.* New York: Macmillan, 1997.

Major League Scorecards and Newsletters, 1946–64. Joyce Sports Collection. Notre Dame University Library, South Bend IN.

Melville, Tom. *Early Baseball and the Rise of the National League.* Jefferson NC: McFarland and Co., 2001.

Miller, Marvin. *A Whole Different Ball Game: The Inside Story of Baseball's New Deal.* New York: Fireside, 1991.

Moffi, Larry, and Jonathan Kronstadt. *Crossing the Line: Black Major Leaguers, 1947–1959.* Jefferson NC: McFarland and Co., 1994.

National League. *National League Green Book.* New York: National League Service Bureau, 1946–51.

———. *National League Green Book.* Cincinnati: National League Service Bureau, 1954–65.

New York Yankees Baseball Club. General Ledger and Cash Books, 1913–44. National Baseball Hall of Fame, Cooperstown NY.

Pietrusza, David. *Major Leagues: The Formation, Sometimes Absorption and Mostly Inevitable Demise of 18 Professional Baseball Organizations, 1871 to Present.* Jefferson NC: McFarland and Co., 1991.

Pluto, Terry. *The Curse of Rocky Colavito.* New York: Simon and Schuster, 1994.

Quinn, Kevin, and David Surdam. "The Case of the Missing Fans: Do Owners Act Opportunistically?" (unpublished MN, 2007).

Quirk, James. "An Economic Analysis of Team Movements in Professional Sports. *Law and Contemporary Problems* 38, no. 1 (Winter–Spring 1973): 42–66.

Quirk, James, and Rodney D. Fort. *Pay Dirt: The Business of Professional Team Sports*. Princeton NJ: Princeton University Press, 1992.

Ribowsky, Mark. *A Complete History of the Negro Leagues, 1884 to 1955*. Secaucus NJ: Citadel Press, 1995.

Riess, Steven A. *Sport in Industrial America, 1850–1920*. Wheeling IL: Harlan Davidson, 1995.

Rossi, John P. *A Whole New Game: Off the Field Changes in Baseball, 1946–1960*. Jefferson NC: McFarland and Co., 1999.

Rottenberg, Simon. "The Baseball Players' Labor Market." *Journal of Political Economy* 64, no. 3 (June 1956): 242–58.

Rust, Art, Jr. *Get That Nigger Off the Field: The Oral History of the Negro Leagues*. Brooklyn: Book Mail Services, 1992.

Scherer, F. M., and David Ross. *Industrial Market Structure and Economic Performance*. 3rd ed. Boston: Houghton Mifflin, 1990.

Scully, Gerald W. *The Business of Major League Baseball*. Chicago: University of Chicago Press, 1989.

Seagrave. *Drive-in Theaters: A History from Their Inception in 1933*. Jefferson NC: McFarland and Co., 1992.

Seymour, Harold. *Baseball: The Early Years*. New York: Oxford University Press, 1960.

———. *Baseball: The Golden Age*. New York: Oxford University Press, 1971.

Smiley, Robert. "Empirical Evidence on Strategic Entry Deterrence." *International Journal of Industrial Organization* 6 (June 1988): 167–80.

Spalding, Albert G. *America's National Game: Historic Facts Concerning the Beginning, Evolution, Development and Popularity of Base Ball*. 1911. Reprint, Lincoln: University of Nebraska Press, 1992.

Sporting News. *The Sporting News Complete Baseball Record Book—1998 Edition*. St. Louis: Sporting News Publishing Co., 1998.

———. *The Sporting News Complete Baseball Record Book—2003 Edition*. St. Louis: Sporting News Publishing Co., 2003.

———. *The Sporting News Dope Book*. St. Louis: Sporting News Publishing Co., 1955–57, 1964–65.

———. *The Sporting News Official Baseball Guide*. St. Louis: Charles C. Spink and Son, 1947–65.

Sullivan, Dean, ed. *Early Innings: A Documentary History of Baseball, 1825–1908*. Lincoln: University of Nebraska Press, 1995.

Sullivan, Neil J. *The Dodgers Move West*. Oxford: Oxford University Press, 1987.

Sumner, Benjamin, ed. *Minor League Baseball Standings: All North American Leagues, through 1999*. Jefferson NC: McFarland and Co., 2000.

Surdam, David. "The American 'Not-So-Socialist' League in the Postwar Era:

The Limitations of Gate Sharing in Reducing Revenue Disparity in Baseball."
Journal of Sports Economics 3, no. 3 (August 2002): 264–90.

———. "The Coase Theorem and Player Movement in Major League Baseball."
Journal of Sports Economics 7 (2006): 201–21.

———. "Non-Price Determinants of Demand for New York Yankees Baseball
Games" (working paper, 2008).

———. "A Tale of Two Gate-Sharing Plans: The National Football League and the
National League, 1952–1956." *Southern Economic Journal* 73, no. 4 (2007):
931–46.

———. "Television and Minor League Baseball: Changing Patterns of Leisure in
Postwar America." *Journal of Sports Economics* 6 (2005): 61–77.

Thomas, David C. "Baseball's Amateur Draft—An Abstract Analysis." *Baseball
Research Journal* 23 (1994): 92–96.

Thorn, John, Pete Palmer, and Michael Gershman, eds. *The Official Encyclopedia
of Major League Baseball: Total Baseball*. 4th ed. New York: Viking, 1995.

———, eds. *Total Baseball: The Official Encyclopedia of Major League Baseball*.
7th ed. Kingston NY: Total Sports, 2001.

Thorn, John, Pete Palmer, Michael Gershman, and David Pietrusza, eds. *Total
Baseball: The Official Encyclopedia of Major League Baseball*. 6th ed. New
York: Total Sports, 1999.

Topkis, Jay H. "Monopoly in Professional Sports." *Yale Law Review* 58, no. 5
(April 1949): 691–712.

Turkin, Hy. *Radio and TV Baseball: The Major League Handbook*. New York:
A. S. Barnes and Co., 1953.

Tygiel, Jules. *Baseball's Great Experiment: Jackie Robinson and His Legacy*. New
York: Vintage Books, 1983.

U.S. Congress. *Organized Baseball: Hearings before the Subcommittee on Study
of Monopoly Power of the Committee on the Judiciary*. Serial no. 1, pt. 6. 82nd
Cong., 1st sess. Washington DC: Government Printing Office, 1952.

———. *Organized Baseball: Report of the Subcommittee on Study of Monopoly
Power of the Committee on the Judiciary Pursuant to H. Res. 95. Documents
and Reports*. House Report no. 2002. 82nd Cong., 1st sess. Washington DC:
Government Printing Office, 1952.

———. *Organized Professional Team Sports: Hearings before the Antitrust
Subcommittee of the Committee on the Judiciary*. Serial no. 8. 85th Cong.,
1st sess. Washington DC: Government Printing Office, 1957.

———. *Telecasting of Professional Sports Contests: Hearing before the Antitrust
Subcommittee of the Committee on the Judiciary*. 87th Cong., 1st sess.
Washington DC: Government Printing Office, 1961.

U.S. Department of Commerce, Bureau of the Census. *Census of Housing: 1950*.
Vol. 1, *General Characteristics*, pt. 1, *United States Summary*. Washington DC:
Government Printing Office, 1953.

———. *Census of Housing: 1960.* Vol. 1, *States and Small Areas*, pt. 1: *United States Summary.* Washington DC: Government Printing Office, 1961.

———. *Census of Population: 1960.* Vol. 1, *Characteristics of the Population*, pt. A, *Number of Inhabitants.* Washington DC: Government Printing Office, 1961.

———. *Eighteenth Decennial Census of the United States: Census of Population, 1960.* Vol. 1, *Characteristics of the Population*, pt. 1, *United States Summary.* Washington DC: Government Printing Office, 1964.

———. *Historical Statistics of the United States: Colonial Times to 1970.* 2 vols. Washington DC: Government Printing Office, 1975.

———. *Seventeenth Census: Census of Population, 1950.* Vol. 1. Washington DC: Government Printing Office, 1952.

———. *Seventeenth Census: Census of Population, 1950.* Vol. 2, *Characteristics of the Population.* Washington DC: Government Printing Office, 1952.

———. *Statistical Abstract of the United States, 1964.* 85th ed. Prepared under the direction of Edwin D. Goldfield. Washington DC: Government Printing Office, 1964.

———. *Twelfth Census: Population.* Washington DC: Government Printing Office, 1901.

U.S. Senate. *Organized Professional Team Sports: Hearings before the Subcommittee on Antitrust and Monopoly of the Committee on the Judiciary.* 85th Cong., 2nd sess. Washington DC: Government Printing Office, 1958.

———. *Organized Professional Team Sports: Hearings before the Subcommittee on Antitrust and Monopoly of the Committee on the Judiciary.* 86th Cong., 1st sess. Washington DC: Government Printing Office, 1959.

———. *Organized Professional Team Sports: Hearings before the Subcommittee on Antitrust and Monopoly of the Committee on the Judiciary.* 86th Cong., 2nd sess. Washington DC: Government Printing Office, 1960.

———. *Professional Sports Antitrust Bill—1964: Hearings before the Subcommittee on Antitrust and Monopoly of the Committee on the Judiciary.* 88th Cong., 2nd sess. Washington DC: Government Printing Office, 1964.

———. *Professional Sports Antitrust Bill—1965: Hearings before the Subcommittee on Antitrust and Monopoly of the Committee on the Judiciary.* 89th Cong., 1st sess. Washington DC: Government Printing Office, 1965.

———. *Status of UHF and Multiple Ownership of TV Stations: Hearings before the Subcommittee on Communications of the Committee on Interstate and Foreign Commerce, Senate.* 83rd Cong., 2nd sess. Washington DC: Government Printing Office, 1954.

Veeck, Bill. *The Hustler's Handbook.* New York: Putnam, 1965.

———. *Veeck as in Wreck.* New York: Putnam, 1962.

Voigt, David Q. *American Baseball: From Gentleman's Sport to the Commissioner System.* Norman: University of Oklahoma Press, 1966.

————. *American Baseball: From the Commissioners to Continental Expansion.* 1970. Reprint. University Park: Pennsylvania State University Press, 1983.

White, G. Edward. *Creating the National Pastime: Baseball Transforms Itself, 1903–1953.* Princeton NJ: Princeton University Press, 1996.

Whyte, William. *The Organization Man.* New York: Simon and Schuster, 1956.

Woodard, Milt. *So You Want to Run a Ball Club.* St. Louis: Charles C. Spink and Son, 1951.

Index

Aaron, Henry ("Hank"), 38, 182, 183, 184, 191, 258, 291
Abel, Robert, 145
Abernathy, Ted, 298
Adams, Val, 305
African American players. *See* black players
Agee, Tommie, 184
Alexander, Charles, 43, 141, 382n32
All-American Football Conference, 103
Allen, Dick, 185, 269
Allison, Bob, 22, 42, 196
All-Star Game, 54, 133
Allyn, Arthur, Jr., 114, 221–22, 295
Allyn, John, 296
Alou, Felipe, 38
Alou, Jesus, 38
Alou, Matty, 38
Alyea, Brant, 270
Amaro, Ruben, 297, 303
amateur draft, 200–207, 208, 270, 292. *See also* draft
American Association (AA), 166, 213, 215, 225, 233
American Association (minor league), 160, 228, 251
American Broadcasting Company (ABC), 129–30
American Football League, 103, 130
American League (AL), 5, 9, 15–16, 18–19; attendance in, 8–9, 15, 16–19, 28, 31, 59, 60, 96, 125, 136, 167, 173–74, 192–93, 198–99, 278–81, 300–301, 308–9, 352; baseball statistics (postwar) of, 313; and draft, 205–7, 208; expansion of, 22, 198–99, 224, 232, 233–43, 263, 300; and farm system, 36–37; and

franchise relocations, 191, 192–96, 197–99, 207–8, 249–57, 258, 259, 263–65, 280; and integration, 7, 9, 181, 182–83, 184, 185–91; and length of games, 114; and night games, 91, 92–93, 333–34; payrolls of, 67–69, 72, 73, 76, 328, 331; and player movement, 42–58; profits of, 62–63, 80–82, 84, 140, 141; and revenue sharing, 60, 163–64, 167–74, 179–80, 345–47; and television, 139–40, 177–78; and ticket prices, 27, 60–61; win-loss records of, 311. *See also specific teams*
American Safety Razor Corporation, 128
Anaheim Angels, 199. *See also* Los Angeles Angels
antitrust exemption, 79, 198, 250, 262; and league expansion, 211–12; and player movement, 217, 220, 273, 277; and television contracts, 130, 145
Antonelli, Johnny, 259
Aparicio, Luis, 39, 40, 42, 184
Appling, Luke, 39
Areeda, Phillip, 213
Arledge, Roone, 129
Astrodome, 112
Atlanta Braves, 153, 163; relocation of, from Milwaukee, 259–63, 303. *See also* Boston Braves; Milwaukee Braves
attendance: in American League, 8–9, 15, 16–19, 28, 31, 59, 60, 96, 125, 136, 167, 173–74, 192–93, 198–99, 278–81, 300–301, 308–9, 352; and black fans, 121–24; and crowd behavior, 116–17; decline in, of Yankees, 6, 12, 13, 19–20, 27–28, 31, 171–72, 278–81, 285, 288–89, 297, 300–301, 305;

attendance (*cont.*)

and demographics, 89–90, 124–25; and facilities, 99, 100, 106–14, 259, 282, 285; and franchise relocations, 192–97, 199–200, 248, 249, 251–52, 253, 259–61; and homerun record (1961), 12, 23–27; and leisure-time activities, 102–4, 124–25; in Minor League Baseball, 103, 154–55, 158–59, 161–62; in National League, 8, 13, 16–19, 31, 125, 182, 196–97, 257–58, 281, 300–301, 309–10, 352; and night games, 21, 91, 92–94, 96, 334; and opinion polls, 96–101, 114–15; and pennant races, 19–21, 22–23, 28–29, 31, 33–34, 138, 195; postwar boom in, 13–14, 16, 90, 124, 167; and profitability, 80–82; and promotions, 90–96, 101–2, 105–6, 125; for road games, 19, 26, 27, 28–29, 170–74, 175, 182, 280; and television, 101, 126, 130, 135–41, 154–55, 162; and ticket prices, 60, 97, 117, 264

Automatic Canteen Company of America, 287

automobiles, 86–87, 107. *See also* parking

Autry, Gene, 296

Bahnsen, Stan, 191

Baker, Frank ("Home Run"), 12, 54

Baltimore Colts, 194, 195

Baltimore Orioles, 5, 15, 21, 23, 25–26, 28–29, 41, 78, 93, 97, 251; and broadcast revenue, 140; facilities of, 113; payroll of, 40; and player movement, 35, 42; profits of, 81; relocation of, from St. Louis, 171–72, 178, 180, 191–95, 197–98, 200, 207–8; and ticket prices, 61, 62–63. *See also* St. Louis Browns

Bando, Sal, 205

Banks, Ernie, 183, 184, 185, 189–90, 291

Barber, Red, 305

Barnes, Donald, 193

Barnes, Henry, 282

Barrow, Ed, 58, 284, 285, 286, 399n12

Battey, Earl, 39, 42, 196

batting averages, 18–19, 354n18

Bauer, Hank, 47

Baumann, Frank, 75, 266

Beane, Billy, 18

Beazley, Johnny, 56

Beckert, Glenn, 270

Belinsky, Bo, 270

Bench, Johnny, 205

Berra, Yogi, 14, 34, 38, 46, 188, 201; salary of, 37, 70, 229; as Yankees manager, 285, 286, 292

Better Homes and Gardens, 102

blacklists, 217, 218

black players, 4, 9, 18, 121–24, 156, 202; and National League, 38; and Yankees, 3, 6–7, 291–92, 298, 300. *See also* integration

Blackwell, Ewell, 34, 44, 48

Blue, Vida, 184

Boehmer, Len, 297

Bollweg, Don, 36

bonus payments, 157, 202, 204–5, 208, 230, 265–72, 276, 364n57. *See also* salaries

Boston Braves, 56, 94, 104, 120, 182; facilities of, 113–14; and farm system, 38; payroll of, 67–68; relocation of, to Milwaukee, 16, 110, 191–92, 196–97, 223. *See also* Atlanta Braves; Milwaukee Braves

Boston Celtics, 11

Boston Red Sox, 5, 16, 27, 38, 40, 64, 117, 298–99, 305; attendance of, 14, 26, 28, 199–200; and draft, 205; and integration, 183; and night games, 93; and player movement, 12, 35, 56; profits of, 80–81; and revenue sharing, 171; and television, 127, 140; and ticket prices, 27, 60, 119

Boudreau, Lou, 48, 50

Bouton, Jim, 36, 288

box seats, 61–62, 67, 93, 117, 248. *See also* ticket prices

Boyer, Clete, 42, 45, 47, 50, 51, 52, 53–54, 303

Boyle, Robert, 123
The Boys of Summer (Kahn), 1
Brannick, Eddie, 77, 248
Bravman, M. Francis, 73–74
Breadon, Sam, 193, 222
Breslin, Jimmy, 283
Briggs, Walter O., 93
Briggs, Walter O., Jr., 68
Briggs Stadium, 107, 109, 222
broadcast revenue. *See under* revenue
Brock, Lou, 18, 184
"Bronx Bombers." *See* New York Yankees
Brooklyn Bridge, 1
Brooklyn Dodgers, 1, 4, 6, 8, 64, 99,
    104, 159; expenses of, 76, 78; and
    integration, 121–22, 181–82, 190;
    payroll of, 71; and player movement,
    38, 40–42; profits of, 63; relocation
    of, to Los Angeles, 5, 77, 222, 245–46,
    248–49; and revenue sharing, 174; and
    television, 126, 132; and variable ticket
    pricing, 118–19. *See also* Los Angeles
    Dodgers
Brouthers, Dan, 215
Brown, Bobby, 202
Bruton, Billy, 182
Bryan, Billy, 304
Bryant, Howard: *Shut Out*, 183
Bryson, Bill, 38, 40, 75, 276
Burdette, Lew, 35, 51
Burk, Robert, 221
Burke, Mike, 305
Busby, Jim, 40
Busch, August, 106, 193, 224
Byrd, Harry, 35, 54, 55, 188
Byrne, Tommy, 55

Callison, Johnny, 39, 42
Camden Yards Stadium, 195
Campanella, Roy, 38, 185, 186
Campanis, Al, 269
Candlestick Park, 81, 110, 111
Cannon, Robert, 221
Carbo, Bernie, 205
Carey, Andy, 75, 202
Carmichael, John P., 148

Carpenter, Bob, 55
Carrasquel, Chico, 40
Carroll, Lou, 273–74
Carroll, Parke, 51, 57
Carroll, Tommy, 75, 202
cartel practices, 9, 209–11, 212–14, 244;
    and antitrust exemption, 211–12,
    277; and bonuses and salaries,
    265–69; and Continental League,
    222–32, 242; and draft, 269–77; and
    franchise relocations, 244–65; and
    league expansion, 232–43; and player
    movement, 214–22, 230–32, 242
Casey, Ben, 178
Cash, Norm, 22, 39, 42, 303
Castro, Fidel, 149
Celler, Emanuel, 130, 132–33, 250, 256,
    293, 294
Cepeda, Orlando, 38, 183, 184, 298
Cereghino, Ed, 202
Cerv, Bob, 35, 45, 47, 54, 241
Chamberlin, Wilt, 159
Chandler, Albert ("Happy"), 56, 127–28
Chavez Ravine (stadium), 81, 111, 112,
    134, 238–39, 246, 249, 250–51
Chicago Cubs, 6, 64, 77, 94, 106, 124,
    163, 189–90; and television, 128, 140
Chicago Tribune, 3
Chicago White Sox, 4, 5, 15, 16, 19, 29,
    60, 83, 140, 186, 207, 304; attendance
    of, 17, 21–22, 28; concessions revenue
    of, 64, 65, 94; facilities of, 106, 108,
    113, 114; and farm system, 36, 39, 40,
    42, 158–59, 218; and integration, 182;
    and player movement, 34, 39–40; and
    revenue sharing, 171, 179; and ticket
    prices, 120
Chiti, Harry, 50
Cicotte, Al, 55
Cincinnati Reds, 6, 34, 61, 79, 91, 127,
    205, 235; facilities of, 225–26; payroll
    of, 67–68; and variable ticket pricing,
    118, 119
Cincinnati Red Stockings, 165
city size, 245, 335, 379n22; and
    Continental League, 226; and

city size (*cont.*)
demographics, 89–90; and expansion franchises, 222–24, 233, 236–38, 243; and Minor League teams, 150, 161, 342; and player movement, 40–42, 206
Clarke, Horace, 191
Clemente, Roberto, 5, 183, 184
Cleveland Indians, 5, 14, 16, 21, 29, 35, 61, 64, 83, 171, 250, 263–65; attendance of, 15, 93, 104, 173, 174, 248, 279; facilities of, 108; and farm system, 36, 37, 207; and integration, 182, 186, 190; marketing by, 94, 95, 264; payroll of, 76; and player movement, 34, 41; profits of, 80; and television revenue, 66, 137, 140, 289
Clinton, Lu, 297, 304
Closter, Al, 297
Coase, Ronald, 32
Coase Theorem, 32, 42, 58, 216
Cobb, Ty, 3
Cochrane, Mickey, 195
Cohen, S. Jerry, 295
Colavito, Rocky, 22, 264, 384n66
Cold War, 2–4, 24
Coleman, Jerry, 35, 36, 202
Colt Stadium, 112, 114
Columbia Broadcasting System (CBS), 4, 7, 83, 127, 128, 130, 131, 178, 292–98, 300
Columbus Clippers, 124
Comiskey, Charles, 194
Comiskey, Charles, II, 50, 146
Comiskey Park, 95, 106, 108, 109, 110, 114
concessions revenue. *See under* revenue
congressional hearings, 43, 143, 147, 212, 250, 362n32; and reserve clause, 219–20, 221, 230–32; and revenue, 59–60, 64; and revenue sharing, 164, 165. *See also* antitrust exemption
Connie Mack Stadium, 78, 108, 109
consumer price index (CPI), 60, 61, 69, 75, 76
consumer spending, 86–88, 139, 148. *See also* leisure-time activities

Continental League, 224, 226–32, 235, 236, 239, 240, 242–43, 251, 253
Cooper, Cecil, 205
Cooper, Morton, 56
costs, 36, 67–76, 78, 81, 254–55, 256–57, 329–30; and franchise relocations, 75, 76–77, 79; of stadiums, 112, 114, 246–47, 254–57; of travel, 76–78, 81, 198, 382n32. *See also* salaries
Cotton States League, 123
Coughlan, Robert, 67
County Stadium, 109, 110, 262
Courtney, Clint, 34
Covington, Wes, 182
Cox, Bobby, 297
Cox, William, 182
Coyne, Robert, 79–80
Craft, Harry, 46
Craig, Peter, 213
Creamer, Robert, 263–64
Cronin, Joe, 73, 115, 118, 235, 237, 240, 295
Crosley, Powell, 225–26
Crosley Field, 225–26
Crystal, Billy, 2, 23
Cuba, 149
Culp, Ray, 272
Curtis, Jack, 205

Daley, Arthur, 286, 293
Daley, Bud, 53, 57
Daniel, Dan, 96, 116, 141, 186, 190; and free agent draft, 273; and image of Yankees, 20–21; and night-game attendance, 136–37; and Yankee trades, 45, 51–52
Dark, Alvin, 183
Davidson, Billy Joe, 75
Davis, Lance, 213
DeMaestri, Joe, 45, 51, 52
DeOrsey, Leo, 275
Detroit Tigers, 16, 17, 80, 82, 193, 233, 303; attendance of, 23, 25, 28–29, 279; and box seats, 61; and farm system, 36; marketing by, 95, 120; and night games, 93; payroll of, 68, 76; and

player movement, 12, 41; and revenue sharing, 171, 173, 179; and television, 137, 140
Devine, Bing, 103, 268–69
DeWitt, Bill, 71, 117, 146–47, 179, 192–93, 240
Dickey, Bill, 13, 58
Dickson, Murray, 45, 48
DiMaggio, Joe, 1, 13, 14, 37, 58, 201, 292
DiMucci, Dion: "(I Used to Be a) Brooklyn Dodger," 1
Ditmar, Art, 46, 47, 48, 50, 51, 53–54, 57, 358n43
Dixon, Paul, 147, 219–20
Dixon, Sonny, 45
Dobson, Pat, 269
Doby, Larry, 182, 183, 185, 190–91
Doerr, Bobby, 298–99
Donovan, Dick, 39–40
Downing, Al, 36, 304
Doyne, John, 261–62
Drabowsky, Moe, 270
draft, 200–207, 208, 270, 272–77, 292; and league expansion, 240–42, 243
Drebinger, John, 47, 49–50
Dugan, Joe, 12
DuMont networks, 127
Dunn, Jack, 218
Duren, Ryne, 46, 47, 49, 50, 53–54
Durslag, Melvin, 134
Durso, Joseph, 195

earned run averages (ERA), 46, 58, 354n18
Earnshaw, George, 218
Easter, Luke, 182, 183
Ebbet, Charles, 194–95
Ebbets Field, 109, 111, 118–19, 181
Ehlers, Art, 62–63
Embree, Red, 55
entertainment. See leisure-time activities
Epstein, Theo, 18
Escuela, Chico, 271
Essick, Bill, 292
Etten, Nick, 55
expansion, league, 22, 27, 198–99, 224,

232–43, 263, 300, 351. See also franchise relocations

Fagan, Paul, 219
Fain, Ferris, 42
Falstaff Brewing Corporation, 128
farm system, 6, 36, 41–42, 56, 207, 268, 290, 314, 384n65; and Minor Leagues, 142, 147, 157–58, 217–18; and Yankees, 13, 20, 34, 35, 36, 37–39, 58, 191, 292, 300, 303. See also Minor League Baseball
Federal Communications Commission (FCC), 132
Federal League, 210, 214, 216, 217, 222–23
Feeney, Chub, 98
Feller, Bob, 1, 74
Fenway Park, 109
Ferdenzi, Til, 19, 287, 288
Ferraro, Mike, 304
Fetter, Henry, 291
Fetzer, John, 126, 131, 132, 136, 295, 296
Fiery, Benjamin, 160
Finch, Bob, 144
Finigan, Jim, 36, 54–55
Finley, Charles O. ("Charlie"), 28, 44, 57, 295; and franchise relocations, 6, 259, 303, 393n45; and free agent draft, 275, 277; and lease with Kansas City, 254–57
first-year player rule, 203
football, 211; and reserve clause, 221, 273; rising popularity of, 103–4, 125, 194, 195; and television, 130–31, 133, 137, 293–94
Forbes Field, 81
Ford, Whitey, 15, 17, 35, 38, 58, 191, 292, 296–97, 303; behavior of, 187, 286; salary of, 70, 174
Fort, Rodney, 82, 168–69, 298
Fox, Nellie, 39, 42
Foxx, Jimmie, 56, 195
Frain, Andy, 106
franchise relocations, 211, 222; effects of, 191–200, 207–8, 280; and expenses,

franchise relocations (*cont.*)
75, 76–77, 79; history of, 244–65; and
Minor League compensation, 228, 238
Frank, Stanley, 114
Frazee, Harry, 12, 294
free agency, 7–8, 16, 32–33, 41, 42, 58,
160, 272–77, 301. *See also* player
movement
Fregosi, Jim, 269
Frey, Lon, 56
Frick, Ford, 147–48, 160, 250, 262,
270, 272–73, 295; and admission tax,
79–80; and Continental League, 227,
228–29, 231, 232; and homerun record
(1961), 23–25; and league expansion,
233, 236, 237, 238–39, 240, 242; and
"Let's Play Ball" week, 101–2; and
reserve clause, 219–20; and surveys,
100; and television contracts, 129, 130,
132, 145, 159
Friend, Bob, 221, 297
Furlong, William, 95

Galehouse, Denny, 56
Game of the Day, 143
Game of the Week, 128–29, 131, 158,
177–78, 294
Gardella, Danny, 216–17
Garver, Ned, 42, 57
gate sharing, 167–74, 179–80, 279–80.
See also revenue sharing
Gehrig, Lou, 3, 13, 58, 292
Geiger, Gary, 203
Gentile, Jim, 22
Gibbs, Jake, 191
Gibson, Bob, 184, 185
Giles, Warren, 118, 146, 148, 237, 262
Gillette, 129–30
Glick, Jeffrey, 244
Gomez, Lefty, 13, 58
Goodwin, Doris Kearns: *Wait till Next
Year*, 1
Gordon, Joe, 34
Gorman, Tom, 44, 49, 54
Graham, Frank, 148
Grba, Eli, 241

Green, Elijah ("Pumpsie"), 183
Green, Howard, 144–45
Greengrass, Jim, 34, 51
Griffith, Calvin, 63, 178, 219, 239, 263,
391n11; and relocation of Senators, 28,
81, 159–60, 196, 234–35, 249–52
Griffith, Clark, 43–44, 68, 81, 135, 147,
183, 300
Griffith Stadium, 109, 110, 251
Grim, Bob, 35, 36, 49, 191
Groat, Dick, 46
Grove, Lefty, 56, 195, 218

Haas, Walter, 393n45
Hadley, Kent, 45
Halberstam, David: *Summer of '49*, 14
Hamey, Roy, 72, 202, 269, 284, 286
Haney, Fred, 241
Hannegan, Bob, 135–36
Hansen, Ron, 42
Harridge, William, 177
Harry M. Stevens Inc. concessions, 64, 65,
66, 109–10, 282, 287
Harshman, Jack, 39–40
Hart, Phil, 231, 293
Hatton, Grady, 40
Haupert, Michael, 33
Hayes, O. W. ("Bill"), 145
Hebner, Richie, 74
Hegan, Mike, 304
Heifetz, Jascha, 30
Held, Woodie, 48, 54
Henrich, Tommy, 14, 37, 298–99
Herlong, A. S., Jr., 144
Herrmann, Ed, 270
Hirshberg, Al, 185–86
Historical Statistics of the United States,
138
Hodges, Gil, 71–72, 74
Hofheinz, Roy, 293, 296
Holway, John, 159
homeruns, 18–19, 22, 47–48, 54, 184;
record for (1961), 12, 23–27, 72, 280
Hopp, Johnny, 56
Horn, Huston, 123
Houk, Ralph, 15, 203, 284, 287, 296–97,
305

Houston Colt .45s, 112, 117, 153, 241, 242, 243
Howard, Elston, 35, 36, 186–89, 191, 201, 291, 292, 296, 303; and segregation, 123; as winner of MVP award, 183, 184
Howard, Frank, 243
Howser, Dick, 297
Hoyt, Waite, 12
Hulburt, William, 166, 225
Hundley, Randy, 269
Hunt, Ken, 241
Hunter, Billy, 35, 53
Hunter, Jim ("Catfish"), 277, 301
Huntley, Chet, 293
Huston, Tillinghast, 12, 286

income, per capita, 85–86. See also consumer spending
Indianapolis Clowns, 124
Inglehart, J. A. W., 295
integration, 3, 4, 6–7, 121–24, 156, 181–91, 291–92. See also black players
interleague play, 235–36
International League, 142, 148, 228
Irvin, Monte, 186
"(I Used to Be a) Brooklyn Dodger" (DiMucci), 1

Jackson, Reggie, 185, 300, 301
Jacobs Brothers concessions, 64
Jenkins, Fergie, 185, 298
Jensen, Jackie, 38
Johnson, Arnold, 43–44, 253, 254–55, 290, 300; and trades, 5, 46, 49–50, 51–52, 54, 57
Johnson, Deron, 47, 57
Johnson, Edwin, 144, 145, 149, 230, 231
Johnson, Johnny, 272
Jones, Sam, 182
Jordan, Jerry N., 137
Joseph S. Ward and Associates, 18–19
juvenile delinquency, 2–3

Kaat, Jim, 42
Kachline, Clifford, 81, 276

Kahan, Oscar, 270
Kahn, Roger: The Boys of Summer, 1
Kaline, Al, 267
Kansas City Athletics, 6, 15, 76, 187, 263; and farm system, 37–38; and player movement, 5, 42–58, 356n30, 357n33; relocation of, from Philadelphia, 140, 172, 173, 191–92, 195, 197–98, 207–8, 245; relocation of, to Oakland, 253–57, 393n45; and revenue sharing, 178, 180; and ticket prices, 60, 61. See also Oakland Athletics; Philadelphia Athletics
Kansas City Monarchs, 124
Kansas City Royals, 263, 301, 302
Kazanski, Ted, 75, 267
Keane, Johnny, 292, 305
Keating, Kenneth, 231–32
Kefauver, Estes, 230, 232, 250, 270
Kell, George, 40
Keller, Charley, 37
Kennedy, John F., 73
Kenney, Jerry, 191
Keough, Marty, 266, 267
Kerner, Ben, 258
Killebrew, Harmon, 22, 42, 196, 267
Kinder, Ellis, 42, 56
King, Joe, 28
Kitt, Howard, 202
Kline, Ron, 46
Knoop, Bobby, 270
Knowles, Glenn, 33
Konstanty, Jim, 35, 55
Koppett, Leonard, 141, 277, 291, 304
Korean War, 3
Koufax, Sandy, 267, 268
Kralick, Jack, 297
Kramer, Jack, 56
Kritchell, Paul, 201, 292
Kryhoski, Dick, 44
Kubek, Tony, 36, 115–16, 134, 190, 191, 292, 296
Kucks, Johnny, 35, 36, 49, 191
Kuenn, Harvey, 53, 267, 384n66
Kuhn, Bowie, 393n45
Kuzava, Bob, 34

Ladies' Days, 90, 92, 94–96, 120–21, 124, 125

Landis, Kenesaw Mountain, 157, 182, 217–18

Lane, Frank, 50, 52, 53, 57, 135, 203, 264, 267, 384n66

Lanier, Max, 217

Larsen, Don, 35, 49

Lazzeri, Tony, 13

Lee, Bill, 205

leisure-time activities, 6–7, 8, 30, 88, 90, 101, 102–5, 125; and air-conditioning, 88–89, 103, 125, 156; and consumer spending, 86–88, 139, 148; in New York City, 30

Lemon, Jim, 22

"Let's Play Ball" week, 102

Lewis, Duffy, 12

Lieb, Frederick, 115

Lindemann, Carl, Jr., 131

Linz, Phil, 286, 288

Little League baseball, 102–3, 156

Lollar, Sherm, 39, 55, 201

Long, Dale, 56, 241

Long, Edward, 255–56

Lopat, Eddie, 14, 34, 39

Lopez, Hector, 45, 49, 51, 183

Los Angeles Angels, 16, 120, 163, 240–41, 243; attendance of, 27, 174, 198–99; facilities of, 112–13, 239

Los Angeles Coliseum, 81, 234, 238, 246

Los Angeles Dodgers, 4, 28, 65, 119, 163, 198, 199, 205, 235, 239; attendance of, 17, 31, 197, 248–49, 299; facilities of, 111, 250–51; payroll of, 71–72; profits of, 81; relocation of, from Brooklyn, 77, 245–46, 248–49; and television revenue, 66, 132, 140. See also Brooklyn Dodgers

Lumpe, Jerry, 47, 49, 54

Lundquist, Carl, 101

"Lutheran Nights," 95

Lyle, Sparky, 270

Lynch, Jerry, 203

Maas, Duke, 46, 47, 57, 241

Mack, Connie, 54, 195, 289

MacPhail, Bill, 177–78

MacPhail, Larry, 74, 82–83, 91–92, 135, 188, 220, 290

MacPhail, Lee, 177–78, 188, 276

Major League Baseball Players' Association, 74

Maloney, Jim, 272

Manley, Effa, 122–23, 190–91

Mantle, Mickey, 1, 17, 22, 32–33, 38, 46, 191, 221, 288, 292, 296–97, 303; behavior of, 187, 286, 380n13; and homerun record (1961), 2, 12, 23–24, 280; salary of, 20, 37, 70, 72–73, 174, 229, 241

Marichal, Juan, 38

Maris, Roger, 17, 19, 22, 47, 48, 50, 191, 264, 288, 296–97, 303; and homerun record (1961), 2, 12, 23–27, 280; salary of, 72–73, 174, 241; trade of, 45–46, 51, 52–54, 356n30

marketing, 61–62, 66; and Minor League Baseball, 144–45, 146, 159; and night games, 21, 65, 91–93, 96, 136–37; and promotions, 90–91, 94–96, 102, 119–21, 124–25, 248, 287–88; and season-ticket sales, 62–63. See also specific promotions

Marquez, Louis, 186

Martin, Billy, 48, 187, 284, 286, 380n13, 399n12

Mathews, Eddie, 258

Mauch, Gene, 19

May, Rudy, 270

Mays, Carl, 12

Mays, Willie, 1, 8, 38, 183, 184, 190, 191, 291

McAndrew, Jim, 205

McCarthy, Joe, 286, 399n12

McCarthy, William, 147, 151–52, 161–62

McCormick, Mike, 38

McCovey, Willie, 38, 110, 183, 184

McDonald, Jim, 34, 35

McDougald, Gil, 37, 38, 191

McDowell, Sam, 269

McGlothen, Lynn, 205

McHale, John, 52, 260, 261

McRae, Hal, 205
Mehl, Ernest, 45, 50, 51, 253, 356n30
Metropolitan Stadium, 250, 252
Meusel, Bob, 12–13, 286
Mexican League, 216–17, 227
Michael, Gene, 191, 297
Millan, Felix, 270
Miller, John, 304
Miller, Marvin, 221
Milwaukee Braves, 5, 6, 41, 78, 97–98, 119–20, 139, 204, 257–59; facilities of, 110, 255; and farm system, 38; and integration, 182; relocation of, from Boston, 191–92, 196–97, 223; relocation of, to Atlanta, 259–63; and revenue sharing, 174. *See also* Atlanta Braves; Boston Braves
Milwaukee Brewers, 263
Minnesota Twins, 28, 29, 42, 180; profits of, 81; relocation of, from Washington, 191–92, 195–96, 207–8, 249–52, 258; and revenue sharing, 163, 178. *See also* Washington Senators
Minor League Baseball, 37, 92, 227, 231, 232, 241, 251, 253, 267–68, 340–42; attendance in, 103, 154–55, 158–59, 161–62; contraction of, 149–58, 159–61; and draft, 200–207, 208, 217–19; marketing by, 144–45, 146, 159; and night games, 93–94; and television, 141–49, 151, 152–55, 157, 158, 160–62. *See also* farm system
Minoso, Minnie, 39, 182, 183, 184, 185
Miranda, Willie, 35
Mize, Johnny, 34, 55–56
Monday, Rick, 205, 277
Montreal Expos, 163
Moon, Wally, 183
Morgan, Joe, 185
Morgan, Tom, 35, 49, 53
movies. *See* leisure-time activities
"Mrs. Robinson" (Simon), 1
Mullane, Tony, 215
Mundt, Karl, 2, 211–12, 250
Municipal Stadium (Cleveland), 107, 108, 137, 264–65, 279

Municipal Stadium (Kansas City), 109
Munson, Thurman, 191, 292
Murcer, Bobby, 191, 292, 300, 304
Murphy, H. Gabriel, 146
Murphy, Robert, 220
Murray, James, 108–9, 185, 248–49
Musial, Stan, 1, 6, 221

National Association for the Advancement of Colored People, 124
National Association of Professional Baseball Clubs, 142–43
National Association of Professional Base Ball Players, 165–66, 225
National Broadcasting Company (NBC), 128, 129, 130, 131
National Football League (NFL), 103–4, 130–31, 137, 272, 293–94. *See also* football
National League (NL), 5–6, 18, 63, 77, 78–79, 84, 114, 121; attendance in, 8, 13, 16–19, 31, 125, 182, 196–97, 257–58, 281, 300–301, 309–10, 352; baseball statistics (postwar) of, 312; and draft, 205–6; expansion of, 22, 27, 233–43; and farm system, 38; and franchise relocations, 16, 191–92, 193, 196–97, 198, 246, 248–49, 259–63; and integration, 181, 183–86; payrolls of, 67–68, 71, 73, 76, 328, 331; and revenue sharing, 165–67, 168, 174; and stadiums, 113–14; and television, 139–40; and ticket prices, 61, 67. *See also specific teams*
Negro League, 38, 122, 124, 185, 189–90
Nelson, Earl, 64
Newcombe, Don, 184, 185
New York Giants, 4, 64, 67, 76, 78, 98–99, 114; attendance of, 8; and farm system, 38; and integration, 182, 186; and player movement, 41; relocation of, to San Francisco, 5, 6, 38, 77, 246–48, 249; and revenue sharing, 174. *See also* San Francisco Giants
New York Mets, 4, 48, 66–67, 241, 242, 243; competition of, with Yankees,

New York Mets (*cont.*)
281–86, 299; facilities of, 112, 114,
230; and variable ticket pricing, 119
New York Yankees, 63, 79, 163;
attendance of, 12, 13–14, 17, 19–21,
26–29, 31, 91–92, 200, 278–81, 287,
288–89, 297, 299–300, 305; and black
players, 3, 6–7, 123, 183, 186–91,
291–92, 298, 300; CBS ownership of,
292–98, 300; concessions revenue of,
64–66, 287; dominance of, 1–5, 6,
8, 11, 13, 14–17, 28, 59, 164, 207,
209, 278–80, 291, 296, 300, 302; and
draft, 200–203, 205; early history of,
12–13; earned run average (ERA) of,
14–15; and farm system, 6, 12–13,
20, 34, 35, 36–39, 51, 58, 191, 207,
292, 300, 303; franchise appreciation
of, 82–83; and free agency, 301; and
homerun record (1961), 12, 23–27, 72,
280; image of, 285–88, 399n12; and
interleague play, 235–36; marketing
by, 94, 120, 121, 285, 287–88; and
Mets, 281–85; monopoly of, in New
York, 225, 233–34; and night games,
91–92, 93; and opinion polls, 99;
payroll of, 68–73, 75–76, 202, 269;
pennant wins of, 11, 12, 14–15, 17,
19–21, 22–23, 27–29, 31, 72–73,
173, 200, 307; and player movement,
5, 12–13, 33–36, 40–41, 42–58, 69,
201, 297–98, 356n30, 357n33; profits
of, 289–91, 292, 299; and revenue
sharing, 163, 170–74, 175, 180; road-
game attendance of, 19, 26, 27, 28–29,
170–74, 175, 182, 280; secrecy of, 213;
slump (1960s) of, 297–98, 300–301,
303–5; and television revenue, 66, 126,
128, 131, 136–37, 140–41, 143–44,
176–78, 289, 297; and ticket prices,
26–27, 30, 60–62, 170, 278, 283;
World Series appearances of, 4–5, 11,
14, 63, 164, 299, 301
Nicholson, Dave, 75
night games, 21, 65, 91–93, 96, 136–37,
333–34

Noren, Irv, 53
Nugent, Gerald, 55

Oakland Athletics, 28, 163; relocation of,
from Kansas City, 253–57, 393n45. *See
also* Kansas City Athletics; Philadelphia
Athletics
O'Connor, Leslie, 157–58, 218, 274–75
Oglivie, Ben, 205
Oliva, Tony, 42
O'Mahoney, Joseph, 220
O'Malley, Walter, 63, 66, 71, 112, 119,
158, 193, 197, 204, 271–72, 273–74;
and franchise relocations, 222, 228,
238–39, 245–46, 247–49; and night
games, 92; on stadiums, 110–11; and
television revenue, 131, 132–34, 146,
177
opinion polls, 96–101
Owens, Paul, 277

Pacific Coast League, 159, 193, 218–19,
228, 238, 246–47, 251
Page, Joe, 14
Paige, Satchel, 182
Palmer, Pete, 37, 40, 206, 300
Pappas, Milt, 42
parking, 8, 98–99, 100–101, 106;
inadequate, 107, 109, 110, 148,
225–26; at new stadiums, 111–14, 196,
246
Partee, Roy, 55
Pascual, Camilo, 42, 196
Pasquel, Bernardo, 216
Pasquel, Jorge, 216
Paul, Gabe, 100, 156, 264
Paula, Carlos, 183
payrolls. *See* salaries
pennant races, 11, 13, 14–15, 17, 27,
72–73, 171–72, 173, 279, 301, 307;
and attendance, 19–21, 22–23, 28–29,
31, 33–34, 138, 195; and ticket prices,
61
Pennock, Herb, 12
pensions, player, 220, 229, 385n24. *See
also* salaries

Pepitone, Joe, 36, 191, 288, 292, 303, 400n21
Perini, Lou, 158, 236, 257–59, 294
Peters, Gary, 39
Pettit, Paul, 75
Philadelphia Athletics, 5, 15, 16, 20, 37–38, 43, 64, 76, 80, 104, 108, 167, 278–79; and farm system, 37–38; and integration, 182; and player movement, 12, 36, 55; relocation of, to Kansas City, 173, 191–92, 195, 197–98, 207–8, 245; and revenue sharing, 167, 171; and ticket prices, 60. *See also* Kansas City Athletics; Oakland Athletics
Philadelphia Phillies, 5–6, 31, 61, 120, 182, 199, 200, 222, 225, 233; expenses of, 76, 78, 79; and player movement, 35; and television, 131, 144
Piersall, Jimmy, 116
Pipgras, George, 12
Pipp, Wally, 12
Piton, Philip, 143
Pittsburgh Pirates, 5–6, 61, 64, 68, 117, 225; expenses of, 78, 79; and player movement, 42; profits of, 81; and revenue sharing, 163, 174; and television, 137, 139
player depreciation rule, 74, 83–84
player movement, 32–33, 39–42, 178–79, 190, 192, 195, 201, 315, 379n22; between Kansas City Athletics and Yankees, 42–58; between leagues, 214–17; and free agency, 7–8, 16, 32–33, 41, 42, 58, 160, 272–77, 301; and unionizing, 220–21; and Yankees, 12–13, 34–42
Players' League, 167, 214
politics, 210, 270; and Cold War, 2–4; and congressional hearings, 43, 59–60, 64, 143, 147, 164, 165, 212, 219–20, 221, 230–32, 250, 362n32; and franchise relocations, 255–56, 261–62; and league expansion, 198, 223, 235; and television, 132–33, 134–35
Polo Grounds, 99, 107–8, 109, 112, 237–38, 246

Popular Mechanics, 102
Popular Science, 102
Porter, Paul, 80
Povich, Shirley, 131
Powell, Boog, 42
Power, Vic, 36, 51, 54, 184, 187–88, 284
Prell, Edward, 50, 237
profits. *See* revenue
promotions. *See under* marketing
Proxmire, William, 262

Quesada, Elwood ("Pete"), 112, 235
Quinn, Bob, 94
Quinn, John, 263
Quirk, James, 82, 168–69, 224, 298

radio, 66, 128, 135, 143, 145, 151–52, 161, 176
Raschi, Vic, 14, 69–70
Raymond, Claude, 203
Reagan, Ronald, 73
Reese, Rich, 270
Reichardt, Rick, 273, 277
relocations, franchise. *See* franchise relocations
reserve clause, 217, 275, 277; and competitive balance, 7–8, 32–33, 41; and preventing new leagues, 214–16, 218, 219–22, 230–31
Reston, James, 24
Reuss, Henry, 262
revenue, 33, 59–60, 62, 80–82, 140, 248–49; broadcast, 66, 70–71, 84, 112, 126–35, 140–41, 176–78, 258, 262, 289, 297; concessions, 63–66, 94, 96, 248, 255, 257; and variable ticket pricing, 118–21
revenue sharing, 9, 60, 163–64, 167–74, 179–80, 279–80, 345–47; alternatives to, 174–79; history of, 164–67
reverse-order draft, 203–5, 208. *See also* draft
Reynolds, Allie, 14, 34
Rheingold Brewery, 66–67
Ribowsky, Mark, 190–91
Richards, Paul, 20, 52, 136, 191, 194, 201, 203, 272

Richardson, Bobby, 36, 292, 303–4

Rickey, Branch, 6, 121–22, 181–82, 183, 185, 267, 284; and Continental League, 226–31, 236, 242

Rivera, Jim, 39

Rizzuto, Phil, 14, 37, 190

Roberts, Robin, 221, 266

Robinson, Aaron, 34

Robinson, Brooks, 42

Robinson, Eddie, 35, 54, 55, 188

Robinson, Frank, 183, 184, 191, 291, 298

Robinson, Jackie, 3, 18, 38, 121–23, 181–82, 183–84, 185, 186, 284

Rogovin, Mitchell, 84

Romano, Johnny, 39, 42

Roseboro, John, 184

Rosenthal, Harold, 98, 110, 185, 225

Ross, David, 212

Rottenberg, Simon, 220

Routzong, Art, 67, 270

Ruffing, Red, 12

Rumill, Ed, 91–92

Ruppert, Jacob, 12, 58, 285, 286, 290

Ruth, Babe, 3, 12, 23, 25, 280, 286

Ryan, Blondy, 55

Ryan, Ellis, 135

Ryan, Nolan, 205

Saigh, Fred, 128, 135, 177, 217

Sain, Johnny, 35, 48, 55–56

salaries, 7, 20, 229; and bonuses, 37–38, 75, 230, 265–72, 276, 364n57; and player negotiations, 115–16, 220–21, 298–99; of teams, 67–75, 76, 290, 302, 328, 331, 360n26, 362n32

Sanders, Ken, 269

Sanford, Fred, 55

San Francisco Giants, 77, 111, 140, 198, 199; and player movement, 38; profits of, 81–82; relocation of, from New York, 246–48, 249. *See also* New York Giants

San Francisco Seals, 37, 219

Scarborough, Ray, 35

Schang, Wally, 12

Scherer, F. M., 212

Schneider, Russell, 276

Schofield, Dick, 297

Score, Herb, 384n66

Scott, Frank, 124, 385n24

scouting bureau, 79

Scully, Gerald, 168–69

"Season of the Pitcher" (1968), 19

Senior Citizens' Nights, 120

Seymour, Harold, 164–65, 166

Shantz, Bobby, 42, 46, 47, 53–54, 241

Shaplen, Robert, 284

Shaughnessy, Frank, 142, 148

Shawkey, Bob, 12, 54

Shea, William, 2, 234, 282–83, 291; and Continental League, 226–32, 236

Shea Stadium, 230, 282

Sherman Anti-Trust Act, 217. *See also* antitrust exemption

Sherony, Keith, 33

Shore, Ernie, 12

Shut Out (Bryant), 183

Siebern, Norm, 45, 47, 54

Sievers, Roy, 42

Simmons, Al, 195

Simmons, Harry, 165

Simon, Paul: "Mrs. Robinson," 1

Simons, Herbert, 226–27, 232

Simpson, Harry, 182, 183

61*, 2, 23

Skizas, Lou, 47–48

Skowron, Bill ("Moose"), 35, 36, 188, 191

Slaughter, Enos, 35, 45, 51, 54, 55–56

Smena, 2–3

Smiley, Robert, 212, 213, 214

Smith, Charley, 297

Smith, Elmer, 12

Smith, Hal, 35

Smith, Red, 61–62, 93–94, 212

Smith, Reggie, 185, 270

Snider, Duke, 1

Snyder, Richard E., 102

South Atlantic League, 154–55

Southern Association, 154–55, 156

Spahn, Warren, 258

Spalding, Albert, 166

spatial preemption, 210, 222–24

Spink, C. C. Johnson, 261
Spink, J. G. Taylor, 101, 240
Sports Network Inc., 131
Stadium Club. *See* Yankee Stadium Club
stadiums, 7, 95, 107–13, 125, 195,
    229–30, 237, 238–39, 246–47, 253,
    260; location of, 105–6, 122; and
    parking, 8, 98–99, 100–101, 106, 107,
    109, 110, 111–14, 148, 196, 225–26,
    246; rent for, 112, 254–57. *See also
    specific stadiums*
Stallard, Tracy, 26
Stann, Francis, 239
Stanton, Frank, 293–94
Stargell, Willie, 185
Starr, Dick, 55
Steinbrenner, George, 4, 11, 83, 298, 300,
    301
Stengel, Casey, 14–15, 20, 46, 49, 54,
    188–89, 202, 282, 284; and "color,"
    285, 399n12
Stephens, Vern ("Junior"), 56, 217
Stevens, Bob, 268
Stevens Brothers concessions. *See* Harry
    M. Stevens Inc. concessions
St. Louis Browns, 5, 13, 16, 64, 80, 83,
    222, 278–79, 280; and farm system,
    37, 40; and integration, 182, 186;
    and night games, 92–93; and player
    movement, 34, 41, 42, 55, 56, 178–79,
    192; relocation of, to Baltimore,
    171–72, 180, 191–95, 207–8; and
    revenue sharing, 167, 171. *See also*
    Baltimore Orioles
St. Louis Cardinals, 6, 31, 61, 64, 106,
    193, 194, 199, 222; and farm system,
    38, 41, 56; payroll of, 68, 69–70;
    profits of, 81; and television, 137, 151;
    and ticket prices, 67, 200
St. Louis Perfectos. *See* St. Louis Cardinals
stolen bases, 18
Stoneham, Horace, 82, 228, 245, 249,
    257; and night games, 92; and stadium
    conditions, 107–8, 237–38, 246; and
    television revenue, 132, 133

Stottlemyre, Mel, 36, 38, 288, 292
Sturdivant, Tom, 35, 36, 49, 191
Subscription Television Inc. (STV), 133–35
Sullivan, John L., 106
Summer of '49 (Halberstam), 14
Symington, Stuart, 256

taxes, 73–74, 117–18; federal admission,
    79–80; and player depreciation rule,
    74, 83–84
Taylor, Tony, 203
"Teenage Nights," 120
television, 138–39, 152, 155, 336–39;
    impact of, on baseball attendance,
    6, 8, 100–101, 126, 130, 135–40;
    and Minor League Baseball, 141–49,
    151, 152–55, 157, 158, 160–62; and
    revenue, 66, 70–71, 84, 112, 126–34,
    140–41, 176–78, 258, 262, 289, 297.
    See also specific networks
Tenace, Gene, 205
Terrell, Roy, 156–57
"Territorial Definition Committee," 233
Terry, Ralph, 46, 47, 49, 50, 51, 54
theater. *See* leisure-time activities
Thomas, David, 205–6
Thomas, Frank, 259
Thompson, Fresco, 271
Thomson, Bobby, 1
Thorn, John, 37, 40, 206, 300
Throneberry, Marv, 48, 202
ticket prices, 26–27, 28, 30, 60–62, 97,
    181, 200, 213, 248, 259, 264, 278,
    283, 316–19, 395n68; for children,
    119–20; and revenue sharing, 168, 170;
    and taxes, 117–18; variable pricing of,
    118–21
Tillotson, Thad, 297
Tolan, Bobby, 270
Topping, Dan, 43, 74, 83, 251, 290, 294,
    296; and integration, 123, 188–89; and
    league expansion, 233, 237; and player
    trades, 56, 57; and television revenue,
    131, 178
Topping, Dan, Jr., 285
Torre, Joe, 269

"total baseball rankings" (TBR) system, 37–38, 40–41, 53–54, 56, 300, 384n65; and black players, 184–85; and draft, 206

trades. *See* player movement

Trautman, George, 142–43, 147, 157, 159, 161, 202–3

Tresh, Tom, 36, 75, 191, 303

Triandos, Gus, 35, 188, 201

Trucks, Virgil, 45

Tugerson, Jim, 123

Tugerson, Leander, 123

Turley, Bob, 35

Turner, Donald F., 213

Umont, Frank, 116

Union Association, 167, 213

Urban, Jack, 49, 53

Urness, Ed, 266

Veeck, Bill, 26, 50, 83, 103, 112–13, 116, 283, 286, 300; on baseball's fan base, 105–6; and concessions revenue, 64, 65; and franchise relocations, 193–94, 197, 198, 249, 260, 262; and integration, 182, 186, 190–91; and league expansion, 238; marketing by, 21–22, 24–25, 94, 95, 125, 263–64, 285; and player depreciation rule, 74; on reserve clause, 275; and revenue sharing, 168, 175; and television, 128, 135, 140, 177; and trades, 52–53, 56

Veeck, Mary Frances, 95

Vietnam War, 3–4

Virdon, Bill, 35, 46, 51, 183

Virgil, Ozzie, 183

Wagner, Robert, 234

Wait till Next Year (Goodwin), 1

Walker, Luke, 270

Ward, Arch, 44

Washington Nationals, 163

Washington Senators, 5, 15, 16, 20, 63, 64, 180, 243, 247; attendance of, 27–28; facilities of, 112, 113; and integration, 182–83; payroll of, 68, 75;
and player movement, 34, 42, 55; profits of, 80, 81; relocation of, to Minnesota, 191–92, 195–96, 198, 207–8, 234–35, 249–52, 258, 391n11; and revenue sharing, 164, 173; and television revenue, 140. *See also* Minnesota Twins

Weaver, Sylvester ("Pat"), 133

Webb, Del, 74, 83, 158, 290, 296; and integration, 189; and league expansion, 113, 198, 224, 239, 243

Weiss, George, 14, 21, 72, 190, 230, 236, 284–85, 291–92; and farm system, 20, 58; and Mets, 282, 283, 286; and player acquisitions, 35, 37, 46, 48, 50, 55, 57, 187–88, 203; and player salaries, 69–70, 202, 229, 267, 269, 298, 302; and television, 136, 146

Western Association Minor League, 144

Western International League, 145

Whitaker, Steve, 304

White, Bill, 184, 298

White, G. Edward, 249

White, Roy, 300

Whyte, William H., 116

Wiley, Alexander, 2

Williams, Bernie, 302

Williams, Billy, 185

Williams, Edgar, 198

Williams, Ted, 1, 26, 73, 221, 298

Wills, Maury, 18, 184, 298

Wilson, Artie, 186

Wood, Wilbur, 269

Woodling, Gene, 34, 35, 221

Woods, Ron, 191

World Series, 4–5, 56, 125, 196, 207, 234; appearances of Yankees in, 4–5, 11, 14, 63, 164, 299, 301; and revenue, 63; and television, 127, 128, 130, 133, 135

Wright, Harry, 165

Wrigley, Philip K. ("P. K."), 77, 126–27, 193, 240, 247–48

Wrigley Field (Chicago), 106, 107, 109, 124

Wrigley Field (Los Angeles), 112, 238–39, 247

Wyatt, John, 297

Wynn, Jim, 185

Yankee Stadium, 43–44, 82–83, 107, 109, 110, 190, 229–30, 289, 290–91
Yankee Stadium Club, 61, 66
Yawkey, Thomas, 5, 40, 266, 299
Yost, Ed, 221

Young, Dick, 178

Zarilla, Al, 56
Zimmerman, Jerry, 266
Zipfel, Bud, 241